# THE ULTIMATE STAR TREK AND PHILOSOPHY

The Blackwell Philosophy and Pop Culture Series
*Series editor William Irwin*

A spoonful of sugar helps the medicine go down, and a healthy helping of popular culture clears the cobwebs from Kant. Philosophy has had a public relations problem for a few centuries now. This series aims to change that, showing that philosophy is relevant to your life–and not just for answering the big questions like "To be or not to be?" but also for answering the little questions: "To watch or not to watch *South Park*?" Thinking deeply about TV, movies, and music doesn't make you a "complete idiot." In fact it might make you a philosopher, someone who believes the unexamined life is not worth living and the unexamined cartoon is not worth watching.

Already published in the series:

# THE ULTIMATE STAR TREK AND PHILOSOPHY

## THE SEARCH FOR SOCRATES

Edited by
**Kevin S. Decker**
and
**Jason T. Eberl**

WILEY Blackwell

This edition first published 2016
© 2016 John Wiley & Sons Ltd

*Registered Office*
John Wiley & Sons Ltd, The Atrium, Southern Gate, Chichester, West Sussex, PO19 8SQ, UK

*Editorial Offices*
350 Main Street, Malden, MA 02148-5020, USA
9600 Garsington Road, Oxford, OX4 2DQ, UK
The Atrium, Southern Gate, Chichester, West Sussex, PO19 8SQ, UK

For details of our global editorial offices, for customer services, and for information about how
to apply for permission to reuse the copyright material in this book please see our website at
www.wiley.com/wiley-blackwell.

The right of Jason T. Eberl and Kevin S. Decker to be identified as the authors of the editorial
material in this work has been asserted in accordance with the UK Copyright, Designs and
Patents Act 1988.

*Library of Congress Cataloging-in-Publication Data*

Names: Eberl, Jason T., editor. | Decker, Kevin S., editor.
Title: The ultimate Star Trek and philosophy / edited by Jason T. Eberl and Kevin S. Decker.
Description: Malden, MA : John Wiley & Sons, 2016. | Includes bibliographical references and
   index.
Identifiers: LCCN 2015038416 (print) | LCCN 2015041167 (ebook) | ISBN 9781119146001
   (pbk.) | ISBN 9781119146018 (Adobe PDF) | ISBN 9781119146025 (ePub)
Subjects: LCSH: Star Trek television programs–History and criticism. | Star Trek films–History
   and criticism.
Classification: LCC PN1992.8.S74 U58 2016 (print) | LCC PN1992.8.S74 (ebook) |
   DDC 791.45/75–dc23
LC record available at http://lccn.loc.gov/2015038416

A catalogue record for this book is available from the British Library.

Set in 10.5/13pt SabonLTStd by Aptara Inc., New Delhi, India
Printed and bound in Malaysia by Vivar Printing Sdn Bhd

1   2016

# Contents
## Voyaging Defiantly through the Philosophical Galaxy

# Acknowledgments
## The Command Staff of Utopia Planitia

Every Federation starship, from the original *Constitution*-class *Enterprise* built in the San Francisco Yards—or in Riverside, Iowa, in the Abrams-verse—to the *Sovereign*-class *Enterprise*-E, has a dedication plaque noting those individuals who were instrumental in the design and construction of these mighty machines. Although a book like this is less likely to travel to the farthest reaches of the cosmos or be instrumental in making first contact with extraterrestrial intelligent species, there is nonetheless a veritable army of personnel no less crucial to its construction. First and foremost, without the authors who wrote the chapters you're soon to enjoy, there would be no book to begin with—just a cordrazine hallucination on the part of the editors. Furthermore, this volume is but one member of a larger fleet headed up by Admiral William Irwin, under the sector command authority of Admiral Liam Cooper at Starbase Wiley-Blackwell, whose command staff headed by Allison Kostka devoted countless hours to its final preparation that may have been better spent preparing for the next Borg or Dominion invasion.

Finally, Captains Decker and Eberl have benefitted from Starfleet's 24th-century policy of allowing families to accompany deep-space missions, meaning that that Jennifer and August, as well as Suzanne, Kennedy, Ethan, and Jack, have had to endure Borg cutting beams, Klingon *bat'leths*, Romulan disruptors, and Ferengi counterfeit gold-pressed latinum in trying to eke out lives coexistent with wannabe Starfleet officers who've indulged in too much synthehol and spent too many hours in the holodeck. Hopefully, their sacrifices will be worth it to readers of this literary starship that we're finally ready to launch into the final frontier of philosophical imagination.

# Introduction
## A Guide to Living Long and Prospering

GET A LIFE, will you people? I mean, for crying out loud, it's just a TV show! ... You've turned an enjoyable little job that I did as a lark for a few years into a COLOSSAL WASTE OF TIME! ... It's just a TV show dammit, IT'S JUST A TV SHOW!

One of the saddest days in *Star Trek* fan history was in 1986 when, in a *Saturday Night Live* skit, the incomparable William Shatner revealed to pudgy fans in Spock ears that there's more to life than *Trek*. Of course, most fans knew this already, but to hear it put so bluntly by "the Captain" himself was almost too much to bear. So let's just get it right out there, front and center: *Star Trek* is indeed just a TV show. But that fact alone doesn't render wasted the thousands of hours spent watching Kirk battling the Gorn, Troi sensing that somebody's "hiding something," or Archer feeding cheese to Porthos. By the way, you heard that right: *thousands* of hours—based on the reasonable assumption that a fan who's ranged omnivorously over all the series has watched each of the over 700 hours of *Trek* programming at least three times (some more, some less of course: Compare your frequency of *Wrath of Khan* viewings vs. the abominable VOY episode "Threshold" or, dare we say it, "Spock's Brain").

Certainly, there are more important matters demanding one's attention: work, school, family, *Star Trek* trivia (sorry, fell off the wagon there). As Jerry Seinfeld once exhorted his friend George Costanza, "We're trying to have a society here!" Given the human need to produce and consume, to have gainful employment, meaningful relationships, an SUV, and two plasma TVs, all of which require time and

*The Ultimate Star Trek and Philosophy*, First Edition. Edited by Kevin S. Decker and Jason T. Eberl.
© 2016 John Wiley & Sons, Ltd. Published 2016 by John Wiley & Sons, Ltd.

effort, do multiple viewings of "The City on the Edge of Forever" constitute "time suckage"? No, because *Star Trek* clearly has something worthwhile to say.

Okay, but *what* does *Star Trek* say? Of course, there's that "hopeful vision of the future" thing that can be heard in every interview about Gene Roddenberry's legacy. But are there other metaphysical, moral, social, or political lessons we can glean from the Great Bird of the Galaxy's vision? In 2008, the intrepid, forward-seeing (and humble) editors of this volume sought to answer this question by producing *Star Trek and Philosophy: The Wrath of Kant*, eighteen chapters on diverse topics in metaphysics, ethics, politics, religion, and logic—a veritable Babel conference on philosophy beyond the final frontier. The intellectual scope of the *Star Trek* universe, however, demanded that we set out on another journey. Just as the Federation expanded its exploration into the Gamma and Delta Quadrants (thanks to the Bajoran Prophets and the Caretaker, respectively), so we, too, have expanded our exploration into the *Trek* saga to mine it, not for dilithium or latinum, but for its treasure trove of intellectual riches.

Over the course of thirty-one chapters, our fellow explorers have tackled the kind of difficult questions that Q will probably challenge humanity to answer hundreds of years from now. In the realm of *ethics*, we examine the moral psychology of the elite individuals who rise to the rank of starship captain, as well as the reasons that justify the Prime Directive they've each sworn to uphold (with the occasional bending, ignoring, or outright violation). While Captains Kirk, Picard, Sisko, Janeway, and Archer often appear justified in their flagrant rule breaking, there are some instances in which their interference is evidently harmful: Why is Kirk so hellbent on destroying utopian civilizations? Is it out of jealousy for having "no beach to walk on" himself?

Other chapters examine the *social* and *political* ideas that underpin various nonhuman cultures: Why are the Klingons so different and yet seem so familiar to us? Do the Borg actually embody values that we might evolve into holding? Is the Federation economic system sustainable in a way that Ferenginar's unbridled capitalism isn't (at least until Rom takes over as Grand Nagus)? Is there a universal meaning of "justice" by which we as finite humans can judge the morality of the Q Continuum?

As a work of science fiction, *Star Trek* is able to raise *metaphysical* questions in a way ordinary TV dramas can't: Should we consider Data or *Voyager*'s holographic Doctor as "persons"? What would it take for an individual to recover her identity once she's lost it in a collective consciousness? Would it have made a real difference if Commander William Riker had died and Lieutenant Tom Riker had taken his place on the *Enterprise*-D? Does it make sense that more highly evolved beings won't have bodies that can move, touch, and feel? How can we know we're not living in a holodeck right now, and would it really matter to us if we were?

The attempt to provide answers to speculative inquiries like these has inspired not only millennia of *philosophical* wisdom, but also the emergence of various *religious* belief systems. Roddenberry, an avowed secular humanist, envisioned a future in which humanity no longer relied upon faith-based answers to unresolved metaphysical or moral questions. Still, religious beliefs and values are treated seriously as essential aspects of Klingon, Bajoran, and other alien cultures in *Trek*. Is human culture of the future better off having divested itself of such superstition, or is there something to be gained by gathering "a few laurel leaves"?

This book is an expression of our "continuing mission" to explore the philosophical frontier of Roddenberry's enduring legacy. As we celebrate a half-century of *Star Trek* on television and in cinema, and with the crew of the Abrams-verse *Enterprise* embarking on their five-year mission in *Star Trek Beyond*, we can confidently say this book won't be the final volume on *Star Trek and Philosophy*, for indeed "the human adventure is just beginning.... "

# Part I
# ALPHA QUADRANT: HOME SYSTEMS

# "The More Complex the Mind, the Greater the Need for the Simplicity of Play"

## Jason T. Eberl

This chapter's title comes from "Shore Leave" (TOS), in which the *Enterprise* crew encounters an "amusement planet" designed by an advanced civilization—they return to this world in "Once Upon a Planet" (TAS). It may seem counterintuitive for highly intelligent beings to need a realm for fantasy entertainment. Some forms of play, however, may be not only beneficial but also *necessary* for intellectual, moral, and spiritual beings to *flourish*. Edifying play isn't aimed at mere pleasure seeking, but rather can lead each of us to a greater understanding of our own self, the world in which we live, and what reality, if any, may lie beyond this world. Along these lines, Josef Pieper (1904–1997) argues that beings capable of understanding the world around them, as well as inquiring into the deeper reality that may transcend the physical world, *must* seek intellectual, moral, and spiritual fulfillment through forms of play that take them out of their workaday lives. In a phrase reminiscent of my *Trek*-inspired title, Pieper says, "The more comprehensive the power of relating oneself to the world of objective being, so the more deeply anchored must be the 'ballast' in the inwardness of the subject."[1] In other words, "Know thyself," as the Oracle at Delphi proclaimed. Indeed, this idea was seized upon by Socrates as the starting point of all philosophy.

Pieper follows a philosophical tradition set down by Plato—who bears only a superficial relationship to "Plato's Stepchildren" (TOS)—Aristotle, and Thomas Aquinas, all of whom could find some affinity with *Star Trek* and other sci-fi/fantasy adventures that tell a good morality tale or stretch the limits of human imagination. As

*The Ultimate Star Trek and Philosophy*, First Edition. Edited by Kevin S. Decker and Jason T. Eberl.
© 2016 John Wiley & Sons, Ltd. Published 2016 by John Wiley & Sons, Ltd.

Aristotle points out, humans, as *rational* animals, aren't satisfied with mere pleasure seeking, but are driven to reflect upon the limitless possibilities of existence. Continuing that line of thought, Aquinas states, "The reason why the philosopher can be compared to the poet [or the sci-fi writer?] is that both are concerned with wonder."[2] Truly, a sense of wonder pervades *Trek*, in which the judicious use of visual effects and theatrical acting—just look at the endless crew reaction shots in *The Motion Picture* while the *Enterprise* flies through V'Ger—helps convey and inspire such wonder while "rebooting" wondrous mythological themes from Homer, Virgil, Dante, and others.

Aristotle notes that "we work in order to be at leisure."[3] But Pieper adds that we need to break out of the economic cycle of *productivity* and *consumption* to fully access our sense of wonder and explore the "final frontier" of reality and consciousness. We need to allow ourselves the leisure necessary to *contemplate* the universe and our place within it. But leisure isn't simply "recharging our batteries." Rather, it's taking time to reflect upon those all-important questions of humanity, reflection that doesn't produce immediate, tangible goods that can be traded on the floor of the Ferengi stock exchange. Leisure is *not* idly twiddling one's thumbs; yet, Pieper finds there to be a "festive" element to human leisure that allows us to develop ourselves intellectually and culturally in a way that simple, pleasure-seeking *hedonism*—in the form, say, of Landru's "red hour"—fails to provide: "The leisure of man includes within itself a celebratory, approving, lingering gaze of the inner eye on the reality of creation."[4] Leisure, in all its proper forms, is a necessary element that must be reintegrated into the modern concept of a "happy life." With that in mind, our mission will be to review Pieper's concept of leisure and consider how contemplating *Star Trek* can be a stimulating and edifying form of play.

## Life Is Not for the Timid

The philosopher Robert Nozick (1938–2002) offered an ingenious thought experiment in which people would reject a method for getting as much pleasure as they'd ever want. Nozick asks us to consider an "experience machine" to which a person could be hooked up for an extended period of time or perhaps their entire life—think of the virtual reality of "The Thaw" (VOY) but without the creepy clown.[5] During their time "in the machine," they'd experience nothing but pleasurable experiences that had been pre-programmed, all the while being unaware that their experiences are artificially generated. Nozick thinks that rational persons would reject being plugged into the machine because we want to *do* certain things, not merely *have the experience* of doing them, and because we want to *be* a certain type of person. Nozick thus contends, "There is no answer to the question of what a person is like who has long been in the tank."[6] Ultimately, Nozick claims we also want to be in contact with a *deeper reality* than the artificially constructed world of the machine.

The problem with the idyllic enticement of the experience machine isn't that it's *ideal*, but rather that it's *idle*, presenting us with a mode of life that has lost its purpose. We have no unsatisfied desires, and there's no striving to change or to grow. In such a scenario, Q's ultimate verdict on humanity's guilt is all but assured and we suffer the "tedium of immortality."[7] It's not that the experience machine would make us immortal, but we'd endure the same purposelessness of continued existence that led to the first suicide of a Q in "Death Wish" (VOY). Philosophers from Aristotle to Alfred North Whitehead (1861–1947) have argued that *change* is the fundamental engine that drives reality forward, and that purposeful change is necessary if rational beings are to better themselves intellectually, morally, or spiritually—without it, they might *live*, but wouldn't *flourish*.[8]

Many depictions of similar "experience machines" in sci-fi also lead to the allegorical conclusion that human beings aren't meant to live in such a purely hedonistic environment. Consider "This Side of Paradise" (TOS), in which a group of human colonists become infected by spores that render them completely happy, peaceful, and healthy (even healing old scars). The "dark side" of life on Omicron Ceti III is that the colonists are *stagnant*. They produce only the bare minimum they need to survive and maintain a comfortable status quo. Once the *Enterprise* crew frees the colonists from the spores' hold—after initially succumbing to the spores' effects themselves—Kirk wonders: "Maybe we weren't meant for paradise. Maybe we were meant to fight our way through. Struggle, claw our way up, scratch for every inch of the way. Maybe we can't stroll to the music of the lute, we must march to the sound of drums."[9] There's more to life than mint juleps.

In what sort of activity should we engage? Humanity's "prime directive," particularly in Western societies as analyzed by Pieper, but increasingly in Eastern societies as well, seems to be "Work! Produce! Buy! Contribute!" But wait, this sounds suspiciously like the *Borg's* prime directive. The Borg certainly aren't idle: they're always working, producing, consuming, and all quite *efficiently*—no time is ever wasted on a Borg cube or unicomplex. What makes humanity different from the Borg? For one set of answers, see the last four seasons of *Voyager* as Captain Janeway strives to help former Borg drone Seven of Nine regain her self-identity.[10] For another, we can return to Pieper's analysis of the value of leisure. Pieper argues that the difference between Borg and human productivity stems from a difference between two types of goods: *bonum utile* and *bonum commune*. The first is the good of "utility": what's *useful*. The second refers to the "common good" in which we seek the flourishing of each individual member of the community. Since there are no individuals within the Borg Collective, there can be no *bonum commune*; there's only the utility that each drone brings to the Collective. This difference, says Pieper, is also found in modern industrialized society, where employers often conceive of workers as little more than drones, and marketing gurus see consumers as absorbent, pleasure-seeking sponges.

So why isn't a perfectly pleasurable life under the spores' influence on Omicron Ceti III enough for a *happy* human life? Natural law ethicists Patrick Lee and Robert George place the value of pleasure within the larger context of "genuinely fulfilling" human goods, concluding that "pleasure is good (desirable, worthwhile, perfective) if and only if attached to a fulfilling or perfective activity or condition. Pleasure is *like* other goods in that a fulfilling activity or condition is better with it than without it. But pleasure is *unlike* full-fledged goods in that it is not a genuine good apart from some other fulfilling activity or condition."[11] Lee and George point to the case of "sadistic pleasures," pleasures that are attendant upon immoral acts, to show that the experience of pleasure alone doesn't suffice as a genuine good for us.[12]

Certainly there are various goods, unlike pleasure, that are both intrinsically desirable and "really perfective or fulfilling" for human persons. But the pursuit of mere pleasure is "disordered" because it involves treating one's body as merely an instrument to attain a goal. It also involves a retreat from reality into *fantasy*. Now, retreating from reality into fantasy may indeed interfere with living a genuinely fulfilling life—just think of the proverbial "couch potato" sitting in front of the television with over 500 channels at their disposal (and still nothing good on!), or individuals who habitually view pornography instead of cultivating healthy sexual relationships, or Lieutenant Barclay's "holodiction."[13] Despite this, a rich, imaginative fantasy life could support the pursuit of genuinely fulfilling goods for human persons. First of all, flights into fantasy aren't inherently bad for us, as we see with the need to dream for our psychological well-being—as the crew of the *Enterprise*-D discovers in "Night Terrors" (TNG). Furthermore, various forms of fantasy entertainment—in particular, well-written and produced sci-fi—allow us to pursue the genuinely fulfilling goods of intellectual and moral contemplation.

The main way in which science fiction provides these kinds of goods is through *thought experiments*. Just like Nozick's test of our intuitions about hedonism by use of the "experience machine," these "What if?" scenarios let us test metaphysical, moral, and other hypotheses we can't examine by the methods of empirical science. As Ray Bradbury (1920–2012) famously put it, "science fiction may be one of the last places in our society where the philosopher can roam just as freely as he chooses."[14] Sci-fi holds up a mirror to contemporary society by placing ethical, political, social, and other issues in a different context, inviting us to reflect without kneejerk emotional or cultural reactions. After peering "through the looking glass," our metaphysical and moral intuitions may be either challenged or confirmed—or we may be left in that state of puzzlement, called *aporia*, in which Socrates left many of his dialogue partners. So one value of thought experiments lies in the role they play in Pieper's concept of leisure: the use of time in which mental and physical energy is directed away from merely productive or consumptive work and toward intellectual contemplation and the active pursuit of spiritual and moral goods that can lead to human flourishing in every dimension of our being.

## Mrs. Sisko, Can Bennie Come Out and Play?

Pieper opens his book with the following passage from Plato:

> But the gods, taking pity on human beings—a race born to labor—gave them regularly recurring divine festivals, as a means of refreshment from their fatigue; they gave them the Muses, and Apollo and Dionysus as the leaders of the Muses, to the end that, after refreshing themselves in the company of the gods, they might return to an upright posture.[15]

Perhaps with the loss of the Muses in mind, Charles Taylor charts the movement in Western culture from an "enchanted" religious worldview to the secular world in which we live today. One of the hallmarks of this gradual shift in attitude is the waning of sacred or "higher" times. These include religious feasts that take a community out of the realm of profane or "ordinary" time to remember events of spiritual and cultural significance. They also include times of communal leisure when the members of a community don't just break from their various labors, but engage in rituals that put them in a collective mindset, making present historical moments that have shaped their culture. The Christian celebration of Good Friday, for example, isn't a mere *remembrance* of Christ's suffering and death, but an event that makes his redemptive sacrifice *present* with the attendant spiritual graces:

> Higher times gather and re-order secular time. They introduce "warps" and seeming inconsistencies in profane time-ordering. Events which are far apart in profane time could nevertheless be closely linked.... Good Friday 1998 is closer in a way to the original day of the Crucifixion than mid-summer's day 1997. Once events are situated in relation to more than one kind of time, the issue of time-placing becomes quite transformed.[16]

It should be noted that, because of these comments about discontinuous times being close to each other, Taylor's field studies are currently under review by Agents Lucsly and Dulmur of the Federation's Department of Temporal Investigations ("Trials and Tribble-ations," DS9).

The value of festive pursuits during "higher times" is grounded in the connection between human and divine minds. Pieper notes that Aquinas "speaks of *contemplation* and *play* in a single breath: 'Because of the leisure of contemplation the Scripture says of the Divine Wisdom itself that it "plays all the time, plays throughout the world." ' "[17] The link between play and contemplation shows that leisure isn't merely resting or being idle. Rather, its purpose is to allow space for intellectual, moral, and spiritual development through religious rituals, charitable work, and the study of the *liberal arts*, which Pieper, following John Henry Newman (1801–1890), distinguishes from the *servile* arts aimed at providing the necessities of life as opposed to directly supporting the flourishing of the human intellect and spirit.[18] Anticipating in some ways *Star Trek*'s "money-less" economy, though not doing away with capital altogether, Pieper recommends certain practical steps to effect the "de-proletarization" of the modern labor– and consumer-driven culture in order to restrict the servile arts to benefit the liberal arts: "building up of property from wages, limiting the power of the state, and overcoming internal poverty."[19] He further distinguishes two types of merit-based compensation for the two different types of arts: *honoraria* for those engaged in the liberal arts and *wages* for labor in the servile arts.[20]

Pieper understands leisure to involve the same "warping" of time that Taylor describes.[21] The contemplative possibilities that leisure affords take us outside of the routine cycle of mere work and rest to reflect upon the eternal truths that ultimately define existence. We can see this in the sense of *eternity* or "no time" experienced in the practice of various Western or Eastern meditative arts,[22] or by those who commune with the Bajoran Prophets in their Celestial Temple. These possibilities also lie in the capacity for well-done history and forward- or past-looking fiction to bring various truths about the nature of the world and the human condition to light, truths that would otherwise be obscured by the press of immediate happenings we see or hear about in the 24/7 news cycle.

At the heart of Pieper's view of the *philosophical act* is the ability "to see the deeper visage of the real so that the attention directed to the things encountered in everyday experience comes up against what is not so obvious in these things."[23] In this way, *Star Trek* provides a vision of what humanity might become in the future, a setting for thought experiments of both moral and metaphysical varieties. This imagined future also serves as a source of *aspiration* for us: we can believe in our social evolution toward achieving—and meriting—a better society, one in which, as Gene Roddenberry describes, "there will be no hunger and there will be no greed and all the children will know how to read."[24]

In *ST: First Contact*, Picard says of life in the 24th century, "The acquisition of wealth is no longer the driving force in our lives. We wish to better ourselves and the rest of humanity." He's describing a path for personal self-realization based on Aristotle's idea that "all human beings by nature desire to know."[25] Knowledge, according to Aristotle, is not only *speculative* in nature, encompassing scientific and theoretical reasoning, but also *practical*—that is, technical and ethical reasoning. The fact that Starfleet officers don't earn a wage, but are rewarded with the means to support their needs and also merit-based honors, shows that their service as explorers, protectors, and peacemakers is not seen as *servile,* but rather as a *vocation,* supporting their overall flourishing and that of humanity and other alien species. Their work provides the freedom to pursue the liberal arts, as evidenced by how well versed characters like Picard and Spock are in history, literature, philosophy, and religion, in addition to the various sciences and the technical details of running a starship.

*Star Trek* also underscores Pieper's idea of leisure as an opportunity for a different kind of labor: study and contribution to the liberal arts and intellectual, moral, and spiritual development. In "The First Duty" (TNG), Picard forcefully reminds young cadet Wesley Crusher, "The first duty of every Starfleet officer is to the *truth*, whether it's scientific truth, or historical truth, or personal truth." Rather than mere escapism, *Star Trek* and other time-honored sci-fi ought to be seen as entertaining, edifying preparation for thinking through the problems that the future will throw at us. *Star Trek*'s utopian vision isn't of a society in which all difficulties have been resolved, but of a community of individuals who *know*—in Aristotle's senses of "knowledge" as both speculative and practical—how to face such difficulties.[26]

Starfleet is fundamentally an *exploratory* body. Nonetheless, it utilizes military tropes—such as the chain of command and naval parlance—that make sense given the numerous phaser battles that ensue week after week. Starfleet also calls to mind the "band of brothers" mentality that's both a crucial and a natural quality emergent from the shared intensity of training and combat, as well as the shared commitment to the *mission*.[27] When the *Voyager* crew travels back in time to 1996 to stop someone from destroying the future, they elicit the help of a "local" who expresses amazement at the intrepid crew's sense of duty: "All this running around you do, your mission," she observes. "You're so dedicated, you know, like you care about something more than just your own little life." If we go back to Plato's picture of a utopia in his *Republic*, we find him recommending that the Guardians of the city should live in community, where all property, and even family, is shared such that each Guardian will learn to care just as much for the well-being of others as for his or her own well-being.[28] This communal ethic was later emphasized in the 19th century by utilitarians Jeremy Bentham and John Stuart Mill, who held that we should seek "the greatest good for the greatest number of people" and that, in determining the just distribution of benefits and burdens in society, every individual member should "count as one and no more than one"—or, as axiomatically put by Mr. Spock, "The needs of the many outweigh the needs of the few or the one."[29]

The Vulcan race has adopted a particular philosophy of logic and morality, the essence of which is captured by the motto "Infinite Diversity in Infinite Combinations." This pluralistic ideal is witnessed in the classic triumvirate of Captain Kirk, Mr. Spock, and Dr. McCoy, with Kirk representing the balanced integration of reason and emotion in ethical decisions; in the specialized expertise of each Starfleet crew member, working *cooperatively* to run the ship and accomplish the mission at hand; in Captain Picard's leadership style, consulting with his senior officers before making decisions with significant moral implications, availing himself of their unique perspectives and expertise instead of acting unilaterally; and finally in the *respect*—not merely tolerance—for intercultural differences, particularly in the case of *Deep Space Nine* where Humans, Bajorans, Ferengi, Cardassians, Klingons, and others who hold vastly different worldviews must learn to live and effectively work together. As these examples show, thoughtful viewing of *Star Trek*, both as a form of entertainment in itself and as a speculative depiction of future human life, is a fine example of just the sort of "play" that leads toward the ideal of human flourishing in our intellectual, moral, and spiritual nature.

## Our "Continuing Mission"

Philosophy and science fiction both call us to the task of unceasing reevaluation of who we are as individuals and as a people, not resting content on the laurels of past accomplishments, but preparing ourselves—both practically and morally—to work toward an optimal future for ourselves and the generations who'll follow us. Socrates set the standard for our communal and individual self-exploration when he emphatically said that "the unexamined life is not worth living."[30] Such inner searching mirrors the stellar exploration depicted in *Star Trek* and other sci-fi literature, television series, and films. Pieper thus refers to the philosophical act as "a step which leads to a kind of 'homeless'-ness: the stars are no roof over the head."[31] He describes human beings as "essentially *viatores*, travelers, pilgrims, 'on the way,' we are 'not-yet' there."[32] To coin a phrase, we are boldly going "where no one has gone before."

Hence, watching the occasional *Star Trek* marathon can actually be a beneficial intellectual exercise—a true form of human leisure à la Pieper. Even when facing death in *ST: Generations*, Kirk can't help but find fighting Soren to have been "fun"—and the same should go for any worthwhile human endeavor. It doesn't follow from this that *anything* that's fun is automatically worthwhile. But it does mean that if you aren't *enjoying* what you do in order to be a productive, contributing member of society, then maybe you've been fed the wrong message. So just because something is entertaining, it doesn't follow that it isn't *illuminating* as well. A simple, hour-long, sci-fi television story can often evoke the most complex and challenging of philosophical questions and ideas—a worthwhile retreat into fantasy that provides, as Pieper says, "that stillness that is the necessary preparation for accepting reality."[33] Perhaps that's why I see so many other professors dressed up as Vulcans and Klingons at sci-fi conventions.

# Notes

1. Josef Pieper, *Leisure: The Basis of Culture* (South Bend, IN: St. Augustine's Press, 1998), 90.
2. Thomas Aquinas, *Sententia super Metaphysicam*, bk. I, lect. 3; as quoted in Pieper, *Leisure*, 62.
3. Aristotle, *Nicomachean Ethics*, bk. X, ch. 7, 1177b4–6; as quoted in Pieper, *Leisure*, 4.
4. Pieper, *Leisure*, 33.
5. Robert Nozick, *Anarchy, State, and Utopia* (New York: Basic Books, 1974), 42–5.
6. Ibid., 43.
7. See Bernard Williams, "The Makropulos Case: Reflections on the Tedium of Immortality" in *The Metaphysics of Death*, ed. John Martin Fischer (Stanford, CA: Stanford University Press, 1993).
8. For elucidation of Whitehead's metaphysical worldview, see Melanie Johnson-Moxley's chapter in this volume (Chapter 20).
9. For a contrary assessment of the value of the utopian lifestyle afforded on Omicron Ceti III, see David Kyle Johnson's chapter in this volume (Chapter 5).
10. Seven of Nine's journey toward self-identity is aptly charted by Nicole Pramik in her chapter in this volume (Chapter 18).
11. Patrick Lee and Robert P. George, *Body-Self Dualism in Contemporary Ethics and Politics* (New York: Cambridge University Press, 2008), 115.
12. Ibid., 107.
13. For discussion of the paradoxical value of the pursuit of pleasure as depicted in *Star Trek*, see Robert Arp, "Mind Your Ps and Qs: Power, Pleasure, and the Q Continuum" in *Star Trek and Philosophy: The Wrath of Kant*, ed. Jason T. Eberl and Kevin S. Decker (Chicago: Open Court, 2008). For more on the ethics of holodeck use, see Philip Tallon and Jerry L. Walls, "Why Not Live in the Holodeck?" also in *Star Trek and Philosophy*; while metaphysical questions raised by holodeck use are explored in Dara Fogel's chapter in this volume (Chapter 26).
14. As quoted by *Star Trek* creator Gene Roddenberry; from the "Inside Star Trek with Gene Roddenberry" bonus CD included with the 20th-anniversary edition of the soundtrack to *Star Trek: The Motion Picture* (Los Angeles: Columbia/Legacy, 1998).

15. Pieper, *Leisure*, 2; the quotation from Plato isn't cited.
16. Charles Taylor, *A Secular Age* (Cambridge, MA: Harvard University Press, 2007), 55.
17. Pieper, *Leisure*, 18; quoting Aquinas, *Scriptum super libros Sententiarum*, bk. I, dist. 2 (*expositio textus*), which quotes Wisdom 8:30.
18. See ibid., 21–2.
19. Ibid., 44. For further discussion of future "Trekonomics," see Jeff Ewing's chapter in this volume (Chapter 11).
20. See ibid., 45.
21. See ibid., 34.
22. For discussion of Eastern meditation in comparison with Vulcan meditative practices, see Walter [Ritoku] Robinson, "Death and Rebirth of a Vulcan Mind," in *Star Trek and Philosophy* (2008).
23. Pieper, *Leisure*, 100.
24. For reasons why we should aspire to live in the Federation, see Jason Murphy and Todd Porter's chapter in *Star Trek and Philosophy* (2008).
25. Aristotle, *Metaphysics*, bk. I, ch. 1.
26. For further discussion of how *Star Trek* exemplifies how we ought to approach difficult dilemmas, see Courtland Lewis's chapter in this volume (Chapter 13).
27. For more detailed discussion of how military ethics is embodied in *Star Trek*'s ethos, see Tim Challans's chapter in *Star Trek and Philosophy* (2008).
28. Plato, *Republic*, bk. III, 416d–e and bk. V, 462a–471b.
29. For further explication of utilitarianism as depicted in *Star Trek*, see Greg Littmann's chapter in this volume (Chapter 12).
30. Plato, *Apology*, 38a.
31. Pieper, *Leisure*, 94.
32. Ibid., 107.
33. Ibid., 31.

# 2

# Aristotle and James T. Kirk: The Problem of Greatness

*Jerold J. Abrams*

If … there be some one person, or more than one, although not enough to make up the full complement of a state, whose excellence is so pre-eminent that the excellence or the political capacity of all the rest admit of no comparison with his or theirs, he or they can be no longer regarded as part of a state; for justice will not be done to the superior, if he is reckoned only as the equal of those who are so far inferior to him in excellence and in political capacity. Such a man may truly be deemed a God among men. Hence we see that legislation is necessarily concerned with those who are equal in birth and in capacity; and that for men of pre-eminent excellence there is no law—they are themselves a law.[1]

Aristotle (385–322 BCE), in his *Politics*, imagines the appearance of a "god among men"—an actual superhuman—who can't be a citizen of the state because no merely human law can constrain such a spectac-ular being, and any attempt to do so would be like trying to restrain Zeus himself. Citizens have only two mutually exclusive options: they can exile—or even execute—a "god among men," or they can submit to superhuman monarchy. Aristotle thinks any state would choose the former, but finds the latter option superior and argues the citi-zenry *should* submit to the superhuman monarch because that's pre-cisely what ideal citizens *would* do if such a being appeared in their society. This problem posed by such a hypothetical superhuman may seem outlandish, but Aristotle actually finds this same antagonism between excellence and equality—in less extreme forms—to permeate all human culture, and to appear vividly in great works of literature.

*The Ultimate Star Trek and Philosophy*, First Edition. Edited by Kevin S. Decker and Jason T. Eberl.
© 2016 John Wiley & Sons, Ltd. Published 2016 by John Wiley & Sons, Ltd.

The same problem also appears in great cinema and perhaps nowhere more powerfully than in J. J. Abrams's *Star Trek* and *Star Trek Into Darkness* with the character of James T. Kirk. Like Aristotle's god among men, as well as the closely related figure of the "great-souled man" (*megalopsychos*), Kirk possesses surpassing intellectual genius and nobility of character; however, this very greatness inevitably antagonizes the rest of Starfleet. As the equal of no man, Kirk speaks openly from love and hate even to his superiors, thinks their rank is merely titular compared to his own natural superiority, follows virtually no laws except his own, and thinks himself a different kind of man, a different kind of being. He can no more be a mere crewmember of a starship than Aristotle's god among men can be a citizen of any merely human state, and must ultimately either be exiled to the wilderness or impose his own law from the captain's chair.

## Kirk and *Megalopsychia*

In his *Nicomachean Ethics*, Aristotle describes a man he calls the *megalopsychos*—the "great-souled man" or the "proud man." This man isn't superhuman, so he can still be recognized as human—unlike the god among men in the *Politics*—yet he appears to be beyond humanity, and thinks himself so.[2] The *megalopsychos* is brilliant and noble, speaks with a deep and powerful voice, walks slowly and will never be hurried, and won't revolve around another's life—except another *megalopsychos*. He speaks openly, whether from love or hate, thinks there's nothing great in society and thus lives apart from others, and possesses all the virtues, with pride at their crown. He holds back from contests and offices in society, thinking them inferior to his own natural rank and honor; but he *will* enter society for the very highest honors to be bestowed on the very highest men, men like himself:

> Again, it is characteristic of the proud man not to aim at the things commonly held in honor, or the things in which others excel; to be sluggish and to hold back except where great honor as a great result is at stake, and to be a man of few deeds, but of great and notable ones.[3]

Kirk—especially as depicted in Abrams's films—is one of these great-souled men: he is brilliant, brave, rebellious, and excessively proud. He lives apart from society on farmland, without any desire to become involved in grand organizations like Starfleet. He doesn't submit to authority, even when challenged to a fight and outnumbered four-to-one by Starfleet cadets trained in combat. Instead he stands his ground and mocks their numbers, telling them they need more guys to make it "an even fight."

After the fight, Captain Christopher Pike discovers the identity of the still proud but badly beaten Kirk, and asks him why the genius son of a hero captain chooses to live beyond society. Again, Kirk speaks with ridicule for rank:

PIKE:   Your aptitude tests are off the charts. So what is it? You like being the only genius-level repeat offender in the Midwest?

KIRK:   Maybe I love it.

PIKE:   So your dad dies. You can settle for a less than ordinary life. Or do you feel that you were meant for something better, something special? Enlist in Starfleet.

KIRK:   Enlist? [Kirk laughs at Pike.] You guys must be way down on your recruiting quota for the month.

Challenged to join Starfleet and to do better than his father—who, as captain of the *U.S.S. Kelvin* for a mere twelve minutes, saved 800 lives—Kirk decides that this is a challenge of the highest honor and enlists the next morning. First, though, he haughtily informs Pike that he'll complete Starfleet training faster than anyone: "Four years? I'll do it in three." But like the *megalopsychos*, Kirk's natural brilliance, pride, and disdain for authority inevitably create antagonisms with the Starfleet hierarchy. As a result, like the god among men who can be no mere member of the state, Kirk can be no mere member of Starfleet.

## Kirk as a Law unto Himself

The *Kobayashi Maru* is a Starfleet test in which a cadet "commanding" a simulated starship is faced with the rescue of the crew of a stranded civilian ship while battling three Klingon D-7s. After having failed the test twice, Kirk decides to take it a third time:

KIRK:   Bones, it doesn't bother you that no one's ever passed the test?

BONES:  Jim, it's the *Kobayashi Maru*. No one passes the test. And no one goes back for seconds, let alone thirds.

Kirk's genius is instrumental, strategic, and creative, perfectly suited to unscripted and dangerous games, which is just what the *Kobayashi Maru* challenge represents. But Kirk has discovered that the unbeatable *Kobayashi Maru* isn't really a true game at all, for a true game is potentially winnable. So, Kirk reprograms the game, rewrites the rules, and reverses the game's logic: instead of an assured loss, he determines an assured win. Commander Spock, who designs and administers the test, calls Kirk to answer in a formal hearing for cheating:

KIRK:   Let me ask you something, I think we all know the answer to. The test itself is a cheat, isn't it? You programmed it to be unwinnable.

SPOCK:  Your argument precludes the possibility of a no-win scenario?

KIRK:   I don't believe in no-win scenarios.

SPOCK:  Then not only did you violate the rules, you also failed to understand the principle lesson.

KIRK:   Please, enlighten me.

SPOCK:  You of all people should know, cadet Kirk, a captain cannot cheat death.

KIRK:   I of all people?

SPOCK:  Your father, Lieutenant George Kirk, assumed command of his vessel before being killed in action, did he not?

KIRK:   I don't think you like the fact that I beat your test.

SPOCK:  Furthermore you have failed to divine the purpose of the test.

KIRK:   Enlighten me again.

SPOCK:  The purpose of the test is to experience fear. Fear in the face of certain death. To accept that fear and maintain control of oneself and one's crew. This is a quality expected in every Starfleet captain.

Spock and Kirk debate the *Kobayashi Maru*'s theoretical foundations: Spock argues that the game, while unwinnable, still functions to educate. Kirk, however, presumes that any game must be winnable, which means Spock's game is not a game. Thus the same charge of deception (or cheating) may be set against the game and, indeed, against Spock himself. In transforming Spock's game, however, Kirk *does* actually play and win a game of his own design. Kirk rejects the presumption of a no-win scenario, and imposes his own rules. These rules allow him to defeat the Klingons and rescue the *Kobayashi Maru* without suffering any casualties among his own crew, which is the (presumed) objective of Spock's no-win "game." Kirk renders this objective possible only by rewriting the game, which is in fact the *ultimate objective of any*

*Starfleet captain in a real battle*: to reason strategically and creatively through an apparently insoluble problem in order to accomplish the mission at hand while safeguarding ship and crew. So, Kirk doesn't play Spock's game at all, but rather his own game in which Spock's game has become the opponent. He further assumes a strategy of deception, thereby mimicking, at a more foundational level, the strategy of the programmed simulation. Yet, Kirk's game isn't for just anyone to play, but only for truly godlike individuals who are laws unto themselves.

Kirk proudly declares himself such a godlike man, a man for whom even Starfleet's Prime Directive doesn't apply, to his superior, Admiral Pike, in *Star Trek Into Darkness*. The *Enterprise* had attempted to save a primitive civilization without being seen, but when Spock's life is in danger and a line-of-sight transport is required, Kirk commands the *Enterprise* to rise, like a god from the sea, in plain view of aliens who've "barely invented the wheel." Pike reprimands Kirk for this ultimate violation:

PIKE:   You think the rules don't apply to you because you disagree with them.

KIRK:   That's why you talked me into signing up in the first place. It's why you gave me your ship.

PIKE:   I gave you my ship because I saw greatness in you. And now I see you haven't got an ounce of humility.... You were supposed to survey a planet, not alter its destiny! You violated a dozen Starfleet regulations and almost got everyone under your command killed.

KIRK:   Except I didn't! You know how many crew members I've lost? Not one!

PIKE:   That's your problem, you think you're infallible! You think you can't make a mistake. It's a pattern with you! The rules are for other people!

KIRK:   Some should be!

PIKE:   And what's worse is you're using blind luck to justify your playing God!

Again, like the *megalopsychos*, Kirk speaks openly about the division between superior individuals and other members of Starfleet, even though, as superior, he serves these others as his crew and loves them as family. But, like the god among men, he can't be assimilated to the laws of society, knows himself to be a law unto himself, and thus openly declares himself above the Prime Directive. Pike, while frustrated, knows that this is *exactly* what he admires in Kirk, and that he shares this quality with his father. Kirk knows it too.

## Exile to Delta Vega

In his *Politics*, Aristotle recognizes that any society faced with a god among men would choose the god's exile over domination by a super-human monarch, and acknowledges this solution to appear even in ancient mythology with the exile of the demigod Heracles, who could be no crew member of any ship: "Mythology tells us that the Argonauts left Heracles behind for a similar reason; the ship Argo would not take him because she feared that he would have been too much for the rest of the crew."[4] In Abrams's *Star Trek*, the *Enterprise* must also leave Kirk behind because, even though he isn't literally superhuman, he is, like Heracles, simply *too much* for the ship's crew. His very presence undermines the unity of the crew, and Spock, in command after Pike's capture by the Romulan captain Nero, can hardly bear this antagonism any more than Aristotle's citizenry can bear the striking superiority of the god among men. Kirk speaks openly in disdain for Spock's unwillingness to engage the Romulans and rescue Pike.

KIRK:     I will not allow us to go backwards, and run from the problem, instead of hunting Nero down.

SPOCK:     Security, escort him out.

Kirk fights the guards, but Spock drops him with a Vulcan neck pinch and exiles him to Delta Vega.

Kirk awakens on a frozen world beyond all civilization, teeming with gigantic beasts. In his *Politics*, Aristotle contends that only human beings can be members of the state, and those who by nature are beneath or above humanity, the beasts and the gods, must live beyond the state in the wilderness: "he who is unable to live in society, or who has no need because he is sufficient for himself, must be either a beast or a god: he is no part of a state."[5] Kirk, the godlike exile in the wilderness of Delta Vega, faces two vicious beasts until finally escaping into an ice cave where he finds Spock Prime, who explains that, in the future, he and Kirk are great friends. Indeed, the friendship between these two fits Aristotle's definition of genuine friendship in which virtuous individuals—such as two *megalopsychoi*—revolve around each other as "second selves."[6] But Kirk informs the elder Vulcan that they're *not* friends, and Spock Prime, perfectly understanding Kirk's "first, best destiny," tells Kirk he must take control of his own ship in order to defeat Nero and in order for their friendship to grow.

So Kirk must play another round of the *Kobayashi Maru*, this time designed by Spock Prime for Kirk to win against the younger Spock. The elder Spock, who's learned much from his old friend Kirk, teaches the younger Scotty transwarp theory—discovered, of course, by the Mr. Scott of Spock Prime's universe—enabling Kirk to beam aboard the *Enterprise* while it travels at warp speed. Spock Prime thus enables Kirk to again impose an alternative set of rules on an apparently no-win scenario against Spock by applying the physics of the future to the present. But first, Spock warns Kirk not to reveal to the younger Spock the identity of Spock Prime:

SPOCK:    Under no circumstances can he be made aware of my existence. You must promise me this.

KIRK:    You're telling me I can't tell you that I'm following your own orders, why not? What happens?

SPOCK:    Jim, this is one rule you cannot break. To stop Nero, you alone must take command of your ship.

Spock knows Kirk's nature and character, knows he's already broken many rules, knows Kirk is a natural captain who's a law unto himself, and warns him *not to break this one rule*, not to tell the younger Spock of his elder self. Later, upon meeting the Spock of Kirk's universe, Spock Prime explains to him how he deceived Kirk into thinking the universe would collapse if Kirk broke his promise, thereby revealing to the younger Spock how much he has yet to learn from the supreme game-playing intelligence of his future friend and great-souled captain, Kirk.

## Captain of the *Enterprise*

After successfully beaming aboard the *Enterprise*, Kirk openly antagonizes Spock, eye-to-eye, haughty like the *megalopsychos*, declaring that Spock felt nothing for the death of his mother, that he's an unfeeling robot, and little more than the "green-blooded hobgoblin" Bones takes him for. Spock explodes in a rage of mortal combat, but brings himself back from killing the exile and instead, quite rationally, relieves himself of duty as captain, all according to Kirk's plan as spelled out by Spock Prime. The crew looks disconcerted, but Kirk, awaiting no discussion of rules or procedures, eases himself comfortably into the captain's chair, finally attaining his appropriate position of superiority, and immediately takes the ship to war.

Aristotle defines the two solutions to the problem of greatness—exile or monarchic rule—as mutually exclusive, but Kirk is able to progress from exile on Delta Vega to the captain's chair—the former seeming "hypothetically necessary" for the latter.[7] Kirk must suffer exile by Spock to the realm of the beasts and the gods in order to discover and fulfill his true destiny as captain of the *Enterprise*, a destiny in which his greatest friend is none other than Spock, who himself takes *his* rightful position as first officer by Kirk's side. Spock returns to the bridge and advises Kirk on the logic and physics of their attack plan, two great-souled men with different powers, who'll continue to revolve around one another for the duration of their lives as "second selves" to each other. Together they defeat Nero and rescue Pike, and later defeat an even more formidable enemy: Khan, a superhuman being, "genetically engineered to be superior" and "forced into exile," cryonically suspended but then revived, and who can also no more live among humanity than Aristotle's god among men.[8]

## Notes

1. Aristotle, *Politics*, trans. B. Jowett, in *The Complete Works of Aristotle*, ed. Jonathan Barnes (Princeton, NJ: Princeton University Press, 1984), III.13.1284a1–18.
2. See Aristotle, *Posterior Analytics*, II.13.97b16–24. While the *Nicomachean Ethics* IV.3 doesn't describe *megalopsychia* as superhuman, in the *Posterior Analytics* Aristotle names Alcibiades, Ajax, Lysander, Socrates, and Achilles (who is also superhuman).
3. Aristotle, *Nicomachean Ethics*, trans. W.D. Ross, IV.3.1124b22–6.
4. Aristotle, *Politics*, III.13.1248b15.
5. Aristotle, *Politics*, I.2.1253a25–30.
6. See Aristotle, *Nicomachean Ethics*, IX.4.1166a30–3.
7. See Aristotle, *Parts of Animals*, I.1.639b26–640a1.
8. I am very grateful to Jason Eberl, Kevin Decker, and Bill Irwin for reading and commenting on an earlier draft of the chapter. Of course, any mistakes that remain are my own.

# The Moral Psychology of a Starship Captain

*Tim Challans*

Now, look, Jim. Not one man in a million could do what you and I
have done. Command a starship. A hundred decisions a day, hundreds
of lives staked on you making every one of them right.
—Commodore Stone to Captain Kirk, "Court Martial" (TOS)

I wish I were on a long sea voyage somewhere. Not too much deck
tennis, no frantic dancing, and no responsibility. Why me? I look around
that bridge, and I see the men waiting for me to make the next move.
And Bones, what if I'm wrong?
—Captain Kirk to Dr. McCoy, "Balance of Terror" (TOS)

The burdens of starship command are incalculable and it's under-
standable that many individuals might fold under the pressure, no
matter how many pretty yeomen bring meals to one's cabin, or the
unlimited availability of cups of Earl Grey tea, or even having one's
pet beagle onboard. Captain R.M. Merik of the *S.S. Beagle* went
into the merchant service after failing "a psycho-simulator test" at
Starfleet Academy due to "a split second of indecision" ("Bread and
Circuses," TOS). Merik's career ended tragically on planet 892-IV following morally questionable decisions he made that led to his entire
crew becoming enslaved and dying in gladiatorial games on a world
that resembled "a 20th-century Rome." *Starship* captains must make
decisions constantly in which they're compelled to balance the best
interests of their crew, their mission, the United Federation of Planets, and any alien species they encounter. And, unlike Merik, they

*The Ultimate Star Trek and Philosophy*, First Edition. Edited by Kevin S. Decker and Jason T. Eberl.
© 2016 John Wiley & Sons, Ltd. Published 2016 by John Wiley & Sons, Ltd.

typically—though not always—succeed. Success in moral decision making, however, requires having well-integrated rational and emotional motivations. Though the intrepid captains who've graced our television screens and cinema for the past five decades are by no means perfect human beings, their leadership qualities make them exemplary case-study subjects in *moral psychology*.

Moral psychology investigates the connections between our thoughts and emotions, both of which are action guiding. We're familiar with various practical programs related to the importance of our emotions in our personal and professional lives: emotional intelligence, the Myers-Briggs Type Indicator® (MBTI) personality inventory, learning style inventories, and so on. But long before we developed these social scientific tools, philosophers set the stage to help us understand the connection between our moral life and our emotional nature. Philosophical questions about moral psychology differ from scientific questions in that the latter are *empirical*, that is, they are questions about the way we actually express emotions. Philosophers ask questions in order to build ideas and concepts that constitute *theories*. Philosophers who inquire into the topic of moral psychology seek to reconcile our emotional responses with our moral character, intentions, actions, and moral responsibility—asking normative questions as well as empirical ones.

It's a fact of human nature that much of the time people are out of synch with their moral emotions; humans simply find it hard to feel emotions such as pride, shame, guilt, regret, and remorse at the right time, in the right place, in the right way, for the right reason, and so on.[1] The rare possession of a *healthy* moral psychology might be an important qualification for being that one-in-a-million person, a starship captain.

## "I Don't Believe in No-Win Scenarios"

*Star Trek* always features a central cast with a captain reminiscent of Plato's (429–347 BCE) metaphorical charioteer, whose responsibility is to balance the reins of two horses pulling in different directions—one driven by passion, the other by intellect. In TOS, Captain James T. Kirk is the charioteer, balancing the pull between Dr. Leonard McCoy, who navigates with his feelings, and Mr. Spock, who leans in a rigorously logical direction. The captain is able to steer the ship by bringing together the best of what each of these two advisors has to offer. And he's able to do so because he can balance *his own* passion and reason, like a good charioteer harnessing two wild steeds. Kirk is thus able to manifest the appropriate emotional response to deal with each situation appropriately, balancing the full range of emotions between *pride* and *humility*.

Plato's student Aristotle (385–322 BCE) considered *magnanimity*— or generosity out of pride—a virtue. Dante (1265–1321), by contrast, considered pride one of the seven deadly sins, and ever since, pride has been suspect as a feature of our common moral psychology. But commanding a starship is anything but common, so pride just happens to be one of those virtuous feelings that actually qualifies Captain Kirk to be that one-in-a-million person who can do the job. Proper pride enables a person to be self-possessed, maintain self-respect, and remain confident when others are doubting. In "Court Martial," Kirk is framed to look as if he'd faltered under pressure during an ion storm, acting prematurely in jettisoning a research pod that allegedly caused a crewman's death. As Kirk humbly endures his trial, Spock is convinced his captain couldn't have faltered—precisely because Kirk exudes a kind of well-founded charisma of pride based on his unwavering, steadfast competence and self-control. Spock testifies, "Human beings have characteristics just as inanimate objects do. It is impossible for Captain Kirk to act out of panic or malice. It is not his nature."

The harmonious combination of reason and emotion enables Kirk to be a skillful *master and commander* of his starship. He also projects a pride—tempered with humility—that gives him the ability to instill trust in those he leads. For the Greeks pride was referred to as *hubris* or magnanimity, for the Romans it was called *superbia*—yet whatever its local terminology may be in any corner of the galaxy, Kirk's pride is what enables him to consistently say that he doesn't believe in a "no-win scenario."[2]

## "I Would Have Told Him Anything"

In *A Theory of Justice*, John Rawls (1921–2002) distinguishes between *shame* and *guilt*.[3] Essentially, we feel shame when we violate a private code of ethics, and we feel guilt when we violate a public code of ethics. Shame is thus self-regarding, whereas guilt is other-regarding. At the same time, the virtue of *integrity* sustains one's adherence to the private code, while the virtue of *honor* does the same for the public code.

In "Chain of Command" (TNG), Captain Jean-Luc Picard demonstrates proper shame and guilt when he's interrogated and tortured by the Cardassian Gul Madred. Taking a brainwashing page out of George Orwell's *1984*, Madred repeatedly works to coerce Picard to admit that he sees five lights in the interrogation chamber, when in fact there are only four. After his rescue, Picard confides to Counselor Deanna Troi that, at the time of his rescue, he was ready to tell Gul Madred that there were five lights—that he would've told him anything—and, even more disturbingly, he actually *saw* five lights. Picard feels guilt due to his experience, since he'd come close to letting down his friends, his crew, and his ship—that is, violating the public code. More damaging may be the shame he felt, having violated his own personal code.

Contemporary philosopher Nancy Sherman names a new concept in the case of military service members who experience guilt and shame while engaged in conflict: "moral injury."[4] It's particularly harmful when it motivates shame. The ancient Greek origin of *shame* had to do with the feeling one has when completely unclothed. Sherman draws attention to the connection between the high rate of suicide among today's service members and the prevalence of their feelings of shame and guilt, but particularly shame. When a person feels shame, it's not simply that they recognize they've done something wrong. Rather, they're no longer the same person—they've essentially lost their self-identity.

Picard literally loses his self-identity when he's assimilated by the Borg and becomes "Locutus"—mouthpiece of the Borg Collective—in "The Best of Both Worlds" (TNG).[5] Picard's guilt over his role in the destruction of over forty starships at Wolf 359 and his shame at not being able to stop the Borg from using him in this way cause him to break down in a moment of humble vulnerability to his older brother in "Family" (TNG):

PICARD: You don't know, Robert. You don't know. They took everything I was. They used me to kill and to destroy, and I couldn't stop them. I should have been able to stop them! I tried. I tried so hard, but I wasn't strong enough. I wasn't good enough. I should have been able to stop them. I should! I should!

ROBERT: So, my brother is a human being after all. This is going to be with you a long time, Jean-Luc. A long time. You have to learn to live with it.

Picard recovers from these experiences, but it's safe to conclude that he had to do much work to integrate and process these more difficult aspects of the development of his moral psychology and the maturation and evolution of his self-identity.

## "I Have a Chance to Change All That"

In TOS, we see the introduction of the Prime Directive—the proscription against interfering with other cultures on alien worlds.[6] The Prime Directive in TOS evidently provides indirect commentary against U.S. involvement in Vietnam—particularly given episodes in which it's explicitly invoked, such as "A Private Little War" and "The Omega Glory." In *Star Trek Into Darkness*, Admiral Pike dresses down a young Captain Kirk for violating the Prime Directive by allowing a primitive culture to see the *Enterprise*. Pike tells Kirk that his ship will be taken from him because he's not ready for command. Interestingly, in terms of moral psychology, young Kirk registers no shame, guilt, regret, or remorse over his actions. By contrast, the mature Jim Kirk we see in *ST V: The Final Frontier* has experienced much guilt, shame, regret, and remorse—perhaps even over certain instances in which he'd violated the Prime Directive. Nonetheless, he refuses to avail himself of the opportunity that Spock's half-brother Sybok offers to help him reckon with and dispose of his pain:

SYBOK:   Now learn something about yourself.
KIRK:    No. I refuse.
MCCOY:   Jim, try to be open about this.
KIRK:    About what? That I've made the wrong choices in my life? That I turned left when I should've turned right? I know what my weaknesses are. I don't need Sybok to take me on a tour of them.
MCCOY:   If you'd just . . . .
KIRK:    To be brainwashed by this con man?
MCCOY:   I was wrong. This 'con man' took away my pain!
KIRK:    Dammit, Bones, you're a doctor. You know that pain and guilt can't be taken away with the wave of a magic wand. They're things we carry with us, the things that make us who we are. If we lose them, we lose ourselves. I don't want my pain taken away. I *need* my pain!

Kirk's pain reminds him who he is; it's an essential part of his self-identity.

In ENT, the *Enterprise* crew ventures into unexplored space on a mission to find the mysterious Xindi who attacked Earth, killing over 7 million people. Just as TOS provided political commentary about Vietnam, ENT provided commentary about the U.S. reaction to the 9/11 attack. The United States sought revenge and, in its pursuit of the enemy, did many things that it still needs to come to terms with—disproportionate violence, torture, and arguably even murder. Similarly, Captain Jonathan Archer and his crew do many morally questionable things in their pursuit of the Xindi—including torturing a prisoner for information ("Anomaly"), killing an innocent man to save his chief engineer ("Similitude"), and pirating a warp coil from an alien ship ("Damage"). In "Home" (ENT), after being in space for a few years, Archer confides in his peer and former romantic interest Erika Hernandez during a mountain-climbing trip. Archer is in need of rest and relaxation for he's simply not himself, full of self-doubt, and feeling distraught about how his initially optimistic mission of *exploration* that started three years prior—without his ship even being armed with phasers—evolved into one of seemingly endless conflicts. When Erika asks him if he's all right, he responds that he's not even sure what *all right* means anymore. He's not proud of much of what's happened and sarcastically tells her he doesn't remember reading the chapters about torture and marooning innocent people in their Starfleet handbook. Archer feels *regret* for what he's done, an emotion that can be based on wrong or harm brought to others that can't be changed. Regret thus involves a kind of acceptance of what's happened.[7] Even though he's deeply wounded as he regrets his wrongdoings, Archer is eventually able to resume his command.

*Remorse* is related to regret, but it is a more powerful emotion. In "Endgame" (VOY), we see an Admiral Janeway who's successfully brought her ship home after spending twenty-three years making it back from the Delta Quadrant. She feels something deeper than regret because of the circumstances that have developed regarding several members of her crew. Seven of Nine has died, and Janeway could never accept her death. She also regrets Chakotay having suffered Seven, who'd become his wife, dying in his arms after being mortally injured on an away mission. Tuvok has succumbed to a neurological disorder and is doomed to spend the rest of his life in a deteriorating deranged state because *Voyager* couldn't get back to the Alpha Quadrant in time for him to be cured. Janeway's lack of acceptance of her crew's present reality motivates her to go back in time and change the past—thus violating the Temporal Prime Directive. Meeting up with her younger self, Admiral Janeway convinces Captain Janeway to help her use the Borg's transwarp conduits to get home, while almost simultaneously destroying the conduits to deny the Borg quick access to cross quadrants. Her bold plan works, and while the admiral dies facing off with the Borg Queen the captain makes it home with her crew. Admiral Janeway felt a very deep kind of guilt that's stronger than regret. Whereas regret always involves *acceptance* of what's happened in the past and one's current state, remorse *never* does. Because remorse is *other-regarding*, the only way to deal with it is to address the wrong one believes one has done to others. Janeway took advantage of an opportunity to change reality through time across two galactic quadrants in order to save her crew: an amazing display of the *right stuff*.

## "No Better Than the Enemy"

Good education, training, and experience can provide the basis for a sound moral psychology. Reliable feelings that emerge from a sound moral psychology guide Captain Picard's actions: he can trust his intuitions, so to speak. But that doesn't mean that he hasn't stopped developing his moral psychology or that he's incapable of learning more. While his intuitions may guide the captain for the most part, it's also possible that his intuitions could use some improvement. In other words, there's a role in moral psychology for second thoughts. In "I, Borg" (TNG), Picard is initially willing to follow the recommendations of his officers who want to allow the return of a drone to the Borg Collective—but weaponized with a virus that would wipe out the Borg altogether. His moral intuitions have developed in a way that the destruction of the Borg with so little risk seems a reasonable and worthy venture. But after listening to Geordi LaForge, who's given the Borg drone a name, Hugh, and Guinan, whose homeworld was destroyed by the Borg and thus has an even stronger initial motivation for revenge that she later tempers, Picard eventually has second thoughts about sending Hugh back to commit genocide. Picard was able to redescribe his situation, allowing him to change his beliefs about autonomous individuality, even when displayed by a Borg; and, along with Geordi and Guinan, his feelings changed because his ideas changed. Picard's revised beliefs were actually more consistent with his overall moral psychology, for after he changed his mind he realized his initial feelings were based on the traumatizing experience he had when the Borg had assimilated him.

One contemporary philosopher, Martha Nussbaum, aptly describes emotions as "upheavals of thought."[8] Charles Taylor, another contemporary philosopher, analyzes how we can change the way we feel about ourselves—whether we feel good or bad about what we've done or how we might judge ourselves through redescription that results in changing our ideas—when considering these kinds of "emotions of self-assessment."[9] In other words, if we can explicitly and precisely describe and redescribe our beliefs, then we can change our emotions. We'd be able to rationally change our feelings, as well as our judgments about things, because we change our beliefs. We may believe one way and feel pride, but we could change our beliefs and later feel shame because our ideas are different. In *ST: First Contact*, Picard calls Worf a "coward" for wanting to use the escape pods in the face of a Borg takeover of the *Enterprise*-E. Later, realizing that his own obsession with the Borg motivated his cruel words, the captain agrees to abandon ship and tells Worf that he's the bravest man Picard's ever known.

Some philosophers argue that our emotions are deeply connected to our beliefs, termed *propositional attitudes*. A proposition is an idea that can be either true or false, and a propositional attitude denotes the type of feeling we have when adopting or expressing an idea that we believe is true or false. This way of understanding the connection of beliefs to emotions seems to establish a kind of priority of idea over emotion, which implies two things: that proper emotions are dependent upon our ideas, and that thoughts precede emotions in time. The word *supervenience* describes how emotions are connected to thoughts: namely, emotions supervene, or are logically dependent upon, the content of our thoughts. Our emotions change as our ideas change. Or, in philosophical language, supervenience occurs when two sets of qualities change in a one-way relation of logical dependency across one individual. ENT provides a biological example of supervienience when considering the different classes of Xindi: aquatic, arboreal, avian, insectoid, primate, and reptilian. The physical qualities (phenotypes) supervene upon genetic qualities (genotypes) as we see the physical characteristics of the Xindi supervene over the genetic ones: fins, nails, wings, tentacles, fur, and scales (yet all made of the same substance, keratin). Analogously, for moral psychology, the qualities of our emotions (the nature of our feelings) change as the qualities of our thoughts (their content) change; emotions supervene upon our thoughts.[10]

But not everyone thinks reason has priority in relation to the emotions, instead believing that reason is dependent upon the emotions. David Hume (1711–1776), for instance, contends that emotions have priority and famously refers to reason as being a "slave of the passions."[11] Likewise, modern psychological behaviorists—following the views of B.F. Skinner (1904–1990)—consider ideas to be secondary to emotions.

## "The Tapestry of My Life"

Captain Picard arguably displays the mature and balanced harmony of his moral emotions informed by his understanding. The emotional makeup of a starship captain is demanding; in addition to the required skills, most people simply don't have the ego required to be under such pressure and hold that level of responsibility. We see this clearly in "Tapestry" (TNG) when Picard is given the chance to go back in time and prevent himself from being stabbed through the heart by a Nausicaan. As he replays his life and is confronted by the aliens, he's able to avoid the fight. Q fast-forwards him to the present, and Picard finds himself disoriented. He's a lieutenant (j.g.) and a science officer doing research and writing reports for Lieutenant Commander Geordi LaForge. He's not the captain, for when he changed the past he started on a path where he was a different person. He's humiliated, poignantly depicted when he has to gangway (get out of the way) for a couple of junior officers—as captain, people routinely gangway for *him*. He no longer feels the magnanimity, superbia, and pride that are requisite for starship command, and he can't live with that. He tells Q that he'd rather die as *Captain* Picard than live the life he's been able to glimpse without his pride, a dreary man who "is bereft of passion and imagination."

Clearly, not everyone can become a starship captain. The role requires possession of a sound moral psychology, and this might explain why the vast majority of us are not made to sit in the captain's chair. Even if we passed our Starfleet exams and got posted on a starship, the vast majority of us still wouldn't have our quarters directly above Ten Forward, where Captain Picard can directly view whatever the ship will encounter next. We wouldn't be, literally and metaphorically, encountering and handling the unknown head-on. The future is better off with the right people serving as starship captains, and our exploration into the moral psychology of such elite individuals helps to explain why those we see in *Star Trek* are made of *starship stuff.*

## Notes

1. Aristotle, *Nicomachean Ethics*, trans. Terence Irwin (Indianapolis, IN: Hackett, 1999).
2. For further analysis of Kirk's moral character—which started out less tempered by humility in his alternate youth, depicted in *Star Trek* (2009) and *Star Trek Incto Darkness*—see Jerold J. Abrams's chapter in this volume (Chapter 2).
3. John Rawls, *A Theory of Justice* (Cambridge, MA: Harvard University Press, 1971).
4. Nancy Sherman, *Afterwar* (Oxford: Oxford University Press, 2015).
5. For further discussion of how Borg assimilation impinges one's self-identity and the difficulty in re-establishing it, see Barbara Stock's and Nicole Pramik's chapters in this volume (Chapters 9 and 18, respectively).
6. The Prime Directive is analyzed in depth by Alejandro Bárcenas and Steve Bein in their chapter in this volume (Chapter 4).
7. Gabrielle Taylor, *Pride, Shame, and Guilt: Emotions of Self-Assessment* (Oxford: Oxford University Press, 1987).
8. Martha Nussbaum, *Upheavals of Thought* (Cambridge: Cambridge University Press, 2003).
9. Charles Taylor, *Philosophy and the Human Sciences*, vols. 1 and 2 (Cambridge: Cambridge University Press, 1985).
10. Jaegwon Kim, *Supervenience and Mind* (Cambridge: Cambridge University Press, 1993).
11. David Hume, *A Treatise of Human Nature*, (Oxford: Oxford University Press, 2000).

# 4

# "Make It So": Kant, Confucius, and the Prime Directive

*Alejandro Bárcenas and Steve Bein*

Some day my people are going to come up with some sort of a doctrine, something that tells us what we can and can't do out here, [what we] should and shouldn't do. But until somebody tells me that they've drafted that directive, I'm going to have to remind myself every day that we didn't come out here to play God.
—Captain Jonathan Archer ("Dear Doctor," ENT)

Two things fill the mind with ever new and increasing admiration and reverence, the more often and more steadily one reflects on them: the starry heavens above me and the moral law within me.
—Immanuel Kant, *Critique of Practical Reason*[1]

In the beginning of *Star Trek Into Darkness*, Mr. Spock descends into the heart of a raging volcano on the planet Nibiru. His mission: to detonate a cold fusion device that will solidify the bubbling magma before it erupts and destroys an entire civilization. Meanwhile, Captain Kirk is on the bridge of the *Enterprise* facing a dilemma. His first priority as captain is the safety of his crew, and that means he's duty-bound to rescue Spock. On the other hand, he's also duty-bound never to violate the Prime Directive. This is the cardinal rule of Starfleet, an absolute ban on exposing pre-warp civilizations to advanced technologies that could change the course of their future. If the only way to rescue Spock is to reveal the *Enterprise* to the primitive civilization at the foot of the volcano, what should he do?

Spock will say the answer is obvious. He can't be saved at this point, because "the needs of the many outweigh the needs of the few"; the

*The Ultimate Star Trek and Philosophy*, First Edition. Edited by Kevin S. Decker and Jason T. Eberl.
© 2016 John Wiley & Sons, Ltd. Published 2016 by John Wiley & Sons, Ltd.

loss of one science officer is nothing in comparison to the fate of an entire culture.[2] But Kirk doesn't see it this way. Following rules is one thing, saving lives is another—and, after all, it's not *certain* that the people of Nibiru will live out a different destiny just because a few inhabitants happened to see the *Enterprise*. As Kirk puts it after he rescues his friend, "Oh, come on, Spock! They saw us. Big deal."

Is it a big deal? Is the Prime Directive worth following, or is it too blunt an instrument for dealing with all the varied situations a Starfleet officer might face during a mission of exploration? Is it true that one *never* ought to interfere with the internal affairs of a foreign culture?[3] Framing the question a different way, what are the consequences of sending a crew into deep space *without* a binding principle like the Prime Directive? What's the point of having such a principle if starship captains are allowed to break it when they see fit?[4]

One thing is certain: it's a difficult problem, and one that has appeared in *Star Trek* from the beginning. One reason it captures our attention is that every one of us has faced a similar situation: what should you do when you want to do what seems to be the right thing, but you know doing so will violate a really important rule? We'll explore two competing solutions to this problem, one that emphasizes the importance of adhering strictly to moral rules, and another that acknowledges the vagueness we often encounter when making moral decisions.

## The Search for Spock's Conscience

One way to address the problem of the Prime Directive is to follow the criteria used by Vulcans: reason and logic.[5] This approach has been highly revered in the history of moral philosophy, and was most convincingly articulated by Immanuel Kant (1724–1804). Kant seems to have had some Vulcan blood in him, because he argues that we ought to carry out moral reasoning through pure reason alone, uncontaminated by emotions or worldly circumstances. He postulates a sort of Prime Directive of his own: the *categorical imperative* (CI). Kant says the CI applies to all *rational beings*—that is, any being capable of moral deliberation, be they human, Klingon, or Ferengi. Lieutenant Uhura is quite upset about Spock's willingness to sacrifice himself just for the sake of the Prime Directive, but for Spock, who takes a Kantian approach to the situation, personal feelings are irrelevant. (Naturally, this makes it pretty frustrating to date a Vulcan!) As long as it's the proper thing to do, Kant tells us, a moral act should be done because of its own worth. Whether we like it or not, what matters is following the rational moral law itself.

Kant formulates the CI in several ways, the first of which amounts to what we might call a *universalization test*: an act is morally right only if it's logically possible, and one could consistently will, that all rational beings behave the same way. According to this test, breaking a promise is wrong because if everyone broke promises, promises themselves would lose all meaning, and it's impossible to break promises in a world where no promises exist. The next important formulation amounts to what we might call a *respect test*: an act is never morally right if it treats rational beings solely as a means to an end, without respecting them as ends in themselves. In both formulations, the aim of the CI is to avoid *subjective bias* in moral reasoning.

To grasp these two ways of understanding the CI, consider the episode "Bread and Circuses" (TOS). Kirk, Spock, and McCoy beam down to an unexplored planet in search of the *S.S. Beagle*. When Mr. Scott learns that the landing party is in trouble, he's faced with a choice: either use the vastly superior technology of the *Enterprise* to rescue the crew, or else uphold the Prime Directive and avoid contaminating a pre-warp civilization. According to Kant, Scotty shouldn't treat any rational beings as if they and their goals are subordinate to his own (the respect test), and he shouldn't behave in a way that would be logically self-defeating if all rational beings were to make the same decision (the universalization test).

If Scotty violates the Prime Directive, he clearly fails the universalization test. If all Starfleet officers were allowed to break the rules in dire circumstances, that would change the very definition of the rules. One can't be *allowed* to break a rule; to break a rule, *by definition*, is to do what's disallowed. If the Prime Directive included a clause that required officers to beam up their captains even if it exposes pre-warp civilizations to transporter technology, then beaming up Captain Kirk wouldn't violate the Directive. But without such a clause, Scotty can only conclude that it's illogical for officers in his situation to make exceptions to the Prime Directive.

Furthermore, using superior technology to get out of trouble can result in disaster. In "A Piece of the Action" (TOS), a whole civilization ends up modeling itself after 20th-century gangster culture just because the crew of an earlier vessel, the *U.S.S. Horizon*, accidentally left behind a book entitled *Chicago Mobs of the Twenties*. But even this is far from the worst-case scenario: in "Time and Again" (VOY),

Captain Janeway's intervention leads to the devastation of an entire planet. As a loyal officer, Scotty values the lives of his shipmates, but as a moral agent observing the CI, he must recognize that the people who captured Kirk, Spock, and McCoy have their own culture, their own agenda, and their own moral values. Mr. Scott can't ignore these just because they don't happen to align with his own. As Kant would put it, he must respect these people as *ends in themselves*.

While such respect for the people of an alien culture prohibits Starfleet officers from engaging in certain actions toward them, it doesn't mean that one must simply accept the other culture's values or that one can't intervene in some fashion. When dealing with an alien culture whose values are contrary to the laws of reason, a Starfleet officer may still take recourse in rational arguments. Captain Picard does exactly this in "Justice" (TNG) when Wesley Crusher is to be executed by the Edo, a people whose legal system is so strict that even Kant might approve.[6] Picard is unwilling to violate the Prime Directive, unwilling to abandon his duty to protect Wesley, and unwilling to simply ignore the Edo's laws. Negotiating with the Edo and even with their god, he exhorts, "There can be no justice so long as laws are absolute. Even life itself is an exercise in exceptions." Commander Riker concurs: "When has justice ever been as simple as a rulebook?" Picard succeeds in delivering Wesley from his death sentence, not by ignoring the rules but rather by navigating the narrow straits between them.

Notice that Kant's CI takes no notice of the one factor that seems to simplify things: the real-world consequences of following rules absolutely. His chief rivals in moral philosophy, the *utilitarians*, define right and wrong solely in terms of consequences. For them, the right action is the one that brings about the greatest benefit for the greatest number, a view Kant wholeheartedly rejects. For one thing, people can use consequences to justify *anything*, no matter how despicable. Is it wrong to sacrifice the lives and futures of one's crew in order to preserve a colony of 8,000 inhabitants? Not necessarily, as Captain Sisko is forced to conclude in "Children of Time" (DS9). What about forcibly relocating an entire people? In *Insurrection*, the Federation and their Son'a allies plan to relocate the Ba'ku. They justify it as potentially saving billions of lives by tapping into the metaphasic radiation of the ring system around the Ba'ku's planet. Picard forcefully challenges Starfleet Admiral Matthew Dougherty on his prioritizing of moral *calculation* over the preservation of moral *principles*:

PICARD:         We are betraying the principles upon which the Federation was
                founded. It's an attack upon its very soul. And it will destroy
                the Ba'ku, just as cultures have been destroyed in every other
                forced relocation throughout history.
DOUGHERTY:      Jean-Luc, we are only moving six hundred people.
PICARD:         How many people does it take, Admiral, before it becomes
                wrong? A thousand? Fifty thousand? A million? How many
                people does it take, Admiral?

Another Kantian argument against utilitarianism is that we're all
too fallible when it comes to predicting the consequences of our
actions. As Picard reminds Dr. Crusher in "Symbiosis," our poor track
record in making such predictions renders the Prime Directive all the
more important: "History has proven again and again that whenever
mankind interferes with a less developed civilization, no matter how
well intentioned that interference may be, the results are invariably
disastrous."

Interestingly, the oh-so-Kantian Vulcans don't wholly reject utilitarian thinking; after all, a bedrock principle of Vulcan morality is that
"the needs of the many outweigh the needs of the few." Later in his
career, even Kant came to acknowledge that the consequences of our
decisions are morally relevant. Even so, they're not so important as to
override the CI. In the end, Kant and Spock share the same concern: if
you start allowing yourself to break rules because of exigent circumstances and immediate foreseeable gains, you compromise the moral
force of the rules themselves.

What does this mean for the Prime Directive? Lieutenant Worf puts
it best in "Pen Pals" (TNG): "The Prime Directive is not a matter
of degree. It is an absolute." By Kantian logic, a rule you're allowed
to violate isn't a rule at all. Moreover, a captain who wants to err
on the side of caution ought to adhere to the Prime Directive at all
times, knowing that when officers violate it—even with the best of
intentions—they make things worse at least as often as they make
things better, and they risk treating other rational beings merely as
means to an end.

## Into Vagueness

That said, we may still ask ourselves what the real problem is here: is
it violating the Prime Directive, or is it doing so *poorly*? Perhaps Kant
and Spock have it all wrong. What if a one-size-fits-all principle is a

misguided approach from the beginning? What happens if we start our moral reasoning from specific situations and work our way up, rather than starting from an abstract principle and working our way down?

This is the approach of Confucius (551–479 BCE). One of the frustrating and fascinating things about reading his *Analects* is that sometimes several students ask him the same question, and to each student he gives a different answer. Why? Because Confucius believes there isn't *one* right answer. Moral responses must be tailored to fit the circumstances.[7]

To this, Kirk might reply, "Hey, that's exactly what I said at my court-martial!" Strangely enough, on this count Confucius actually shares much in common with one of Kant's philosophical forebears, Aristotle (384–322 BCE), who said that "the educated person seeks exactness in each area *to the extent that the nature of the subject allows*."[8] Morality isn't as precise as mathematics, but it has a precision of its own. If your answer to eight plus eight is "somewhere between ten and twenty," that's not precise enough. By the same token, if you're wondering whether or not you should obey the Prime Directive, "never break it" is far too precise. Confucius and Aristotle would agree that while the Prime Directive is usually correct, there will be cases where it's wrong *not* to break it.

So how do you know when to obey the Prime Directive and when not to? The answer comes down to *character*. Confucius and Aristotle are concerned not with one-size-fits-all principles but rather with character traits. We call good traits *virtues* and bad traits *vices*, and the goal of ethics is to cultivate the virtues and stamp out the vices. Using the family as a basic building block of morality, Confucius observes that virtuous people tend to raise virtuous children by serving as role models. The most virtuous people are the ones who emulate the best role models; Confucius calls the very best of all role models the *junzi*, or "exemplary person."[9]

This model extends from the family to the state: the virtuous ruler leads the people by example, and in so doing, the whole kingdom thrives. If Confucius were the superintendent of Starfleet Academy, he'd identify which virtues should be instilled in cadets, and then identify the officers who best embody those virtues—the *junzi* of Starfleet—who would become the faculty. The cadets' job, then, would be not only to master the skills and subjects needed for space exploration, but also to emulate their professors' moral and intellectual character. Picard would certainly seem to qualify as a Starfleet *junzi*, and is even offered the post of Academy Commandant in "Coming of Age" (TNG). His value as a role model is most evident in his relationship with aspiring cadet Wesley Crusher, to whom he offers a book by William James in "Samaritan Snare" (TNG):

PICARD:   There is no greater challenge than the study of philosophy.
WESLEY:   But William James won't be in my Starfleet exams.
PICARD:   The important things never will be. Anyone can be trained in the mechanics of piloting a starship.
WESLEY:   But Starfleet Academy....
PICARD:   It takes more. Open your mind to the past. Art, history, philosophy. And all this may mean something.

When Wesley is finally accepted into the Academy, he goes on one last mission with Picard. The two of them crash-land on an arid planet where the only source of water is guarded by a lethal form of energy. When Picard is badly wounded, Wesley confesses how much of an exemplar of virtue Picard has been for him:

> How many people get to serve with Jean-Luc Picard? ... All of the things I've worked for, school, my science projects, getting into the Academy, I've done it all because I want you to be proud of me. If there is one thing that I've learned from you, it's that you don't quit. And I'm not going to quit now. I've seen you think yourself out of worse problems than this, and I'm going to think us out of this. You're not going to die. I'm not going to let you die. I'll get to the water and I'll keep you alive until they find us. I promise ("Final Mission," TNG).

So what should Wesley and other Starfleet cadets learn about the Prime Directive? If Picard were a *junzi* professor, he'd likely advise caution. But if Kirk were the professor ... well, let's face it, he'd probably be fired in his first semester for hitting on his female students.[10] But if he were somehow able to restrain his ardor, his lesson plan would be quite different from Picard's. We get a glimpse in *Into Darkness* when Admiral Pike tells Kirk he's been relieved of his command after the fiasco on Nibiru. Pike tells Kirk, "You think the rules are for other people." Kirk's response? "Some should be."

According to Confucius, Kirk is right—but only if he's a *junzi*. Pike tells Kirk, "You think the rules don't apply to you because you disagree with them." The *junzi* would politely correct him: "It's not that the rules don't apply *because* I disagree with them. They don't apply *when* I disagree with them, and I only disagree with them when they prevent me from being a virtuous leader." Here we see the justification required for violating the Prime Directive: any rule that prevents the *junzi* from being *junzi* isn't a rule worth following—at least not in that particular instance.[11]

This leaves Starfleet at a crossroads. Ideally, it would appoint only *junzi* professors to teach its cadets, but Confucius himself is the first to admit the exemplary person is a rare breed. There are too many classes to teach, and not enough *junzi* to teach them. Worse yet, even if the Academy's faculty were composed of nothing but *junzi*, the simple fact is that many of the new graduates would fall short of their professors' moral and intellectual standards. Even Wesley falters, much to Picard's disappointment, in "The First Duty" (TNG). While Starfleet may *ask* all of its cadets to emulate their *junzi* officers, most of them won't be up to the task; just look at the misguided cadets running the *U.S.S. Valiant* during the Dominion War ("Valiant," DS9). Even some Starfleet captains with years of accumulated experience won't know when to follow the Prime Directive and when to break it.[12] Better, then, to put Picard in charge and teach cadets to take the Kantian approach.

Except that doing so sometimes results in catastrophe. There are too many cases in which Kant's categorical imperative leads us to counterintuitive conclusions. In "Pen Pals" (TNG), unusual levels of geologic activity threaten to destroy Drema IV, forcing Picard to consider violating the Prime Directive in order to save an entire species of humanoids. As an expression of the CI, the Prime Directive clearly states that there should be no intervention. In fact, Picard reminds his senior staff that one of the functions of the Prime Directive "is to protect *us*. To prevent us from allowing our emotions to overwhelm our judgment." So, is it callous to let an entire people die? Of course. Is it morally obligatory anyway, regardless of how we feel about it? Maybe, if all we have to work with is the CI. But abstract moral principles are *not* all we have to work with. We must apply them in real-world situations. In "Pen Pals," what pulls Picard out of the realm of moral abstraction and into the real world is a plea for help. He reassesses the situation as a *junzi*, and in this instance he concludes, "We cannot turn our backs."

That said, you don't have to be a *junzi* to see what's wrong with answering pleas for help in *every* circumstance. The virtuous person understands that moral decisions can't be made in advance. New social, cultural, and technological innovations create new moral problems for which we have no preexisting rules. The moral landscape is always changing, but the *junzi* will always be able to keep pace with it. Kant would say the same of the CI: it's an overarching principle to govern *all* ethical decisions. Nevertheless, it's clear that novel situations can throw such a rule for a loop. More importantly, the CI oversimplifies the textured, nuanced, finely grained nature of moral interactions. Confucius would accuse Kant of attempting to sculpt stone with a sledgehammer, when what's needed is a very small hammer and a wide array of chisels, plus the skill to know which one to use in which instance. This, of course, is where things get difficult for Starfleet. It's a lot easier to train cadets to swing a sledgehammer than to chisel like Michelangelo.

## The Final Moral Frontier

One theme that *Star Trek* has embraced over the years is that the Prime Directive isn't simply an imaginary rule about meeting other civilizations. There's a deeper meaning behind it. The Prime Directive symbolizes just how difficult making good moral decisions can be. Pat answers can be dangerously shortsighted, and careful consideration is almost always a good idea.

The Prime Directive also shows us that thinking carefully about morality sometimes leads us to question our social and cultural traditions. As Quark says in "Family Business" (DS9), "All it takes is for one impressionable youngster to join Starfleet and the next thing you know, a whole generation of Ferengi will be quoting the Prime Directive and abandoning the pursuit of latinum." At other times, in order to do the right thing, one has to test the rigidity of existing moral rules, and if it really is true that a rule can't be broken, then perhaps—as Janeway admits to Captain Ransom in "Equinox" (VOY)—one ought to "bend it on occasion."

If you're the newest graduate from Starfleet Academy, Admiral Confucius would have you understand the Prime Directive well enough to know when to bend or even break it. Kirk, Janeway, and Sisko would agree with him. But Admiral Kant would have you adhere to the Prime Directive, because a rule that can be violated isn't really a rule at all. Spock and Worf would agree with him. When Kant says "make it so," he's talking about an *action*: whatever you choose to do, you should be ready to hold everyone else to the same rule. But when Confucius says "make it so," he's talking about a *person*: make yourself like your role models, then behave like a role model yourself.

Developing a fine sensitivity to effectively navigate a moral universe is a difficult task. One thing is sure: behaving morally requires a lot of experience. Like even the best Starfleet officers, sometimes we fail and sometimes we hit the mark. Only time will allow us to become exemplary moral agents. Then, and only then, will we be ready to navigate the starry heavens above us, plotting our course by the moral laws within us.

## Notes

1.  Immanuel Kant, *Practical Philosophy*, trans. Mary J. Gregor (Cambridge: Cambridge University Press, 1999), 269.
2.  Spock's *utilitarian* reasoning, in this case and others, is explored in Greg Littmann's chapter in this volume.
3.  This question is also explored in depth by William Lindenmuth in his chapter in this volume.
4.  Another analysis of the ethical foundation of the Prime Directive, particularly in this context, is provided by Jason T. Eberl, "An Inconsistent Triad? Competing Ethics in *Star Trek Into Darkness*" in *The Philosophy of J.J. Abrams*, ed. Robert Arp and Patricia Brace (Lexington: University Press of Kentucky, 2014).
5.  For a more detailed analysis of the role of reason and logic in Vulcan philosophy, see Walter [Ritoku] Robinson, "Death and Rebirth of a Vulcan Mind" in *Star Trek and Philosophy*, ed. Jason T. Eberl and Kevin S. Decker (Chicago: Open Court, 2008).
6.  Kant was an advocate of the death penalty, although he probably wouldn't go so far as to extend it to squishing a few plants. A point of contention in Kant's moral philosophy is whether one can advocate capital punishment and still respect all rational beings as an ends in themselves.
7.  This approach to moral reasoning, sometimes termed "casuistry," is explicated in Courtland Lewis's chapter in this volume.
8.  Aristotle, *Nicomachean Ethics*, trans. Terence Irwin (Indianapolis: Hackett, 1999), I.3.1094b.
9.  Roger T. Ames and Henry Rosemont, Jr., *The Analects of Confucius: A Philosophical Translation* (New York: Ballantine, 1999), 60.
10. At least the Kirk of the alternate timeline depicted in J.J. Abrams's recent films. In the original timeline, Kirk actually was an instructor at the Academy and is described by his former student, Gary Mitchell, as "a stack of books with legs," elaborating, "The first thing I ever heard from upperclassmen was, 'Watch out for Lieutenant Kirk. In his class, you either think or sink'" ("Where No Man Has Gone Before," TOS).

11. As seen in the exchange between Pike and Kirk, a tension is fostered when the *junzi* must justify themselves to others who may not acknowledge the greatness of their virtue. This problem of the "great-souled" person, to use Aristotle's term (*megalopsychos*), is discussed with reference to Kirk in Jerold J. Abrams's chapter in this volume.

12. Examples of captains who have violated the Prime Directive include Captain R.M. Merik of the *SS Beagle* in "Bread and Circuses" (although he wasn't a *starship* captain, having flunked out of the Academy in his fifth year), Captain Ronald Tracey of the *USS Exeter* in "The Omega Glory" (TOS), and Captain Rudolph Ransom of the *USS Equinox* in "Equinox" (VOY).

# 5
# Destroying Utopias: Why Kirk Is a Jerk

## David Kyle Johnson

I have an idea for a bumper sticker: "Happiness is a warm puppy, a sunny day, [and] an anathema to Captain James T. Kirk."
—Computer from *Star Trek*, Mission Log (Episode) 34, "The Apple"[1]

Kirk or Picard? That's a heated question that can't be settled here. But Kirk does have at least one major moral flaw: his willingness to impose his values on others. If you aren't living life how Kirk thinks you should, you *will be* after he's through with you! Just compare how Kirk and Picard handle things in "The Apple" (TOS) and "Justice" (TNG).

In "Justice," Picard does everything he can to not interfere with the scantily clad, amorous, blonde jogging people of Rubicun III. Despite the native Edo's odd sense of justice, he makes no effort to judge or reform their society or destroy the "god" that rules them. He simply convinces their transdimensional god-figure that "there can be no justice as long as laws are absolute" in order to rescue Wesley, and then leaves. But in "The Apple," when Kirk comes across a very similar society on Gamma Triguli VI, he can't destroy their way of life *fast enough*. Their machine-god, Vaal, provides them a tropical utopia, makes them immortal, and asks for only two things in return: Vaal must be fed when hungry, and the natives must not have sex—since "replacements" aren't needed. But since Kirk thinks they need "freedom," he destroys Vaal and then leaves them to fend for themselves.

*The Ultimate Star Trek and Philosophy*, First Edition. Edited by Kevin S. Decker and Jason T. Eberl.
© 2016 John Wiley & Sons, Ltd. Published 2016 by John Wiley & Sons, Ltd.

To be fair, Vaal was also threatening the *Enterprise*. But Kirk makes it clear he would've destroyed Vaal regardless, because he believes it's *the right thing to do*. Dr. McCoy concurs:

> There are certain absolutes ... and one of them is the right of humanoids to a free and unchained environment, the right to have conditions that permit growth.... These humanoids are intelligent, they need to advance and grow.... There's been no progress here in at least ten thousand years. This isn't life, it's stagnation.

Spock, on the other hand, thinks Kirk has kicked them out of paradise—just like Satan once did.

## Kirk Is a Spoiled Spor(e)t

Kirk had already done the very same thing to the farming colony on Omicron Ceti III in "This Side of Paradise" (TOS). The spores that saved the colonists from Berthold radiation also provided perfect health and happiness. Instead of being dead, the farmers were gleefully working the land to produce the food they needed and living wonderfully happy lives. Kirk's response is telling: "We weren't meant for that, none of us. Man stagnates if he has no ambition, no desire to be more than he is." Elias Sandoval, the colony leader, claims that they have everything they need. "Except a *challenge*," Kirk replies— so, bye-bye spores!

While Kirk must also save his command from his spore-infected, mutinous crew, he makes it clear that he would've rid the colonists of the spores regardless: "Maybe we weren't meant for paradise. Maybe we were meant to fight our way through. Struggle, claw our way up, scratch for every inch of the way. Maybe we can't stroll to the music of the lute, we must march to the sound of drums" Once spore-free, even Sandoval agrees: "We've done nothing here. No accomplishments, no progress. Three years wasted." The lesson is simple: living on a world lacking hardships isn't an option, because only by struggling can we progress and live up to our potential. It's a lesson perhaps most succinctly articulated in "I, Mudd" (TOS), when Norman's androids threaten to supply humanity with all it could ever want or need. In a spoof of this "hardship lesson," McCoy and Scotty reject the androids' offer:

MCCOY:   You offer us only well-being.

SCOTT:    Food and drink and happiness mean nothing to us. We must be about our job.

MCCOY:    Suffering, in torment and pain. Laboring without end.

SCOTT:    Dying and crying and lamenting over our burdens.

BOTH:    Only this way can we be happy.

## Mission Log Mayhem

This "hardship lesson" has been a hot-button topic on *Star Trek: Mission Log*—a podcast produced by Gene Roddenberry's son Rod and hosted by John Champion and Ken Ray with the goal of examining the "meaning, messages and morals" of every *Star Trek* episode from TOS to ENT. Ken "Berthold" Ray in particular objects to Kirk's dismantling of the utopias on Omicron Ceti III and Gamma Trianguli VI, raising three separate arguments.

First, Kirk says he's giving the Feeders of Vaal *freedom*, but besides the forthcoming wild orgy, what exactly are they now free to do that they couldn't do before? Vaal had only two rules. What's more, Kirk denies them the freedom to return to the arrangement they had: they're now free to live only the kind of life Kirk approves—which will primarily involve trying to figure out, from scratch, how to survive. McCoy claims that Kirk put them "back on a normal course of social evolution." But given their small numbers and dependence on Vaal, won't they more likely be dead within a week?

Second, the value of a farming life on Omicron Ceti III is too readily dismissed. Sandoval says they weren't able to complete the work they set out to do: "We wanted to make this planet a garden." But isn't that what they did? Even if they originally intended to export food, why shouldn't people seeking the simple, happy lifestyle guaranteed by the spores be allowed to do so? What right does Kirk have to decide, for everyone, that such a life isn't worth living?

Finally, these societies are dismantled in the name of *accomplishment*; but what exactly are they supposed to accomplish? One presumes it's the same things we are; but what are we striving to accomplish? Aren't we trying to eliminate want, need, crime, suffering, and illness? Isn't that, in fact, part of Roddenberry's vision for the future? As Picard later boasts in "The Neutral Zone" (TNG), "We've eliminated hunger, want, the need for possessions. We've grown out of our infancy." And isn't that exactly what these societies had accomplished? Why must Kirk dismantle every society that's accomplished what we're struggling for? Even if we'll never actually achieve this goal, what does it say about us if we can't even tolerate the existence of such a society in our fiction?

A number of replies to Ken's arguments have been considered on *Mission Log*. Let's look at the best ones and see if these arguments can be expanded to answer such objections.

## Drugs Are Bad, Mmkay?

One objection to spore-driven life on Omicron Ceti III initially seems strong: aren't the spores basically just an illicit drug, like heroin, that provides an artificial high? So isn't Kirk just breaking the colonist's nasty drug habit? Sure, the spores make you feel good—but at what price?

Unfortunately, this analogy is flawed. First of all, one dose of the spores is all a person needs—so the colonists aren't *dependent* on them like a drug. Because of the Berthold rays, they do depend on them for survival, but that's a different kind of dependency—the same kind offered by a prescription medication or an inoculation. Second, there seems to be nothing wrong with using something to make you feel happy. The reason that using street drugs like heroin is a bad idea isn't because it'll make you feel happy; it's because it won't make you happy *in the long run*. It'll ruin your health and make you miserable. As Tasha Yar puts it to Wesley in "Symbiosis" (TNG), "Before you know it, you're taking the drug not to feel good, but to keep from feeling bad." But the spores not only make you perpetually happy, they make you even healthier than you would be otherwise. So what "price" is paid by a person infected by the spores? Who exactly is suffering because the colonists are happy, healthy, and have no wants or needs?

"But," one might object, "isn't it an *artificial* happiness caused by the spores' manipulation of brain chemistry to make the colonists feel happy when they really aren't?" No. First of all, *everything* that makes you happy—whether watching *Star Trek*, falling in love, or exposure to spores—does so by manipulating chemicals released in your brain. By the same logic, we'd have to ask, "Is the happiness experienced by people on antidepressants artificial?"

Second, even if spore-induced happiness is "artificial," the suggestion that what's *natural* is inherently superior commits a logical fallacy called the *appeal to nature*—when something being natural is thought to somehow automatically make it more desirable or ethically better. The mistake is clear once you realize that many natural things—like hemlock, hurricanes, and illness—aren't desirable at all, lead to suffering, and should be avoided. Conversely, artifacts like drinking glasses, houses, and modern medicine aren't natural at all, but are vastly superior to and more desirable than their natural alternatives.

And, lastly, it makes no sense to suggest that someone could *feel* happy but not really *be* happy. Can you be in pain without feeling it? You might injure yourself and not feel it—but if you feel pain, then *you're in pain*. Likewise, if you feel happy, *you're happy*.

## They're Not Flourishing!

You can't be happy without feeling it, but you can be happy without enjoying *eudaimonia*, the Greek word for the best kind of life—often translated as "flourishing." Just like you can be mistaken about being healthy, you can also be mistaken about whether you've achieved *eudaimonia* or not. Simply feeling happy all the time is neither necessary nor sufficient for *eudaimonia*. So, perhaps the problem is that the Omicron Ceti spores and Vaal give happiness but prevent flourishing.

Perhaps. But this depends on exactly what the best kind of life is. Aristotle (384–322 BCE) thought it involved using *reason* well, which included doing philosophy; he thought that was our *proper function*, given that reasoning is a distinctive thing that humans can do whereas the rest of nature apparently can't. But neither the spores nor Vaal seem to prevent the use of reason. Those under their influence may have not yet chosen to do so; but, historically, philosophy developed only when people no longer had to continually worry about the basics of survival—and had the leisure to worry about the meaning of life and other matters instead.[2] So even though we don't see any philosophy being done on Omicron Ceti III or Gamma Trianguli VI, there's no reason it couldn't be done given the leisure time granted to their people.

*Eudaimonia* might also require one to have *virtue* and *practical wisdom* so that one values the right things and knows how to accomplish them. But there's no reason to think that any of the classical virtues—self-control, generosity, courage, honesty, justice, and so on—are outside the reach of our utopian inhabitants. So it seems that *eudaimonia* could be within their reach.

## "This Isn't Life—It's Stagnation"

Some might equate *eudaimonia* with *self-actualization*, the highest state of psychologist Abraham Maslow's (1908–1970) "hierarchy of needs." Maslow suggested that once a person has her biological needs met (food, water, and shelter) and feels safe and protected, loved and needed, and accomplished, she can seek self-actualization. To do so, she must fulfill her *potential*—to be able to do all she's capable of doing. Since Kirk and McCoy's complaints center on the spores and Vaal promoting *stagnation*—preventing their subjects from progress, accomplishment, and being more than they currently are—perhaps this is the best way to frame their concerns.

But it's not clear that the utopias in question actually prevent self-actualization. First, the people in those utopias have many characteristics Maslow said self-actualized people have: they're accepting, spontaneous, creative, appreciative of life, honest, responsible, and hardworking—they even maintain deep relationships and have childlike wonder. Second, there's more than one path to accomplishment and progress. Creating art and literature, playing sports, learning, teaching, working—these are all activities Maslow valued, and all seem possible in the spores' and Vaal's utopia.[3] Despite Sandoval's suggestion to the contrary, the colonists even accomplished their goal of making a "garden" out of Omicron Ceti III.

Of course, they can't accomplish what Kirk has accomplished. But why must they? A starship captain may be a paradigmatic example of a self-actualized person—a "paragon of virtue," as Lenore refers to Kirk in "The Conscience of the King" (TOS). But that path is open to only a handful of exceptional individuals. As Commodore Stone tells Kirk in "Court Martial" (TOS), "Not one man in a million could do what you and I have done. Command a starship." It can't be expected of everyone.

In *Mission Log*, Ken Ray defends life under the care of Norman's androids on Mudd's planet as preferable because of its possibilities for self-actualization. After all, it's by performing all "necessary service functions" that the androids freed their original creators to develop a "perfect social order." McCoy mentions how he could spend his entire life studying in their research facilities. Think of what he or any other member of the *Enterprise* crew could accomplish in a lifetime dedicated to a particular cause on Mudd's planet. Such a life may not be for everyone, but it seems foolish to say that it can't be one of self-actualization.

## What's So Important about Self-Actualization?

Perhaps the spores and Vaal are different from Norman's androids in that they eradicate *ambition* and the use of reason and thus make self-actualization impossible. Even so, is self-actualization that important? After all, just like commanding a starship, self-actualization is something only a few can accomplish. Maslow thought only 1 percent of people were in reality self-actualized. So, at worst, conditions that prevent self-actualization harm only the possibilities of a few.

Further, self-actualization is impossible unless our basic biological, safety, and social needs are met—all of which the spores and Vaal guarantee. The spores even saved the colonists' lives. Similarly, Vaal likely saved the civilization of Gamma Trianguli VI. Akuta, the leader of the Feeders of Vaal, said his antennae were given to him during "the dim time." The planet, it seems, was on the verge of destruction—perhaps due to environmental disaster, overpopulation, wars, or more—and Vaal was constructed to solve the problem.

Once one achieves self-actualization, it's easy to pity those who can't attain it; but for those who struggle just to survive, giving up safety and security for an unlikely chance at self-actualization would seem crazy. Think of how "The Apple" might be perceived in a country ravaged by famine, disease, and natural disasters. "It's a horror story!" such viewers might declare. "This society, which has solved all its important problems, is invaded by a monster named Kirk who undoes all their accomplishments!"

After all—how much do *you* really struggle to survive? Do you grow or kill your own food? Do you police your own neighborhood? Did you build your own house or car? Do you make or even wash your own clothes, or does a machine do that for you? Few modern persons will answer these questions affirmatively; what does that say about us? Perhaps nothing good. Indeed, the philosopher Jean-Jacques Rousseau (1712–1778) argued that modern humans were *inferior* to primitive humans. The latter could survive on their own; but, without modern society, most of us would be dead in a month.

But what would we really think if some aliens influenced by Rousseau "Kirk-ed" us—destroyed all our machines and infrastructure to make us "better people"? Would we think they had a point and thank them for interfering? I doubt it. Perhaps it makes us weaker in a way, but modern society has its advantages—not the least of which is that it's delivered the most peaceful and plentiful time to live in history. Although the selective reporting on the news might make it seem otherwise, a smaller percentage of people die today because of wars, poverty, disease, and famine than any other time in history.[4]

Besides, our advances don't necessitate stagnation. In fact, Kirk himself defends technology as something that enables human flourishing in "The Conscience of the King" (TOS):

KARIDIAN:  Here you stand, the perfect symbol of our technical society. Mechanized, electronicized, and not very human. You've done away with humanity, the striving of man to achieve greatness through his own resources.

KIRK:  We've armed man with tools. The striving for greatness continues.

And all this brings up an important point: *what* does Kirk want these people to accomplish anyway? What level of "greatness" should they strive for? Shouldn't eradicating war, disease, famine, poverty, and natural disasters be at the top of everyone's list of "things to accomplish" in order to *flourish*? Vaal and the spores already have done so. Perhaps the reason their utopias can't advance any further is because they've already reached the top. What's more, utopia-creators like Vaal and the spores don't just come from nowhere. Vaal was likely constructed to save his society from disaster. The spores may have been genetically engineered by someone to combat disease and depression. So Kirk is actually undoing the very things that he wants accomplished via a life of hardship.

And how much does *Kirk* struggle to survive? Vaal is supposedly an example of when a machine "becomes too efficient [and] does too much work for you." But is anyone more dependent upon a machine—the *Enterprise*—than Kirk? He even talks to it like his *lover*: "This vessel, I give, she takes. She won't permit me my life. I've got to live hers.... Now I know why it's called 'she'.... Never lose you, *never*" ("The Naked Time," TOS). Kirk telling the farming colonists that their life is too easy would be like Q telling Kirk that his life is too easy. Even if, as Spock exhorts in *The Wrath of Khan*, commanding a starship is Kirk's "first, best destiny," if Kirk really wants to accomplish genuine self-actualization, Kirk should build, pilot, and repair his own ship himself; only in that way could he *fulfill his true potential*.

## But Are They Free?

We might also worry about the *freedom* of the people in these utopias. Given that the spores were forced upon the colonists, perhaps it was best for the *Enterprise* crew to free the colonists from their influence. Of course, if given the choice between death by Berthold rays and the spores, I'm sure they would've chosen the latter. The original situation was, unfortunately, one of a *forced choice*. Ideally, the colonists would've been given information about the spores and their effects beforehand, and then given the choice whether to live under their influence or not.

But the colonists *could've had this choice* at the end of the episode. Away from the influence of the spores, if some had chosen to go back, how could one say that choice wasn't free? And even if they turned it down, I'm sure others would appreciate the opportunity to make that choice; wouldn't Omicron Ceti III be the perfect option for the terminally ill? How would such a choice to live under the influence of the spores be that different from Captain Pike's choice in "The Menagerie" (TOS) to live in the illusory world created by the Talosians with Vina rather than remain an invalid? Yet Kirk doesn't even consider these possibilities as an option for Omicron Ceti III or Gamma Trianguli VI.

What about the Feeders of Vaal? Ray argues that Kirk limited their freedom by forcing them to do things his way. McCoy, however, would likely counter by suggesting that they were only "living to service a hunk of tin" and that Kirk freed them from enslavement. But that (*papier-mâché*) "hunk of tin" provided them everything they needed: not only food for survival, but also a perfect climate and immortality. Sure, they had to feed Vaal, but does that really amount to *slavery*? When it's low, I have to put gas in my car's fuel tank. Does that mean I'm its slave? When Vaal's gong sounds, is that Vaal demanding to be fed or just the sound of his fuel meter running low?

McCoy might also counter by pointing to the fact that Vaal prohibited *sex* and arguing that such a prohibition isn't conducive to paradise. But we live under many laws that restrict sexual expression: Wear clothes. No nude dancing. Don't sell sexual favors. We have laws about marriage—and that's just the tip of the iceberg. All things considered, the Feeders of Vaal seem to enjoy *more* freedom than we do.

Furthermore, it's not clear at all that the Feeders of Vaal—or at least their ancestors—didn't *choose* to live under Vaal's rules. Vaal was likely created to solve a whole planet-full of problems, and the people of Gamma Trianguli VI probably preferred Vaal to some alternative. We all choose to live under certain rules, and we all choose to fuel and maintain the machines that make our lives easier. The Feeders of Vaal were likely doing the same thing.

If anyone is restricting freedom, it's *Kirk*. The libertarian political philosopher Robert Nozick (1938–2002) argued that the best political system is one in which the government's only role would be to protect the citizens against force, fraud, and theft.[5] To truly ensure freedom, such a system must allow its citizens to live how they want. If a group wants to band together and live as communists, return to a simpler agricultural life without technology, or even build a machine to control their weather and grant them immortality, they should be allowed to do so. So by trying to force everyone to live as he sees fit, Kirk is the biggest threat to freedom of all.

## Kirk Is a Jerk

I have an idea for a T-shirt. On the front it would say, "Kirk is coming, look productive… " and on the back it would say "… or he will irreparably damage your way of life and everything in which you believe."
—Computer from *Star Trek*, Mission Log 34, "The Apple"

As Ken Ray puts it, it's not Nomad ("The Changeling," TOS) or Landru ("Return of the Archons," TOS) that's the precursor to the Borg. It's *Kirk*. Although the Borg are famous as biomechanical hybrids, their true villainy comes in trying to force their way of life upon everyone else because they assume it's superior: "Resistance is futile."[6] In Kirk's defense, he may just be emulating the attitude of the Federation itself. As ex-Starfleet officer Michael Eddington says to Captain Benjamin Sisko after becoming a Maquis renegade in "For the Cause" (DS9):

Open your eyes, Captain. Why is the Federation so obsessed about the Maquis? We've never harmed you, and yet we're constantly arrested and charged with terrorism. Starships chase us through the Badlands and our supporters are harassed and ridiculed. Why? Because we've left the Federation, and that's the one thing you can't accept. Nobody leaves *paradise*. Everyone should want to be in the Federation. Hell, you even want the Cardassians to join.… You know, in some ways you're worse than the Borg. At least they tell you about their plans for assimilation. You're more insidious. You assimilate people and they don't even know it.

But it's still inexcusable.

While *Star Trek* was generally progressive in its cultural attitudes, Kirk's views seem to be an expression of conservative elements of 1960s culture. In that context, the Omicron Ceti colonists seem to represent the establishment's view of "dirty hippies," who just lay around, make love, and don't accomplish anything. We see this again in "The Way to Eden" (TOS) when the *Enterprise* encounters those "space hippies." As Scotty says, about their impromptu "jam session," "I don't know why a young mind has to be an undisciplined one. They're troublemakers." (I don't know what he was complaining about; Spock was even playing with them, and I thought their jam was "real now.")

The criticisms of Vaal seem to echo the criticisms of communism, and the control a communist government must exercise in providing for its people. When the freedom of democracy and capitalism leaves people hungry in the street, while communism promises to provide food and shelter for all, defenders of democracy and capitalism have to make suffering and the struggle to survive a *good* thing. Even when communism isn't delivering its promises, what communism promises must be painted as an *evil*.[7]

It's the same imperialist attitude the American colonists took toward the Native Americans: they're savages who need Bibles and trousers. It never crossed the mind of European settlers that the natives should be left alone to live their life as they see fit.[8] And it didn't cross Kirk's mind until he actually lived such a life himself in "The Paradise Syndrome" (TOS)—which gives us perhaps the most ironic bit of dialogue in the series:

ELDER GORO:  Have we displeased you? ... Perhaps we have not improved as quickly as the Wise Ones wish.

KIRK/KIROK:  Your land is rich, your people happy. Who could be displeased with that?

*You* could, Kirk! *You* could be displeased with that! You've dismantled entire societies simply because they weren't improving! One wonders if, after "The Paradise Syndrome," Kirk ever thought back to Omicron Ceti III or Gamma Trianguli VI with any regrets.

Now I'm not defending *cultural relativism*.[9] Not all cultures are on a moral par, and intercultural intervention is sometimes justified. It was right, for example, to force "the cloud minders" of the floating city of Stratos to give their zenite miners rights. Tricking the "gamesters of Triskelion" into freeing their slaves was justified. It's wonderful that Kirk broke the "patterns of force" of the Nazi culture on Ekos.

The Federation may even be morally superior to the societies engendered by Vaal, the spores, or even the Maquis. But it's important to emphasize that people have the right to make that determination for themselves and choose how to live their lives. If members of a society aren't hurting anyone, the observation that they have it "too easy" isn't a legitimate reason for dismantling that society. When the corrupted *Enterprise* computer in "The Practical Joker" (TAS) printed "Kirk is a Jerk" on the back of his uniform, I think it was onto something.

## Notes

1. http://www.missionlogpodcast.com/the-apple/ (accessed June 19, 2015).
2. To see the importance of *leisure* for the development of philosophy, and culture in general, see Jason Eberl's chapter in this volume (Chapter 1).
3. See Saul McLeod, "Maslow's Hierarchy of Needs" *Simply Psychology* (2007): http://www.simplypsychology.org/maslow.html (accessed June 19, 2015).
4. See Steven Pinker and Andrew Mack, "The World Is Not Falling Apart" *Slate* (2014): http://www.slate.com/articles/news_and_politics/foreigners/ 2014/12/the_world_is_not_falling_apart_the_trend_lines_reveal_an_ increasingly_peaceful.html (accessed June 19, 2015).
5. See Robert Nozick, *Anarchy, State, and Utopia* (New York: Basic Books, 1974).
6. You're welcome to compare Kirk's cultural dictates to the Borg's technological totalitarianism in Dan Dinello's chapter elsewhere in this book (Chapter 8).
7. Whether communism is *actually* evil is explored by Jeff Ewing's chapter in this volume (Chapter 11).
8. Walter Robinson elaborates on how cultural imperialism affected Native Americans historically, as well as in their depiction on *Star Trek*, in his chapter in this volume (Chapter 19).
9. William Lindenmuth evaluates the merits of cultural relativism in his chapter in this volume (Chapter 24).

# 6

# "We Are Not Going to Kill Today": *Star Trek* and the Philosophy of Peace

## David Boersema

In "A Taste of Armageddon" (TOS). the *Enterprise* finds itself unwittingly caught up in a war between two neighboring planets, Eminiar VII and Vendikar. The war's been going on for 500 years, but in an effort to avoid the horrors of actual warfare, an arrangement has been worked out to wage the conflict using virtual weapons instead of physical ones. Casualties are tallied, and, through enforced acts of duty, victims of virtual "attacks" report to disintegration chambers: "The people die, but the culture goes on." Captain Kirk intervenes by forcing the leaders of the respective planets to face the destruction and suffering that go along with "real" war, remarking, "That's what makes it a thing to be avoided."

Although the notion of a virtual war sounds like fiction, with the emergence of new technologies, as well as social attitudes and military practices, in the past several decades it's become ever more real. Following the events of 9/11, the United States and its allies launched a military campaign to defeat the forces of Al Qaeda, as well as nations and groups seen as supporting them, with military operations beginning in Afghanistan and Iraq. In an effort to reduce military casualties, the United States increased its reliance on *drones*, small planes that could be guided remotely with no humans on board. U.S. government officials implemented a policy of "shock and awe," a massive military campaign to quickly subdue and defeat the enemy. They countered the appearance of an invasion of other sovereign nations by claiming that we could "fight them over here or fight them over there," with "over

*The Ultimate Star Trek and Philosophy*, First Edition. Edited by Kevin S. Decker and Jason T. Eberl.
© 2016 John Wiley & Sons, Ltd. Published 2016 by John Wiley & Sons, Ltd.

there" clearly being the better option. Citizens at home were told to live their lives as normally as possible, showing that Americans were resolute, and thus preventing the terrorists from winning.

Themes of peace and violence arise throughout the *Star Trek* canon. Indeed, *Star Trek* reveals a sweeping understanding of the multiple dimensions and issues related to peace studies, including explorations of various forms, causes, and justifications of violence, along with alternatives to violence.

## Justice, Peace, and a "Right to the Clouds"

If asked to define *peace*, what would you say? Most people say something like "the absence of war or violence." But this way of thinking places *violence* as the central, basic concept, with peace being a secondary, derivative one. While concern about being free *from* hostilities is important for peace, it reflects merely "negative peace"—peace as the *absence of hostilities*. But "positive peace" is at least as important, referring to the conditions for being free *to* fulfill human potentials. Life in a state of poverty or prejudice, fear or degradation, is inherently not peaceful. Murder is violent, but starvation is too. Psychological, emotional, and economic abuses are experienced as violence just as much as physical blows are. Violence can be organized (as in the case of war) or unorganized (as in the case of racism). It can be intended or unintended. Just as someone might be offended by another's remark, even though the remark wasn't intended to offend, one can suffer violence (for example, age discrimination) even though no violence was intended.

This conception of positive peace as inherently and inescapably intertwined with *social justice* is highlighted in "The Cloud Minders" (TOS). The social structure on the planet Ardana is split between the inhabitants of the sky-city of Stratos, who are the ruling intellectual and cultural elite, and the Troglytes—the workers who perform all manual labor down on the surface. Encountering these two classes, the *Enterprise* crew wrestles with various tensions. Those tensions are given voice by Vanna, a Troglyte leader fighting for social justice, as she remarks to a prominent Stratos citizen, "I speak for my people. They have as much right to the clouds as the Stratos dwellers." Her point isn't about living in Stratos per se, but about having legitimate access to the resources of that community. Peace, understood as freedom *to* pursue opportunities and not merely as freedom *from* violence, is intimately related to justice; and any genuine attempt to understand and promote peace requires addressing issues of injustice as both a form and cause of violence.

Equally relevant is the relation between *interpersonal* peace—peace with others—and *intrapersonal* peace—peace within oneself. It's difficult for a person to have inner peace if he or she lives in a context of threats, intolerance, or discrimination. At the same time, it's difficult for a person to get along with others and respond to conflict nonviolently if he or she lives in an inner state of confusion, humiliation, or rage. Vanna's rage raises the issue of fair distribution of the community's resources, but also speaks to the personal indignation and harm resulting from that failure of social justice. When Droxine, the High Advisor's daughter, questions what the Troglytes would do in Stratos, Vanna responds with a claim of basic *dignity*, "Live in the sunlight and warmth, as everyone should."

In exploring the nature of peace, it's useful to comprehend the connections among *conflict*, *violence*, and *force*. *Conflict* involves a struggle over incompatible desired outcomes. When two three-dimensional chess masters sit down to face each other, each wants to win, but only one of them will; they have conflicting desired outcomes. *Violence* is one response to conflict—as when Charlie Evans psychokinetically melts the chess pieces after losing to Spock in "Charlie X" (TOS). But there are other potential responses, such as negotiation, cooperation, compromise, changing perceptions, and nonviolent persuasion. Violence is a form of force, but only one form. *Force* is a power used to bring about some change. To force open a stuck turbolift door isn't an act of violence; the turbolift isn't being attacked or abused. Likewise, a person who fights off an attacker is using force, but not violence. Some acts of force are *defensive*, having the goal of preventing harm or violence. Collective actions such as boycotts, strikes, embargoes, and walkouts are forceful actions, but not violence. Other acts of force are *offensive* and constitute violence. The use of force—even lethal force if necessary—isn't necessarily violence. But if the use of force is offensive, rather than defensive, it is. Nonviolent action can be forceful, as witnessed by the work of Mohandas Gandhi in India and Nelson Mandela in South Africa—pacifism is not passivism.[1] To be committed to nonviolence isn't simply to do nothing, to fail or refuse to sometimes use force, but to use force only to restrict, overcome, and replace violence.

## "We All Have Our Darker Side": Causes of Violence

Violence seems to be universal, and efforts to eliminate it seem futile.
Why is this? What causes us to be so violent? Some accounts suggest that violence is inevitable. Perhaps we're by nature violent beings:
the world includes predators and prey, and humans are among the
predators. This view is stated openly by Anan 7, one of the High
Councilors of Eminiar VII. When Kirk reveals that he's intervened
in order to force the two warring parties to confront the horrors
of "real" war and thus be motivated to sue for peace, Anan 7
retorts, "There can be no peace. Don't you see? We've admitted
it to ourselves. We're a killer species. It's instinctive. It's the same
with you."

This view has also been held by various philosophers and scientists. Thomas Hobbes (1588–1679) famously remarks that our "state
of nature" is a "war of all against all."[2] Sigmund Freud (1856–1939)
holds that we're driven by instinctive pressures to satisfy our biological desires and needs.[3] Konrad Lorenz (1903–1989) considers animals, including humans, to be endowed with genetically "fixed action
patterns," some of which are aggressive.[4] Finally, Edward O. Wilson theorizes that aggression is an adaptive evolutionary trait for
humans and other species to enhance their chances in the struggle
for survival against competitors in environments of limited resources;
violence thus promotes the survival of the fittest by eliminating the
less fit.[5]

Such a view is at the forefront of "The Enemy Within" (TOS), in
which a transporter malfunction results in Kirk being split in two.
The "good" Kirk is weak and indecisive, whereas the "evil" Kirk is
strong and cunning—and wreaks havoc. Kirk complains after his two
halves are reunited, "I've seen a part of myself no man should ever
see." Dr. McCoy, however, offers a more balanced perspective earlier
in the episode:

KIRK:     I have to take him back inside myself. I can't survive without him.
          I don't want him back. He's like an animal, a thoughtless, brutal
          animal, and yet it's me. Me.

MCCOY:    Jim, you're no different than anyone else. We all have our darker
          side. We need it! It's half of what we are. It's not really ugly, it's
          human.

KIRK:     Human.

MCCOY:     Yes, human. A lot of what he is makes you the man you are....
Without the negative side, you wouldn't be the Captain. You
couldn't be, and you know it. Your strength of command lies mostly
in him.

This notion that we're inherently violent is essentially folk wisdom,
however, and is often justified by claims that competition, and ensuing
violence, are "natural." But many scholars have challenged this view,
some arguing that *cooperation* evolved as a drive equally strong as
that of competition.[6] Even Hobbes contends that human rationality
leads us to realize that we must form cooperative "covenants" in order
avoid the undesirable "state of nature." Reflecting on Kirk's plight in
"The Enemy Within," Spock tells McCoy, "Being split in two halves is
no theory with me, Doctor. I have a human half, you see, as well as an
alien half, submerged, constantly at war with each other.... I survive
it because my intelligence wins over both, makes them live together."

So while humans have the capacity for violence, the struggle for survival doesn't make it inevitable that we must exercise that capacity—
our intelligence can help us to live together. As Kirk says to the leaders
of Eminiar VII, "We are not going to kill today." It comes out as well in
"Arena" (TOS) when Kirk is forced by an advanced race, the Metrons,
to fight a reptilian Gorn. After a prolonged struggle, Kirk comes out
the victor, but refuses to kill the Gorn. Likewise, in "The Gamesters
of Triskelion" (TOS), Kirk is forced to engage in combat with aliens
for sport; but at the climax of the struggle, both Kirk and the alien
Shanna refuse to kill the other.

Along with the belief that human aggression is natural comes the
view that aggression is directed toward an enemy conceived of as
wholly "Other"—those who are different, not part of our inner circle, are suspect and potentially a threat. In "Balance of Terror" (TOS),
during a standoff between the *Enterprise* and a Romulan Bird-of-Prey,
we learn that Romulans and Vulcans not only look alike but also have
a common ancestry. As events unfold and Spock inadvertently puts
the *Enterprise* in danger, Navigator Andrew Stiles accuses Spock—
and implicitly, all Vulcans—of being an enemy of the Federation. For
Stiles, being Romulan—or even just looking Romulan—is to be Other.
His identity is human; theirs isn't. "Let This Be Your Last Battlefield"
(TOS) makes this point even clearer. The *Enterprise* encounters two
aliens from the planet Cheron, Lokai and Bele. A noticeable difference
between them is the coloration on their faces: Lokai is solid white on

the right side of his body and solid black on the left, while Bele is the opposite. They see each other as two different races with a long history of antagonism and hostility toward each other. These two episodes point out the importance of national, cultural, or ethnic identity as a factor in who's seen as the Other, a legitimate target of supposedly justifiable violence.

## "Some Had to Die That Others Might Live": Justifications for Violence

If we accept the notion that humans are inherently aggressive, it's then a short step to claim that aggression is justified. After all, it's natural! Needless to say, other justifications for aggression and violence have been offered. One is the claim that not only do we have the right of defense—that is, to defend ourselves against aggression and violence— but also we can claim the defense of *right*: it's justifiable to engage in violence if it's in the name of doing what's right, such as freeing others from oppression or enforcing international law. On this view, not only is it acceptable to engage in violence if the cause is just, but also we have a *moral responsibility* to do so. The U.S. government, for example, finding no direct link between Iraqi leader Saddam Hussein and the 9/11 attack, shifted its justification for invading Iraq from defending the United States from terrorism to claiming that it was appropriate to remove Hussein from power since he was brutalizing the Iraqi people.

Sometimes, these justifications are couched in the language of *rights*: if violence is needed in order to protect people's rights, then it is regret-table but acceptable. Other times, these justifications are couched in the language of *duties*: there are cases in which violence might be acceptable because it's our duty to do what's right. Our end is jus-tice, and violence is, regrettably, the necessary means to achieve that end. Sometimes these justifications are couched in the language of *costs and benefits*: if some violence is necessary in order to promote what's good, then, on balance, it's an acceptable means of promot-ing the greater good. This view is explored in "The Conscience of the King" (TOS). Kirk comes to suspect that an actor in a traveling the-ater troupe, Anton Karidian, is in fact Kodos "the Executioner," for-mer governor of Tarsus IV. Kodos had ordered the massacre of 4000 colonists, fully half of a population that had been struck by famine. When confronted by Kirk, Karidian defends Kodos's action:

KARIDIAN:    Kodos made a decision of life and death. Some had to die that others might live. You're a man of decision, Captain. You ought to understand that.

KIRK:    All I understand is that four thousand people were needlessly butchered.

KARIDIAN:    In order to save four thousand others. And if the supply ships hadn't come earlier than expected, this Kodos of yours might have gone down in history as a great hero.

KIRK:    But he didn't. And history has made its judgment.

Karidian's *utilitarian* argument, that the—albeit regrettable—choice was justified because it promoted the greatest good for the greatest number, is challenged by Kirk. But similar arguments are frequently made, especially in the contexts of war or times of emergency.[7]

## "No Kill I": Alternatives to Violence

Examples of choosing not to kill or engage in violence belie the claim that violence is natural for humans. Indeed, *Star Trek* is replete with examples of how to respond to violence in nonviolent ways. In "The Empath" (TOS), not only do Kirk and McCoy offer to sacrifice themselves for the benefit of others, but so, too, does a frail, mute humanoid, who McCoy names "Gem." Her willingness to overcome her natural instinct for self-preservation is indeed just what's being tested by the Vians who torture first Kirk and then McCoy, in order to determine whether her race is worthy of preservation from a coming cataclysm. In response to the Vians' violence toward Kirk and McCoy, Gem responds with nonviolent *compassion*.

A different tactic, aimed at not just coping with but also preventing violence, is *deterrence*: motivating others to refrain from acting violently toward you. During the height of the Cold War, the unstated yet practiced policy of both the United States and the Soviet Union was what came to be called MAD, or *mutually assured destruction*. Each nation stockpiled nuclear weapons and made it clear to the other that it was ready to retaliate should the other make a first strike. By terrifying each other with the threat of complete annihilation, it was argued, the Cold War powers could (and did) "keep the peace," because neither nation was willing to take such a risk. A version of this attitude is displayed in "Balance of Terror" and many other episodes in which the Federation disputes with the Klingons or the Romulans.

In his book *Why Nations Go to War*, John G. Stoessinger surveys the major wars of the 20th century and draws the following conclusion: "The most important single precipitating factor in the outbreak of war is misperception. Such distortion may manifest itself in four different ways: in a leader's image of himself; a leader's view of his adversary's character; a leader's view of his adversary's intentions toward himself; and finally, a leader's view of his adversary's capabilities and power."[8] One of those factors—a distorted view of the adversary's character—is demonstrated various times throughout *Star Trek*.

*Misperception*, sometimes willful but more often arising out of ignorance, sometimes defines our relations with others and our understanding of ourselves, and so colors our interactions with others just as their misperceptions color their relation to us. "The Devil in the Dark" (TOS) provides an example that connects misperception with violence. On the mining colony of Janus VI, an unknown menace is damaging equipment and killing miners. The *Enterprise* is sent to investigate and discovers that, because of the mining operations and opening of new tunnels, the colonists had inadvertently killed the eggs of the native, silicon-based Horta. The destruction of their equipment and the killing of the invading "monsters" by the mother Horta were acts of self-defense, as Kirk chides the colonists: "You've killed thousands of her children.... The Horta is intelligent, peaceful, mild. She had no objection to sharing this planet with you, till you broke into her nursery and started destroying her eggs. Then she fought back in the only way she knew how, as any mother would fight when her children are in danger." The identity of "the devil in the dark" was perceived quite differently by the humans and the Horta!

Although the miners were innocent of malice, prior to the arrival of the *Enterprise*, they never questioned whether they were the wronged party. We know all too well that stereotyping and demonizing those who are seen as adversaries are both unjust and rampant. In the course I teach about the Middle East, on the first day of class students write down what they know about the Middle East and about Islam. The results are predictable: the Middle East is politically monolithic; Muslims are all religiously and socially conservative; most Arabs hate America; the region is essentially oil fields and deserts. At the same time, many Middle Easterners share some stereotypes about America: Americans are culturally insensitive; they care only for themselves; they are fundamentally materialistic and narcissistic; they are out of touch with the rest of the world. Of course, stereotypes don't come from nowhere! There are reasons why Americans see Muslims as religiously fanatical, and there are reasons why Middle Easterners see Americans as materialistic. But stereotypes are misperceptions and lead to demonization, which, as Stoessinger says, leads to violence and its justification. Correcting such misperceptions and attempting to see ourselves from the perspective of others can go a long way toward eliminating at least some causes of hostility and violence and, perhaps, even help to prevent them in the future, a future envisioned in *Star Trek*.

## "Peace and Long Life": *Star Trek*'s Message of Peace

Early in "Is There in Truth No Beauty?" (TOS), Dr. Miranda Jones notes that Spock is wearing the revered Vulcan symbol of IDIC: Infinite Diversity in Infinite Combinations. Spock states that it represents "the ways our differences combine to create meaning and beauty." As Jones prepares to depart the *Enterprise*, she bids Spock farewell with "Peace and long life, Spock," to which he replies with the Vulcan salute "Live long and prosper." These exchanges encapsulate the vision of *Star Trek* as both understanding and also promoting a philosophy of peace: we're all interconnected, and by embracing this fact, we find and create peace.

Though *Star Trek* is filled with conflict and even violence, a prevailing theme is the desirability of peace and the commitment to promoting it. In a *Voice of America* radio broadcast on November 11, 1951, Eleanor Roosevelt famously quipped, "It isn't enough to talk about peace. One must believe in it. And it isn't enough to believe in it. One must work at it." This is true of issues related to both negative and positive peace—showing the horrors of war, refusing to kill even when given the opportunity and an apparent justification for doing so, advocating fairness and equality, negotiating an end to hostilities if possible, and addressing not simply the symptoms of violence but also their causes.

Working for peace, of course, isn't done in a vacuum. Violence happens, often intentionally (as with the Stratos city-dwellers and the Troglytes), sometimes unintentionally (as with the miners on Janus VI). Valuing peace—believing in it and working for it—doesn't mean that we have to be unrealistic about conflict or violence. Rather, it means that we can see a better alternative and are committed to striving for a reality that reduces, if not eliminates, violence. This is the ultimate vision of *Star Trek*, wherein themes of justice, tolerance, freedom, mercy, and compassion are repeatedly put front-and-center. Sometimes explicitly, as seen in the above examples, sometimes implicitly, as seen in the *Enterprise*'s unquestioned inclusiveness in the form of its diverse, yet integrated, crew. *Star Trek* envisions a future of full inclusion. Beings are, in the words of the Revered Martin Luther King, Jr.—who, according to Nichelle Nichols, watched *Star Trek* with his family[9]—judged by the content of their character, not by the color of their skin, the bumpiness of their foreheads, or any other irrelevant factors. Genuine and serious respect for and valuing of others involve a commitment to treating them as *ends in themselves*, not merely as means for our own ends. This involves seeing ourselves as interconnected with others and with the world beyond. Indeed, to "boldly go" is not necessarily a journey into physical space, but into an inner life based on discovering and celebrating interconnections with others. Therein, *Star Trek* tells us, lies peace and long life.

## Notes

1. See Duane L. Cady, *From Warism to Pacifism*, 2nd ed. (Philadelphia: Temple University Press, 2010).
2. Thomas Hobbes, *Leviathan*, ed. Edwin Curley (Indianapolis, IN: Hackett, 1994).
3. Sigmund Freud, *The Ego and the Id* (original title: *Das Ich und das Es*) (Vienna: International Psycholanalytischer Verlag, 1923).
4. Konrad Lorenz, *On Aggression* (original title: *Das sogenannte Böse*) (Berlin: Methuen, 1963).
5. Edward O. Wilson, *On Human Nature* (Cambridge, MA: Harvard University Press, 1979).
6. See David P. Barash, *Buddhist Biology: Ancient Eastern Wisdom Meets Modern Western Science* (Oxford: Oxford University Press, 2014).
7. For more detailed discussion of utilitarian ethical reasoning, see Greg Littmann's chapter in this volume (Chapter 12).
8. John G. Stoessinger, *Why Nations Go to War*, 7th ed. (New York: St. Martin's, 1998), 211.
9. http://www.npr.org/2011/01/17/132942461/Star-Treks-Uhura-Reflects-On-MLK-Encounter (accessed June 17, 2015).

# Part II

# BETA QUADRANT: DANGEROUS RIVALRIES

# Klingons: A Cultural Pastiche

## Victor Grech

Outside of the Vulcans, Klingons are the most enduringly famous humanoid race in the *Star Trek* universe, a fearless and fearsome interstellar military power in the Beta Quadrant. Originally cast as the "bad guys of the week" in TOS, they morphed in TNG into grim but worthy Federation allies. As TNG—and later DS9 and VOY—explored Klingon culture in greater depth, they became not simply a "one-note" species representing some singular aspect of human culture—as the Ferengi reflect unchecked capitalistic greed or the Betazoids the empathic aspect of our psyche. Rather, the Klingons are singularly intriguing as a veritable pastiche—a motley conglomeration—of various human cultures. Additionally, events in the Klingon Empire have served as metaphors for contemporary events. Klingon culture is so well developed, in fact, that they're the only *Star Trek* race to have had their language published in a dictionary for fans who wish to nurture their inner warrior spirit.[1]

Let's explore some of the human cultural representations that we find in our favorite bumpy-headed, *bat'leth*-swinging, *raktajino*-drinking aliens that can help us reflect on how human society has evolved and where we may be headed in our own future. Perhaps, instead of the peace-loving Federation Roddenberry envisions for us, we may be more inclined to follow "the way of the warrior."

*The Ultimate Star Trek and Philosophy*, First Edition. Edited by Kevin S. Decker and Jason T. Eberl.
© 2016 John Wiley & Sons, Ltd. Published 2016 by John Wiley & Sons, Ltd.

## First Appearances: "They're Animals!"

The TOS writers who initially created the Klingons described them as "Oriental, hard-faced.... Think of the Mongol Hordes with space-ships and ray guns."[2] Klingons were portrayed as swarthy, musta-chioed menaces in the mold of Genghis Khan and Fu Manchu. Starting with *The Motion Picture*, Klingons got an even fiercer look through the acquisition of forehead ridges, which can function as a head-butt weapon either in the heat of battle or in a friendly bar-fight on Qo'nos.[3]

In "Blood Oath," *Deep Space Nine*'s Constable Odo complains, "Every time Klingons visit the station, I wind up with a Klingon after-noon." Starfleet cadet Nog later experiences what a "Klingon after-noon" means: "It's their attitude, sir. It's bad. ... They're loud, obnox-ious, and if I may say so, sir, generally intoxicated" ("Blaze of Glory," DS9). Klingons are often considered uncouth by outsiders—even their body odor is considered foul smelling by some (*The Undiscovered Country*; "Trials and Tribble-ations," DS9). But they are a paradoxi-cal mix: liberally quoting Shakespeare, which they translate from "the original Klingon," while behaving in ways that would make a Russian like Chekov call them "*nekulturny* Cossacks"—uncultured barbar-ians. Accustomed to eating live *gagh* with their hands, they're some-times uncertain how to use conventional utensils at dinner, as Uhura and Chekov note disdainfully in *The Undiscovered Country*: "Did you see the way they eat? ... Terrible table manners." Klingon food itself is depicted as barbaric—Commander Riker eats a tasty banquet-full of Klingon delicacies to prepare for temporary transfer to a Klingon Bird-of-Prey in "A Matter of Honor" (TNG). An apparent act of brav-ery in itself, consuming dishes like rokeg blood pie, pipius claw, and heart of targ "brings courage to one who eats it" ("Day of Honor," VOY).

## "The Way of the Warrior"

Far from being simple-minded, vicious, animalistic barbarians, Klin-gons are a technologically advanced culture and maintain ancient cus-toms and rituals associated with the warrior ethos that has defined their society since the time of Kahless the Unforgettable. While, to out-siders, Klingons may appear to be little more than a bloodthirsty gang bent on indiscriminate killing at the merest slight to their pride, the

Klingon honor code has been developed over 1500 years and exhorts specific actions in response to specific infringements on one's honor. Jadzia Dax, for example, clarifies to her crewmates on DS9 exactly how violence can be properly executed aboard a Klingon warship:

O'BRIEN: Serving on a Klingon ship is like being with a gang of ancient sea pirates. You advance in rank by killing the people above you. So everywhere you turn you're surrounded by potential assassins.

KIRA: Well that's crazy! How could a ship function like that?

DAX: It's not quite that chaotic. The social and military hierarchy of a Klingon vessel is very strictly enforced. A subordinate can only challenge a direct superior and only under certain conditions.

BASHIR: What sort of conditions?

DAX: Dereliction of duty, dishonorable conduct, cowardice.

O'BRIEN: Cowardice?! A Klingon?

DAX: It's been known to happen. The Klingons are as diverse a people as any. Some them are strong and some of them are weak.

Klingon mythology, which is similar to Viking and Greek legends, led to a code of behavior that closely emulates Bushidō, the "Way of the Warrior-Knight" developed in Japan between the 9th and 12th centuries. This code emphasized frugality, courage, veracity, compassion, and stoicism. Like the Imperial Japanese, Klingons emphasize unquestioning obedience to strong rulers who've proven themselves:

Do not forget that a leader need not answer questions of those he leads. It is enough that he says to do a thing and they will do it. If he says to run, they run. If he says to fight, they fight. If he says to die, they die. ("Rightful Heir," TNG)

Klingon culture also reflects Eastern culture by its form of martial art, *mok'bara*, which emulates "some form of tai chi chuan" ("Second Chances," TNG).

Klingons are a "culture [that] finds honor in death," from valorous combat that is actively sought ("Broken Bow," ENT). Not content with menial duties, General Martok is exuberant when given a convoy escort mission through space rife with Jem'Hadar raiders: "A vital mission, impossible odds and a ruthless enemy, what more could we ask for?" ("Sons and Daughters," DS9). In fact, although their capacity for longevity is biologically much greater than that of humans—especially with the evolution of redundant organ systems and a reinforced skeletal structure ("Ethics," TNG)—Klingon warriors don't expect, or hope, to live to a ripe old age: "There are no old warriors," Commander Riker is told in "A Matter of Honor" (TNG). Failing to die at an enemy's hands could even bring dishonor to oneself and one's family:

KLAG: My father was captured in battle by Romulans and not allowed to die. He eventually escaped.

RIKER: Where is he now?

KLAG: He is on our planet. He waits.
[Riker looks quizzically at the Tactics Officer]

TACTICS OFFICER: He waits for his death.

KLAG: He will eventually fade of a natural illness and die, weakened and useless. Honorless. I will not see him.

RIKER: He's your father!

KLAG: A Klingon is his work, not his family. That is the way of things.

The Klingon battle cry, "Today is a good day to die!" while perfectly summing up a Klingon warrior's willingness to embrace an honorable death, shouldn't be understood as a morose, fatalistic surrender to one's inevitable demise (there are situations that call for a Klingon to commit ritual suicide—as Worf's brother, Kurn, desires in "Sons of Mogh," DS9). Going into battle with a suicidal mind-set, however, is actually a sign of weakness that endangers not only oneself but also one's fellow warriors—as Jadzia chides Kang when she realizes he has no intention of surviving their coming battle against "the Albino" who murdered his child. "I think you Klingons embrace death too easily," she admonishes him. "You treat death like a lover. I think living is a lot more attractive" ("Blood Oath," DS9). In fact, far from being merely angry, vengeful vehicles of violence, Klingons should take *joy* in their successes—as Klingon *Dahar* Master Kor exhorts Worf, "The way of the warrior is not a humble path. Show some pride in your accomplishments!" ("Once More untoiThe Breach," DS9). When, in "Rightful Heir" (TNG), Worf battles the "resurrected" Kahless, the latter stops the combat when he observes the dour visages of those watching, "What is wrong? Is there only anger and bloodlust in your souls? Is that all that is left in the Klingon heart? We do not fight merely to spill blood, but to enrich the spirit! Look at us, two warriors, locked in battle, fighting for honor! How can you not sing, for all to hear? WE ARE KLINGONS!"

The Klingon warrior ethos also justifies the annexation of territory from perceived inferior races, since they consider themselves something like *Übermenschen*, "supermen" in the philosophy of Friedrich Nietzsche (1844–1900): noble beings who value courage, mastery, creative leadership, and self-reliance.[4] In "You Are Cordially Invited" (DS9), Martok declares to Worf, "We don't embrace other cultures, we conquer them." Klingons are extremely *territorial*, and thus there's no such thing as an "insignificant corner of Klingon space" ("Bounty," ENT). This is typified in General Chang's proclamation at dinner in *The Undiscovered Country* that Klingons "need breathing room," to which Captain Kirk sardonically replies, "Earth, Hitler, 1938," pointing out the obvious echo of the Nazi ideology of *Lebensraum*—the desire for more "living space." But Klingons don't engage in conquest merely for its own sake. Rather, they're driven by the same basic needs that drive any society to violence. As Kang's wife, Mara, educates Kirk in "Day of the Dove," (TOS): "We have always fought. We must. We are hunters, Captain, tracking and taking what we need. There are poor planets in the Klingon systems, we must push outward if we are to survive."

## "Our Gods Are Dead. Ancient Klingon Warriors Slew Them Millennia Ago"

The Klingon religion is an interesting combination of mythical and spiritual elements, along with a grounded *humanism* that characterizes Gene Roddenberry's fundamental vision of the future by eschewing the contemporary existence of deities. In the Klingon wedding ceremony seen in DS9's "You Are Cordially Invited," the presider proclaims, "With fire and steel did the gods forge the Klingon heart ... the strongest heart in all the heavens. None can stand before it without trembling at its strength.... The Klingon hearts destroyed the gods who created them." In "Homefront" (DS9), Worf explains that the Klingon gods "were more trouble than they were worth." Whether Worf literally believes this story, Klingon mythology here echoes Nietzsche's proclamation, "God is dead. God remains dead. And we have killed him."[5] Nietzsche considers humanity to have appealed to supernatural explanations for various phenomena and to ground our sense of morality in the past; but rational discoveries in science and philosophy during the Enlightenment and beyond have rendered such divine appeals superfluous and nothing more than mere superstition.

Although Klingons don't believe in all-knowing, all-powerful deities as many monotheistic religious believers do, they do revere as a semidivine figure "the first warrior-king": Kahless the Unforgettable ("The Sword of Kahless," DS9). In physical feats, he was comparable to the classical Greek hero Hercules, having completed several quests, the crowning achievement of which was slaying the tyrant, Molor, and unifying the Empire ("Firstborn," TNG). Like other Messianic figures, Kahless was promised to return one day, and dedicated clerics awaited him at the Boreth monastery until they decided to engineer a clone from his blood implanted with constructed "memories" of Kahless's life as recorded in Klingon legend. Although an unorthodox way for Kahless to "return," it was agreed that the clone could serve as a moral figurehead for the Klingon people as "Emperor." Worf, however, is disappointed that it wasn't the *real* Kahless who returned, and he continues to feel spiritually empty.[6] Kahless's clone, imbued with his progenitor's wisdom, consoles Worf:

> Kahless left us, all of us, a powerful legacy. A way of thinking and acting that makes us Klingon. If his words hold wisdom and his philosophy is honorable, what does it matter if he returns? What is important is that we follow his teachings. Perhaps the words are more important than the man. ("Rightful Heir," TNG)

Yet another religious coming was envisaged in ancient Klingon texts, the *Kuvah'magh*, whose appearance was prefigured, in almost biblical terms, by many predictions that seemed to point to the daughter of Tom Paris and B'Elanna Torres in VOY's "Prophecy."

The Klingon conception of the afterlife follows the Messianic belief embodied by Kahless with dashes of Norse and Greek mythology. When warriors die, their eyes are forcibly opened and all Klingons present roar in order to warn the dead, "Beware, a Klingon warrior is about to arrive," while the warrior's body is considered "only an empty shell" ("Heart of Glory," TNG). Warriors who died honorably join Kahless in Sto'Vo'Kor, a paradise wherein, like the Viking Valhalla, feasting and battle are eternal. Klingons who die in dishonor are ferried by Kortar across the "River of Blood" on the "Barge of the Dead" to Gre'thor, where they'll be tormented for all eternity by Fek'lhr, a satanic analog ("Devil's Due," TNG).[7] Klingon souls on the Barge are tempted by voices and images masquerading as friends and family, attempting to lure them off the barge and into the river ("Barge of the Dead," VOY). This parallels Greek mythology, in which the ferryman, Charon, carries the souls of the newly deceased across the rivers Styx and Acheron from the world of the living to the world of the dead in Hades. The tempters who endeavor to lure souls off the barge are similar to the "sirens" in Homer's *Odyssey*.

Elements of Arthurian legend, in combination with the search for Christian sacred relics, such as the Holy Grail, are manifest when Kor acquires an ancient shroud: "You see?... The imprint on the cloth.... This held the Sword of Kahless," which had been stolen from the Empire. The cloth isn't merely a clue to a revered object, but is itself "holy" due to the sacredness of what it had held. Similarly, the "Shroud of Turin" is revered by Christians who believe it to have held the dead body of Christ prior to his resurrection. Kor rejoices:

> I am on a quest ... for the most revered icon in Klingon history ... more coveted than the Emperor's crown!... Think of the glory, the honor.... To return the Sword to our people. I would give my life for that chance.... Children will sing our names for a thousand years. They'll erect statues of us in the Hall of Heroes. ("Sword of Kahless," DS9)

As with many cultural and religious traditions, Klingon culture is shot through with *ritual*, to the point that some note jocularly that Klingons "have rituals for everything except waste extraction" ("Looking for *par'Mach* in All the Wrong Places," DS9). Klingon rituals are particularly reminiscent of certain traditional cultures, such as that of feudal Japan, which include a "tea ceremony" ("Up the Long Ladder," TNG). As with more severe forms of *asceticism* practiced by avowed religious adherents, Klingon rituals are replete with sacrifice, including a four-day fast along with trials involving "blood, pain, sacrifice, anguish, and death" in preparation for a marriage ceremony ("You Are Cordially Invited," DS9).

The Klingon willingness to undergo personal sacrifice makes them the ultimate *stoics*. "A warrior does not complain about physical discomfort," Worf declares in "Clues" (TNG). This extends to coming-of-age rituals, such as the Klingon "Rite of Ascension," the second level of which involves the infliction of pain by a series of warriors employing "pain sticks," much like the old Native American custom of running the gauntlet. In "The Icarus Factor" (TNG), Data explains the purpose of the ritual: "The true test of Klingon strength is to admit one's most profound feelings while under extreme duress."

## "I Don't Care What You Look Like, You Are No *Klingon!*"

Worf—the only full-blooded Klingon to wear a Starfleet uniform—was brought up among humans from a young age. However, although he was "raised and loved by human parents"—Sergey and Helena Rozhenko—Worf strives to retain his Klingon heritage: "I was born a Klingon. My heart is of that world. I do hear the cry of the warrior" ("Redemption, Part I," TNG). Yet, he suffers throughout most of his life as an outcast from Klingon society. By the same token, he never quite fits comfortably into human society either, describing himself in his youth as "the uncontrollable one ... the biggest, the strongest, most fearless child on the entire planet. I fought hard, played hard, I did as I pleased ("Let He Who Is without Sin," DS9). Worf's aggressive tendencies led to a tragic accident, resulting in Worf becoming more stoic and self-controlled than just about any other Klingon. Riker (in "A Matter of Honor," TNG) and Guinan (in "Redemption, Part I," TNG) observe that Worf seldom laughs heartily the way other Klingons readily do:

GUINAN: You know, I had a bet with the Captain that I could make you laugh before you became lieutenant commander.

WORF: Not a good bet today.

GUINAN: I've seen you laugh. I like it.

WORF: Klingons do not laugh.

GUINAN: Oh, yes, they do. Absolutely they do. *You* don't. But I've heard Klingon belly laughs that'd curl your hair.... Your son laughs. He's Klingon.

WORF: He is a child and part human!

GUINAN: That's right. And you're not; you're a full Klingon, except you don't laugh.

WORF: I do not laugh because I do not feel like laughing.

GUINAN: Other Klingons feel like laughing. What does that say about you?

WORF: Perhaps it says that I do not feel like other Klingons.

Although the *Enterprise*'s mostly human crew comprise his surrogate family, this isn't sufficient for Worf to truly feel as if he *belongs*. When Worf is acting particularly "Worfish" as he approaches the tenth anniversary of his First Rite of Ascension, Wesley observes, "Worf doesn't have any Klingon friends ... we don't practice Klingon tradition and we're not Klingons. Worf is feeling culturally and socially isolated" ("The Icarus Factor," TNG).

Worf's heritage was further elided by his career choices. He "joined Starfleet … something no Klingon had ever done" ("The Sword of Kahless," TNG) and thus became subservient to Federation mores and customs. In order to conform, he actively represses his passions in almost Vulcan fashion: "Those feelings are part of me. But I control them. They do not rule me" ("Heart of Glory," TNG). On several occasions, Worf is taunted by other Klingons to prove his Klingon nature, from Chancellor Gowron to two renegade Klingons who seek to overturn the Khitomer accords:

> Tell me, what it is like for the hunter to lie down with the prey? Have they tamed you, or have you always been docile? Does it make you gentle? Has it filled your heart with peace? Do glorious battles no longer inspire your dreams? ("Heart of Glory," TNG)

Even Worf's own brother questions whether he's fit to lead their house: "Perhaps your blood has thinned in this environment" ("Sins of the Father," TNG).

The elision of Worf's Klingon nature appears to be due to the application of "Occidentalism," a term coined by French philosopher Roland Barthes (1915–1980) to denote the Westernization of non-Western cultures. In Worf's case, the Federation and Starfleet consciously and unconsciously manipulate Worf with an almost hegemonic influence. While intercultural values are respected, limits are imposed when one serves aboard a Federation starship. Picard chastises Worf after he kills Duras, claiming the Klingon Right of Vengeance following K'Ehleyr's murder in "Reunion" (TNG):

> The *Enterprise* crew currently includes representatives from thirteen planets. They each have their individual beliefs and values and I respect them all. But they have all chosen to serve Starfleet. If anyone cannot perform his or her duty because of the demands of their society, they should resign.

Worf must constantly assimilate to Federation values, entailing a process of *acculturation*—the psychological enslavement resulting from the imposition of one's culture on another. The effects of this phenomenon, like Occidentalism, are usually manifest on multiple levels—usually in a one-way process. In Worf's case, his acculturation actually leads to what could be considered well-meaning, but nevertheless condescending, praise by Picard in "Redemption, Part I" (TNG):

> I felt that what was unique about you was your humanity, compassion, generosity, fairness. You took the best qualities of humanity and made them part of you. The result was a man who I was proud to call one of my officers.

## "The Federation Is No More Than a *Homo sapiens*–Only Club"

Picard's imputation of "humanity" to Worf shows just how blind Starfleet officers, as well as members of any socially dominant culture, can be to other cultural perspectives. On the one hand, Starfleet's Prime Directive of noninterference with other cultures appears as a near-absolute principle. It seems to embrace *cultural relativism*, the view that an individual's beliefs and activities can and should be judged only by peers within the same culture.[8] On the other hand, 23rd- and 24th-century humans persist in unfairly judging Klingons as coarse and barbarous. At the awkward dinner party in *The Undiscovered Country*, Chekov asserts, "We do believe all planets have a sovereign claim to inalienable human rights"—at least he didn't claim the concept of "human rights" was invented in Russia! The Klingon chancellor's daughter, Azetbur, disdainfully replies, "Inalien.... If only you could hear yourselves. '*Human* rights.' Why the very name is racist."

Starfleet officers are typically shown to be flexible and culturally adaptive, as evidenced when Riker eagerly volunteers to serve on a Klingon ship in "A Matter of Honor" (TNG). Surprisingly, though, they remain generally reluctant to embrace, or even comprehend, Klingon culture. Even the ever open-minded Picard confesses in "Where Silence Has Lease" (TNG), "I think it is perhaps best to be ignorant of certain elements of Klingon psyche."

Within the *Star Trek* universe, Klingon culture largely remains "Other," and, in the case of acculturated individuals like Worf, the influence is pretty much one-way. Ironically, *outside* of the fictional 24th-century world, Trekkers have been responsible for cultural appropriation in the *other* direction, adopting elements of a minority culture—in this case, Klingon—outside of their original cultural context. Many Trekkers engage in cosplay with quite authentic-looking Klingon armor, learn the *mok'bara* and how to fight with a *bat'leth*, and even become proficient in the Klingon language and marry each other in the same Klingon manner that Worf and Jadzia did in "You Are Cordially Invited" (DS9). There may be an element of poetic justice in this, since *Star Trek* by and large imparts an idealistic vision based on values of contemporary Western liberalism; Klingons represent anything *but* such values. More specifically, this cultural appropriation may constitute poetic justice for Klingons, who liberally quote from Shakespeare while claiming the Bard as one of their own![9]

# Notes

1. See Marc Okrand, *The Klingon Dictionary* (New York: Pocket Books, 1992). There's even an online Klingon Language Institute: http://www.kli.org (accessed June 15, 2015).
2. The first part of this quotation is from Gene L. Coon, who wrote the first episode in which the Klingons appeared, "Errand of Mercy"; the latter part is from David Gerrold, who wrote "The Trouble with Tribbles."
3. This drastic discrepancy in appearance was finally given an in-universe explanation in the ENT episode "Divergence."
4. Friedrich Nietzsche, *Thus Spoke Zarathustra*, trans. Walter Kaufmann (New York: Viking Penguin, 1954). It is important to note, however, that Nietzsche did not intend the *Übermensch* as a racial concept.
5. Friedrich Nietzsche, *The Gay Science*, trans. Walter Kaufmann (New York: Random House, 1974), §125.
6. For a detailed discussion of Worf's "crisis of faith" in light of Kahless's apparent return, see Heather Keith, "The Second-Coming of Kahless: Worf's 'Will to Believe'," in *Star Trek and Philosophy*, ed. Jason T. Eberl and Kevin S. Decker (Chicago: Open Court, 2008).
7. The characterization of Fek'lhr as a "satanic analog" needs to be squared with Kang's statement in "Day of the Dove" (TOS) that Klingons "have no devil." There are a few potential explanations: (1) Kang was expressing his own personal disbelief in Fek'lhr's existence; (2) Klingons *used* to believe in Fek'lhr but have largely since abandoned that belief, having "killed" him just as ancient Klingon warriors slew the rest of the Klingon gods; or (3) less an analog for Satan, Fek'lhr is more like the demonic canine Cerberus who guards the gates of Hades (http://en.memory-alpha.wikia.com/wiki/Fek'lhr). This last option, however, has to be squared with B'Elanna's claim in "Barge of the Dead" (VOY) that Fek'lhr *tortures* the dishonored dead, a role more analogous to Satan than to Cerberus.

8. For a more in-depth discussion of cultural relativism, see William Lindenmuth's chapter in this volume (Chapter 24).

9. The Shakespearean play *Hamlet, Prince of Denmark* has in fact been "restored to the original Klingon" by Nick Nicholas and Andrew Strader of the Klingon Language Institute (New York: Pocket Books, 2000).

# 8

# The Borg as Contagious Collectivist Techno-Totalitarian Transhumanists

## Dan Dinello

Cybernetically enhanced humanoids, the Borg assimilate entire civilizations using advanced technology. Genocidal destroyers, the Borg's ultimate goal is perfecting their species through the imperialistic incorporation of other species' biological and technological distinctiveness. Perfect villains for the digital age, they don't seek to rule other worlds or negotiate treaties; rather, they pursue their objective to upgrade themselves with the relentless, implacable, cold logic of a computer. Neurally linked into a collective consciousness and mechanistically emotionless, the Borg represent what Captain Jean-Luc Picard calls "almost pure evil."

Anxieties about the Borg focus on their invincible militarism, genocidal threat, ruthless cruelty, totalitarian collectivism, torturous technology, and physical monstrousness. Their bodies are functional automatons and broadly identical: ghostly pallor and blank faces reflect an absence of free will; metal, wires, and tubes grotesquely pierce their heads, limbs, and torsos; and they're encased in tight black rubber outfits. Their repulsiveness derives from the grotesque intertwining of the organic and the mechanical. The Borg express a dark vision of fetishized, mutated, posthuman cyborg bodies and unrestrained, antihumanist technology.

This representation of the Borg as malevolent machines contrasts strongly with the generally positive stance *Star Trek* takes toward technology. When the *Enterprise* experiences breakdowns—warp core breaches, transporter accidents, or radiation shield failures—these are typically attributed to external forces rather than failings of the ship's

*The Ultimate Star Trek and Philosophy*, First Edition. Edited by Kevin S. Decker and Jason T. Eberl.
© 2016 John Wiley & Sons, Ltd. Published 2016 by John Wiley & Sons, Ltd.

technology or the crew. In "Contagion" (TNG), for example, the *Enterprise* starts to experience crippling malfunctions similar to those that had just destroyed her sister ship, the *Yamato*. While the crew is initially concerned that there may be a fundamental design flaw in the *Galaxy*-class starships, they eventually discover that an ancient alien program is rewriting the ship's software and wreaking havoc on its systems. The *Enterprise* remains a good ship—although perhaps not as good as Commander Riker's former ship, the *Lollipop* ("Arsenal of Freedom," TNG).

Like starships and tricorders, cyborgs aren't inherently evil. Well-behaved, humanoid cyborgs populate the *Star Trek* crews: Picard operates with an artificial heart, Geordi LaForge sports a VISOR, Nog walks with an artificial leg after an unfortunate run-in with the Jem'Hadar, and former Borg drone Seven of Nine still has both external and internal implants. Most significantly, the artificial techno-creature Data personifies *Star Trek*'s philosophy of positive humanist technology.

## Cybernetic Servitude

Lieutenant Commander Data is extremely nice and morally as good as anyone on the *Enterprise* or, for that matter, on any planet in the universe. Courteous, gentle, and tolerant, he earns our admiration with intelligent, decisive, and honest actions. Along with standard robotic traits—logic, humorlessness, and intelligence—Data functions with high-minded moral standards. His basic programming includes a strong inhibition against harming living beings that incorporates author Isaac Asimov's (1920–1992) laws of robotic ethics.

Reacting to what he called the "Frankenstein complex" of fearsome, evil machine-men in 1940s pulp science-fiction magazines, Asimov wanted to change the image of robots. To a great extent he succeeded, strongly influencing sci-fi writers and roboticists with a vision of helpful robots and safe, positive technology: "I saw them [robots] as machines—advanced machines—but machines. They might be dangerous but surely safety factors would be built in…. I determined to write a robot story about a robot that was wisely used, that was not dangerous, and that did the job it was supposed to do."[1] Asimov thus specified his three Laws of Robotics:

1  A robot may not injure a human being, or, through inaction, allow a human being to come to harm.

2  A robot must obey the orders given it by human beings except where such orders would conflict with the First Law.
3  A robot must protect its own existence as long as such protection does not conflict with the First or Second Law.[2]

These laws—what might also be called the Three Commandments of Robotic Subservience—formed an ethical system guaranteeing robot servitude and human dominance. Yet, Asimov's robots, as they developed over forty stories and several novels, became more caring, more sensitive, and more "human" than humans. Asimov imagined robots that behaved like saints—meek, humble, selfless, pro-human do-gooders. Still, while pointing to robotic moral superiority and human failings, Asimov's robots—in deference to the ethical laws—obey even the most idiotic human.

Asimov influenced roboticists like Hans Moravec, who urged "the installation of an elaborate analog of Isaac Asimov's 'Laws of Robotics' in every intelligent machine."[3] His laws are foundational for the nascent philosophy of "Roboethics."[4] Indeed, Asimov provided the blueprint for good, likeable, slave-like sci-fi robots like Data, among many others.[5]

In "Datalore" (TNG), we discover that the great cyberneticist, Dr. Noonien Soong, based Data's artificial intelligence on a sophisticated "positronic" brain—the fictional type of brain Asimov invented for his robots. Data is intellectually and physically more powerful than any human, yet completely obedient to them and their humanistic ideology. He even wants to become human: he paints, plays violin and classical guitar, performs Shakespeare, and reads mystery novels.

Like a good Asimovian robot, Data puts greater value on the lives of the humanoid *Enterprise* crew than on his own life. In *ST: Nemesis*, Data makes the ultimate sacrifice, giving his life to save his shipmates. Data embodies the central *Star Trek* concept that, despite their flaws, the ideals of liberal humanism—individuality, political freedom, personal autonomy, respect for life—reign supreme and will be defended and expanded, rather than endangered, by advanced technology. At least, this is the case for Federation-created technology.

## "Resistance Is Futile, You Must Comply"

If Data is the dream of a perfect technology, the Borg are the nightmare: relentless, destructive, compassionless, and utterly indifferent. "In their collective state, the Borg are without mercy, driven by one will alone, the will to conquer. They are beyond redemption, beyond reason," Picard wrote in a report later read by *Voyager* Captain Kathryn Janeway. Unlike the humanist Data, who is guided by his "ethical subroutine" informed by Asimov's laws, the Borg demonstrate an alternative vision of technology as antihuman, out of control, and imperialist.

In line with philosophers who are critical of technology, like Jacques Ellul and Langdon Winner, the very existence of the Borg counters the notion that technology is politically neutral and subject to human control. Far from being neutral, Borg technology pursues its own course apart from human desires and calculations. Ellul could've been describing the Borg when he says, "Technique has become a reality in itself, self-sufficient, with its special laws and its own determinations. Technique tolerates no judgment from without and accepts no limitation. The power and autonomy of technique are so well secured that it plays the role of creator of a new civilization."[6]

Langdon Winner reinforces Ellul's thesis: technological systems move autonomously, transforming everything in their path: "Human beings still have a nominal presence in the [technological] network, but they have lost their roles as active, directing agents. They tend to obey uncritically the norms and requirements of the systems which they allegedly govern."[7] As such, technology thwarts human control and tends to modify and dominate the environment, including the psychology, motives, and behavior of society.

Ellul further argues that technology is "anthropomorphic": a sensing, thinking, deciding, and demanding subject. The Borg symbolize the perception of technology as possessing lifelike properties: consciousness, will, and implacable movement. Reflecting human assimilation by the Borg, Ellul argues that humans have become thoroughly *technomorphic*: having invested in a mass of methods, techniques, machines, organizations, and networks, humans must comply with technology or perish. As Winner puts it, "Virtually everything in reach will be transformed to suit the special needs of the technical ensemble. Anything that cannot be adapted (for whatever reason) is eliminated."[8] When Picard, as Locutus, sizes up Data, he declares him to be a "primitive artificial organism" and that he'll "be obsolete in the new order" ("Best of Both Worlds, Part II," TNG).

Like technology, the Borg can't self-replicate. Their mechanical prosthetic parts make them sterile and nonsexual, so that propagation and evolution require parasitizing others.[9] They assimilate and incorporate humans and other intelligent life forms through injections of nanoprobes. Borg technology infiltrates the cells of an individual like a virus, seizing control, altering biochemistry, and mutating its host to support the Borg's survival, evolution, and improvement while transforming the person into a Borg fashion victim. A sinister contagion, the Borg represent both malignancy and mental enslavement.

In this view of technology as an independent, quasi-biological life form, humans are reduced to secondary status as reproductive vessels: "Each generation extends the technical ensemble and passes it on to the next generation. The mortality of human beings matters little, for technology is itself immortal and, therefore, the more significant part of the process."[10] Like a biological species that lives on even though the individual members perish, the technological virus uses humans, not so much as participants, but as a breeding ground that combines and recombines technological structures to produce new mutations. Q sums it up best in "Q Who?" (TNG): "The Borg is the ultimate user.... They're not interested in political conquest, wealth, or power as you know it. They're simply interested in your ship, its technology. They've identified it as something they can consume."

Voracious in their urge to possess and engulf—scooping up entire cities from planetary surfaces—the Borg represent what Winner calls the "technological imperative": a self-perpetuating, self-enhancing transformative force for the total adaptation, integration, and incorporation of the material and human world. Through the absorption of individuals, raw materials, and other technologies into their collective, the Borg reflect our own vast technological systems, creating webs of mutual dependency required for the system to function, develop, and perfect itself. "Technology is a source of domination that effectively rules all forms of modern thought and activity," says Winner. "Whether by an inherent property or by an incidental set of circumstances, technology looms as an oppressive force that poses a direct threat to human freedom."[11] Ellul bluntly concludes that technology is inherently *totalitarian*.[12]

## "We Wish to Improve Ourselves"

Using technology, the Borg strive to achieve *perfection*, which they envision as invincible military might, mental and physical healing techniques, communal harmony, and machine-like efficiency. They rigorously implement their desire to escape the limitations of organic flesh through genetic and cybernetic augmentation of their bodies and brains. In contrast to Locutus's dismissal of Data as "primitive" and "obsolete," the Borg Queen is enamored with Data in *ST: First Contact* as he represents the ideal to which the Borg aspire. Beyond these progressive improvements, the Borg overcome aging and death with regeneration modules that revive mental and physical energies. In their obsession with "achieving perfection" via technology, the Borg echo and ultimately critique the techno-utopian philosophy of transhumanism.

Not content with surrendering to the natural inevitability of growing old and dying, transhumanists believe that scientists will eventually attain control of biological evolution at the molecular level and gain the ability to upgrade the human species. By fusing various enhancement and repair technologies, scientists are expected to engineer a disease-proof, super-cyborg species that will eventually supersede humanity in its current form. Philosopher Max More summarizes the transhumanist program:

> We challenge the inevitability of aging and death. We see humans as a transitional stage standing between our animal heritage and our posthuman future. When technology allows us to reconstitute ourselves physiologically, genetically and neurologically, we will transform ourselves into posthumans—persons of unprecedented physical, intellectual and psychological capacity, self-programming, potentially immortal, unlimited individuals.[13]

More believes that this techno-transformation will be accelerated by means of genetic engineering, life-extending biosciences, intelligence intensifiers, neural-computer integration, worldwide data networks, virtual reality, artificial intelligence, synthetic biology, off-planet migration, and molecular nanotechnology.

In accordance with Borg philosophy, life will be enhanced and prolonged through both genetic engineering and cyborgization: body-improving prosthetic technology will replace deteriorating body parts. Artificial machinery will replace organic machinery: instead of Geordi's VISOR replacing a lack of vision, humans born with functional biological eyes may nevertheless replace them with the spectrally enhanced VISOR. "We are on a path to changing our genome in profound ways," says transhumanist roboticist Rodney Brooks. "The distinction between us and robots is going to disappear."[14]

Max More points out that transhumanism derives from the Enlightenment philosophy of the 17th and 18th centuries in its dismissal of divine forces, belief in a materialistic worldview, exaltation of science, and emphasis on human progress toward perfection—all resulting in the *posthuman superman*. The philosophical assumptions that underlie transhumanism can be traced to French philosopher René Descartes (1596–1650), who provided the foundation for Enlightenment philosophy and scientific advancement.

Descartes describes the physical world, including humans, in mechanical terms: "I consider the body of man as being a sort of machine so built up and composed of nerves, muscles, veins, blood and skin."[15] Descartes's dualistic conception of a human being as an immaterial conscious mind conjoined with a mechanical body was popularized in the first decades of the computer age when cybernetics, artificial intelligence, and information theory defined the human brain as an extremely complex biological information-processing machine. Defining a person's psychological identity as simply patterned information allows transhumanists to believe that eventually a person's mind could be digitally recorded and uploaded into a cybernetic structure like Asimov's fictional "positronic brain." This is precisely the route to virtual immortality that Dr. Ira Graves attempted in "The Schizoid Man" (TNG) when he uploaded his consciousness from his failing organic body into Data's artificial neural network.

"In the end, we will find ways to replace every part of the body and brain, and thus repair all the defects that make our lives so brief," says artificial intelligence pioneer Marvin Minsky. "Needless to say, in doing so we will be making ourselves into machines."[16] In the envisioned posthuman future, biotechnology will engineer stronger, more efficient replacement organs by redesigning their constituent cells and constructing them with more durable materials—perhaps by utilizing nanotechnology as seen in "Evolution" (TNG) or in the form of Borg nanoprobes. Once our bodies have been replaced with stronger, better designed artificial organs, we won't need to waste time eating and excreting. Like the Borg, posthumans will be "beyond nature."

While relatively minor medical artifices upgrading defective organs are acceptable in the *Star Trek* universe, the Borg are demonized for the grotesque extensiveness of their cybernetic augmentation. Anxiety about extreme cyborgization reflects antipathy toward the body being transgressed, hybridized, and made monstrous. The paranoia exhibited on *Star Trek* in the face of posthuman technology reflects the confusion of a clear demarcation or boundary between humanity's *interaction with* technologies and its *assimilation by* technologies.

Described as "bionic zombies" in *ST: First Contact*, the Borg look and behave like monsters. The Borg process of evolving and improving themselves—the genocidal assimilation of other species—is befitting of Nazi doctor Josef Mengele. Like the Borg, Mengele used technology to torture, maim, and destroy humans as experimental subjects in the name of utopian goals. While no one accuses transhumanists of this sort of murderous fanaticism, their potential for monstrosity centers on the inequitable consequences of what some perceive as their eugenics project. In the early 20th century, a eugenic movement swept Europe and North America, encouraging selective breeding based on the physical or social value of inheritable traits. The authority of science was invoked to impose a scheme devised by one section of society on another. Eugenics was embraced by the "wealthiest, most powerful and most learned men against the nation's most vulnerable and helpless. The intent was to create a new and superior mankind."[17]

The perfectionist goal of the transhumanist project might lead to discrimination against those not wealthy enough to afford the genetic and cybernetic enhancements that become available. Furthermore, along with better healthcare access and medical technologies, the path to human progress has historically been sought through *social* improvements rather than upgrades to individual bodies: "Dreams of human equality and solidarity embraced by liberals, utopians, socialists, and pragmatists of earlier generations have no standing in theories of a post-humanist future," Winner writes. "Obligatory expressions of ethical concern about tensions between old-fashioned inferiors and newly engineered superior specimens are typically given short shrift."[18]

## "Freedom Is Irrelevant"

Focused exclusively on their tyrannical perfectionism, the Borg care nothing about equality, democracy, freedom, or respect for others. Their single-minded megalomania derives from their single mind—a collective consciousness that permits no individual thought, no debate. Each Borg mind is neurally linked through a sophisticated subspace network that ensures each member is subject to constant supervision and guidance. All traces of individuality are eradicated. Being part of the collective offers significant biomedical advantages to the individual drones. The mental energy of the group consciousness can help an injured or damaged drone heal or regenerate damaged body parts or technology; conversely, when Seven of Nine is separated from the Borg in "The Gift" (VOY), her body begins to reject her implants.

Militarily, the collective mind gives the Borg the ability to adapt quickly to defensive tactics used against them. As a society of literally *one* mind, the Borg is the ultimate *totalitarian* state. The fundamental philosophical premise that makes the Borg collective consciousness possible is shared by transhumanism: thoughts, memories, and personality traits are reducible to patterns of neural energy in the brain, and these patterns can be electronically simulated, transmitted, changed, or controlled. Transhumanist philosopher James Hughes argues that "radical cognitive enhancement would change every constituent element of consciousness.... The prospect of radical neuroscience has made the erasure of the illusion of personal identity tangible."[19] Hughes claims that neurotechnologies might replace individual identity with a completely collective identity. In this regard, "Borgism" and transhumanism are aligned and judged negatively by the *Star Trek* ethos. A group mind or collective civilization is diametrically opposed to the values of liberal humanism represented and promoted by the Federation. "My culture is based on freedom and self-determination," Picard declares emphatically to his Borg captors in "The Best of Both Worlds, Part I" (TNG).

Freethinking is suppressed in the Borg collective mind because it produces doubt, confusion, and inaction. The Borg mock the clumsiness and inefficiencies associated with autonomy. In the VOY episode "Scorpion, Part II," Seven of Nine denounces the *Voyager* crew: "You're erratic, conflicted, disorganized. With every individual giving their own small opinion, you lack harmony, cohesion, greatness." As the ultimate collectivist regime, the Borg lack not only individual consciousness and compassion, but also any internal distinctions of property, privacy, friendship, or family. Such a collectivist regime and ideology constitute a threat to Federation values.

When Picard is assimilated, it's a knife to the Federation's ideological heart. Passionate in his commitment to humanistic ideals of progress, self-improvement, tolerance, and individuality, Picard represents what's best about Starfleet. His assimilation exemplifies the powerful Borg threat of the extinction of human identity and individuality at the hands of a collectivist technological system. Picard's transformation into a cyborg is also a *physical* assault: instruments penetrate and probe, invading the integrity of his flesh. He isn't merely cyborgized; he's robbed of his humanity. But in a striking close-up, we see a tear running down Picard's face: his individuality remains intact against the Borg onslaught on his personhood. Ultimately, Picard's victory over the Borg in "The Best of Both Worlds, Part II" (TNG) comes, not in his suggestion to Data of putting the Borg "to sleep," but in his ability to reach out to Data *as Picard* in the first place. Analogously, Riker is able to defeat Locutus and save Picard by throwing away the metaphorical book Picard wrote as captain of the *Enterprise*, and devising his own "brilliantly unorthodox strategy" as captain in his own right. Individual innovativeness, the force of will, and the superiority of creative imagination are key elements that enable the *Enterprise* crew to defeat the Borg.

In later encounters with the Borg, human creativity continues to be the antidote to the invasive and dehumanizing effects of collectivist technology. In "I Borg" (TNG), a solitary drone is captured and held prisoner on the *Enterprise*. Separated from the collective and befriended by the crew, he begins to respond as an individual. By the end of the episode, it—now "he"—has acquired the name "Hugh," affirmed the crew's individual rights through his friendship with Geordi, and rejected the Borg's right to assimilate them. It's clear from Hugh's transformation, as well as Seven of Nine's rehumanization, that Borg collectivity is *imposed* on its members. Borgism is a monstrous foreign ideology that subverts humanistic values and represents the ultimate techno-totalitarian dystopia. Borg drones are inherently individuals, but are controlled, oppressed, and manipulated by a tyrannical technological system. Referring to Hugh's return to the Borg, Picard says, "The sense of individuality which he has gained here will be transmitted throughout the collective. Every one of the Borg will have the opportunity to experience the feeling of singularity. Perhaps that would be the most pernicious program of all: the knowledge of self, spread through the Borg collective in that brief moment, might alter them forever." Humanity's survival depends, not on the extent to which we can use technologies or brute force, but on our ability to exploit enduring liberal humanist values of freedom, creativity, and individuality.

While *Star Trek* prioritizes these values and implies that they're inherent in human nature, transhumanism emphasizes technological enhancement as its sole objective. Humanistic values are inessential, even contradictory, to its proposed program of liberating humans from biological constraints. If implemented, transhumanism would seemingly lead to a polarized, discriminatory, and unequal division between superior posthumans (the "GenRich") and inferior retrohumans ("Naturals"); these would be "entirely separate species with no ability to cross-breed, and with as much romantic interest in each other as a current human would have for a chimpanzee."[20]

Furthermore, the proposed reengineering of humans into a technologized posthuman species would, by definition, alter human nature. As such, the transhumanist agenda risks a dehumanization that undermines humanity's distinctiveness based upon the demarcated boundary between the biological and the technological. This is precisely the horror that the Borg represent to *Star Trek*'s liberal humanist ideology: a technological assimilation of human nature that compromises the integrity of human identity and robs humanity of its inherent values.[21]

## Notes

1. Isaac Asimov, *Robot Visions* (New York: Penguin, 1991), 6–7.
2. Ibid., 8.
3. Hans Moravec, *Robot: Mere Machine to Transcendent Mind* (New York: Oxford University Press, 1999), 140.
4. The First International Symposium on Roboethics was held in Sanremo, Italy, in 2004. See also Patrick Lin, Keith Abney, and George Bekey, eds., *Robot Ethics: The Ethical and Social Implications of Robotics* (Cambridge, MA: MIT Press, 2011).
5. It's well known that Asimov was good friends with *Star Trek* creator Gene Roddenberry and, long before Roddenberry created the character of Data for TNG, he had envisioned a helpful Asimovian robot in his television movie, *The Questor Tapes* (1974).
6. Jacques Ellul, *The Technological Society*, trans. John Wilkinson (New York: Vintage, 1964), 134.
7. Langdon Winner, *Autonomous Technology: Technics-out-of-Control as a Theme in Political Thought* (Cambridge, MA: MIT Press, 1977), 29.
8. Ibid., 208.
9. Although Riker observes a "Borg baby" in the *Enterprise*'s first encounter with the Borg in "Q Who?" (TNG), it appears he misinterpreted what he was seeing and that the baby had been assimilated from another species.
10. Winner, *Autonomous Technology*, 59–60.
11. Ibid., 3
12. Ellul, *The Technological Society*, 105.
13. Max More, "Extropian Principles 3.0": http://www.highexistence.com/the-extropian-principles/ (accessed February 27, 2015)
14. Robert Brooks, *Flesh and Machine: How Robots Will Change Us* (New York: Pantheon Books, 2002), 236.
15. René Descartes, *The Philosophical Works of Descartes*, vol. 1, trans. Elizabeth S. Haldane and G. R. T. Ross (Cambridge: Cambridge University Press, 1968), 195.

16. Marvin Minsky, "Will Robots Inherit the Earth?" *Scientific American* (October 1994), 109.

17. Edwin Black, *War against the Weak: Eugenics and America's Campaign to Create a Master Race* (New York: Four Walls Eight Windows, 2003), 9.

18. Langdon Winner, "Are Humans Obsolete": http://homepages.rpi.edu/~winner/AreHumansObsolete.html (accessed February 15, 2015).

19. James Hughes, "Transhumanism and Personal Identity," in *The Transhumanist Reader*, ed. Max More and Natasha Vita-More (Malden, MA: John Wiley & Sons, 2013), 227, 229.

20. Lee M. Silver, *Remaking Eden: Cloning and Beyond in a Brave New World* (New York: Avon Books, 1997), 7.

21. Thanks to Maureen Musker for her criticism of earlier versions of this chapter.

# Assimilation and Autonomy

## Barbara Stock

<table>
<tr><td>THE BORG:</td><td>Resistance is futile…. We will add your biological and technological distinctiveness to our own. Your culture will adapt to service ours.</td></tr>
<tr><td>PICARD:</td><td>Impossible! My culture is based on freedom and self-determination!</td></tr>
<tr><td>THE BORG:</td><td>Freedom is irrelevant. Self-determination is irrelevant. You must comply.</td></tr>
</table>

—"The Best of Both Worlds, Part I" (TNG)

This exchange between the Borg and Captain Jean-Luc Picard illustrates what's truly horrifying about the Borg. They don't just kill you. They don't just enslave you. They *subsume* you, destroying your individuality and your ability to think for yourself, making you a mere cog in their machine—a drone. Picard, after being assimilated by the Borg and then freed by his shipmates, laments, "They took everything I was. They used me to kill and to destroy, and I couldn't stop them" ("Family," TNG).

Put in philosophical terms, the Borg strip the assimilated of their *autonomy*. Definitions of autonomy vary, but they center on the notion of choosing for yourself, deciding freely what you will do. We'll explore questions relating to autonomy through the lens of the Borg, such as: What exactly is autonomy, and why is it important? Is autonomy compatible with being influenced by other people? Could the Borg Collective ever be autonomous? Beyond respecting

*The Ultimate Star Trek and Philosophy*, First Edition. Edited by Kevin S. Decker and Jason T. Eberl.
© 2016 John Wiley & Sons, Ltd. Published 2016 by John Wiley & Sons, Ltd.

others' autonomy, should we also take steps to *enhance* autonomy—perhaps by helping non-autonomous beings attain it? What if the non-autonomous don't want such enhancement? What if they *like* being Borg?

Two episodes from the *Star Trek* canon will be especially helpful in our inquiry. First is "I, Borg" (TNG), in which the *Enterprise* crew finds an injured adolescent Borg, whom they name "Hugh." As Hugh develops individuality, the crew debates the ethics of using him as a weapon to deliver a virus to destroy the collective. Second, we'll talk about "The Gift" (VOY), in which Captain Kathryn Janeway forcibly prevents Seven of Nine from rejoining the Collective, arguing that since Seven isn't yet autonomous, Janeway must make her decisions for her. At the same time, Janeway plays a supportive role in Kes's development as an autonomous person.

## Autonomy Analyzed

In "I, Borg," Geordi LaForge explains to Hugh the difference between humans and Borg: "I choose what I want to do with my life. I make decisions for myself." *Choice* is essential to autonomy, but autonomy means more than the freedom to act on whims. It also includes the idea of *reasoned self-governance*: Geordi can consider various options for what he wants out of life, determine which he thinks is best, set goals, and select actions that support these goals. Naturally, he doesn't do this for *every* decision—that would've made him an inefficient helmsman! Yet he can from time to time step back and evaluate his choices, making "course corrections" to his life trajectory as needed. This ability distinguishes truly autonomous beings—like humans, Vulcans, or Klingons—from creatures with no capacity for rationality: the latter might act freely, but they aren't able to *deliberate*. Nothing forced the tribbles to start eating the grain destined for Sherman's Planet, but it would be odd to say that they "decided" to do so, for any reason.

Although we usually think of autonomy in terms of deciding what I *want* to do, that's not always how it works:

GEORDI:  Don't you understand, Hugh? We're giving you a choice.
HUGH:  Choice?
GEORDI:  Yes, a choice. Do you want to go back with the Borg or stay with us?
HUGH:  I could stay with you?
PICARD:  We could grant you asylum, Hugh.

HUGH: Choose what I want? I would choose to stay with Geordi, but it is too dangerous. They will follow. Return me to the crash site. It is the only way.

GEORDI: Hugh, think about this. Are you sure?

HUGH: Yes.

At this point in the episode, Hugh is thinking like an individual and can make the choice to do what he thinks is *right*, even though it's against his personal preferences. Immanuel Kant (1724–1804) would approve: "morality lies in the relation of actions to the autonomy of the will—that is, to a possible making of universal law by means of its maxims."[1] Autonomous beings are able to make decisions morally by reasoning out whether a potential action should, or should not, be adopted by all people, such that it becomes a "universal law." Suppose the *Enterprise* receives a distress call from an unknown vessel. Should the crew investigate and offer aid? Sure, if they don't have a more pressing mission. Who knows—maybe next time they'll be the ones in distress, so they would want other starships in the vicinity to feel obligated to help. If you're considering whether to put a friend in the path of the Borg, think about whether it would be reasonable to want *everybody* to make their friends targets for the Borg; it isn't, so don't do it yourself! Hugh probably didn't reason exactly this way in making his decision, but his choice to *not* do what he wants demonstrates that he's assimilated the moral aspect of autonomy.

It should be apparent at this point that "autonomous" can be applied to two different sorts of things: there are autonomous *beings* and autonomous *actions*. Beings that can rationally deliberate in the face of a moral choice are called "autonomous," and many, though not all, of their actions display autonomy. It's important to grasp that both concepts are a matter of degree. There's a *lot* of ground between non-autonomous tribbles and autonomous adult Klingons: this ground covers young children, the cognitively limited Pakleds ("Samaritan Snare," TNG), and Borg drones in the process of regaining individuality. What all these share is that they can make some choices well, governing themselves to a greater or lesser extent, though not as much as a typical adult can. Tom Beauchamp and James Childress nicely capture the range that applies to autonomous *actions* by offering three rules. Autonomous actions are done "(1) intentionally, (2) with understanding, and (3) without controlling influences that determine [them]."[2] Doing something intentionally is *absolute*—you either meant to do it or you didn't—but the other two admit of degrees: our understanding of the situation may be more or less complete, and we might be more or less swayed by external input. Because (2) and (3) vary according to situations, we should aim toward a "substantial" degree of understanding and freedom; but we rarely, if ever, perfectly achieve them.

Many philosophers from Plato to Kant stress the value of autonomy. But why, exactly, is it important? First, it's *subjectively* important to the beings who have it. Many regard its loss, whether through Alzheimer's or assimilation—or the neural neutralizer from "Dagger of the Mind" (TOS)—as a fate worse than death. Second, disrespect for another person's right to make his or her own decisions points to a disturbing lack of regard, which Kant describes as treating that person as a "means" rather than an "end in themselves." If Picard had sent Hugh, with the transmissible recursive paradox program Geordi and Data had devised, back to the Borg without giving him a choice in the matter, he would've been using Hugh as a means to destroy the Collective, rather than treating him as important in his own right. Third, there's a sense in which *all of ethics* rests on the importance of autonomy. Imagine a world made up only of tribbles and tribble-eating glommers ("More Tribbles, More Troubles," TAS); the tribbles reproduce prodigiously and the predators eat them. One might feel sympathy for the cute little fluff-balls, but do any ethical judgments seem appropriate here? Only *autonomous* beings can be held responsible for their actions—be praised or blamed—since they're the only ones that can reflectively govern their own actions. So, while we can't blame the glommers for eating tribbles, we could hold morally accountable the armada of Klingon warriors who took part in "the great tribble hunt" and "obliterated the tribbles' homeworld" ("Trials and Tribble-ations," DS9).

## "*Voyager* Is My Collective"

As crucial as the idea of autonomy seems to be to our moral life, it's also been criticized for relying on a highly individualistic and overly rationalistic notion of humanity. The "autonomous man"—and feminist philosophers point out that the example is typically a man—coolly surveys his options and his interests; he's self-sufficient and beholden to no one. But this isn't the situation in which most of us frequently find ourselves. Consider the crew of a starship: Lt. Sulu can't just decide to fly the *Enterprise* wherever he wants, even if he has good reasons; Lt. Worf can only "fire at will" when his captain tells him he can. What freedom they have exists within a *power structure*, their choices constrained by rank and duty.

Of course, Sulu and Worf freely chose to join Starfleet, and they have the option of resigning should they reconsider—as Worf does temporarily in "Redemption, Part I" (TNG). But many of the power structures we find ourselves subject to were *not* freely chosen, and extricating ourselves from them wouldn't be as easy as just removing our combadge. We're born into families that are embedded within societies, which fundamentally shape our decisions in subtle and complex ways. In extreme cases, social forces can distort an individual's sense of agency to the point that it becomes hard to say whether the individual or their actions are autonomous. Suppose an intelligent and articulate Ferengi female says that she's perfectly happy going without clothing and owning no property, that she *chooses* to remain within her home, chewing food for her male offspring. She may indeed feel satisfied with her lot in life. Yet this satisfaction seems to be the result of some internalized oppression. She lives in a culture in which profit is everything, and she's been told since birth that she'll never earn any. How could she help but make submissive "choices"? Given this, Quark's description of Ferengi marital life is fairly chilling: "husbands and wives never argue—there's no divorce, no broken homes—nothing but peaceful, conjugal bliss" ("Fascination," DS9).

In response to these criticisms, *relational* accounts of autonomy have emerged, emphasizing how interactions with others can enable or suppress our autonomous decision making, and how social conditions may even partially create the conditions for our autonomous decisions. This focus on relationships isn't surprising when you think of how we get to be autonomous beings in the first place: we're raised by parents and teachers who, in the process of helping us to make our way in the world, also aid us in developing the cognitive and emotional skills we need to be able to deliberate and make independent decisions. Parents, for instance, imbue their children with their own value system and nudge them toward certain goals; but they also give them tools to question received wisdom and figure out their own paths. This capacity for critical reflection is crucial for relational views of autonomy; we need to remember that while none of us *created* our own values and preferences, we *make them our own* when we exercise our ability to sift through them and accept or reject them.[3]

Well, you might say, that's just how we *develop* autonomy. Once we become adults, we become independent and others ought to leave us alone to make our own decisions, right? Wrong. For one thing, there's no clear biological or psychological line marking out childhood from adulthood. More importantly, even as adults we're deeply imbedded in social relations. While we don't want others to *control* our actions, we can certainly expect them to try to *influence* our actions. Captain Janeway demonstrates this in "The Gift," when Kes tells her that her amped-up psychokinetic powers and bouts of cellular flux aren't a medical problem to be solved, but a transformation Kes wants to see through:

JANEWAY:    What if it's not true? What if you're simply being swept up in the excitement of something you think is happening, but it's not real? On the basis of a feeling, an intuition, you're asking me to let you go, quite likely forever? Kes, I just can't do that.

KES:        It's my decision. My fate. Would you really try to stop me?

JANEWAY:    No. But argue with you? Even plead with you to reconsider? Absolutely, for as long as it takes.

Far from undermining Kes's autonomy, Janeway's arguing and pleading support its exercise. Since autonomous choice involves evaluating goals and plans designed to achieve them, what better way to do this than to have a friend pushing you to question your conclusions and consider matters more deeply?

As we've seen, some relational accounts specify that interactions with others are *enabling* conditions of autonomous decisions.[4] Although it makes sense to emphasize human individuality when contrasted with the Borg, humans aren't isolated beings. Janeway draws upon this idea to comfort Seven of Nine: "I can't give you back to the Borg, but you're not alone. You're part of a human community now. A human collective. We may be individuals but we live and work together. You can have some of the unity you require right here on *Voyager*" ("The Gift"). But Seven is unimpressed with this reasoning, and taking Janeway's attitude seriously might lead us to a counterintuitive conclusion: perhaps the Borg are autonomous after all!

Imagine a decision-making processes that might happen on *Voyager*: Kes goes to Janeway for advice and also bounces ideas off of Neelix and seeks Tuvok's counsel. And these are just the explicit, voluntary requests for input. Crewmembers also offer Kes unsolicited advice, share philosophical outlooks, and make comments that might bear on future decisions. In addition, Kes gets relevant information from nonliving beings, including the Doctor, as well as the ship's computer and various other tools and technologies.

In the philosophy of mind, *extended cognition* stands for the notion that "many cognitive processes are carried out by a hybrid coalition of neural, bodily, and environmental factors." Think of Kes's deliberation and its dependence upon the ship's computer, a holographic physician, and her fellow shipmates: "extended cognition" might entail that responsibility for her resulting actions belongs to "wider entities of which individual persons are only parts."[5] Combining this idea with the relational concept of autonomy, perhaps the "autonomous agent" responsible for Kes's decision isn't just Kes, but Kes plus her relational network (past and present) and the physical objects she uses. From there, it's not much of a stretch to consider the Borg as a hybrid of brains, bodies, and technology that interact in complex ways to arrive at decisions and initiate its own autonomous actions. Seen in this light, we can understand how the Collective can express itself either as "we" through a harmonized cacophony of multiple voices, or as "I" through the singular voice of the Borg Queen. We can also make sense of this enigmatic exchange between the Queen and Data in *First Contact*:

QUEEN: I am the Borg.
DATA: That is a contradiction. The Borg have a collective consciousness. There are no individuals.
QUEEN: I am the beginning, the end, the one who is many. I am the Borg.
DATA: Greetings. I am curious, do you control the Borg Collective?
QUEEN: You imply disparity where none exists. I *am* the Collective.

Of course, characterizing the Borg Collective as autonomous doesn't mean that individual drones have autonomy, any more than Kes and her relational network having autonomy implies that the tricorder Kes uses is an autonomous being.

## Evangelical Autonomy

So far, we've established that autonomous beings can choose their own actions in accordance with their goals and plans—which they can also critically evaluate. Autonomy is a good thing that we can encourage in others by helping them develop deliberative skills and by interacting with them during decision making. The Borg, as a whole, *might* be considered autonomous, but that's no help to you if they assimilate you—you'll just be a drone. This leads to the question: should Starfleet crews de-assimilate Borg whenever they can? More pointedly, was Captain Janeway acting ethically when she forcibly de-assimilated Seven of Nine?

Janeway's de-assimilation of Seven actually includes several separate decisions, some of which are more controversial than others. At the end of "Scorpion, Part II," Janeway initiates a plan that severs Seven from the Collective as *Voyager* flees Borg space. At the beginning of "The Gift," Seven demands to be returned to the Borg, or at least left on a planet with a subspace transmitter, but Janeway refuses. When Seven's human immune system starts reasserting itself, Janeway authorizes surgery to remove her Borg implants, despite believing this choice to be "the last thing Seven of Nine would want." Janeway later implies that if Seven regained her individuality and still wanted to rejoin the Collective, she wouldn't allow it.

While the first three decisions are quite defensible, the last is morally problematic. Severing Seven from the Collective was a tactical decision designed to save *Voyager* from the Borg. Even if this decision wasn't in Seven's best interest, it was in the best interest of the *Voyager* crew. Thus, Janeway can make a utilitarian argument on the grounds that, as Spock puts it, "the needs of the many outweigh the needs of the few or the one." Similarly, turning the ship around and bringing Seven back to the Borg would've been tactically stupid. At the time that Seven requested she be left on a planet, she wasn't medically stable. Agreeing to her demand at that point might've been tantamount to negligent manslaughter.

This effectively puts Janeway's decision in the same moral ballpark as her decision to override Seven's presumed preference for death rather than separation from the Collective. Alternatively, as the Doctor notes, "If a patient told me not to treat them, even if the situation were life-threatening, I would be ethically obligated to honor that request." But this assumes that the patient is *competent* to make such a decision, and I think a good case can be made that Seven, at that moment, wasn't competent. She hadn't yet become an autonomous agent, and moreover, she was confused and emotionally distraught. If she were thinking through her options clearly, she might rank her preferences as: (1) rejoin the Collective, (2) die, and (3) live as an individual. Her second option cuts off all possibility of attaining her first, while tolerating the indignities of the third option temporarily might present an opportunity to attain option 1. So, despite Seven's great distress at the prospect of becoming an individual, someone acting on Seven's behalf might reasonably conclude that preserving her life against her express, but non-autonomous, wishes is the best match for her long-term goals.

Of course, Janeway wouldn't want to see Seven run back to the Collective later. And that's where she treads on ethically shaky ground:

JANEWAY:    I've met Borg who were freed from the Collective [referring to the events in "Unity" (VOY)]. It wasn't easy for them to accept their individuality, but in time they did. You're no different. Granted, you were assimilated at a very young age, and your transition may be more difficult, but it will happen.

SEVEN:      If it does happen, we will become fully human?

JANEWAY:    Yes, I hope so.

SEVEN:      We will be autonomous. Independent.

JANEWAY:    That's what individuality is all about.

SEVEN:      If at that time we choose to return to the Collective, will you permit it?

JANEWAY:    [pause] I don't think you'll want to do that.

SEVEN:      You would deny us the choice as you deny us now. You have imprisoned us in the name of humanity, yet you will not grant us your most cherished human right: To choose our own fate. You are hypocritical, manipulative. We do not want to be what you are. Return us to the Collective!

JANEWAY:    You lost the capacity to make a rational choice the moment you were assimilated. They took that from you, and until I'm convinced you've gotten it back, I'm making the choice for you. You're staying here.

SEVEN:      Then you are no different than the Borg.

Janeway's pregnant pause before saying "I don't think you'll want to do that" makes her statement sound to me exactly the way Seven interpreted it—that Janeway would *not* let Seven go back to the Borg, even if she autonomously chose to do so. Or, rather, Janeway would view Seven's choosing to go back to the Collective as proof that she wasn't truly autonomous, and therefore that her decision may be overridden.

Janeway could try to justify her move on the grounds that it can't be rational for someone to freely choose to give up their future freedom to choose. Similar reasoning has been offered on the inherent irrationality of suicide. But this line of argument doesn't work in either case. While many people who choose to end their lives are suffering from mental illness and aren't competent choosers, it's still possible to rationally choose death over something you find intolerable, such as intractable pain, permanent disability, or dishonor—as Worf chooses initially in "Ethics" (TNG) or his brother Kurn later chooses in "Sons of Mogh" (DS9).[6] Similarly, it's at least possible for you to rationally choose to give up all future prospects for rational choice. Hugh did so—as do many other characters, most of them not Borg, who sacrifice their lives for others. Granted, Seven's reasons would be less noble than Hugh's, but the point is that such a choice is neither impossible nor meaningless.

Of course, it all works out in the end. By the time Seven develops into an individual autonomous agent, she no longer wishes to rejoin the Collective. When it comes to Captain Janeway's indomitable will, resistance is, indeed, futile.

## Notes

1. Immanuel Kant, *Groundwork of the Metaphysics of Morals*, trans. H.J. Patton. (New York: Harper and Row, 1956).
2. Tom Beauchamp and James Childress, *Principles of Biomedical Ethics*, 4th ed. (Oxford: Oxford University Press, 1994), 123.
3. A good source for information on relational accounts of autonomy is Catriona Mackenzie and Natalie Stoljar, eds., *Relational Autonomy: Feminist Perspectives on Autonomy, Agency, and the Social Self* (Oxford: Oxford University Press, 2000).
4. As another example, neo-Aristotelian philosopher Alasdair MacIntyre argues that we must acknowledge our inherent interdependence through which we develop as "independent practical reasoners"; see his *Dependent Rational Animals: Why Human Beings Need the Virtues* (Peru, IL: Open Court, 1999).
5. Mason Cash, "Extended Cognition, Personal Responsibility, and Relational Autonomy," *Phenomenology and the Cognitive Sciences* 9 (2010): 645–71. A couple good primers on the "extended cognition" thesis are Andy Clark, *Supersizing the Mind: Embodiment, Action, and Cognitive Extension* (New York: Oxford University Press, 2010); and Alva Noë, *Out of Our Heads: Why You Are Not Your Brain, and Other Lessons from the Biology of Consciousness* (New York: Hill and Wang, 2009).
6. Saying that something is a rational choice doesn't necessarily mean it's the best possible choice. It just means that the chooser is able to deliberate, and that the choice makes sense based on his or her assessment of the options available. Many humans, not sharing Worf's traditional Klingon beliefs, would rationally choose to live and continue to lead productive lives with the same disabling condition or with only 70% mobility, which Dr. Crusher can provide at most using standard therapies at her disposal.

# 10

# Q: A Rude, Interfering, Inconsiderate, Sadistic Pest—on a Quest for Justice?

*Kyle Alkema and Adam Barkman*

The nearly omnipotent character known only as "Q" dramatically enters the *Star Trek* universe when he puts all humanity—in the person of Captain Jean-Luc Picard—on trial in the first episode of TNG. The charge? Being "grievously savage" ("Encounter at Farpoint"). Acting as self-professed prosecutor, judge, and jury, Q promises Picard an "absolutely equitable" trial, only to coerce Picard into pleading "guilty" by threatening to kill his crew. Picard tries to object by referencing Q's earlier assurance of a fair trial, but Q dismisses his objection as "entirely irrelevant," refusing to give any reasons for his actions. Picard finally gets through to Q by asking this mysterious inquisitor to test him and his crew to see if humans have progressed beyond their past savagery. The *Enterprise*-D crew pass the test, seeming to prove that they've become peaceful and benevolent, and Q grudgingly lets them continue on their mission, claiming that "generosity has always been my weakness."

If Q is as unpredictable and whimsical as he seems, then it's unclear why he honors his bargain with Picard. If he wanted to, he could simply carry out whatever punishment he liked against humanity, regardless of any evidence or plea from the humans themselves. It's also unclear why he puts on the façade of a public trial to begin with, or why he cares whether humans are savage or not. What *is* clear, however, is his power to do whatever he wants, as he's quick to demonstrate time and again. What gives Q the right to put humanity on trial in the first place? What justifies his self-proclaimed authority over Picard and company?

*The Ultimate Star Trek and Philosophy*, First Edition. Edited by Kevin S. Decker and Jason T. Eberl.
© 2016 John Wiley & Sons, Ltd. Published 2016 by John Wiley & Sons, Ltd.

Q might derive his authority from his power, if it's true that "might makes right." Q could be like the "Leviathan" of Thomas Hobbes (1588–1679), an absolute sovereign who has the power to keep people from warring with each other, but who can't be held accountable or subject to any civil law in the use of that power. Or Q might be subject to a higher authority, just as human rulers are. This higher power might justify Q putting humanity on trial, or perhaps condemn Q's actions as unjust. John Locke (1632–1704) would say that humans, as rational creatures, are justified in making laws for their own self-government, but that the justification for these laws is based on *natural law*: objective, universal, unchanging principles. As a rational creature—albeit of a different plane of existence—Q might have to answer to the same objective values and duties we do.

In this chapter, we'll argue that we can, indeed, call Q to account for his actions, and not on the basis of the Federation's rules or our own civil laws. Enlisting Hobbes and Locke, we'll examine the motives behind Q's enigmatic actions and see what Q, deep down, might believe about justice. So let's try to find out what's behind Q's frustratingly perplexing charades. *Let's put Q on trial.*

## Solitary, Nasty, Brutish, and Q

To say that Q is a curious creature is as much of an understatement as saying that Spock likes logic. Our pitiful human minds are unable to comprehend Q's true nature, just as our eyes are unable to see his true form. What's clear to us is the conflict swirling inside Q between his disconcerting lack of concern for others and something like a conscience that causes him to save a planet from disaster in "Déjà Q" (TNG). Perhaps he might claim absolute sovereignty over others because he has *absolute power*, and thereby doesn't need to justify what we perceive as his meddling. His power gives him the right to pursue his own conception of what's good, and he doesn't need to give any other reasons for this pursuit. However, he's not strictly omnipotent, if omnipotence is defined as being able to do anything that is *logically* possible.[1] Q's power apparently extends to any *physical* possibility, such as changing the gravitational constant of the universe, as he recommends Geordi to do in "Déjà Q." Yet, Quinn, another Q we'll return to later, admits that the Q are not omnipotent, and their power is limited at least by the power of the other members: Q couldn't make himself immune from attacks by other Q during the Continuum's civil war ("Death Wish" and "The Q and the Grey," VOY). So even Q has his limits.

Q asserts his authority over Picard and the rest of humanity due to his assessment of us as a "dangerous, savage, child-race"—indeed, for poignant dramatic effect, he makes the setting for humanity's trial the "post-atomic horror" between World War III and humanity's first contact with the Vulcans in 2063. Similarly, Captain Kirk is put on trial in "The Squire of Gothos" (TOS) by the self-entitled General Trelane—*retired*—who displays both tremendous power and a character as impulsive and volatile as Q's. Indeed, Trelane is an immature member of the Q Continuum.[2] Trelane claims that he can do anything he wants and describes human passion as "primitive fury" and the "very soul of sublime savagery." Like Q, Trelane dresses up in judge's garb and accuses Kirk of treason against a higher authority, of conspiracy, and of fomenting insurrection. Neither Trelane nor Q offer any justification for their "judicial" authority. They both do whatever they want simply because they can, for their own amusement, or out of boredom. And since both bring humanity—or at least particular humans—to trial based on our perceived "savagery," they might defend their authority on a Hobbesian basis.

Hobbes published *Leviathan* in 1651, near the end of the English Civil War.[3] This time of political turmoil undoubtedly influenced his view on what humanity would be like in a "state of nature." Left on our own, he argued, we find ourselves in a brute "war of all against all." A restless desire for survival, power, and glory in each of us leads to conflict, unless there exists a common power able to keep us in check. Otherwise, we're left to fend for ourselves in this depraved condition, where there's no law, no notion of right and wrong, and no justice or injustice.

Hobbes begins with a basic *right of nature* that all people possess: our liberty to ensure the preservation of our own life. A *law of nature*, for Hobbes, is a general rule that compels a person to survive and forbids self-destructive actions. Because everyone is compelled by this law, each person naturally acts as though he had a right to everything he would need to ensure his survival. The fight for survival is a common theme, and one witnessed in many *Star Trek* episodes. Q not only manipulates it in the numerous survival tests he imposes upon the *Enterprise*-D crew—whether pitting them against "vicious animal things" in "Hide and Q," exposing humanity's unpreparedness against the Borg in "Q Who?", or probing Picard's willingness to die for love in "Qpid"—but also has trouble avoiding it himself when he's condemned by the rest of the Continuum and made mortal in "Déjà Q." While Hobbes's first and fundamental law of nature is to seek peace in order to survive, his second is that we can and should defend ourselves. But we also, Hobbes says, give up our "right to everything" in order to further the cause of peace and form "covenants" with each other—what are also referred to as *social contracts*. *Justice* now exists to the extent that each of us adheres to the terms of the covenants into which we've entered—we each have to keep up our side of the bargain, no exploitative "Ferengi print" in our social contracts ("Captive Pursuit," DS9).

With the creation of a "commonwealth" comprising the various covenants we've made with each other comes the possibility of conserving peace and justice. A group of people can become a commonwealth—be "made one person"—when they're represented by one person; but this requires the *consent* of everyone in that group. Through the social contract, authority is transferred from each person to a source of authority, the "sovereign," who represents them all. This transfer of authority is *absolute*, and therefore the representative can't be held accountable for its actions. Hobbes's commonwealth isn't like a representative democracy where those elected are accountable to those they represent—allowing for impeachment when a head of state misbehaves. There's no such thing as "misbehaving" when it comes to the sovereign's actions—unlike Trelane, its parents won't materialize in this dimension to scold and punish it. The submission of individual wills to the sovereign's will—the forsaking of each person's proper right of nature—is what Hobbes means by a *Leviathan*: a political creation, a "mortal god" to which the people of a commonwealth owe their peace and defense. Just as Starfleet personnel must submit to those in command when they join the service, those in Hobbes's commonwealth agree to give up a portion of their liberty.

The Leviathan's power is absolute and can't be taken away by popular vote; the Leviathan can't even be accused of misconduct, let alone found guilty. It is the judge, jury, and executioner, as it were. Since the Leviathan is responsible for both prescribing the rules and upholding the peace and unity of the commonwealth, Hobbes concluded that it *transcends* the civil laws it imposes: it decides what constitutes right and wrong, good and evil. Hobbes gets the idea of the Leviathan from the Bible: "Nothing on earth is its equal—a creature without fear. It looks down on all that are haughty; it is king over all that are proud" (Job 41:33–4). Whatever the biblical Leviathan was, this mysterious creature was much to be feared in ancient times. The fearsome

General Trelane—*retired*—figuratively looks down on the puny humans and flamboyantly scoffs at them, as does Q from his floating dais.

Q has no equal in our dimension. Like Hobbes's sovereign, Q's purpose *could* be the conservation of peace in the universe: if humans are hopelessly savage, then perhaps Q is right in delivering his verdict, "It's time to put an end to your trek through the stars, make room for other more worthy species." If Q has a legitimate claim as the Leviathan through some kind of social contract, then he merely has to act in the interest of future peace for the greatest number of rational beings, which justifies his actions and legitimates his claim as judge and executioner. But rarely does Q appear to be acting out of concern for future peace; rather, Q's "claim" to authority seems based on his power alone.

## Liberty, yet Not Q License

According to Hobbes, Q can't be a proper sovereign since he lacks the *consent* of humanity. He has no right to be our representative or our judge, unless we've already acknowledged that. But is there anything that could underwrite Q's authority? Perhaps the future good his interventions might bring. By the end of many episodes, "Q the misanthrope" seems concerned with the future good in some way—saving the inhabitants of Bre'el IV, teaching Picard a lesson about love or not regretting his past, or preserving a young girl from execution—while nevertheless appearing as if he doesn't care about anyone other than himself. Q claims that the Continuum does anything it wants ("True Q"). When asked if the Q ever use their power to help people, he evades the question. Ultimately, it's unclear whether Q cares for any sort of future good, for humanity or otherwise.

In "Déjà Q," Guinan accuses Q of toying with lower lifeforms, teasing and tormenting them for his own pleasure. Picard calls him the "next of kin to Chaos" ("Q Who?"); and Janeway accuses him of being a "rude, interfering, inconsiderate, and sadistic pest" ("Death Wish"). Q is clearly many of these things, even if his IQ is 2005. More drastically, Picard describes Q as "devious and amoral and unreliable and irresponsible and definitely not to be trusted" ("Qpid"). But is Q *truly* amoral? This is highly unlikely, considering how often morality is woven through the episodes involving Q.

The themes of law and justice run deep with Q. Things come full circle when he reappears in the TNG finale informing Picard that humanity, as "a barbarous species," is guilty "of being inferior." Picard retorts, "It is not for you to set the standards by which we are to be judged," to which Q replies, "Oh, but it is. And we have" ("All Good Things ... "). After Picard challenges Q's right to judge the disposition of Q-offspring Amanda Rogers in "True Q," Q simply defends his position as one of "superior morality." Picard doesn't buy it, though:

> Your arrogant pretense at being the moral guardians of the universe strikes me as being hollow, Q. I see no evidence that you are guided by a superior moral code, or any code whatsoever. You may be nearly omnipotent, and I don't deny that your parlor tricks are very impressive, but morality, I don't see it! I don't acknowledge it, Q! I would put human morality against the Q's any day.

If Q does indeed possess a superior morality, then he should have to back it up. Thus, while there are shades of Hobbes's Leviathan in Q, neither the "might makes right" argument nor social contract theory seems to resolve the tension between his allegedly "superior morality" and his torment of lesser species like the "very intelligent, but very flighty" Calamarain ("Déjà Q").

## eQual by Nature

Like Hobbes, Locke believed that the state of human nature is one of individual liberty and freedom. But Locke was more optimistic about our prospects in our natural state. Rather than a "war of all against all," he saw the possibility of peace and harmony; freedom can be found within the bounds of the natural law that governs every rational being. Locke thus built his political philosophy on the foundation that *reason* teaches us what we ought to do, even in the state of nature. Self-preservation—Hobbes's "right of nature"—is important, but it's not the ultimate basis of political authority. Unlike Hobbes, Locke argued that reason prompts us to acknowledge certain moral obligations to others, even in the state of nature.

The natural law consists of eternal, universal, and unchanging principles, which can be either absolute or general. For example, the *general* principle of piety states that, all things being equal, we should obey those in authority over us. A general prohibition, such as "Don't kill," might have notable exceptions, as in the case of self-defense or war. An *absolute* principle implies zero exceptions to carrying it out.[4] Our basic human rights—such as the right to self-preservation—are in harmony with the obligation to respect the rights of others. Hence, Q does have the right to pursue his own happiness, but that doesn't justify tormenting "lower species" without just cause. Since everyone is subject to the same law, we can hold each other accountable and punish injustices.

According to Locke, there may be people or institutions in authority over us that we have a duty to follow, so long as that authority is held accountable to the same principles of natural law. Q may or may not have legitimate authority over humans, but if he did then he'd still have to answer to what's right by natural law. Locke holds that legitimate *political* authority stems from a similar social contract to Hobbes's conception, but *moral* obligations are rooted in the natural law alone, which enshrines values that should be shared across all rational species.[5]

The natural law functions even in the Delta Quadrant. In "Death Wish," Janeway has to mediate a moral dilemma: should she give another Q—given the human name "Quinn"—asylum onboard *Voyager* so that he may be made mortal and commit suicide, or should she allow the Continuum to imprison him for eternity under cruel conditions, trapped inside a comet? Janeway follows Starfleet procedure for when someone requests asylum, acting as judge for the case after obtaining consent from both Qs. There are many factors she must consider. For instance, Hobbes's Leviathan could justifiably prevent suicide for two reasons: because it goes against an individual's basic right to self-preservation—although maybe an individual could give up that right—*or* in order to protect the future peace of the commonwealth. Q argues, "He's putting his selfish wishes over the welfare of everyone else," contrasting "social order versus anarchy," similar to Hobbes's argument in favor of a commonwealth against humanity's natural condition of war.

Quinn sums up Q's argument and puts it in a different light: "They feared me so much they had to lock me away for eternity. And when they did that, they were saying that the individual's rights will be protected only so long as they don't conflict with the state's." Janeway eventually rules in Quinn's favor, granting him asylum, and Q has to hold up his end of the bargain by granting Quinn mortality, allowing—and even helping—him to commit suicide. Q's motivation isn't merely to honor the agreement. Arguably, he feels *morally obligated* to help Quinn once he's shamed into acknowledging that he'd surrendered his previous "irrepressible" individuality to the conformist authority of the Continuum. Natural law is the backbone of this episode, since it concerns the pursuit of justice—as applicable to both humans and the nearly omnipotent Q—through carefully weighing general principles, as well as the evidence and reasoned arguments for both sides, in order to decide what is objectively right in this case.

Q shows himself to have a moral side, just as the rest of the Continuum does. The Q appear bound by the same principles of right and wrong as we are. When Q accuses humans of being "savage lifeforms" who "never even follow their own rules," he's implying that nonsavage lifeforms *should* follow their own rules ("Encounter at Farpoint"). During another test in "Hide and Q," Q tells Worf that "fairness is such a *human* concept," but then tells the crew to "carefully obey the rules of the game." He also claims to always keep his arrangements ("Q Who?"), and when Q gives Picard his personal guarantee, Q does stick to his word ("Tapestry").

To whom does Q answer? He seems to be held accountable by the Continuum—until he starts a civil war over the question of liberty in "The Q and the Grey." When Q tries to get out of a wager he made with Picard, the captain reminds him, "I'm sure your fellow Q remember that you agreed never to trouble our species again" ("Hide and Q"). Thunder rolls and Q looks to the heavens, then lets out a scream as he's teleported to who-knows-where. In "True Q," Picard challenges the Continuum's directive to kill Amanda Rogers, a member of the Q who's just discovered she isn't human. Q tells Picard, "Don't be naïve. You have no idea what it means to be Q. With unlimited power comes responsibility. Do you think it is reasonable for us to allow omnipotent beings to roam free through the universe?" He even notes that "on rare occasions"—as with Amanda's parents—*executions* of Q are "necessary and warranted," again appealing to some norm of justice ("Death Wish"). In line with Locke's natural law approach, Q further qualifies, "And the decision to proceed is only made after great deliberation by the entire Continuum." But Q can't have it both ways: he can't sometimes stress the importance of rational deliberation and duty, and other times act without either.

Though Q can go almost anywhere in time and space, he can't escape his underlying morality, his conscience. Maybe the powerful Q could be more actively constructive and beneficial toward the myriad "lower species"; but they're neither amoral nor anarchic. Q, as a member of "the vaunted Q Continuum, the self-anointed guardians of the universe," perhaps has a heavier responsibility than he'd care to admit ("Death Wish").

## Qumanity

The key to this discussion, and the resolution of the tension within Q, can be found in the theme of *self-sacrifice* contained in most Q episodes. In "Encounter at Farpoint," Picard offers himself to Q to be punished, pleading for the lives of his crew; similarly, Kirk offers to sacrifice himself for his crew, beseeching Trelane on their behalf, but to no effect. After the young Q Amanda Rogers vows not to use her power—at the risk of death—she decides to use it to save innocent lives ("True Q"). Finally, Q brings his rebellious and immature son to *Voyager* in "Q2" in the hopes of Janeway providing moral correction and opportunities for character growth; Q-junior passes the test when he's willing to sacrifice himself to save his mortal friend, Icheb.

Q himself gets in on the self-sacrificing action—twice. When he has his powers taken away by the Continuum and is reduced to being human, those he tormented in the past come to take vengeance. After some personal growth fostered by Data's example, Guinan's admonishment, and one of Picard's "wonderful speeches" Q enjoys coming for, he steals a shuttle in order to give himself up without endangering the rest of the *Enterprise* crew—though he sarcastically claims he'd rather die than live as a human. Another Q witnesses his "selfless act" and restores his powers ("Déjà Q"). In "The Q and the Grey," Q sacrifices himself again during the Continuum's civil war, this time for the principles of freedom and individuality for which he fought so hard—following the example of Quinn's "final gift to my people" in "Death Wish." Self-sacrifice is able to transcend justice without contradicting it; indeed, it's his self-sacrifice that shows the justice deep down in Q, hidden underneath his wit and bravado. This self-sacrifice doesn't mesh well with Hobbes's fight for survival as a basic right of nature; but going beyond the call of duty for the sake of others is in line with Locke's natural law.

Compared to our view of Q at the beginning of this chapter, it might come as a surprise to discover that sacrificial love is at the core of Q's relationship to justice. His inner tension is resolved by his embrace of *conscience*, which rationally informs him of the right thing to do according to natural law. As we witness the path Q travels away from the dusty desert hell of the Continuum represented in "Death

Wish," we're able to watch him toss away his sadism, rudeness, and all-around pestilentiality, like one might dispose of a Markoffian sea lizard or a Belzoidian flea. Well, at least to a certain extent. Q remains Q, after all, and the tension is still there from start to finish.

The Q Continuum's morals thus might not be so different from ours. Q is a member of a race almost incomprehensible to us, and yet we learn that Q and his fellows are not so alien. Picard speculates after Q saves the people of Bre'el IV, "Perhaps there's a residue of humanity in Q after all"—though Q is quick to appear and counter, "Don't bet on it, Picard!" ("Déjà Q"). Q isn't always right, though. He's guilty of having a conscience; he's guilty of being contaminated with a residue of humanity. The priestly robes of Locke's natural law look better on him than the judge's robes of Hobbes's Leviathan, though his wardrobe includes both. This court stands adjourned.

## Notes

1. This excludes being able to do logical nonsense, such as trying to determine what would happen if an unstoppable force met an immovable object.
2. As revealed in Peter David's novel *Q-Squared* (New York: Pocket Books, 1994).
3. Thomas Hobbes, *Leviathan*, ed. Edwin Curley (Indianapolis, IN: Hackett, 1994).
4. A critical analysis of a rigid, absolutist moral system, with Starfleet's Prime Directive as an example principle, can be found in Alejandro Bárcenas and Steve Bein's chapter in this volume.
5. John Locke, *The Second Treatise of Government*, ed. C.B. Macpherson (Indianapolis, IN: Hackett, 1980).

# 11

# Federation Trekonomics: Marx, the Federation, and the Shift from Necessity to Freedom

*Jeff Ewing*

*Star Trek* centers on the United Federation of Planets, a spacefaring, interplanetary federal republic organized around the principles of liberty, rights, and equality. This much is clear. But how should we characterize the Federation's *economic* system—does it align with these principles? The Federation, since the late 22nd century, has abandoned currency-centric economics—organized around gaining capital and personal property—in favor of a postscarcity economy focused on *self-enhancement*. The idea isn't without its forerunners: Karl Marx (1818–1883) claims that a *classless society* and the "realm of freedom," in which the development of human capacities is both a central goal and organizational principle, can arise only when the "realm of necessity"— that is, material limitations or scarcity—is overcome. I will argue that the Federation's economic system reflects one version of the transitional stage toward Marx's envisioned classless society. I'll show how the transcendence of scarcity and profit and growth-oriented economic activity both reflect Marx's vision of classless society and form the background to central Federation principles—such as the Prime Directive, the prioritization of scientific knowledge and self-realization, and the Federation's orientation toward peace rather than conquest or war.[1]

*The Ultimate Star Trek and Philosophy*, First Edition. Edited by Kevin S. Decker and Jason T. Eberl.
© 2016 John Wiley & Sons, Ltd. Published 2016 by John Wiley & Sons, Ltd.

## Capitalism Is Most Illogical

ROM:      There's only one thing I have to say to you. Workers of the world,
          unite! You have nothing to lose but your chains.
QUARK:    What's happened to you? ("Bar Association," DS9)

The Federation is composed of over 150 planetary governments representing a large number of member species, unlike many other galactic powers, such as the Romulan Star Empire or the Cardassian
Union. While much of *Star Trek*'s drama focuses on interstellar crises,
problems posed by science and technology, and the ethics of exploration, aside from a few scattered references, fans are left wondering
about the nature of the Federation's economic system. Theories have
ranged from calling the Federation a "proto-postscarcity economy"
to viewing it as a "well-defined general equilibrium production-
exchange economy with a large government presence," "participatory economics," or even "in essence, a communist society."[2] One
thing that's clear is that the Federation's economic system is *explicitly not* a capitalist economy—at least not capitalist in the way we
know it now. As an economic system, capitalism is characterized by
(1) privately owned "means of production" (the tools, machines,
plans, and resources used in the processes of economic production)
and (2) production oriented toward profit and growth, where (3) this
profit rests predominantly on the exploitation of wage labor—where
workers produce more than they need to meet their own needs, and the
capitalists who own the means of production take the surplus. How
far from these traits is the Federation, and what does that mean for
what it is?

The Federation was formed in 2161 by humanity and its allies
after the Earth–Romulan War. Planets join the Federation by consent and hold equal voting rights on the Federation Council. As
Captain Picard explains, "If there is one ideal that the Federation holds most dear, it is that all men, all races can be united"
(*Star Trek: Nemesis*). This ideal—and the Federation's unity—can
be maintained because, as Captain Kirk states, the Federation is
a "democratic body" ("Errand of Mercy," TOS), the culture of
which is "based on freedom and self-determination" ("The Best of
Both Worlds, Part I," TNG). To promote these ends, the Federation built a formidable Starfleet, which, while well capable of exercising military force, focuses primarily on exploration, science, and
defense.

Of the Federation's economic system, we know far less. Picard states that in the 24th century "material needs no longer exist" ("The Neutral Zone," TNG) and the challenge in life has become "to improve yourself. To enrich yourself." Picard highlights the fact that "people are no longer obsessed with the accumulation of 'things.' We have eliminated hunger, want, the need for possessions." In *Star Trek: First Contact*, Picard notes that "money doesn't exist in the 24th century" and that "the acquisition of wealth is no longer the driving force in our lives. We work to better ourselves and the rest of humanity." Outsiders also recognize—even if they don't necessarily agree with—the central value defining the Federation's economic system. The Ferengi Nog, for example, describes humans as having abandoned "currency-based economics in favor of some philosophy of self-enhancement" ("In the Cards," DS9).[3]

Thanks to a trip back through time to the 19th century ("Time's Arrow, Part II," TNG), we also have a conversation between Deanna Troi and Samuel Clemens, aka Mark Twain, which serves to further clarify the class relations of the Federation:

TROI:      He's one of the thousands of species that we've encountered. We live in a peaceful Federation with most of them. The people you see are here by choice.

CLEMENS:   So there're a privileged few who serve on these ships, living in luxury and wanting for nothing. But what about everyone else? What about the poor? You ignore them.

TROI:      Poverty was eliminated on Earth a long time ago, and a lot of other things disappeared with it. Hopelessness, despair, cruelty.

CLEMENS:   Young lady, I come from a time when men achieve power and wealth by standing on the backs of the poor, where prejudice and intolerance are commonplace and power is an end unto itself. And you're telling me that isn't how it is anymore?

TROI:      That's right.

In short, Federation economics is oriented toward equal opportunities for individual growth and self-determination, made possible by a triumph over scarcity of material resources. It's implied that, in direct opposition to the central features of capitalism, *exploitation* as a generator of economic wealth has also been abandoned. Meanwhile, the accumulation of wealth is no longer the goal of economic activity, and currency, as we know it at least, has largely been abandoned.

Some form of currency *has* remained, though, and so has a degree of private ownership—here lies the source of debate about

Federation economics. Kirk tells Spock that "the Federation has invested a great deal of money in our training" ("Errand of Mercy," TOS), and Beverly Crusher charges a roll of cloth to credit on Deneb IV ("Encounter at Farpoint," TNG). In *Star Trek III*, McCoy negotiates the price of a transfer to the Genesis planet, and Scotty makes reference to buying a boat in *Star Trek VI*. Evidently, ownership of more than just personal property continues: there's the Sisko family restaurant in New Orleans ("Homefront," DS9) and the Chateau Picard vineyard in France ("Family," TNG). So how should we understand these apparently conflicting references to wealth and property in the Federation? As we go forward, we'll see that the Federation is but one possible form that the first, transitional stage to a Marxian classless society may take—but first, what *is* Marx's vision for classless society?

## Dammit, Marx, I'm a communist, not a Communist!

Just as a reconstruction of the Federation's economic system has to be pieced together from scattered references throughout a large canon, so must the canon of Marx and Friedrich Engels (1820–1895) be combed through for their picture of a classless, communist society. Reconstructing what communism *really is* in the minds of Marx and Engels is complex for at least three reasons. First, they didn't write a systematic treatment of the topic, requiring us to dig for scattered references from their vast array of works to piece together an account. Second, both Marx and Engels were hesitant to lay out a perfect, concrete, Utopian vision outside the contest of struggle and history— indeed, "constructing the future and settling everything for all times"[4] is not Marx's project. Finally, communism, as Marx seems to have conceived of and advocated for it, was entirely different than the Communist political structures of the USSR or China, both of which have been organized around rigid and politically determined hierarchies, where "the state" is vastly more powerful than the populace. Marx himself advocated democracy and suggested the state would "wither away" in a classless society. These contradictions of, and confusions about, Marx's vision were aided and abetted by the tendency of both these Communist states—as well as liberal democratic powers like the United States—to conflate the ideals of Marx's project with Soviet or Chinese reality. Some characteristics of Marx's communist vision, however, can be pulled out from the varied treatments of the topic by Marx and Engels. They succinctly summarize communism in the *Communist Manifesto* as "abolition of private property,"[5] but not *personal* private property. Rather, Marx and Engels refer to the abolition of "bourgeois" or capitalist property, understood as the means of production, and consequently the abolition of the exploitation of labor—just the way Troi characterizes the Federation's economy in her discussion with Clemens.

More specifically, and with greater rhetorical flourish, Marx in the *1844 Manuscripts* refers to communism as "the *positive* supersession of *private property* as *human self-estrangement*,"[6] that is:

> The sensuous appropriation of the human essence and human life [not] understood only in the sense of *direct*, one-sided *consumption*, of *possession*, of *having*. Man appropriates his integral essence in an integral way, as a total man.[7]

In short, communism's success rests on a classless society where private ownership of the means of production ends. In Marx and Engels's view, this allows for a dramatic improvement in human freedom and well-being based on a shift in focus from *having* to *being*, from one-sided development of crippled potential to a focus on the development of a whole and complex personhood. Think of life aboard the *Enterprise*-D. In addition to their primary duties, crewmembers have been shown taking painting classes ("A Matter of Perspective," TNG), performing theater ("The Nth Degree," TNG), holding chess tournaments ("Data's Day," TNG), and playing guitar ("Silicon Avatar," TNG). In addition, virtually any situation can be experienced or skill developed via the holodeck. Marx argues that diverse "free conscious activity" such as this is the crucial trait that distinguishes humanity from nonhuman species—that people consciously *choose* their activity, rather than being driven by instinct.[8] As a consequence, human nature is characterized by both *creation* of our external world (through production) and *self-creation*. Marx thus rejects anything that inhibits the free self-creation of humanity, and (for our purposes) focuses on two specific *kinds* of limitations to free, conscious self-creation: (1) *material* limitations, or lack of economic opportunities; and (2) social limitations, by which a person's activity is constricted primarily because of hierarchical social relations and power arising from the ability to control economic systems and resources.

*Material* limitations provoke Marx to emphasize that material, technological developments are vital prerequisites to overcoming class society and to liberation:

> The realm of freedom really begins only where labor determined by necessity and external expediency ends; it lies by its very nature beyond the sphere of material production proper.[9]

Engels thus argues that "communism has only arisen since machinery and other inventions made it possible to hold out the prospect of an all-sided development, a happy existence, for all members of society."[10] Development of technology and science under capitalism generates the increasing potential to overcome these material needs for everyone, and to eliminate the most dangerous and degrading forms of work. The limitations intentionally placed on that potential by capitalist social relations remain a major impetus for revolution.

For Marx, one of the primary social causes of stifled self-creation is the rigid division of labor, both *detailed* and *social*. The *social* division of labor—involving a clear demarcation of different positions within a total economy—also occurs in economic systems before capitalism (like feudalism). The *detailed* division of labor, involving a subdivision of tasks within a productive process, is exclusively a capitalist development. Since these divisions narrow the possibilities for human self-development to a significant degree—I can't choose my activity, after all, if only one type of activity is available to me—Marx rejects divisions of labor, particularly the detailed variety:

> Some crippling of body and mind is inseparable even from the division of labor in society as a whole. However, since manufacture carries this social separation of branches of labor much further, and also, by its peculiar division, attacks the individual at the very roots of his life, it is the first system to provide the materials and the impetus for industrial pathology.[11]

The division of labor, which in a class society is formed by private ownership of the means of production, cuts off avenues for self-creation because the potential for workers' self-creating activity is diverted into profit-seeking or capital-maximizing forms. Consequently, Marx rejects both private property in the means of production and the domination of human possibility by money, perceiving them as obstacles to self-creation. Thus, for Marx, self-creation under communism is accompanied, and facilitated by, the abandonment of

money—much like within the Federation—since "with collective production, money capital is completely dispensed with."[12] Marx, however, argues that "there is no reason why the producers should not
receive paper tokens permitting them to withdraw an amount corre-
sponding to their labor time from the social consumption stocks. But
these tokens are not money; they do not circulate."[13] Private property
and money are out; labor tokens and total "being over having" are in.

One final feature of Marx's classless, communist society is found in
the recognition that full, classless communism involves a long process
of change that resolves into two stages. The first stage of communist
society, having recently emerged from capitalism, involves individuals
*politically* winning "the battle of democracy" and using the democratic state "to wrest, by degrees, all capital from the bourgeoisie, to
centralize all instruments of production in the hands of the state, i.e.,
of the proletariat organized as the ruling class."[14] Economically, the
working class in this stage would receive in consumption exactly what
their labor entitles them to; and, for any individual worker, "the same
amount of labor he has given to society in one form, he received back
in another."[15] By contrast, in a more advanced phase of communist
society,

> when labor is no longer just a means of keeping alive but has itself
> become a vital need; when the all-round development of individuals has
> also increased their productive powers and all the springs of cooperative
> wealth flow more abundantly—only then can society wholly cross the
> narrow horizon of bourgeois right and inscribe on its banner: From
> each according to his abilities, to each according to his needs![16]

Politically, Marx theorizes that this final stage is characterized by the
dissolution of the state as we know it—a coercive, ruling institution
separate from and subordinating the population. With this understanding of some of the nuances of a Marxian classless society in mind,
let's take a fresh look at the Federation.

## Set Phasers to "Revolution"

In the context of Marx and Engels's work on a communist, classless society, how might we characterize the Federation? First, it really
*does* seem that the Federation operates without dependence on the
domination of certain classes by scarcity, money, or an orientation
toward accumulation of personal property or capital. Unfortunately,

most of our glimpses of life in *Star Trek* pertain to Starfleet practices, not the day-to-day lives of civilians. Even so, we can take the statements by different Starfleet captains at face value: economic life doesn't rely on money and is oriented toward the development of individual capacities. These priorities are reflected in the nature of Starfleet ships themselves: they're first and foremost deep-space exploratory vessels with adequate defensive technologies *rather* than military craft such as Klingon Birds-of-Prey or Dominion battlecruisers. What little evidence we have about civilian occupations in *Star Trek* also seems to support Marx and Engels's view that individuals should be able to choose effectively whichever occupations they wish—the Sisko family includes a Starfleet captain, a restaurateur, a writer, and a freighter captain. This new economic orientation is consistent with Marx's depiction of postcapitalist classless society.

Furthermore, the world of *Star Trek* rests on a relative triumph over scarcity, exactly in the way Marx theorized in terms of the shift from "necessity" to "freedom." The fact that famines and natural disasters are possible—such as the fungus-caused food shortage on Tarsus IV in "The Conscience of the King" (TOS)—does *not* disqualify the Federation from being a postscarcity economy, as some analyses have posited,[17] but rather stands in acknowledgment that real crises can and do happen. Postscarcity economic systems don't render accidents impossible, but instead improve the ability to respond to them in a quick, egalitarian manner—as we see the *Enterprise* and its successors respond effectively to various disease outbreaks or other disasters (e.g., "The *Galileo* Seven" and "The Cloud Minders" (TOS); and "Hide and Q," "The Child," "Déjà Q," and "Lessons" (TNG)). Indeed, Marx argued that any program for a classless society necessarily had to involve allotments for "a reserve or insurance fund in case of accidents, disruption caused by natural calamities, etc."[18] Overall, the Federation's triumph over economic scarcity allows its citizens to focus on personal development, as well as to participate in scientific and cultural exchange with other societies and races. Military engagements, such as they are, are effects of the Federation's being one galactic power among many, with others at one point or another representing potential military threats—the Klingon, Romulans, Borg, Dominion, or the Typhon Pact.[19]

In this context, the existence of Federation credits and personal property is less of a curiosity than it first seems. Marx didn't reject the potential use of "labor notes" of some kind in the transitional stage to classless society. And even in fully developed communism,

Marx argued against the rejection of *personal* privately owned property. Federation credits make sense if thought of as part of a transitional stage in which labor is still coupled to consumption potential. They also make sense in terms of a context in which trade may occur between the Federation and non-Federation worlds or galactic powers—Starfleet officers need *some* form of currency to pay their tab at Quark's bar! Hence, the references to "money" in TOS are probably best understood as references to Federation credits.

Like Marxian communism, the Federation is a political democracy with each planet having democratic votes in making Federation policy, and the central planet of the Federation is a United Earth. Earth is united despite the fact that many nation-states and confederations seem to retain some territorially organized boundaries and identities that correspond to their historical boundaries and cultures—but they aren't independent powers or even federated territories. We can assume, however, that the United Earth government and the Federation aren't *direct* democracies in which popular voting settles every issue—thus the Federation Council. We can also assume that the political structure of both the United Earth and the Federation retain the state's hierarchical structure as an institution, at some level, "over" its citizenry—it didn't "wither away," as Marx had predicted.[20] In this sense, the politics of the Federation seems to be, like Federation credits, firmly located in a transitional period *rather* than at the level of a fully developed classless communism.

The biggest contradiction to reconcile is the apparent inherited ownership of private business like Sisko's Creole Kitchen or Chateau Picard. They could also be explained by treating the Federation as a *transitional* stage on the way to, rather than as the achievement of, a fully classless society—but that isn't entirely satisfactory: Chateau Picard has been producing wine for at least a hundred years, a longevity that speaks to a lack of social movement to classlessness. That said, Marx never advocated a singular, context-independent transitional path to communism; and while certain demands in the *Communist Manifesto* must be considered as independent of the national context of the time, the timing of their implementation is something that can best be understood *within* a historical process of transition. Perhaps the Federation's triumph over scarcity is considered so complete that inherited ownership is no longer seen as a means to subordinate others. Suffice it to say, the economic system of the United Federation of Planets has a number of central features attributed to Marx's vision of a classless society, and the eccentricities that exist make the most sense if we picture the Federation within the first, transitional phase toward, rather than as the complete and final phase of, classless society.

## To Boldly Conclude ...

The Federation's abandonment of a profit-and-growth-based economic system and money in favor of an economic system designed to facilitate personal development is a product of future successes in overcoming scarcity. As we've seen, Federation "trekonomics" can be well described in terms of Marx's own vision of the first stage of a postscarcity, money-free, classless society. The difficulties of interpretation that have provoked debate—the existence of Federation credits, the visible hierarchy in Starfleet, and the family ownership of some specialized means of production, such as restaurants and vineyards—can be resolved if we acknowledge that Marx consistently described a first, complex transitional stage to full communism.

Perhaps it is this overcoming of a profit-and-growth-oriented economic system that's responsible for the Federation's vast successes in attracting disparate planets into a democratic union of species, as well as for other characteristic aspects of the Federation. For example, its prioritization of scientific knowledge and self-realization is made possible by the direction of economic imperatives toward group advancement and the good of individual Federation citizens. The Federation's ability to maintain the Prime Directive as a policy may be seen as a consequence of its lack of need for "foreign" labor or resources: unlike early colonial capitalist nations, the Federation has no interest in strip mining, enslavement, or territorial conquest. Similarly, this self-sufficiency may account for the Federation's hesitancy to engage in interstellar warfare. The Federation can clearly be seen as the transitional stage to full Marxian communism. Given more time to develop, the Federation would boldly go the rest of the way.

## Notes

1. For further analysis of *Star Trek*'s philosophy of *peace*, see David Boersema's chapter in this volume (Chapter 6).
2. For the Federation as a "proto-post scarcity economy," see R. Webb, "The Economics of *Star Trek*: The Proto-Post Scarcity Economy,"

Medium.com (2013): https://medium.com/@RickWebb/the-economics-of-star-trek-29bab88d50. For a "general equilibrium production-exchange economy," see J. Gans, "That Star Trek Economy Thing," Digitopoly.org (2013): http://www.digitopoly.org/2013/11/19/that-star-trek-economy-thing/. For a participatory economics interpretation, see M. Grinder, "The Economics of *Star Trek*," Thepointistochangeit.org (2012): http://thepointistochangeit.org/2012/09/30/the-economics-of-star-trek/. Finally, for the Federation as a communist society, see P. Frase, "Anti-*Star Trek*: A Theory of Posterity," PeterFrase.com (2010): http://www.peterfrase.com/2010/12/anti-star-trek-a-theory-of-posterity/ (all accessed June 19, 2015).

3. By way of contrast, for an in-depth analysis of Ferengi economic values, see Jacob M. Held, "'The Rules of Acquisition Can't Help You Now': What Can the Ferengi Teach Us about Business Ethics?" in *Star Trek and Philosophy*, ed. Jason T. Eberl and Kevin S. Decker (Chicago: Open Court, 2008).

4. Karl Marx, "Marx to Ruge," *Letters from the Deutsch-Französische Jahrbücher* (1843): https://www.marxists.org/archive/marx/works/1843/letters/43_09.htm (accessed June 19, 2015).

5. Karl Marx, "Manifesto of the Communist Party," in *The Revolutions of 1848*, vol. 1 (London: Penguin, 1992), 80.

6. Karl Marx, "Economic and Philosophical Manuscripts," in *Early Writings* (London: Penguin, 1992), 348.

7. Ibid., 351.

8. The importance of this type of self-creative activity, for which *leisure* from productive labor is necessary, is discussed in Jason Eberl's chapter in this volume (Chapter 1).

9. Karl Marx, *Capital: A Critique of Political Economy*, vol. 3, trans. D. Fernbach (New York: Penguin, 1990), 958–9.

10. Freidrich Engels, "Draft of a Communist Confession of Faith," in *Birth of the Communist Manifesto* (New York: International Publishers, 1971): https://www.marxists.org/archive/marx/works/1847/06/09.htm (accessed June 19, 2015).

11. Karl Marx, *Capital: A Critique of Political Economy*, vol. 1, trans. B. Fowkes (New York: Penguin, 1990), 484.

12. Karl Marx, *Capital: A Critique of Political Economy*, vol. 2, trans. D. Fernbach (New York: Vintage Books, 1981), 434.

13. Ibid.

14. Marx, "Manifesto of the Communist Party," 86.

15. Karl Marx, "Critique of the Gotha Programme," in *The First International and After*, vol. 3 (London: Penguin, 1992), 346.

16. Ibid.

17. Webb, "The Economics of *Star Trek*."

18. Marx, "Critique of the Gotha Programme," 344.

19. The "Typhon Pact" is a confederation consisting of the Romulans, Breen, Gorn, Tzenkethi, Tholians, and Kinshaya. Its formation is covered in the *Typhon Pact* series of novels published by Pocket Books in 2010–2012.
20. An insightful look into the Federation's political structure is provided by Keith R.A. DeCandido's *Star Trek: The Next Generation* novel *Articles of the Federation* (New York: Pocket Books, 2005).

# 12

# "The Needs of the Many Outweigh the Needs of the Few": Utilitarianism and *Star Trek*

## Greg Littmann

Captain Kirk slumps dying against the wall of the reaction chamber, his DNA shattered by the radiation leak. Looking up at Mister Spock through the transparent hatch, he gasps, "How's our ship?"

"Out of danger … you saved the crew," Spock tells him quietly.

"You used what he wanted against him. That's a nice move."

"It is what you would have done."

"And this … this is what you would have done." Kirk sighs. "It was only logical."

In *Star Trek Into Darkness*, both Kirk and Spock are willing to sacrifice their lives for others. Kirk dies by exposing himself to radiation so that he can realign the warp core and save the *Enterprise*. Spock *almost* dies in a volcano on the planet Nibiru while trying to save the primitive natives, even refusing a subsequent rescue attempt by *Enterprise* for fear of revealing the ship and influencing Nibiru's natural development.

No matter the timeline, this is just how Kirks and Spocks behave. In "The *Galileo* Seven" (TOS), when Spock is pinned by a rock as the spear-wielding giants of Taurus II advance on his landing party, he insists that his crewmates leave him behind to save themselves. Likewise, in "The Squire of Gothos" (TOS), Kirk allows the god-like, but foppish, Trelane to hunt him for sport in return for sparing the *Enterprise*. In *The Wrath of Khan*, Spock gives up his life by

*The Ultimate Star Trek and Philosophy*, First Edition. Edited by Kevin S. Decker and Jason T. Eberl.
© 2016 John Wiley & Sons, Ltd. Published 2016 by John Wiley & Sons, Ltd.

exposing himself to radiation in the engine room while restoring the warp drive—the counterpart to Kirk's sacrifice in *Into Darkness*. Heroic self-sacrifice even runs in the Kirk family. In *Star Trek* (2009), Kirk's father, George, dies by ramming the *U.S.S. Kelvin* into Nero's *Narada*, saving 800 lives; while, in *The Search for Spock*, Kirk's son, David, dies by throwing himself in front of a Klingon *d'k tahg* knife to save Lieutenant Saavik.

Why should anyone sacrifice themselves like this? Spock sees sacrificing himself for others as simply being rational. When his crewmates rescue him in "The *Galileo* Seven," he complains, "The logical thing for you to have done was to have left me behind." In *Into Darkness*, Kirk justifies his sacrifice in the same way. Leaning against the transparent wall of the reaction chamber, he groans to Spock, "This is what you would have done. It was only logical." But what is so logical about self-sacrifice? In *The Wrath of Khan*, Spock makes his reasoning explicit. Propping himself up against the transparent wall of the reaction chamber, he groans to Kirk, "Don't grieve, Admiral. It is logical. The needs of the many outweigh … " " … the needs of the few," continues Kirk, who's heard it all before. Spock makes the same argument in *Into Darkness* when urging *Enterprise* not to break the Prime Directive by saving him on Niburu. In reply to McCoy's protests, he reasons, "Doctor, the needs of the many outweigh the needs of the few."

*Utilitarianism* is the theory that whether an action is morally right or wrong depends entirely on how beneficial or harmful it will be for everyone involved—only the net balance of benefit and harm matters. If sacrificing your own life realigning a warp core will save the lives of a starship full of people, then sacrificing yourself is the right thing to do and not sacrificing yourself would be morally wrong. After all, sacrificing yourself would bring much greater benefit, saving many lives at the cost of one. Even the rebellious young Kirk of *Star Trek* (2009) recognizes the importance of acting to benefit large numbers of other people. Captain Pike sells Kirk on joining Starfleet by reminding him of the benefit the Federation provides: "You understand what the Federation is, don't you? It's important. It's a peacekeeping and humanitarian armada." In *Into Darkness*, Spock speaks of utility as if it's the most important thing in life, telling Uhura, "Your suggestion that I do not care about dying is incorrect. A sentient being's best chance of maximizing utility is a long and prosperous life."[1]

# "Illogical" Human Emotions

ROBOT ALICE #471:    Please explain "unhappy."
SPOCK:    Unhappiness is the state which occurs in the human when wants and desires are not fulfilled.

—"I, Mudd" (TOS)

Most utilitarians believe that the only thing valuable in itself is *happiness*, and the only thing bad in itself is *suffering*; so, to maximize utility is to maximize happiness and minimize suffering. In the words of one of utilitarianism's founders, English philosopher Jeremy Bentham (1748–1832): "it is the greatest happiness of the greatest number that is the measure of right and wrong."[2] Utilitarians would be baffled by the common Vulcan view that emotions are best gotten rid of. Spock tells McCoy in "Dagger of the Mind" (TOS): "We disposed of emotion, Doctor. Where there's no emotion, there's no motive for violence." Utilitarians would ask what value being unemotional can have if it doesn't make anyone happier. Besides, creatures with no emotion would have no reason to do anything ever. As the Scottish philosopher and non-engineer David Hume (1711–1776) argued, reason alone can't tell us to want or value anything.[3] Creatures with no emotion have no motive for violence, but they have no motive for anything else either—like knowledge, peace, or survival.

Utilitarians are more accepting of the view that emotions simply need to be kept in check. In *Star Trek* (2009), Spock's father, Sarek, explains to him that "emotions run deep in our race," but you must have "control of feelings so that they do not control you." The original Spock (or Spock Prime) gradually learns to value emotion, in defiance of Vulcan teaching. In *Star Trek: The Motion Picture*, he explains to Kirk, "[The robot] V'ger is now as I was when I came aboard. Empty, in search. Logic and knowledge are not enough." *The Voyage Home* ends with Spock finally coming out to his mother about having feelings, sending her the message, "I feel fine."[4] Later, in *The Undiscovered Country*, he passes along the sage advice to his protégé that "logic is the beginning of wisdom, Valeris, not the end."

Bentham thought that all pleasure of equal intensity is equally valuable.[5] However, not all utilitarians agree. Bentham's pupil, John Stuart Mill (1806–1873), accepted that all pleasure is good, but thought that "higher pleasures," which are intellectually demanding, are better than "lower pleasures," which are not.[6] Higher pleasures would include the joy of activities like studying science, appreciating fine Vulcan lyre music, or playing three-dimensional chess. Lower pleasures would include things like drinking Saurian brandy, petting a tribble, and McCoy's pastime of making fun of Spock's appearance.

Mill argued that higher pleasure must be more valuable than lower pleasure, because people who've experienced both will choose higher pleasures over lower ones. However, this doesn't ring psychologically true. We can make perfect sense of a character like Kirk, who's brilliant but loves pleasures of the flesh. We learn in *Star Trek* (2009) that Kirk's intelligence is "genius level," but there's nothing baffling about the fact that he loves a bar fight and casual threesomes with Caitian catwomen. Likewise, from TOS, we know that Kirk is a brilliant strategist, a poetry lover, and a master of three-dimensional chess, able to defeat even Spock. Yet it's no surprise that he still devotes time to lower pleasures like rock climbing, horseback riding, and appreciating female beauty. For instance, in "Wolf in the Fold," we find Kirk on shore leave with McCoy and Scotty, watching erotic dancing in a club on the hedonistic world of Argelius II. He makes it clear at the end of the episode that he's a connoisseur of such establishments, trying to entice Spock to join him by promising, "Mister Spock, I know a cafe where the women are so ... " We never get to hear the end of his sentence, but it's a fair guess he wasn't going to say, " ... good at playing chess and writing poetry." In case you think that people like Kirk don't exist in the real world, note that Albert Einstein was twice as randy as Captain Kirk and half as discriminating, while Mozart's and Benjamin Franklin's ideas of fun would make a green Orion dancing-girl blush orange.

Entertainment in *The Next Generation* better reflects Mill's take on psychology, but is predictably implausible. When the crew of *Enterprise*-D hit the holodeck for virtual adventures, they inevitably opt for something like improvisational theater, rather than obvious alternatives like pornographic adventures or wild shoot-'em-ups with body counts in the thousands. This stands in stark contrast to the way people use computers for recreation today. Even players of the MMORPG *Star Trek Online* are far less likely to be found roleplaying than zapping Klingons with phasers. More plausible uses of holotechnology are seen in *Deep Space Nine*. Quark's personal favorite holosuite program is "Vulcan Love Slave"—all three volumes; Klingons get to fight the "Battle of Klach D'Kel Brakt"; and

Miles O'Brien and Julian Bashir indulge in Viking wars, the Battle of the Alamo, and shooting down "Jerries" in the Battle of Britain.

## The Limits of Sacrifice

KIRK:  I am used to the idea of dying. But I have no desire to die for the likes of you.

—"Errand of Mercy" (TOS)

Despite the above evidence to the contrary, Vulcan philosophy apparently teaches that utilitarianism is *false*. When a pre-adolescent Spock is being trained by computers in *Star Trek* (2009), he answers a question we don't hear by stating, "When it's morally praiseworthy but not morally obligatory." The computer confirms that this is the right answer. But if utilitarianism is correct, then nothing is ever morally praiseworthy but not obligatory. If you *can* raise utility, you have an obligation to do so. Some philosophers think this makes utilitarianism too demanding. It places a heavy duty on us to sacrifice our own best interests for those of others, placing "the good of the many" over "the good of the one." Most people accept that self-sacrifice for the greater good is *heroic*; but is it always *required*, as utilitarians believe?

In his final film, *Generations*, Kirk Prime sees no such obligation. He initially refuses to leave his idyllic life on his virtual play-farm just because Captain Picard offers him a chance to save millions of lives. Kirk complains that devotion to duty never got him anything but "an empty house." Even when he finally agrees to come with Picard, he doesn't do it for the millions of innocents, but because he misses feeling important: "Ever since I left Starfleet, I haven't made a difference." Is it fair to blame him for thinking of himself first for once?

Utilitarianism doesn't just imply that we must sacrifice *ourselves* for the greater good, but also that we must sacrifice *other people* if that serves the greater good. The *Star Trek* television series takes an ambivalent attitude toward such sacrifices. In "The Ultimate Computer" (TOS), Kirk plans to let the *Enterprise* be destroyed to eliminate the M-5 computer that has taken it over and is threatening four other starships. The captain explains to his skeleton crew, "Our nineteen lives will buy the survival of over a thousand of our fellow starship crewmen." Yet, Spock is seen as callous in "The *Galileo Seven*" when he suggests leaving someone behind in order to make the shuttle light enough to take off, explaining to a horrified McCoy, "It is more rational to sacrifice one life than six, Doctor." Likewise, in "A Taste of Armageddon" (TOS), Kirk refuses to allow his crew to be killed in accordance with the rules of the war game between Eminiar VII and Vendikar, even though doing so would spare millions of people on the two planets from the horrors of real war.

Attitudes toward sacrificing civilians are just as inconsistent, though tending strongly to the view that it mustn't be done. In "Operation: Annihilate!" (TOS), Kirk would rather slaughter the population of Deneva than allow the plague of violent insanity they suffer from to infect other planets, declaring, "I cannot let it spread beyond this colony, even if it means destroying a million people down there." Yet, in "Charlie X" (TOS), Kirk can't bring himself to kill the well-meaning teenage Charlie, even though the mentally disturbed young psychic has already destroyed the starship *Antares* and poses a threat to the entire Federation. Likewise, in "The Conscience of the King" (TOS), Kirk is disgusted by Kodos "the Executioner," former governor of Tarsus IV, who responded to a supply shortage by killing 4000 eugenically selected colonists so that 4000 others could survive. In "The Cloud Minders" (TOS), Kirk even intervenes to stop a political prisoner from being tortured, though he acknowledges that "physical discomfort" can be very effective and that the prisoner has information that could cure a plague on Merak II. The high advisor of Stratos asks in astonishment, "Is it preferable to spare Vanna and allow an entire planet to be destroyed?"

Captains in later *Star Trek* series often show a similar ambivalence. Picard refuses to allow Admiral Dougherty and the Son'a to relocate the Bak'u, even though doing so would allow the Federation to harness the youth-restoring powers of their planet for general benefit (*ST: Insurrection*); yet he surrenders the prefix codes of the *U.S.S. Phoenix*, opening it up to a fatal attack, to prevent sparking a war with Cardassia ("The Wounded," TNG). Sisko colludes in the assassination of a Romulan senator to bring the Star Empire into the Dominion War ("In the Pale Moonlight," DS9). But he admits to Worf, after reprimanding him for putting Jadzia's life ahead of an important mission on Soukara, that he probably would've done the same thing if it had been his wife's life on the line ("Change of Heart," DS9). Janeway may be the most consistently utilitarian captain, stranding her crew in the Delta Quadrant rather than sacrifice the Ocampa to the Kazons ("Caretaker," VOY); later, she kills an innocent person, Tuvix, in order to bring back two others, Tuvok and Neelix, who'd been fused in a transporter accident—an act that the holographic Doctor's ethical program wouldn't allow him to perform ("Tuvix," VOY). Finally, though Archer opts repeatedly throughout the third season of *Enterprise* to sacrifice the interests of innocent individuals to complete his Earth-saving mission to find and defeat the Xindi—torturing an Osaarian pirate ("Anomaly"), killing Trip's clone to save him ("Similitude"), and stranding an Illyrian vessel by stealing their warp coil ("Damage")—each is portrayed as a negative, *morally compromising* choice.

## Friendship and Loyalty

KIRK: I want you to know why I couldn't let you die … why I went back for you.

SPOCK: Because you are my friend.

*—Star Trek Into Darkness*

According to utilitarianism, our duty to put the needs of the many ahead of the needs of the few extends even to people we have personal relationships with, like our friends and family. Some philosophers reject utilitarianism on the grounds that treating everyone equally violates the special loyalties and obligations we have to people who are close to us.[7] The protagonists of the *Star Trek* franchise would seem to agree, as they generally place personal loyalty over public duty. In *Into Darkness*, Kirk's first question after he returns from the surface of Nibiru is not "Did we save Nibiru?" but "Where's Spock?" When faced with a choice between rescuing Spock and respecting the Prime Directive by not revealing the *Enterprise*, Kirk rescues his friend. Later, when he's trying to justify his actions to Pike, he focuses on the fact that he managed to save Spock, while the fact that he managed to save Nibiru is barely mentioned. Kirk expects Spock also to place the needs of his friends first. After learning that Spock presented Starfleet with an honest report of the events at Nibiru, Kirk accuses, "I am familiar with your compulsion to follow the rules. But I can't do that. Where I come from, if you save someone, they don't stab you in the back." Spock doesn't share these values. As McCoy notes, if Kirk's and Spock's positions had been reversed, "He'd let you die."[8]

In "City on the Edge of Forever" (TOS), Kirk briefly approves of placing public utility over private loyalty. He ingratiates himself with his love interest, the 1930s charity worker, Edith Keeler, by speaking approvingly of a poet who recommends the three words "let me help" (a utilitarian commitment) over "I love you" (a personal one). Kirk proves himself a man of his word when he allows Edith to die in order to prevent the Nazis from winning World War II. More typical, though, is his attitude in "The Gamesters of Triskelion" (TOS), in which he assures his love interest, the green-haired gladiator, Shahna, "Love is the most important thing on Earth."

Like his counterpart in the alternative timeline, this Kirk doesn't let his duty to the Federation get in the way of his loyalty to his crew. When he learns in *The Search for Spock* that McCoy is carrying the mind of his dead Vulcan friend, he and his old crew hijack the *Enterprise* to recover Spock's body and restore him to life. What's more, he explicitly rejects the principle that the needs of the many outweigh the needs of the few. When the resurrected Spock asks, "Why would you do this?" Kirk explains, "Because the needs of the one outweigh the needs of the many."

Spock is initially firmly on the side of placing utility over personal loyalty. For instance, in "Journey to Babel" (TOS), he refuses to "jeopardize hundreds of lives [and] risk an interplanetary war" by relinquishing command long enough to donate blood for a life-saving operation for his father. Over time, though, his personal loyalties grow stronger. By *The Voyage Home*, he's willing to jeopardize their Earth-saving mission in order to rescue a captured and injured Chekov from the FBI. Kirk asks, "Is that the logical thing to do, Spock?" "No," Spock replies, "but it is the *human* thing to do." By *The Final Frontier*, it's no surprise that Spock refuses an order to shoot his brother, Sybok, even though Sybok threatens the *Enterprise*.

## Your Orders, Captain?

SPOCK:     Without facts, the decision cannot be made logically. You
           must rely on your human intuition.

—"Assignment: Earth" (TOS)

Moral theories can't be proved or disproved by logic alone. Spock often speaks as if they can, but, as Scotty might say, "Ye cannae change the laws of logic!" In moral matters, we must rely ultimately on our intuitions. So what do *you* think? Is it true, as utilitarians claim, that morality requires us to place the needs of the many ahead of the needs of the few? Are we really required to sacrifice ourselves if, like Kirk in the reaction chamber, we bring a greater benefit to others than we lose by the sacrifice? Must we really put the needs of our loved ones behind the greater needs of strangers, like Spock when he refuses to give blood to save his father while there is a war that needs averting?

You'll have to make up your own mind, but I think that the utilitarians are correct. The heroes of *Star Trek* generally think otherwise; but, then, *Star Trek* adventures have a habit of not showing harm happen to the many when a hero chooses to prioritize the needs of the few. The plague on Merak II never spreads to other worlds because Kirk stopped Vanna's torture; no battles are lost when Kirk hijacks the *Enterprise* to search for his dead best friend; Spock agrees to rescuing Chekov from the FBI without dooming the Earth; the Federation doesn't lose the Dominion War because Worf doesn't make his rendezvous on Soukara; and, at least as far as we know, no bloody religious wars are fought by the people of Nibiru over differing interpretations of how to best serve the *Enterprise*-god.

One notable exception to this trend occurs in *Into Darkness*, when Section 31 agent Thomas Harewood favors the one over the many by detonating a bomb in the agency headquarters for Khan, in return for Khan providing a cure for his daughter's fatal disease. Most of us would agree that Harewood does something morally wrong in carrying out the bombing, even though he only does it out of love for his daughter. Yet the results of, say, Spock choosing to save his father could've been even worse: an interplanetary war in which the death toll would far exceed the forty-two people killed in Harewood's attack. Likewise, in *The Voyage Home*, when Spock recommends endangering the mission to save Earth by taking time to rescue Chekov—what if they hadn't gotten to the whales in time to save them from the whalers?—he's gambling with the lives of billions of people. Would his crewmates still think him a hero if they returned to the 23rd century with a healthy Chekov only to find that most of our world had been drowned by the storms caused by the alien probe? If we accept that catastrophes for the many are genuinely likely in this and other cases we've discussed, favoring the few becomes harder to defend, just as it is hard to defend Harewood for putting his daughter's life ahead of the lives of his victims. As the disgusted Eminiarian counselor Anan 7 demands of Kirk in "A Taste of Armageddon," "Are those five hundred people of yours more important than the hundreds of millions of innocent people on Eminiar and Vendikar? What kind of monster are you?"

In the *Star Trek* universe, humanity has largely rejected the idea that it's morally okay to favor people who are of our own race, gender, or nationality. If we accept that such discrimination is wrong, it seems arbitrary to believe that it's right to discriminate in favor of people we're close to and, likewise, against strangers. Since all people are equal, the good of all people should be valued equally. This flies in the face of the way humanity has acted throughout history, but sometimes you just have to be bold enough to go where no one has gone before.

# Notes

1. The utilitarian sympathies of Federation society are best demonstrated by its attitude to conflict resolution, seeking win–win solutions rather than aiming at defeat and punishment. Violent criminals are routinely sent for humane psychiatric treatment and rehabilitation. As Kirk notes approvingly in "Dagger of the Mind" (TOS), penal colonies are "more like resort colonies now." Warring peoples are encouraged to make peace, sort out their differences, and cooperate for mutual benefit, like the rulers and miners of Ardana in "The Cloud Minders" (TOS), the communist Comms and rebellious Yangs of Omega IV in "The Omega Glory" (TOS), and the feuding black-and-white and white-and-black races of Cheron in "Let That Be Your Last Battlefield" (TOS). This attitude is quite unlike the villain-crushing approach of other popular space operas made at around the same time as the original series, such as the *Flash Gordon* and *Buck Rogers* TV series of the 1950s, contemporary *Lost in Space* and *Doctor Who*, and the *Star Wars*, *Blake's 7*, and *Battlestar Galactica* franchises born in the 1970s. Television space wouldn't get this friendly again until *Star Trek: The Next Generation* appeared in 1987, bringing us a universe in which even the Klingons have been turned into friends and allies.
2. Jeremy Bentham, *A Fragment on Government* (Cambridge: Cambridge University Press, 1988), 3.
3. David Hume, *A Treatise of Human Nature*, ed. David Fate Norton and Mary J. Norton (Oxford: Clarendon Press, 2007), bk. I, ch. 2, §3.3.
4. For additional discussion of the value of emotions for Vulcans and other humanoids, see Harald Thorsrud, "Humans Smile with So Little Provocation," in *Star Trek and Philosophy* (2008).

5.   See Jeremy Bentham, *An Introduction to the Principles of Moral and Legislation* (Oxford: Clarendon Press, 1879; orig. 1789), ch. 4, §4.
6.   John Stuart Mill, *Utilitarianism* (Cambridge: Cambridge University Press, 2014), 8–11.
7.   American philosopher Josiah Royce (1855–1916), for instance, considers loyalty to be a bedrock of morality; see his book *The Possibility of Loyalty* (New York: The MacMillan Company, 1908).
8.   For further analysis of the inherent tension between the utilitarian mandate and an ethic of loyalty as depicted in *Star Trek Into Darkness*, see Jason T. Eberl, "An Inconsistent Triad? Competing Ethics in *Star Trek Into Darkness*," in *The Philosophy of J. J. Abrams*, ed. Patricia Brace and Robert Arp (Lexington: University Press of Kentucky, 2014).

# 13

# Casuistry in the Final Frontier

## Courtland Lewis

*Star Trek* doesn't just entertain, it teaches. More precisely, it teaches lessons through *casuistry*: using case studies to engage and enlighten viewers about truths concerning deep philosophical questions and the human condition. *Star Trek* is a series of philosophical thought experiments that challenges viewers to arrive at consistent positions about some of life's toughest questions. It isn't an exaggeration to say that, with very few exceptions, *Star Trek* has done more to teach audiences about the nuances of reality, science, morality, and friendship than any other show in the history of television. Why does it so consistently set itself apart from other shows? Is it simply because Gene Roddenberry had a brilliant idea for a science fiction program? Is there something special about *Star Trek*'s creative team—the writers, producers, designers, animators, and actors? Did Q decide to do something nice for humanity for once? Simply stated, the answer is "yes." All of these factors—yes, even Q—play their role in weaving the tapestry of casuistry that is *Star Trek* in all its incarnations.

## Set Phasers to Learn

Mention "educational show" to most kids, and they'll run like they just saw a Klingon under their bed. Call it *Star Trek* and throw in some phasers, a transporter, and some really strange aliens, and it's like offering a Ferengi a free trip to Vegas—you won't be able to

*The Ultimate Star Trek and Philosophy*, First Edition. Edited by Kevin S. Decker and Jason T. Eberl.
© 2016 John Wiley & Sons, Ltd. Published 2016 by John Wiley & Sons, Ltd.

keep them away. It takes skill to present something both entertaining and educational, but that's exactly what *Star Trek* does. It presents a philosophical investigation into human existence through a series of episodic case studies. The entertainment gets your attention, the stories engage your mind as thought experiments, and each episode encourages you to ponder the intricacies of the cases presented, consider resolutions, and apply each lesson learned to your everyday life.

Casuistry is a method of analysis that makes use of case studies, either real or fictional, in order to examine what should happen in similar real-life situations. It's most common in discussions of applied ethics, but casuistry is also helpful in science, politics, and religion. By presenting cases, casuistry tests and gauges people's *intuitions*— that is, our "gut feelings." The idea behind casuistry is that, if we look at typical cases, examining the subtleties of the facts of each, we'll arrive at a general understanding of what should be done in similar cases. From these paradigmatic cases, we move to more difficult, more nuanced cases, constantly revising our conclusions in light of new evidence and data. Advocates of casuistry point out that pure theorizing leads to endless disagreement, whereas our intuitions often provide satisfactory conclusions about particular cases without the benefit of theories.[1] If we bracket theoretical questions and focus on our intuitions, we'll often achieve broad agreement about what's true and what should happen in similar cases.

Consider how fans disagree over which is better: TOS versus TNG, or maybe *The Wrath of Khan* versus *Star Trek Into Darkness*. These sorts of disagreements are based on different theoretical assumptions about what makes for a good viewing experience. Fans of TOS hold assumptions that value the characters and adventures of the TOS crew over those of the TNG crew, and vice versa—contrasting, for example, Kirk's bold, headstrong leadership with Picard's more cerebral and collaborative style. Or fans value the pace, story, and cinematography of *Star Trek Into Darkness* over *The Wrath of Khan*, and vice versa— not to mention Montalban versus Cumberbatch as the quintessential Khan. Our theoretical assumptions are important, but they shouldn't prevent us from enjoying and learning from all versions of *Star Trek*. All we need do is accept a "mixed approach" that allows us to hold on to our theoretical assumptions, yet focus on the particularities of individual cases.[2] So, no matter our favorite *Star Trek* series or films, we retain the ability to learn broadly similar lessons from each intrepid adventure.

## Boldly Going Where No Genre Can Go

*Star Trek*'s casuistic power is grounded in the fact that it's a *science fiction* show. In one sense, then, it's no different than other sci-fi on television. What sets *Star Trek* apart is its creative approach to storytelling, which purposefully engages and teaches fans. Some science fiction shows merely tell a story that fits into the genre. *Star Trek*, by contrast, takes full advantage of the virtues of sci-fi to present characters, ideas, and concepts in a deeply—often subconsciously—educational way.

Hugo Gernsback—founding editor of *Amazing Stories*—coined the term *science fiction* in 1929.[3] It was also around this time that science fiction became a literary genre in its own right, distinguished from fantasy, horror, and similar genres. What sets science fiction apart is how it combines the facts of science and the freedom of fiction: "science" provides the genre with reason, rationality, and a particular method for solving problems, and "fiction" provides writers and readers with the freedom to explore the unlimited potential of their imaginations.[4]

The combination of science and fiction creates three virtues that *Star Trek*'s creative team pushes to their boundaries in order to constantly engage viewers to be active watchers and thinkers. The first virtue is that *Star Trek*'s stories are "constrained" by science. No matter how fantastical the story, it must take place in a world governed by scientific principles and be resolved with explanations that are scientifically plausible. Although the writers are often forced to invent "technobabble" to devise solutions to whatever "problem of the week" threatens the *Enterprise, Deep Space Nine*, or *Voyager*, the fictional "tech" solution is envisioned as a plausible extension of our current technological prowess that doesn't violate known scientific laws. The second virtue is that science's "constraint" creates a *flexible realism* that allows *Star Trek*'s creative team to test the limits of human experience and understanding, while keeping stories grounded in such a way that fans are capable of understanding and incorporating real-life lessons. The third virtue is that *Star Trek*'s stories are essentially thought experiments. Philosophers use thought experiments to make sense of particularly difficult questions, because they test our intuitions about what's true and false. As a result, *Star Trek* is particularly good at promoting curiosity and intellectual growth. With these virtues combined, *Star Trek* creates a casuistic experience that would make even the most logical Vulcan giddy.

# SCIENCE!!! … I Mean, KHAAAN!!!

The laws of science constrain much—if not all—of what we do. When I heat water to make "tea, Earl Grey, hot," science is at work, and I'm unsurprised when water comes out of the kettle instead of Romulan ale—though I sometimes wish it were. However, we shouldn't see this as a constraint, at least not in the ordinary sense that something is being prevented from happening. Instead, all that's meant by "constraint" is that *this is just the way things are*. If Romulan ale ever comes out of my tea kettle, I'll assume there's some sort of logical explanation for why it does. So, what is *science*? It's a methodological approach to examining the world. It provides a structure of analysis to critically examine observable data, offer hypotheses that explain phenomena, and arrive at conclusions based on testing and disproving false hypotheses. How does this apply to *Star Trek* and casuistry?

Science is the basis of technology and, as such, provides us with tools and devices that continually influence our lives and stretch the limits of what's possible and plausible. When we combine science with fiction, we get "an effort to predict the future on the basis of known facts, culled largely from present-day laboratories."[5] This fusion creates futuristic worlds, ingenious gadgets, and a litany of ships and life forms by taking what's known and applying the scientific method to determine what might be possible. The *scientific method*, then, provides a foundation on which to build fictional stories that push the limits of our understanding of what's possible.

Understood in this way, science is no constraint at all. The 2005 documentary *How William Shatner Changed the World* illustrates how *Star Trek* inspired computers, cell phones, and many other contemporary advances in technology.[6] *Star Trek* has even inspired physicists to formulate the creation of transporters, replicators, and warp engines.[7] Science is the basis of technology, and because *Star Trek* is science based, its "fantasies" are based in reality. As a result, *Star Trek* is *real*, in a sense. We might not have replicators yet; but since *Star Trek* is based in the reality of science, fans recognize that what they're watching is possible and so they're engaged in a very real and tangible way. *Star Trek* isn't merely about flying around to alien planets; it's about challenging our understanding of the present and foretelling possible futures. This only happens if it remains grounded in science.

Science, therefore, provides a mechanism by which to tell the story. Storylines should be guided by a rational structure of hypothesizing, testing, and evaluating results. Consider a typical *Star Trek* episode, like the TNG episode "Clues." On their way to investigate a mysterious planet, all of the crew except Data fall unconscious. Shortly thereafter, the crew begin noticing strange occurrences. Dr. Crusher's experimental flora have miraculously grown; Worf's wrist is injured; Counselor Troi is "unfocused"; and the ship's chronometer has been tampered with. Throughout the episode, the crew uses a critical scientific approach to gather data, form hypotheses, and arrive at conclusions. This scientific approach leads them to the truth, even if it's a truth they're uncomfortable with: Data is *lying*.

Now, imagine how different the episode—and the series—would have been if the crew relied instead on superstition and wild conjecture. Instead of looking for the truth, imagine if they simply said, "It must be the spirit of Captain Kirk haunting the ship"; and instead of using science, they used the ship's wizard—Gandalf, of course—to exorcise the spirit. It might be interesting, but it wouldn't be *Star Trek* or science fiction. It would be fantasy set in space, which is essentially *Star Wars*.[8] While it's still possible to derive moral and philosophical lessons from more fantastical tales, from a casuistic perspective, to take such an approach runs the risk of causing fans to "tune out" and disconnect.

Take, for instance, the 2015 *Doctor Who* (technically in the same universe as *Star Trek*) episode "Kill the Moon." When a creature smaller than the moon gave birth to the moon, fans cried "foul." There appeared to be no plausible scientific explanation for this event, and so fans accused the show of ceasing to be science fiction. Sometimes *Star Trek* skirts the edges of fantasy. Q's appearances always add a bit of fantasy, and the spirit of Jack the Ripper in "Wolf in the Fold" (TOS) and Chakotay's visions in "Tattoo" (VOY) involve the fantastic. Nevertheless, the basic assumption of *Star Trek* is that even when the crew encounters "fantastic," unexplained phenomena, there's ultimately a scientific explanation. They might not always find the explanation, but they assume there is one, and thus fans stay engaged in the story because it's "real."

A prime example is the VOY episode "Emanations," in which Ensign Harry Kim must die in order to return to *Voyager*, which has been exploring the asteroids of a planetary ring system populated by the decaying corpses of an alien species. While this species believes in an afterlife, the scientific evidence at hand indicates that their bodies simply appear on one of these asteroids and decay. Nevertheless, *Voyager*'s sensors record highly organized energy patterns within the ring system, perhaps indicating the persistence of the aliens' consciousness beyond death. While not definitely resolving the question one way or the other, Captain Janeway is open to the possibility of some sort of afterlife for these aliens that's consistent with her scientific understanding of the universe.

## Is There a Bones in the House?

*Star Trek* must remain firmly grounded in science to retain the engaging casuistic force that it has, but what about its *fictional* component? What if *Star Trek* were more "realistic"? If realism is good, then wouldn't more realism make for a better thought experiment? The simple answer is "no." Arguably, the goal of realistic fiction is to reproduce experiences recognizable to audiences By contrast, science fiction is an imaginative fiction that produces spectacular things not found in our world.[9] Yet, these spectacular things—environments, planets, aliens, and time travel—are recognizable and relevant to viewers only because they're grounded in the reality of science.

There are wonderful examples of "science fact" shows—like *House M.D.*—that do an incredible job of giving viewers a glimpse into the moral, social, and political issues that arise while practicing medicine. Even though these shows push the boundaries of normal medical drama and examine ethical and medical issues from an impressive number of perspectives, they lack *Star Trek*'s second virtue—its storytelling *flexibility*: "The science fiction film has simply proven to be one of our most flexible popular genres—and perhaps for that very reason, one of our most culturally useful."[10] Science fiction's flexibility has been lauded as "a popular fictional genre that engages with (and visualizes) cultural debates around one or more of the following: the future, artificial creation, technological invention, extraterrestrial contact, time travel, physical or mental mutation, scientific experimentation, or fantastic natural disasters."[11] It's *Star Trek*'s ability and *willingness* to explore the limits of science *fiction* and the human condition that make it such a powerful casuistic teaching tool.

Think about the TOS episodes "The Mark of Gideon" and "Miri." In the former, scientists have eradicated all illness, and in the latter, researchers discover a way of prolonging life. Both storylines could appear in a "science fact" film, but the examination of the issues would be limited by the program's factual framework. Science fact programs are confined to particular places and settings. *Star Trek*'s flexibility, on the other hand, provides a storytelling space in which fantastic case studies are created, a space in which the curing of all illness leads to overpopulation, misery, and the need to reintroduce sickness that causes death; and attempts to prolong life lead to the near extinction of the planet's population. As fictional, *Star Trek* gives us a more nuanced and complete understanding of the possible features and issues related to such cases, providing viewers an opportunity for a more thought-provoking experience.

As a result, these episodes don't just tell a story. They become thought experiments about proper research techniques and agendas. The episodes don't simply say, "Beware, science!" They say, "Let's be aware of the dangers, and proceed cautiously as we move toward the future." Viewers gain a much broader knowledge base of science and ethics than they would from a science fact program.[12] With its three virtues, *Star Trek* truly sets itself apart as one of the greatest science fiction shows and one of the most important television shows of all time.

## *Star Trek*, You Have Been and Shall Always Be My Friend

Let's consider two prime examples of *Star Trek*'s use of casuistry to make tangible contributions to important philosophical discussions. The first involves *Star Trek*'s engagement with the question of whether or not certain entities are part of the moral community of *persons*, which includes (most) human beings. Relevant episodes include the TOS episode "The Devil in the Dark," where Spock uses a mind-meld in an attempt to determine the nature of the silicone-based entity called the Horta; as well as the TNG episodes "The Quality of Life," in which Exocomps become self-aware, and "The Offspring," in which Data creates a sentient daughter.

The most famous example, however, comes from "The Measure of a Man" (TNG), in which it's determined whether Data is an individual person with rights or the property of Starfleet. Picard successfully defends Data's right to self-determination. What makes this episode so gripping is that, until this point, fans simply *assumed* Data was his own person. The episode pulls no punches. Riker's forced prosecution makes a strong case in favor of Data being merely a "thing," so much so that Picard is forced to give a defense based on emotional pleas, what-ifs, and appeals to ignorance—we don't know for certain if he's alive, so we better not deem him property. I'm not criticizing Picard, but the point is that Data provides an incredibly challenging case study. He appears so human; yet, as Spock observes in "Unification, Part II," his "efficient intellect, superior physical skills and no emotional impediments" make him appear utterly alien in behavior. Every time we see Data, we're challenged to consider his metaphysical and moral status.

The second prime example occurs in the VOY episode "Nothing Human," concerning research ethics. Captain Janeway must choose between using data gathered from inhumane experiments, or not using the data and letting B'Elanna Torres die. The episode challenges viewers to consider whether or not data obtained through immoral experiments—like the Nazi and Japanese experiments during the Second World War—should be used for potentially beneficial medical research. As the episode illustrates, people remain divided over what should happen to such data. Does using it legitimize inhumane research? Does it denigrate the memories of those who suffered? Or does the use of such data make something good out of something bad?

*Voyager*'s holographic Doctor creates an interactive program to help him remove a life-threatening parasite from Torres. Unaware of any controversy, the Doctor looks through the historical records and recreates a hologram of the most qualified and experienced exobiologist in history—the Cardassian doctor, Crell Moset. Moset, however, is infamous for performing horrible experiments on unwilling patients during Cardassia's occupation of Bajor. Consequently, his holographic presence makes *Voyager*'s Maquis crew—comprising several Bajorans—uncomfortable, hostile, and indignant.

Crell Moset is analogous to the infamous Nazi doctor Josef Mengele, who performed inhumane experiments during the Second World War.[13] The episode also touches on issues found in other examples of inhumane experimentation, like the Tuskegee Syphilis Study.[14] As you can imagine, these cases still incite heated debate. *Star Trek*'s use of science and fiction, however, allows the show to present a case study that illustrates the complexities of these real-life cases in a "safe" way. Instead of seeing the moral issues in terms of Nazis and racism, we see the issues framed in terms of Cardassians and holographic doctors. And instead of just speaking of *hypothetical* medical advances, we see a "real" case of ill-gotten data that could save a life.

Fans aren't left on the sidelines; *Star Trek* keeps them engaged throughout. They've heard every side of the issue and had a chance to follow their intuitions to arrive at their own conclusions. In the end, Janeway allows the procedure in order to save Torres. Thankfully, *Star Trek* doesn't give us a simplistically moralistic ending. Instead of just saying, "It's okay to use ill-gotten research," the case study continues.

After saving Torres's life, the Doctor erases Crell Moset from the computer. Even though the holographic program's knowledge is valuable, his progenitor's means for getting that knowledge are unjustifiable. So, in an attempt to honor those living and dead, the Doctor erases him.

Fans feel the difficulty of such decisions because they took part in the deliberation, and thereby they've learned from the experiences depicted in the episode. This is precisely the power of casuistry. With the various types of philosophical case studies presented in these and many other episodes discussed throughout this book, it's easy to see the effectiveness and importance of *Star Trek* and its use of casuistry.

## Live Long and Use Casuistry

What other show is willing to tackle such controversial issues in such an engaging fashion? *Star Trek* takes issues and presents them in a way that captures their subtle nuances. Its basis in science, flexibility in fiction, and willingness to use thought experiments to explore some of humanity's toughest philosophical questions make it a casuistic force that—whether fans realize it or not—piques viewers' intellectual curiosity in a way that irrevocably changes their lives. The audience comes away with the power to apply what they've learned to their everyday lives to make the universe a better place—some even going so far as to wear a Starfleet uniform while serving on a jury in a high-profile case as a symbol of the civic values embraced by the Federation.[15] It's through this process that *Star Trek*'s mission becomes real.

*Star Trek* does all of this without overburdening viewers with the "scary" real-life details that might make them shut down or retreat into their deeply ingrained positions. It gets viewers to imagine the world through the prism of the fantastic, to see how different ways of *reasoning* and different situations affect the actual decisions we make. It takes different actions and people, alien moralities, futuristic technologies, and the infinite universe to create a—hopefully—never-ending case study of reality and the human condition. When all is said and done, *Star Trek* and its wonderful creative team boldly go where other series can't or refuse to go. Thanks, "Mon Capitaine!"[16]

## Notes

1. Stephen Toulmin and Albert Jonsen, *The Abuse of Casuistry* (Berkeley: University of California Press, 1998).

2. Mark Kuczewski, "Casuistry and Principlism: The Convergence of Method in Biomedical Ethics," *Theoretical Medicine and Bioethics* 19:6 (1998): 509–24.

3. Eric Link and Gerry Canavan, *The Cambridge Companion to American Science Fiction* (Cambridge: Cambridge University Press, 2015).

4. J.P. Telotte, *Science Fiction Film* (Cambridge: Cambridge University Press, 2001), 3.

5. John W. Campbell Jr., as quoted in Telotte, *Science Fiction Film*, 3.

6. William Shatner, *I'm Working on That: A Trek from Science Fiction to Science Fact* (New York: Pocket Books, 2002).

7. Lawrence Krauss, *The Physics of Star Trek* (New York: Harper Perennial, 1995).

8. For discussion of various philosophical questions raised within the *Star Wars* saga, see Jason T. Eberl and Kevin S. Decker, eds., *The Ultimate Star Wars and Philosophy* (Malden, MA: Wiley-Blackwell, 2016), as well as their *Star Wars and Philosophy* (Chicago: Open Court, 2005).

9. Adam Roberts, *Science Fiction* (London: Routledge, 2000).

10. Telotte, *Science Fiction Film*, 10.

11. Keith M. Johnston, *Science Fiction Film: A Critical Introduction* (New York: Berg, 2011), 1.

12. Another key area where science and ethics collide that's explored numerous times throughout various *Star Trek* series and films is genetic engineering and human cloning; see Jason T. Eberl, "'Killing Your Own Clone Is Still Murder': Genetics, Ethics, and KHAAAAAN!" in *Star Trek and Philosophy*, ed. Jason T. Eberl and Kevin S. Decker (Chicago: Open Court, 2008); and Amy Kind, "Is Ignorance Bliss? *Star Trek: Nemesis*, Cloning, and the Right to an Open Future," in *Bioethics at the Movies*, ed. Sandra Shapshay (Baltimore: Johns Hopkins University Press, 2008).

13. See Gerald L. Posner and John Ware, *Mengele: The Complete Story* (New York: McGraw-Hill, 1986); and Robert Jay Lifton, *The Nazi Doctors* (New York: Basic Books, 1986).

14. See James H. Jones, *Bad Blood* (New York: The Free Press, 1981); and Harriet A. Washington, *Medical Apartheid* (New York: Doubleday, 2006).

15. http://www.cnn.com/US/fringe/9603/03-14/trek.html (accessed June 1, 2015).

16. I'd like to thank the editors of this volume for their diligent work, and my wife Jenny for putting up with my *Star Trek* and *Doctor Who* addictions. Most importantly, I'd like to thank *Star Trek*'s creative team for caring enough to change the world for the better, and my wonderful friends, both present and missing, who I've had the pleasure to journey with—as long as we remember, no one ever dies.... LLAP!

# Part III
# DELTA QUADRANT: QUESTING FOR HOME

# "Today Is a Good Day to Die!" Transporters and Human Extinction

## William Jaworski

| | |
|---|---|
| BADGER: | Dude, you are tripping! I'm not dead! I'm on the *Starship Enterprise* mackin' on Yeoman Rand while the Andorian with the disruptor is back on Talos IV or whatever. |
| SKINNY PETE: | What do you think all those sparkles and shit are? Transporters are breaking you apart, man, down to your molecules and bones. They're making a copy. That dude who comes out on the other side—he's not you; he's a color Xerox. |
| BADGER: | So you're telling me every time Kirk went into the transporter he was *killing* himself? So over the whole series there's like a 147 Kirks? |
| SKINNY PETE: | At least! Dude, yo, why do you think McCoy never likes to beam nowhere? Cuz he's a doctor, bitch! Look it up; it's science. |

—*Breaking Bad*, "Blood Money"

You probably think you're human. Most people do. But if you're convinced of that, you shouldn't get anywhere near a transporter. The reason is simple: it would shred you to bits, just as Skinny Pete says. You wouldn't volunteer to be shredded to bits by more conventional means (axes, meat grinders, *bat'leths*)—at least not if you're into survival. Yet that's precisely what a transporter is supposed to do. So if you're into survival, you shouldn't set foot in a transporter.

*The Ultimate Star Trek and Philosophy*, First Edition. Edited by Kevin S. Decker and Jason T. Eberl.
© 2016 John Wiley & Sons, Ltd. Published 2016 by John Wiley & Sons, Ltd.

There are two ways you could resist this conclusion. First, you could give up on believing you're *human*. You could claim that you're a different kind of being, one capable of surviving the transporter process. Second, you could give up on *survival*. You could claim that the convenience of using transporters outweighs the importance of whether you or any other human survives the process. But before considering these responses, it's worth asking whether transporters are possible in the first place.

## "I Cannae Change the Laws of Physics!"

There are good reasons to think *Star Trek* transporters are impossible. Consider another device—a simpler prototype of a *Star Trek* transporter: a *matter–energy–matter (MEM) converter* (Figure 14.1). The MEM converter works in three stages. First, it scans an object and records the positions and states of all of the fundamental physical particles that compose it. Second, the converter disintegrates the object. Third, it assembles an exact replica of the object by repositioning fundamental physical particles according to the record it created during its original scan.

There's reason to think that MEM converters are impossible—namely, the *uncertainty principle*, an implication of quantum theory originally formulated by the physicist Werner Heisenberg (1901–1976).[1] According to this principle, the properties of quantum particles come in pairs, such as their position and momentum. The more we

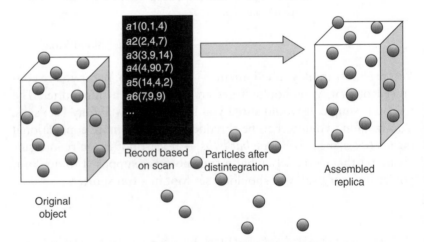

Figure 14.1   How a matter–energy–matter (MEM) converter works.

know about one property of a pair, the less we know about the other; so, the more we know about the position of a quantum particle, the less we know about its momentum and vice versa. For the MEM converter to do its job, it would have to create an exact physical replica of the object inside it. That means it would have to record accurately the properties of all the particles that compose the object. But the uncertainty principle implies that the machine can't do this—not even for a single particle. The more accurate the converter's information about a particle's position, the less accurate its information about that particle's momentum. The MEM converter could thus never get enough accurate information to generate a physical replica.

What's true of the MEM converter is also true of the transporter, since both seem to involve the same kinds of processes. Since the MEM converter is impossible, it follows that the *Star Trek* transporter is impossible as well. Of course, the engineers who designed the *Star Trek* transporter knew about the uncertainty principle and built the device with a "Heisenberg compensator."[2] But this just pushes the problem back since "compensating" for quantum-level uncertainty is itself something that seems impossible in principle.[3]

## "Suppose They Went *Nowhere*?"

Even if transporters were possible, you still shouldn't want to step into one. Would you let yourself be shot by a Varon-T disruptor that tears your body apart molecule by molecule?[4] If you're into survival, then the answer is surely no. Yet, despite the evident lack of pain, this is precisely what the transporter does to you. Of course, the transporter is different in that it doesn't disintegrate the quantum-level bits that compose you, but converts them to energy, transmits them somewhere, and then puts them back together.[5] But what makes you think that the reassembled bits would compose *you* and not merely an exact *replica* of you? You might say, "Well, it's the same bits, and if it's the same bits, then it must be the same person composed of those bits!" The problem is, you can't really believe that.

Here's why: suppose that you're currently composed of a finite number of bits, call them $p_1, p_2, p_3, \ldots, p_n$. Suppose now that you die, and through natural decomposition those bits get scattered throughout the biosphere. Suppose, moreover, that due to a number of chance occurrences over the next 300 years, those bits come to compose some non-human animal, such as a dog or a tribble. There's nothing impossible about that. The basic physical bits that compose you are no different from the basic physical bits that compose dogs and tribbles—and trees and rocks and tables, for that matter. If, in the past, $p_1, p_2, p_3, \ldots,$ $p_n$ came to compose you as you are now, they could certainly come to compose a dog or a tribble or some other kind of thing later on. Do you really think that later thing would be *you*? Having the same component bits doesn't imply that the same individual is composed of those bits.

## "Remember ... "

But maybe you think a *person* can survive being decomposed into bits even if a human can't. What?!? That's right: maybe you think that *persons*, like you and I, can survive being broken down into bits because we're not *humans*. Humans are complex physical systems, members of the primate species *Homo sapiens*. They can't survive extensive decomposition. But maybe you and I are not humans, not members of an animal species, not *physical* beings at all. This is what *substance dualists* claim.[6]

According to substance dualists, we have no physical properties or parts. The human you see in the mirror when you fix your hair, put on makeup, or shave isn't really you—when Deanna Troi and Kira Nerys see their faces reflected with the respective guises of a Romulan and a Cardassian, it's merely their *bodies* that have been altered, but Deanna and Kira are still the same *persons*.[7] You might be connected to the human you see in the mirror in some way. You might take a keen interest in what it does and how it's affected by things. You might even treat it as if it's really you; but, according to substance dualists, it isn't. Persons are instead purely *mental* beings. You have mental states such as thoughts, feelings, and perceptions, but according to substance dualists, none of those states are essentially embodied in the physical parts of humans. In fact, it's possible for you to exist without any physical parts at all—a pure mental *spirit*.

Vulcans seem to be substance dualists. They think that they're nonphysical beings that are merely connected to their bodies. At the end of *The Wrath of Khan*, Spock exposes himself to lethal radiation levels in order to save the *Enterprise*. Before doing so, he places his *katra*—his "living spirit"—within McCoy. Later, in *The Search for Spock*, Sarek tells Kirk that the *katra* is Spock himself: "Only his body was in death," Sarek says. "He entrusted you with his very essence, with everything that was not of the body.... It is the Vulcan way when the body's end is near." When Spock's body is regenerated on the planet Genesis, Kirk sets out to return Spock—his *katra*—to that body. If Sarek is right, then Vulcans are not physical beings. A Vulcan's essence is "not of the body." A Vulcan is instead a nonphysical person who's connected to a Vulcan body, and who could be connected to other bodies—just as Spock connected himself to McCoy.

If Vulcans are nonphysical beings, then it's possible for them to use transporters safely, since they're not affected by what happens to a Vulcan body when it enters a transporter. Suppose that Spock is initially connected to Vulcan Body$_1$. When Vulcan Body$_1$ steps into the transporter, it gets disintegrated, and the transporter generates an exact replica, Vulcan Body$_2$. Since Spock, a nonphysical being, is unaffected by the disintegration process, he can be reconnected to Vulcan Body$_2$. So, even if a Vulcan's body gets energized to bits, the Vulcan person—the nonphysical being—remains intact.

What is true of Vulcans could also be true of us: perhaps we too are nonphysical beings who are merely connected to human bodies. The human you see in the mirror isn't really you; you don't really have hair, eyes, or other physical parts; you don't really have a physical location; you can't really get chopped, blown up, or energized to bits. If that's the case, then you could survive a transporter.

Substance dualism, though, has a number of troubling implications. If we persons are nonphysical beings, how are we able to interact with bodies? Physical interaction requires spatial location. When one billiard ball strikes another, that striking happens at a specific location where the surface of one ball impacts the surface of the other. But if you're a nonphysical being, you have no location. How then are you able to interact with a body? Even if we could account for mental–physical interaction, what accounts for each person interacting with only *one* particular body? If Kirk and Spock are both transported simultaneously, why is it that Kirk interacts at the end of the process with Human Body$_2$, while Spock interacts with Vulcan Body$_2$? If we are nonphysical beings, there's no reason to think that any of us are necessarily tied to only our current bodies. It shouldn't require the elaborate alien technology on Camus II for Janice Lester to take control of Kirk's body in "Turnabout Intruder" (TOS).

Furthermore, if substance dualism is true, many of our moral intuitions are blown out the airlock. Why is killing a human so bad? If substance dualism is true, then humans aren't persons; so in killing a human, you're not killing a person, but merely destroying his or her body. It might be more like an act of vandalism—destroying someone's property. Likewise, think about what happens to the *katra* of the young Spock who's been regenerated on Genesis—yes, his mind is simple, but he has one nonetheless, as evidenced by his suffering *pon farr*. Is it destroyed when Spock's *katra* is restored to it? If so, then isn't the Vulcan priestess T'Lar committing murder by destroying the *katra* of the young regenerated Spock?[8]

## "I'm a Doctor, Not a Soul!"

Maybe you can't bring yourself to believe substance dualism. Maybe you're convinced that you're basically a physical being. Are there any views that claim that you're a physical being but deny that you're human? "What Are Little Girls Made Of?" (TOS) suggests one of them. Kirk is held captive on Exo III by the famous scientist Roger Korby, who's creating experimental androids. Korby creates an android replica of Kirk. The android, he says, is "only a machine," but it didn't have to be. "By continuing the process," Korby tells Kirk, "I could've transferred *you*, your very consciousness into that android—your soul, if you wish, all of you."[9] There's a metaphysical view that makes sense out of Korby's basic idea, one known as *constitutionalism*.[10]

Constitutionalism claims that you and I are *constituted by* humans. To say that X is constituted by Y implies at least two things about X and Y: first, X and Y share all the same parts; and, second, X and Y are different things. Imagine that you shape a lump of clay into a statue of Kahless the Unforgettable. There's no part of the statue that isn't part of the lump, and there's no part of the lump that isn't also part of the statue. Yet, despite having all the same parts, constitutionalists say, the statue and the lump are different things because they have different properties. The lump, for instance, existed before the statue did; and, unlike the statue, it can survive being squashed. A thing can't be different from itself, and because the statue and lump have different properties, constitutionalists conclude that they must be different things.

According to constitutionalists, the same is true of you and the human you see in the mirror. You and that human have all the same parts—all the same limbs, digits, internal organs, and so on. Yet you and that human are different things, say constitutionalists, because you and that human have different properties. Unlike that human, for instance, you could survive the complete replacement of your body parts with robotic parts.

Imagine that we begin the process of replacing your human, biological parts with robotic parts—like what the Borg do to Captain Picard in "The Best of Both Worlds" (TNG). Imagine, however, that instead of leaving some of the original human parts behind, we replace *all* of them. Every one of your original human parts is replaced by a robotic part. According to constitutionalists, it's possible for you to survive such a process and become a robot. Even if your brain were replaced by an artificial positronic implant, many constitutionalists reason that so long as the implant copied your brain's neural processes, it would also copy your mental states—in particular, your *first-person perspective* of yourself and the world around you. And, they say, so long as that first-person perspective exists, you'd continue to exist. When, in "Life Support" (DS9), Dr. Bashir replaces half of Vedek Bareil's cerebrum, Bareil feels somewhat different, but his mental states appear to be largely intact. Although Bashir doesn't believe Bareil could survive complete replacement of his cerebrum—telling Kira, "He may look like Bareil. He may even talk like Bareil. But he won't *be* Bareil"—this may only reflect technological limitations that could be overcome in the future. It isn't possible, however, for the human you currently share your parts with to become a robot. That human is essentially a biological being; it can't become a nonbiological being like a robot. Hence, you can survive different kinds of changes than that human can. A thing can't differ from itself, so you and that human must be different things. Constitutionalists conclude that human isn't you; it merely constitutes you.

Suppose you're a constitutionalist. What can you say about transporters? You can say that initially you are constituted by $Human_1$. When $Human_1$ steps into the transporter, it is disintegrated and replaced by $Human_2$. Since $Human_2$ is an exact replica of $Human_1$, you're now constituted by $Human_2$. What ensures that $Human_2$ constitutes you and not a mere replica of you? According to constitutionalists, you're essentially a mental being. Moreover, what makes you the unique individual you are is that you have the mental states you do, and those mental states are determined by the configuration of your physical parts. Since $Human_2$ has the *same* configuration of physical parts as $Human_1$, it must give rise to the same kinds of mental states. And since $Human_1$ and $Human_2$ give rise to the same kinds of mental states, $Human_2$ must constitute you after the transport just as $Human_1$ constituted you before it.

# Would the Real Riker Please Beam Up?

Constitutionalism is an exciting theory that is the basis for many *Star Trek* episodes. But it faces the *fission problem*, which Commander Riker experiences firsthand in "Second Chances" (TNG). Eight years earlier, while serving as a lieutenant aboard the *U.S.S. Potemkin*, Riker was part of an away team sent to Nervala IV. When beaming back to the ship, the transporter beam was split by an atmospheric distortion field, and two replicas of Riker materialized: one aboard the *Potemkin*, the other on the planet's surface. Here's the problem: according to constitutionalists, an individual's mental states make him or her the unique individual that he or she is. But at the moment they materialized, both replicas of Riker were physically indistinguishable. On the constitutionalist view, that means they must be mentally indistinguishable as well: other than having distinct first-person perspectives, they must have exactly the same mental states. Which of them, therefore, is the *real* Riker?

There are four options: (a) the replica on the planet is the *real* one, (b) the replica on the ship is, (c) both of the replicas are, or (d) neither of them is. Commander LaForge endorses option (c). "Both were materialized from complete patterns," he says, so both are real. But this view can't be right. One thing can't be identical to two things. Moreover, the replica on the ship and the one on the planet have different locations and are constituted by different humans. Upon materializing, each has its own unique first-person perspective continuous with that of the original Riker, and each immediately begins accumulating distinct sets of memories over the next eight years. A thing can't differ from itself, so the replica on the ship and the one on the planet cannot *both* be Will Riker. Option (d) must be rejected since the whole idea is to give an account of how you could survive the transport process, and (d) implies that Riker doesn't survive it.[11] That means constitutionalists must endorse either (a) or (b): only one of the two replicas can be the real Riker.

Since the replica on the ship and the replica on the planet are mentally indistinguishable, there seems to be no principled reason to choose one over the other as the *real* Riker. If an individual's mental states make him or her the unique individual that he or she is, and both replicas have mental states that have perfect continuity with Riker's at the moment he tells the *Potemkin*, "Energize," then they're both equally good candidates for being the real Riker. It seems, then, that constitutionalists have no choice but simply to pick one or the other arbitrarily. But in philosophy, being arbitrary just isn't cool.

## "What's So Damn Troublesome about Not Having Died?"

Whether because of the fission problem or for some other reason, constitutionalism might not appeal to you. Maybe you're convinced that you're really human after all. Must you then avoid transporters? Only if you think *survival* requires *identity*. One way of resolving the fission problem without being arbitrary is to claim that both Rikers are equally "survivors" of the original Riker, though neither is *strictly identical* with him.[12] If survival is just as good as identity, then even if the human who comes out of the transporter isn't really the human who went in—your child, your spouse, your best friend—the replica is still indistinguishable from that human, and you could treat that replica in the same way you would've treated the original. The replica would be mentally continuous with the original—continuous enough to count as his or her "survivor."

One problem with this response is that it appears to be incompatible with *love*, for love is *particular*. When you love a person, the object of your love isn't the characteristics the person has, but the person himself or herself. Someone's kindness, sense of humor, intelligence, and other characteristics might be lovable too; but loving a person's characteristics is different from loving the person himself or herself. Other people might have the same characteristics as your beloved, and yet you might not love *them*. While Commander Riker is "flattered ... sort of" by Troi's burgeoning romance with Lieutenant Riker and she admits finding it hard to separate her feelings for the two of them, Troi doesn't love Lieutenant Riker *just because* he has Riker's characteristics. If love is particular in this way, then it would be no comfort knowing that your loved ones had been annihilated and replaced by replicas that had all the same characteristics, for however lovable those characteristics might be, you'd still be deprived of the real objects of your love: the individuals themselves.

*Star Trek* transporters thus confront you with three options: (1) you give up thinking that you're a human, (2) you give up valuing individual identity and love, or else (3) you take a shuttlecraft or other means of transportation, and be thankful that transporters are probably impossible anyway.

# Notes

1. Werner Heisenberg, "über den anschaulichen Inhalt der quantentheoretischen Kinematik und Mechanik," *Zeitschrift für Physik* 43 (1927): 172–98.
2. http://en.memory-alpha.wikia.com/wiki/Heisenberg_compensator (accessed May 27, 2015).
3. Diehard fans of transporters might argue that even if transporters are physically impossible, they aren't *metaphysically* impossible. If the laws of nature were different, and the uncertainty principle didn't obtain, then in such a world transporters would be possible. This argument assumes that it's possible for the laws of nature to be different from what they are in fact. But if properties are powers to produce certain effects, then it's impossible for the laws of nature to be different from what they are in fact. In that case, transporters aren't just physically impossible— they're metaphysically impossible. They can no sooner exist than married bachelors or square circles can.
4. http://en.memory-alpha.wikia.com/wiki/Varon-T_disruptor (accessed May 27, 2015).
5. See Rick Sternbach and Michael Okuda, *Star Trek: The Next Generation Technical Manual* (New York: Pocket Books, 1991), ch. 9.
6. Substance dualism has a venerable history dating back to Plato (427–347 BCE), who defended a version of it in *The Phaedo*. It was defended in late antiquity and the Middle Ages by Neoplatonists, and in the early modern era by René Descartes (1596–1650) in his *Meditations on First Philosophy*. The latter work was the inspiration for contemporary versions of substance dualism such as the one defended by Richard Swinburne in *The Evolution of the Soul* (New York: Oxford University Press, 1986) and in *Mind, Brain, and Free Will* (New York: Oxford University Press, 2013). For a discussion of Swinburne's views, see my "Swinburne on Substances, Properties, and Structures," *European Journal for Philosophy of Religion* 6 (2014): 17–28.
7. See "Face of the Enemy" (TNG) and "Second Skin" (DS9).
8. There are many technical philosophical objections to substance dualism. I discuss them, as well as a variety of competing theories, in my *Philosophy of Mind: A Comprehensive Introduction* (Malden, MA: Wiley-Blackwell, 2011).
9. Similarly, Dr. Ira Graves transferred his consciousness into Data's body in "The Schizoid Man" (TNG). Data's creator, Dr. Noonien Soong, also survived by using the Exo III technology to transfer himself into an android body; David Mack, *Star Trek: The Next Generation— Cold Equations: The Persistence of Memory* (New York: Pocket Books, 2012), ch. 7.

10. Lynne Rudder Baker defends a version of constitutionalism in her *Persons and Bodies: A Constitution View* (New York: Cambridge University Press, 2000).

11. An astute reader may think that Riker *would* have survived the transport process if it had gone normally; he doesn't survive in this case only because he's split in two. This response falters, however, since it assumes that Riker would survive a normal transport process in which his pattern is replicated only once; but, as LaForge notes, both Rikers were produced out of "complete patterns." How could a double success be a failure in which Riker doesn't survive?

12. See Derek Parfit, *Reasons and Persons* (New York: Oxford University Press, 1984), pt. III.

# 15

# Two Kirks, Two Rikers

## Trip McCrossin

"Captain's Log, Stardate 1672.1. Specimen-gathering mission on planet Alfa 177. Unknown to any of us during this time, a duplicate of me, some strange alter ego, had been created by the transporter malfunction." What ensues in "The Enemy Within" (TOS) is an "unusual opportunity to appraise the human mind," Mr. Spock clinically observes, "or to examine, in Earth terms, the roles of good and evil" in the human condition, and how this may clarify the question, "what is it that makes an exceptional leader?"

Human beings have our "negative side," Spock speculates, consisting in our "hostility, lust, violence," as embodied now in Captain Kirk's duplicate; and we have our "positive side, which Earth people express as compassion, love, tenderness," as embodied by the seemingly original Kirk who emerged first from the transporter. After the evil duplicate is discovered, Spock concludes to Dr. McCoy that Kirk's "evil side, if you will, properly controlled and disciplined, is vital to his strength." He then turns to Kirk. "Your negative side removed from you," he says, "the power of command begins to elude you." In rare agreement, McCoy confirms Spock's conclusion, adding, though, that no less important are certain positive qualities the "good" Kirk possesses: "The intelligence, the logic. It appears your half has most of that. And perhaps that's where [humanity's] essential courage comes from."

Given the period in which this episode first aired, and the nature of *Star Trek* as social-political allegory, it's hard not to see the storyline as designed to have viewers reflect critically on the presidency of Lyndon Johnson and the tragic tension between his "Great Society"

*The Ultimate Star Trek and Philosophy*, First Edition. Edited by Kevin S. Decker and Jason T. Eberl.
© 2016 John Wiley & Sons, Ltd. Published 2016 by John Wiley & Sons, Ltd.

aspirations and his escalation of the war in Vietnam. Aside from this provocative historical idea, the episode provides us with an "unusual opportunity to appraise" the longstanding *metaphysical* controversy regarding the nature of *persons*, be they good or evil. And the opportunity is especially rich, given another, quite different, transporter malfunction many years later, one yielding two William T. Rikers in the TNG episode "Second Chances."

## (Gregorian) 1694 to (Stardate) 1672

Even when he's not being split in two, each time Kirk steps into the transporter and says, "Energize," his body is converted from matter into a cohesive energy pattern that's then transmitted somewhere and reconverted back into its original material form. The transport process alone raises questions of human identity and persistence.[1] Yet even without ever having stepped into a transporter, we might wonder along with Kirk whether he remains the *same* through time—that is, whether he maintains his identity despite changing. Over a certain period of time, natural growth dictates that all the cells of Kirk's body are eventually replaced with new ones; and yet it seems perfectly clear to him, and to others interacting with him, that he's the same person even though his body, taken cell by cell, is in fact a *different* body. The Enlightenment philosopher John Locke (1632–1704) didn't think this material change was a challenge to anyone's identity; for he says, in the 1694 edition of *An Essay Concerning Human Understanding*, that who Kirk *is*, as a *person*, doesn't rest on the nature of his body at all. Rather, as "a thinking intelligent being, that has reason and reflection, and can consider itself as itself, the same thinking thing in different times and places," Kirk's identity as a person is a function of his "consciousness, which is inseparable from thinking," and "can extend to actions past or to come," and it can do so, it seems, independently of what becomes of his body.[2]

Kirk would be comfortable with this idea, having himself lived through a version of Locke's strange example of a prince and a cobbler exchanging bodies. In "Turnabout Intruder" (TOS), the *Enterprise* answers a distress call from Camus II, site of an archaeological expedition excavating an ancient civilization directed by an old flame of Kirk's, Dr. Janice Lester. But the distress call is a trap, and Lester has excavated a device that allows her to transfer Kirk's consciousness into her body and vice versa, allowing Lester to assume command of the *Enterprise*. Once the device has done its work, each retains the memories of things experienced in their former body; although Lester has assumed Kirk's body, she has none of his memories of captaining the *Enterprise*, which helps the crew to uncover the ruse eventually. Locke believes that isolating personal identity is important to seeing past acts as either praiseworthy or blameworthy: to whom do we direct our praise or blame—to the one who *remembers* having done the acts (but whose current body isn't associated with them) or the one who has no such memory (but whose current body was the *vehicle* by which the acts were done)? Before her transfer to Kirk's body, Lester had murdered all but one of her research colleagues. So should *Kirk* be held responsible now that he possesses Lester's body? We routinely invoke the idea of personal identity, Locke contends, because it's a *tool* that we need in addressing the moral dimensions of our daily lives: "In personal identity is founded all the right and justice of reward and punishment."[3] This means that we judge Kirk and Lester morally accountable *only* for actions of which they are each *conscious* of having done—regardless of what others may sincerely believe concerning the *bodies* associated with the same actions. That no one may recognize either Kirk in Lester's body, or Lester in Kirk's, is irrelevant. Our job is to uncover the persons *truly* accountable for the actions we praise and blame.[4]

## Being "Half a Man," but Still a Whole "Double"

"Can half a man live?," Kirk pleads in the closing scenes of "The Enemy Within." Depending on how you look at it, he's pleading with both himself and someone else. The episode's inquiry into what makes for an "exceptional leader" relies on making the original and duplicate captains temperamentally opposite, but each is unable to survive without the temperamental characteristics of the other. It also relies on the duplicates being in other respects "doubles"—individual persons in their own right, however defective.

"Apparently," Spock points out to Kirk, his "double, however different in temperament, has your knowledge of the ship, its crew, its devices." Hence, the double's assault on Yeoman Rand, on the basis of Kirk's prior but suppressed attraction to her, which the double describes now as merely "pretending." According to Locke's view of personal identity, each of the doubles has the original Kirk's knowledge and memories, which would seem to make *both* of them identical with the original. Yet immediately upon their creation, each begins crafting new memories—some more lascivious and violent in the one case. Locke's view is that this makes each of the doubles a person in his own right after the transporter mishap.

Given Locke's perspective that the identity of persons needs only *continuity of consciousness* in order to persist through time, the question arises, what if a person's consciousness were somehow reproduced in several bodies? Wouldn't this result in distinct persons who are yet identical with an earlier one? This would violate a logical law known as the *transitivity of identity*: if A=B and A=C, then B=C, where A is, say, Kirk before he beams up from Alfa 177, and B and C are the "good" and "evil" Kirks whom the transporter malfunction produces. Since the two Kirks each have different conscious experiences once they're separated—one remembers attacking Yeoman Rand, while the other one doesn't—they can't be the same person; yet the law of transitivity of identity says that they must be. This poses a serious problem—some would say an insuperable one—for Locke's view of personal identity.

There are three competing approaches to resolving this problem. First is the suggestion that *both* Kirks survive *as the same person* who was beamed off Alfa 177. Second is the idea that *neither of them* does, in the sense that the Kirks who emerge from the malfunctioning transporter aboard the *Enterprise* are not only distinct from one another, but also distinct from the person beamed off the planet. Finally, there's the possibility that *just one of them* does, the other being an "imposter" of some sort, as the duplicate is initially described before the nature and effect of the transporter malfunction become apparent.

The first alternative seems to be in keeping with the storyline. Even while the crew is understandably confused, Spock and McCoy rally unequivocally around the "positive" Kirk because he's *been* the captain all along. But when the duplicate bellows in the closing scenes, "I'm the captain!," he too seems to be asserting something true. "Isn't it obvious?," he continues. "You know who I am." "Yes," answers the positive Kirk, "I know," and indeed they both "know" by virtue of remembering all the same experiences Kirk had prior to beaming up from Alfa 177. While this would seem to be in keeping with the storyline—because two different things can't be the same as a third—it's at odds with the logic of identity.

The second alternative is more in keeping with the logic of identity, but also more at odds with the storyline. If neither the positive nor the negative Kirk is identical with the Kirk beamed off Alfa 177, then that

Kirk no longer exists and duplication is effectively a form of death for the original Kirk. But this isn't what the storyline implies, as noted above. There's also the strange dog-like creature, similarly duplicated into temperamentally opposite doubles, which Spock calls "the animal" in the singular, referring to the pair together. Finally, the episode concludes with the positive and negative Kirks reentering the repaired transporter and being reunited into a single Kirk. But if the positive and negative Kirks did not share a personal identity with the original one, the newly emerged Kirk would be yet a *fourth* Kirk—akin to the newly created person, Tuvix, formed out of the combined transporter patterns of Tuvok and Neelix ("Tuvix," VOY).

The third alternative seems relatively in keeping with both the storyline and the logic of identity, but it is still not without problems. It supports giving greater legitimacy to the positive Kirk than to the negative one. Even if the crew is confused, Spock and McCoy rally unequivocally around the positive Kirk. But if this accident had occurred in the parallel universe depicted in "Mirror, Mirror" (TOS), where the captain's personality is more defined by "hostility, lust, violence," then the Spock and McCoy of that universe would've just as likely rallied around the negative Kirk. Similarly, if the transporter's malfunction had beamed *only* one or the other of the Kirks aboard (the other's pattern being lost altogether), there'd be no worries about personal identity involved at all. But can being the same person over time really be just a matter of there not being a better candidate who's competing for the title?

This episode, designed to challenge us to think more carefully about the nature of leadership, also challenges our understanding of the nature of personal identity. While setting aside the second alternative above (that Kirk doesn't survive after the transporter mishap), it favors an unspecified mix of the first and third—and in doing so challenges us to wonder whether this "mixed" view is philosophically coherent. We learn that leadership is most effective in those whose positive and negative qualities coexist in a balanced, harmonious relationship. Each of the Kirks will perish without the qualities of the other, even if the positive Kirk seems more like the original than does his counterpart. When the transporter ultimately puts them back together, we understand this to be a *re*unification that brings us *our* Kirk back—a little older, a little wiser, but ultimately the same Kirk who was beamed off the planet earlier in the day.

All of this is facilitated by our competing Kirks being conspicuously different. But things get more complicated if we have competing doubles who, at least at the point of duplication, are indistinguishable, as with the two Rikers in *The Next Generation*'s "Second Chances."

## Two Whole Rikers

"Captain's Log, Stardate 46915.2. The *Enterprise* is orbiting Nervala IV, waiting for an opportunity to retrieve scientific data left there by Starfleet researchers when they were forced to evacuate eight years ago," during which time "a massive energy surge in the distortion field around the planet" led the starship *Potemkin*'s transporter chief to employ an "interesting approach" in beaming then-Lieutenant Riker aboard by initiating a second containment beam. The operation appeared successful insofar as Riker materialized on the *Potemkin*'s transporter pad. Yet, at the same time, a second Riker materialized on the planet as one of the containment beams was deflected by the distortion field. Unknown to the *Potemkin* crew, Lieutenant Riker was abandoned on Nervala IV, where he lived alone for eight years, only to come face to face with "himself" in the form of Commander Riker in "Second Chances."

"Which one is real?," Commander Riker asks. "Both," Geordi LaForge answers, as "both materialized from a complete pattern." "Up until that moment," Doctor Crusher adds, "you were the same person." "But of course," Captain Picard adds in turn, "as you and Lieutenant Riker have lived very different lives for the past eight years, you are now very different people." As different as they are now *from one another*, both Rikers' lives have nonetheless carried on from that common moment when they *were the same person*.

The second of the three alternatives above—that the original Riker has not survived at all—seems just as unattractive in this case as it was in Kirk's. But if the leadership allegory of "The Enemy Within" called for a compromise between the first and third alternatives, the third appears unavailable in this episode. We may prefer "our" Riker to the other now (although Counselor Troi has difficulty sorting out her own feelings concerning each of them), but we would've been unable to distinguish them shortly after the time of duplication. How can only *one* of them be identical to the original Riker when nothing allows us to tell which one it might be?

But the first alternative still has a serious flaw because it's at odds with the logic of identity. Riker and Troi aside, the *Enterprise*-D crew seems to have little anxiety about this. "I suppose it's little like meeting someone's twin," Picard suggests disarmingly of the Rikers' experience of one another, "but no matter how strange it may seem to us, we now have two Will Rikers on board, and as Lieutenant Riker will be with us for several days, I think we should do everything we can to make him comfortable and welcome." For Commander Riker and Counselor Troi, however, encountering Lieutenant Riker offers them an "unusual opportunity to appraise" the nature of romantic love. At the time of the Nervala IV mission eight years earlier, Riker and Troi were involved romantically, but afterward Riker was promoted for "exceptional valor in the evacuation of the research station" and "chose to make his career a priority." As a result, their feelings for one another waned. Now, with the reemergence of Lieutenant Riker, there's an opportunity for him to rekindle Troi's feelings. Commander Riker warns her, though, "If he had gotten off the planet instead of me, don't you think he would have made the same choices that I made?" The episode ends with Lieutenant Riker doing exactly that, leaving the *Enterprise* to serve on the *Gandhi*. The striking similarities in appearance, personality, emotional attachments, and, ultimately, important life choices support the idea that *both* Commander and Lieutenant Riker are the *same person* as the original Riker, despite violating the logic of identity.

Perhaps, as persons, we should be less worried about our *identity* over time and more focused on our *survival*. Derek Parfit, referring to his own, hypothetical version of the situation in which Riker finds himself, contends that the "distinction between successive selves can be made by reference, not to the branching of psychological continuity," which seems to threaten identity, "but to the degrees of psychological connectedness," which seems otherwise to support survival regardless of identity. "Since this connectedness is a matter of degree," he continues, "the drawing of these distinctions can be left to the choice of the speaker and be allowed to vary from context to context."[5] What's remarkable about "Second Chances" isn't so much that it reflects Parfit's interpretation of a Lockean perspective, but that in its use of the malfunctioning transporter motif in support of its romantic love allegory, it makes it seem so *uncontroversial*.

## Kirks and Rikers and What's in the Bathwater

In the 1960s, *Star Trek* was revolutionary television. The reinvention of the duplication challenge to Locke's perspective on personal identity, during this same period, was also revolutionary. In this context, Parfit's defense of it in terms of the idea that "what matters in survival need not be one-to-one" correspondence between identical persons over time was no less revolutionary. Revolutions, though, if successful, become less revolutionary over time. Worries that nagged us at first nag us less eventually, if at all. We may miss being excited, in other words, but we also welcome the comfort; we may become complacent. This may explain the difference in TOS's and TNG's solutions to similar problems.

People who recall those first episodes of the original series going boldly where no one had gone before have likely continued to enjoy the franchise as the decades have rolled on, even while missing that "new starship" smell. The smaller group of us who recall the appearance of Parfit's original proposal likely still engage in the debate about personal identity that's continued in its wake but, in the same spirit, miss that "new theory" smell. The difference in tone, if not in substance, between "Second Chances" and "The Enemy Within" brings together these two sorts of complacency. But while comfort can be a good thing, all things considered, complacency's often not.

There's at least one serious worry, that is, which seems to get less and less play as time goes on. Does the idea that what matters in personal *survival* needn't include personal *identity* mean that personal identity doesn't matter *at all*? If Parfit has successfully scrubbed questions of personal survival clean of questions of personal identity, as is often advertised, should we just go ahead and throw the latter out with the proverbial bathwater? On the face of it, it would seem not. If our survival in spite of the "branching" of persons (like transporter mistakes) is just a matter of sufficient psychological connectedness, then if there were no branching, wouldn't we survive then *as identical* with our past selves? There's an apparent tension here that takes us back to the pre-Parfit debate, and reminds us to continue to worry about something we seem to have been lulled into not worrying about so much anymore.

During the eight years that Lieutenant Riker was stranded on Nervala IV, no one, himself included, knew about the deflection of the second containment beam during the evacuation. As far as everyone was concerned, there was only one Riker. The "mixed" view suggested when the second Riker is discovered suggests to us, on the one hand, that there are "two Will Rikers aboard," as Picard says, the implication being that *both* survive as the original. LaForge insists that "both materialized from a complete pattern." Dr. Crusher adds that, until that point, "you [two] were the same person," and she's speaking to Commander Riker, saying just what she would say if she'd been speaking to Lieutenant Riker. On the other hand, while Troi comes to contemplate entering into a relationship with the newly emerged Lieutenant Riker, in the end we seem to be led to believe that of the two, Commander Riker is somehow the better candidate for *being* the same as the *Potemkin*'s Lieutenant Riker—so much so that, as Lieutenant Riker readies to leave the *Enterprise* for his new assignment aboard the *Gandhi*, we learn that he's decided he's no longer Lieutenant *Will* Riker, but rather Lieutenant *Thomas* Riker.

What's odd here, though, is that if *Will* Riker is now killed, or if he had never emerged from the transporter in the first place, eight years earlier, then *Thomas* would not only survive as the original Will, but also presumably do so *as identical* with him, being the only available candidate. But *how* can Thomas, being identical with the original *Potemkin* Riker, depend on the existence (or lack of existence) of some other thing in the world, namely, the Will who's been aboard the *Enterprise* for the last six years? That is, why does the life of the *Enterprise* Riker make any difference to the *identity* of Thomas Riker with the Will Riker who stepped into the *Potemkin*'s transporter all those years ago? What's odd, in other words, is this. First, the episode clearly suggests, and we seem now complacently to accept, that Will and Thomas both *survive* as the original Riker. Second, assuming they do, neither can be *identical* with the original, as the logic of identity just as clearly dictates. Third, intuitively, each would nonetheless be *identical* with the original, were he instead a *sole* survivor. Finally, this would seem to mean that personal identity is no longer an *intrinsic* property, as it would seem to be—one we have *solely* in our own right, independently of the existence of others—but instead an *extrinsic* one. And, as David Wiggins rightly pointed out just a year after "Enemy Within" aired, this is rather *counter*intuitive. According to what he called the "only *a* and *b*" rule, if *a* and *b* are *the same thing*, in the sense that while we may refer to them in these two ways, still there's just *the one thing*, then *its* existence surely can't depend on the distinct existence of some *other* thing.[6] The complacency threatened by the episode's resolution seems, interestingly, to be undermined by its own structure. This is not to say that there's an obvious resolution here (or in "The Enemy Within," or in the philosophical literature). But our attention to the episode has brought us to a renewed sense that the debate about personal identity and survival is far from over.

Maybe we shouldn't be surprised to find a "To be continued" here. "Second Chances," as a lesson about romantic love, ends inconclusively, but with an eye to the future. Thomas, leaving the *Enterprise*, is newly posted to the *Gandhi* and hoping that Troi is joining him, but it turns out that she's not—"not yet," at least. While he admits that he's not surprised, he also insists that he's not giving up hope. "I waited a long time," he muses, and so "I guess I can wait a little longer." And so it is for us as well. We've waited a long time to sort out the relation between survival and identity: centuries since Locke first got our attention, decades since "The Enemy Within," Wiggins, and Parfit did in turn. As long as we resist complacency about the issues in question, and keep working at them, surely we too can wait a little longer.[7]

## Notes

1. These questions are explored in William Jaworksi's chapter in this volume (Chapter 14).
2. John Locke, *An Essay Concerning Human Understanding*, ed. Peter H. Nidditch (New York: Oxford University Press, 1975), bk. II, ch. 27, §9.
3. Ibid, bk. II, ch. 27, §26.
4. This same issue arises in the DS9 episode, "Dax," in which Jadzia Dax is tried for an alleged crime committed by her previous host, Curzon Dax. While Jadzia's body wasn't the vehicle by which the crime was allegedly committed, the Dax symbiont with which she's physically and consciously conjoined would carry the memory of the alleged deed if in fact Curzon has done it.
5. Derek Parfit, "Personal Identity," *Philosophical Review* 80:1 (1971): 3–27.
6. David Wiggins, *Identity and Spatio-Temporal Continuity* (London: Blackwell, 1971). The rule in question, and personal identity in general, are addressed in additional detail in Wiggins's *Sameness and Substance* (Oxford: Oxford University Press, 1980), and *Sameness and Substances Renewed* (Cambridge: Cambridge University Press, 2001).
7. I'd like thank John Perry and Carol Rovane for all that they've taught me, personally and through their writing, about the nature of personal identity. Of course, though, neither bears any responsibility for what I've done with their insights and encouragement. I'd also like to thank the editors for helpfully drawing attention to the TOS episode "Mirror, Mirror"; DS9 episode "Dax"; and VOY episode "Tuvix," and more generally for their patience and understanding, far above and beyond the call, in the process of completing the chapter's initial draft, and in the editorial process subsequently.

# 16

# Data, Kant, and Personhood; or, Why Data Is Not a Toaster

*Nina Rosenstand*

In an early episode of TNG, the android Data is about to be dismantled by a scientist and possibly killed for the sake of research.
Does Data have the right to refuse to undergo the "procedure"? Not
if he isn't recognized as a *person*. But what is a person? In *Is Data
Human?*, Richard Hanley suggests that the *Star Trek* universe operates with three distinct meanings of the concept *human*: one refers
to someone born of human parents, with human DNA—the *biological* meaning. The second picks out any *humanoid*, any being who
shares the basic human qualities of self-propelled mobility and intelligence, but above all has the same general psychological makeup as
a biological human—the *psychological* meaning. The third and most
interesting meaning of "human" refers to any being, regardless of
appearance or origin, who's capable of asking itself questions about
right and wrong—the *moral* meaning. In other words, a *moral* being is
a *person*.[1] Within the *Star Trek* universe, any person deserves inalienable rights and respect from other persons. But from where did this
concept arise, and how far-reaching is it?

Within the body of *Star Trek* television series and movies, the concept of personhood stands out in one particular episode that may just
be the "best episode ever." Its title, "The Measure of a Man," evokes
the famous saying by Greek pre-Socratic philosopher Protagoras, who
claimed, "Man is the measure of all things." The irony is that the
"measure" here doesn't imply that everything is *relative* to a human
being, which seems to be what Protagoras meant, and what's at stake
isn't the personhood of a human, or even a humanoid, but an *android*.

*The Ultimate Star Trek and Philosophy*, First Edition. Edited by Kevin S. Decker and Jason T. Eberl.
© 2016 John Wiley & Sons, Ltd. Published 2016 by John Wiley & Sons, Ltd.

## "The Measure of a Man"

Think back to the second season of TNG. Data is considered by his colleagues to be a full member of the crew, although he often demonstrates a lack of understanding of quirky human customs, such as giftwrapping. We sense that his greatest wish is to understand humanity and become a human being. Of course that can never be, because Data is artificial; but the question of whether Data is a *person* will be resolved in "The Measure of a Man." A visiting scientist, Dr. Bruce Maddox, approaches Captain Picard with a request to take Data away from the *Enterprise* in order to examine his unique positronic brain and potentially create countless androids like him that could be distributed to each ship in Starfleet and assigned to missions that are too dangerous for a crew of humans and humanoids. This research project involves dismantling Data and downloading his memories into a storage bank, with the risk of permanent loss of consciousness. Data refuses to comply and resigns from Starfleet. But does he actually have the right to refuse and resign, or is he the *property* of Starfleet with no more rights than the *Enterprise*'s computer? A hearing is held to determine Data's future in which Picard speaks for Data. Commander Riker is forced to speak for Maddox. He's presented with the ultimatum by the judge, Captain Philippa Louvois: either he takes on the job in good faith or she'll summarily rule that "Data is a toaster" to be handed over to Maddox.

Riker must take his job as prosecutor seriously despite Data being his good friend. Indeed, he successfully shows that Data is a machine that can be turned on and off, and he even condescendingly calls Data "Pinocchio," reminding us of the old story of the wood puppet who wants to be a real boy. Picard is devastated by Riker's compelling argument and seeks advice from Guinan, who opens his eyes to the ultimate implication of declaring Data the property of Starfleet: the creation of multitudes of Datas without any rights—in other words, a new breed of *slaves*. This gives Picard renewed energy and moral strength to return to the hearing.

Picard asks Maddox how he would define a person with a right to self-determination—in *Star Trek* terminology, a "sentient" being.[2] Maddox doesn't hesitate: a sentient being is one who is *intelligent, self-aware*, and *conscious*. So, asks Picard, is Data intelligent? Of course he is, since he can perform multiple simultaneous computations in his positronic brain. Is he self-aware? Without a doubt, since he talks about his concern about his life being at stake. But is he conscious?

Are two out of three criteria enough? In the future, Starfleet will be judged based on this decision, because this is where the fate of all future "Datas" will be determined—whether they will be persons or mere slaves without rights. The judge, Captain Philippa Louvois, persuaded by the logic of Picard's argument, rules in Data's favor and leaves the question of consciousness open, because it's a question for Data himself to explore—whether Data has a *soul* is a question best left for philosophers, she says! Maddox, finally, also sees Data as a person and not just a thing, referring to him as "he" instead of "it."[3]

## Pinocchios and Future Datas

"Pinocchio" has become a "real boy"—at least under Federation law. And as Pinocchio had the magic of the Blue Fairy, his fairy godmother, Data has the wisdom of Guinan—who's not only a watchful godmother for Data in this case, but also in many instances throughout *The Next Generation*. The moral personhood of both Pinocchio and Data really comes from *within* rather than because of a legal decision: they both learn to be "brave, truthful and unselfish," and "with conscience as their guide,"[4] a moral measure of a human.

Captain Louvois's ruling becomes a watershed for all Starfleet decisions concerning the rights of artificial intelligences. Instances in which her decision is invoked as precedent include Picard's argument to Admiral Haftel that Data's rights as a parent to the android Lal ought to be respected in "The Offspring" (TNG) and Data's recognition in "The Quality of Life" (TNG) that non-humanoid-looking "exocomps" may become self-aware and thereby have rights. Data's precedent extends even to the rights of holographic entities like the Doctor on *Voyager* ("Author, Author," VOY).

Guinan and Picard, arguing for Data's right to self-determination, have succeeded on two fronts. For one thing, the concept of personhood has been expanded from human/humanoid to cover many other conceivable life forms, even artificial ones. For another, Louvois's ruling links the concept of personhood with the right not to be used merely for a purpose, even the pursuit of some greater good. There's a philosophical precedent for both arguments.

## Rational Beings as Ends-in-Themselves

The philosophical underpinnings of Louvois's judgment are found in the ethics of Immanuel Kant (1724–1804). Kant suggests that a truly moral action is one based on a principle that we can frame as a *universal* moral principle for everyone to follow—every truly moral action implies a *duty*. Simply doing good and having nice intentions isn't enough—you have to reason out whether your intention could become a principle guiding the moral decision making of *everyone* in a similar situation. The method by which we identify such a principle is known as the *categorical imperative*.[5] According to Kant, there's no excuse for failing to do your duty according to a moral principle, because a rational person couldn't want everyone else using the same excuse and getting out of their duty—because in that case, who would be there for you when you count on them?

Furthermore, Kant says, as a rational being, you wouldn't want to be treated with disrespect by others. Nobody wants to be reduced to a tool, used by someone else for their own purposes, even if those purposes might be benign and end up benefiting others. Rational beings should be treated as *persons*, with respect for their inherent *dignity* as such, and never treated "merely as a means to an end."[6] Of course, we sometimes have to treat each other as some kind of tool or facilitator: we call the plumber when our toilet won't flush, we go to work and do services for strangers and get paid, and we take classes from professors (professors teach classes for students), all using each other, in a sense, to earn a living, get jobs done, or learn skills. Kant wouldn't say that such relationships are inappropriate. It is possible to temporarily use a person's services without reducing them to being "merely" a tool if we acknowledge their self-worth, dignity, and humanity—in other words, their *personhood*.

That's what Kant calls treating someone as an "end in himself" (or herself). To underscore this, he creates a *practical* version of his categorical imperative: "Act in such a way as to treat humanity, whether in your own person or in that of anyone else, always as an end and never merely as a means."[7] Here, Kant has provided an early concept of *human rights*. If we're being reduced to mere tools for someone's personal goals or some social benefit, or we're treating others that way, one of the deepest, most fundamental moral rules is being violated. This is the rule that obliges us to treat rational beings with respect, simply because they're rational beings.[8]

Around the same time as Kant, another influential view of moral actions was being developed: *utilitarianism*. Jeremy Bentham (1748–1832) argues that the primary goal of moral action, on both small and large scales, is to create the maximum amount of pleasure for the maximum number of people, known as the Principle of Utility or the Greatest Happiness Principle.[9] The Principle of Utility is appealing because it recognizes that human beings all want to escape pain and unhappiness, and all want to obtain happiness and pleasure. Whereas Kant's categorical imperative prohibits reducing a person to a tool, Bentham's utilitarianism allows such reduction for the sake of maximum happiness for the maximum number.[10] Or, as Spock puts it, "the needs of the many outweigh the needs of the few."[11]

## Is Data an End in Himself, or Merely a Means to an End?

Is Picard a Kantian? In "The Measure of a Man" at least, he is.[12] Is Maddox a utilitarian? One might think so. He wishes to create great benefits for Starfleet, resulting in safer conditions for humans and humanoids working in space, by subjecting a smaller group of beings—engineered Datas—to various dangers. Even when Data explains that he doesn't want to risk losing his life in the research process, the fear of one is outweighed by the potential benefits to the many. However, Maddox also reveals himself to be a Kantian, because he wouldn't suggest sacrificing any "sentient" crewmember for the sake of Starfleet. *Both* Maddox and Picard acknowledge only *rational* beings as persons. It's just that their definitions of who or what counts as "rational"—or "sentient"—differ. We thus return to Hanley's definitions of "human." Maddox sees a "sentient being" (read: *sapient, rational* being) as a *biological* or *psychological* human or humanoid, and thus fails to see Data as a sentient *moral agent*. However, Kant anticipated Data's situation, arguing that *any rational being* should be treated as an end in himself or herself. Data is certainly a rational being—and, for Kant, *any* rational being will be able to understand the basic principles of the categorical imperative and thus merit respect as a morally *autonomous* being. So, in Kant's view, we have an obligation to accept aliens and robots as persons and moral agents, as long as they're *rational*.[13]

If Maddox had been a pure utilitarian and Louvois had agreed with him, Data's personhood would've been irrelevant. From a purely utilitarian perspective, as long as greatest happiness for the greatest number has been produced, it does not matter who suffers—human, humanoid, or any other kind of being. From a Kantian perspective, however, since no rational being should ever be used merely as a means to an end, Data, or anyone else, should never be reduced to a mere tool or a slave in violation of their personal dignity, even if it could benefit Starfleet to have an army of Datas at the ready.

## The Bigger Picture

At this point, someone might object that the Data's story is "just a story" and that it'll probably be quite a while before any android/gynoid/robot/fembot can pass the Turing test and be considered conscious, so the question of robotic personhood seems overly hypothetical.[14] Stories, though, are never "just" stories. They are also mirrors of our own lives and carry messages of values and responsibilities beyond their fictional universe.[15] And besides, we'd better be prepared for the day when androids demand rights, whether or not they can *prove* they're conscious. Furthermore, as Maddox is willing to consider Data as a mere tool, so too have humans in most of recorded history been willing to regard certain types of fellow humans as mere tools. The story of Data's fight for recognition as a person is thus a metaphor for the universal quest for social equality, for being a part of humanity with recognized rights. "The Measure of a Man" takes its place in the world of fiction not only along groundbreaking sci-fi stories about robots and aliens such as *I, Robot* (based on a collection of stories by Isaac Asimov), *Blade Runner* (based on a Philip K. Dick novel), *Bicentennial Man*, *District 9*, *E.T.*, *Alien Nation*, *AI: Artificial Intelligence*, and *2001: A Space Odyssey*, but also along mainstream fictional and nonfictional stories of oppressed or disenfranchised humans seeking recognition as fellow human beings.[16] "The Measure of a Man" looks ahead to the future, but it also looks back to our past, and resonates in our collective consciousness. That's why this TNG episode about Data's personhood has become a television classic.

## Notes

1. Richard Hanley, *Is Data Human? The Metaphysics of Star Trek* (New York: Harper Collins, 1998), 10–12.
2. It's become customary in science fiction to use the term *sentience* to describe a being with intelligence, a thinking being. Unfortunately, the original meaning of the term is a being who (or which) can *feel* or *sense*, in particular pain and pleasure. The appropriate philosophical

term would be *sapience*, the ability to think. But as long as we all know what Picard means, we can go along with the "sentience" misnomer.

3. Maddox eventually evolves to become a *defender* of the rights of sentient (sapient) androids, including those of Data's "brother" B-4; see David Mack, *Star Trek: The Next Generation—Cold Equations: The Persistence of Memory* (New York: Pocket Books, 2012), ch. 20.

4. *Pinocchio* (Los Angeles: Walt Disney Studios, 1940).

5. Immanuel Kant, *Groundwork for the Metaphysics of Morals*, 19–20: www.earlymoderntexts.com/pdfs/kant1785chapter2.pdf (accessed June 1, 2015).

6. Ibid., 28–9.

7. Ibid., 29.

8. Before we get too enthusiastic about this principle, which does indeed demand respect for anybody who qualifies as a thinking being, I must add that Kant, in what we might call a blunder of a logical fallacy—the false dichotomy or false dilemma—declares that either you're rational being, a *person*, or you're not, and are just a *thing* that can be used merely as a means to an end. It wasn't until Kant published his *Metaphysics of Morals* (1797) that he added a third option, and thus saved infants, toddlers, severely mentally disabled humans, and other human beings with diminished rational capacity from being labeled mere "things."

9. See Jeremy Bentham, *An Introduction to the Principles of Moral and Legislation* (Oxford: Clarendon Press, 1879; orig. 1789).

10. Another aspect of the Principle of Utility that differs from Kant's moral philosophy and its focus on the rational being is that Bentham widens the scope to *any creature* that can feel pleasure and pain (the true meaning of *sentience*). Thus, utilitarianism becomes the first moral philosophy to include nonhuman animal suffering as morally relevant; see Peter Singer, *Animal Liberation* (New York: Harper Collins, 1975).

11. For further analysis of utilitarianism as depicted throughout *Star Trek*, see Gregory Littmann's chapter in this volume.

12. In "Justice" (TNG), Picard rescues young Wesley from execution on a rule-based planet because of breaking a rule (damaging a plant), by pointing out to the local, very Kantian population that "any mature system of rules must allow for exceptions."

13. On the other hand, Kant doesn't allow for the possibility that *nonhuman animals* could be morally relevant, because he doesn't recognize them as rational. While TNG often goes in a Kantian direction, the writers of TNG weren't afraid to add issues of animal welfare to the moral spectrum—think of Data considering his pet cat, Spot, as a "true and valued friend" worthy of a sonnet ("Schisms" (TNG)).

14. The mathematician Alan Turing devised a test ("Computing Machinery and Intelligence" *Mind* 49 (1950): 433–60) by which a human

test subject tries to determine whether the "person" with whom he or she is playing a computer game is actually a human or a computer. Recently, the programming of computers has become so sophisticated that human test subjects weren't able to tell, in every case, whether they were confronting a person or a computer. They actually ascribed emotional answers to computers and assumed that some humans sounded as cold as computers, and that was without the computers being self-aware (to our knowledge!).

15. For reflection on this point, see the introduction to *Star Trek and Philosophy*, ed. Jason T. Eberl and Kevin S. Decker (Chicago: Open Court, 2008).

16. Additional discussion of the metaphysical and moral status of artificially intelligent entities, with particular reference to Hal-9000 and the robotic boy David in *A.I.*, can be found in Jason T. Eberl, "'Please Make Me a Real Boy': The Prayer of the Artificially Intelligent," in *The Philosophy of Stanley Kubrick*, ed. Jerold J. Abrams (Lexington: University Press of Kentucky, 2007).

# 17

# Humans, Androids, Cyborgs, and Virtual Beings: All aboard the *Enterprise*

## *Dennis M. Weiss*

Putting aside any heated debate over the identity of the *first* episode of TOS (by airdate? production order? pilot one? pilot two?), for the sake of discussion, let's go with "Where No Man Has Gone Before."[1] Besides being the series' second-chance pilot, it institutes Kirk's familiar voiceover from the opening credits of TOS and significantly featured Kirk's best friend, Gary Mitchell, who becomes godlike after the ship passes through the galactic barrier. Mitchell promises his fellow ESPer, Elizabeth Dehner, miraculous powers: "To be like God, to have the power to make the world anything you want it to be." Of course, we know the result. The episode ends with Kirk recording his Captain's Log: "Add to official losses, Doctor Elizabeth Dehner. Be it noted she gave her life in performance of her duty. Lieutenant Commander Gary Mitchell, same notation." Kirk tells Spock, "I want his service record to end that way. He didn't ask for what happened to him."

Having been transformed into a god, Mitchell loses his humanity and ultimately his life. "Where No Man … " is just one of several early TOS episodes that involve stories of transformation that raise questions about the humanity of an individual. "Charlie X" features a human foundling raised by aliens unable to integrate back into human society. The salt-craving alien of "The Man Trap" is able to shapeshift and take on the guise of different human beings. "What Are Little Girls Made Of?" presents a classic *Star Trek* take on a human being becoming technological (Roger Korby) and a machine striving to become human (Andrea).

*The Ultimate Star Trek and Philosophy*, First Edition. Edited by Kevin S. Decker and Jason T. Eberl.
© 2016 John Wiley & Sons, Ltd. Published 2016 by John Wiley & Sons, Ltd.

These tales of transformation connect *Star Trek* to a history of stories going back at least to the ancient Greeks. According to the philosopher Martha Nussbaum, a central preoccupation of Greek myth and morality was stories about transformations from and to the human. Such stories appeal to the audience's imagination to judge what makes the difference between humanity and its absence: "stories of communal self-definition and self-clarification, told to humans (especially to young ones) in order to initiate them into ... the way of life that is constituted by the boundaries that the stories display. By the beast on the one hand, the god on the other."[2]

In its fifty years of robots, androids, cyborgs, and alien others on the small and big screens, *Star Trek* has played a function not unlike that of Greek myth. Whether dealing with actual Greek gods such as Apollo, salt-craving beasts and Hortas, or hive minds and androids, *Star Trek* fashions moderns myths that provoke reflection on what it means to be human and transformations that either preserve or destroy one's humanity. Today, our understanding of what it means to be human is being challenged by developments in a variety of scientific and technological fields, including artificial intelligence, genetic engineering, robotics, and nanotechnology. Journalist Joel Garreau wonders whether, due to such rapid technological innovations, human nature itself will change: "Will we soon pass some point where we are so altered by our imaginations and inventions as to be unrecognizable to Shakespeare or the writers of the ancient Greek plays?"[3] In the context of this question, *Star Trek* becomes an ideal vehicle for modern narratives exploring the nature of being human in a technological age.

## To Be a Man, or at Least a Mind

When thinking about *Star Trek*'s underlying philosophy of human nature, critics typically have taken one of two paths. The first is to simply align *Star Trek* with a tradition of dualistic thinking about human nature that runs from René Descartes (1596–1650) to Alan Turing (1912–1954) to Ray Kurzweil's efforts to upload his mind to cyberspace. This first path can be found in Richard Hanley's book *Is Data Human?* in which the issue of Data's humanity is resolved by referring to a Cartesian model in which humans are rational minds and our bodies are simpy superflous appendages to those minds.[4] The other path is drawn from more recent traditions in philosophy, including cultural studies, poststructuralism, and colonial studies, and can be found in the essays collected in *Enterprise Zones*, whose authors take *Star Trek* to task for its humanist, Enlightenment, utopian, colonialist, and bourgeois ideology.[5] From both paths, *Star Trek* looks pretty typical in its insistence on an Enlightenment model of human nature, in which *rationality* and *autonomy* are the predominant characteristics. This model of human nature says that the *mind* is the locus of individuality and self-identity, whereas the body, passions, and the intersubjectivity of persons are marginalized. Human nature is a historically fixed and universal property, not fundamentally created or altered by our social circumstances.

While there's some truth to this charge, like any sufficiently complex text, *Star Trek* supports multiple interpretations. If we turn to some of *Star Trek*'s beings who aren't quite human and who, in their efforts at transformation, provoke reflection on what it means to be human, we can see an alternative view of human nature implied in *Star Trek*. This view is based on the importance of relationships, interdependence, parenting, responsibility, emotion, and the bodily experience—what might be thought of as a more *feminist* model of human nature.[6] We can see the feminist model in the long processes of development of the android Data, liberated Borg drone Seven of Nine, and *Voyager's* holographic Doctor, and their struggle to understand, if not finally attain, humanity. As we watch these characters attempt to understand what it is to be human, we're given a lesson in which *Star Trek* affirms the importance of human embodiment, emotions, bonds of love between family and friends, and culture. All this suggests that humanity is more an *achievement*—one that's increasingly undertaken in the company of technological others—than an essential, unchanging property.

## "You Need to Learn to Play"

In "Charlie X" (TOS), the eponymous character is a teenager who spent his formative years being raised by purely mental entities, the Thasians. Endowed by them with incredible powers he needed to survive, Charlie ultimately finds it impossible to integrate with humans once he's reunited with his own kind. As the Thasians take Charlie away, he implores his fellow humans, "Don't let them take me. I can't even touch them. Janice! They can't feel! Not like you. They don't love!" Having been raised by aliens and transformed by unique powers, this space-age wolf child finds it impossible to recover his humanity. From its inception, *Star Trek* seems aware that interpersonal bonds, feelings such as love and care, and simple bodily touch are central to our humanity.

Charlie may look human and possess the right DNA, but having lost his family, he hasn't been schooled in humanity. We see interesting parallels with Data, Seven of Nine, and the Doctor, all of whom have tenuous relationships to their "biological family." For an android, Data has a rather full family tree. His great-great-grandfather is Arik Soong, and his grandfather is Ira Graves. He has a father (Noonien Soong), mother (Juliana Tainer), a brother with whom to act out sibling rivalry (Lore), and eventually even a daughter (Lal) and another, more simpleminded, brother (B-4).[7] Unfortunately, Data's memory of his early "childhood" with his parents was erased by Juliana Tainer, and soon after his parents had to flee the Crystalline Entity and leave Data behind.[8] Data isn't conscious of any formative time spent with his parents. The Doctor, too, has an uneasy relationship with his creator, Lewis Zimmerman, who thinks it's a mistake to have left the emergency medical hologram (EMH) activated for so long ("The Swarm" and "Life Line" (VOY)). He's thinking that the Doctor was never given the knowledge base required for extended dealings and interactions with human beings. The EMH is insufficiently developed for the context of *Voyager* being stranded in the Delta Quadrant. Seven's childhood is equally problematic as she and her parents were assimilated by the Borg when she was six ("The Raven" and "Dark Frontier" (VOY)). Since the Borg don't *nurture* their young, Seven, once liberated from the Collective, lacks interpersonal skills, can't empathize with her fellow crewmembers, and consistently finds it difficult to "assimilate" into her new social context.

These characters' lack of childhood development is further underscored by their portrayal as childlike, if not feminized. In contrast to the typically hypermasculine androids, virtual beings, and cyborgs common in much science fiction cinema—just think of Arnold Schwarzenegger's Terminator—the Doctor and Data are presented as somewhat soft and fleshy, not the armored bodies typical of villains like the Borg. The Doctor is often portrayed as wracked with self-doubt, worried about danger and risk. Data too is often portrayed as helpless in the face of complex human interactions. Seven is, if anything, *hyper*feminized. In fact, those who successfully—even if just temporarily—make the transition from machine to human tend to be female: Andrea in "What Are Little Girls Made Of?" (TOS), Rayna in "Requiem for Methuselah" (TOS), and Lal in "The Offspring" (TNG).

These characters' childlike qualities are especially on display in their interactions with actual children. Data is explicitly counseled to be more childlike in *ST: Insurrection*. Data explains to Artim that he "would gladly accept the requirement of a bedtime in exchange for knowing what it is like to be a child." Artim says that if he's to know what it is to be a child, Data needs to learn to play.[9] In "Hero Worship" (TNG), Data forges a relationship with Timothy, who bonds with the android after Data saves him from a wrecked ship. Seven is regularly identified with the youngest crew member of *Voyager*, Naomi Wildman, who often emulates the Borg and looks up to Seven. In "Infinite Regress" (VOY), while suffering from a kind of multiple personality disorder brought on by a malfunctioning Borg vinculum, a childlike Seven and Naomi became best friends. Both the Doctor and Seven are regularly shown to be somewhat petulant and churlish, as children and adolescents can be. They often disobey rules and must be sent to their respective rooms: Seven ordered to her alcove to regenerate, the Doctor deactivated.

## "Spend Some Time with … Family"

As children who were insufficiently socialized into their own families, these three characters face the difficult task of reconstituting families aboard *Enterprise* or *Voyager*. It's among their crewmates that Data, Seven, and the Doctor must learn both how to be cared for and how to care for others. It's through his regular interaction with the *Enterprise* crew, both officially and in his off-duty hours, that Data comes to understand parts of what it means to be human. Data performs for his friends—as a standup comic, a violinist, an actor—attends a regular poker match, learns to paint, and cares for his pet cat, Spot. He comes to understand his own lack of humanity in his interactions with the crew and his failure to respond with care to others. He attempts to have a romantic relationship with Jenna D'Sora in "In Theory" (TNG) and attempts to father a child, Lal, in "The Offspring" (TNG). In each case, Data discovers he has to learn what it means to have an intimate or loving relationship with another. Being human requires being responsive to other humans.

Seven comes to see Janeway and the crew of *Voyager*, even if somewhat warily, as her surrogate family, and eventually refers to *Voyager* as her new "collective" ("Drone" (VOY)). She regularly discusses the process of her "humanization" with Janeway, who serves as a model of what a human being is and regularly reminds Seven that the crew is her new family. When Seven is initially "liberated" from the Borg and brought aboard *Voyager*, Janeway asks the Doctor, "How's the newest addition to our family?" The Doctor also takes on the responsibility of giving Seven assignments meant to foster her socialization skills. It's significant in this respect that Seven of Nine often interacts with Naomi Wildman, for while Naomi often echoes Borg behaviors, she also insists that Seven adopt a more human attitude, playing games with her and taking her to dinner. In "Survival Instinct" (VOY), Seven is troubled by her former relationship to the Borg and turns to Naomi for reassurance, asking her whether she considers Seven to be family. Naomi responds yes and asks Seven whether she thinks of her as family; Seven also answers in the affirmative. After a difficult confrontation with several former Borg, Seven, alone in the astrometrics lab, is joined by Naomi. "I thought maybe you might want to spend some time with ... family," she says, taking her place next to Seven. Clearly, becoming human means becoming an *interdependent* being who's both responsible *for* others and the responsibility *of* others.

The Doctor too is socialized by the intuitive and feminine Kes, who encourages him to develop and evolve his own identity. Kes introduces him to opera and encourages him to enter into relationships. In "The Swarm" (VOY), after having remained online for two years, the Doctor's program begins to fail. A holographic representation of his creator, Lewis Zimmerman, complains that the Doctor's directories are cluttered with useless information like friendships with the crew, love interests, and opera. But Kes argues that it's precisely this stuff that transformed the EMH into a *person*. The Doctor even constructs his own holodeck family so that he might learn how to interact better with the crew, who've lost their own families. In the aptly titled "Real Life" (VOY), the Doctor initially programs the perfect family: a loving wife who keeps perfect house and two adoring, smart, and perfect children. After introducing this holo-family to Kes and B'Elanna Torres, however, they object that he'll never learn anything about having a family from this perfectly simulated version. Torres adjusts the program, making the characters somewhat less predictable, and the Doctor has to learn how to adjust to the new scenario. His initial approach, though, is to try to rationally engineer the family's time together, and this results first in a discontented family and, ultimately, in the death of his holo-daughter.

As his daughter lies dying, the Doctor terminates the program rather than deal with his family tragedy. Later, though, he's encouraged to return and play out the drama. As Tom Paris remarks to him, "You wanted a family. That means taking the good along with the bad. You can't have one without the other." Paris points out that the *Voyager* crew has been brought closer through their shared experience of suffering and that, if the Doctor doesn't finish the program, he'll not only fail to comfort his wife and son, but also fail to realize the comfort they can bring him: "You'll miss the whole point of what it means to have a family." The Doctor returns to his holodeck program, another step in his humanization: coming to understand what it means to be part of a family, having obligations to other family members, learning to put up with their inadequacies, comforting them in times of tragedy, and learning to be comforted by their presence.

## "That Is What It Is to Be Human"

The process of socialization that Data, the Doctor, and Seven of Nine undergo is reminiscent of what Annette Baier characterizes as learning "the arts of personhood." All persons start out as children, born to earlier persons from whom they learn the arts of personhood: "A person ... is best seen as one who was long enough dependent upon other persons to acquire the essential arts of personhood. Persons essentially are second persons, who grow up with other persons."[10] Persons require, according to Baier, successive periods of infancy, childhood, and youth, during which they develop as persons: "In virtue of our long and helpless infancy, persons, who all begin as small persons, are necessarily social beings, who first learn from older persons, by play, by imitation, by correction."[11]

Baier observes that gods, if they were denied childhood, couldn't be persons because "[p]ersons are essentially successors, heirs to other persons who formed and cared for them, and their personality is revealed both in their relations to others and in their response to their own recognized genesis."[12] Though he had a human childhood, the newly godlike Gary Mitchell has no divine elder to teach him the arts of (divine) personhood; he thus fails to learn Kirk's essential foundation for godliness: "Above all else a god needs *compassion*!" Later, the omnipotent and omniscient Q realizes that, not having had his own childhood, he's ill equipped to raise his son in the arts of personhood and relies on Janeway to teach "Junior" how to be a morally responsible member of Q society ("Q2," VOY).[13]

It's our social nature, the facts of mutual recognition and answerability to others, our responsiveness to persons, that shapes and makes possible our personhood: "The more refined arts of personhood are learned as the personal pronouns are learned, from the men and women, girls and boys, who are the learners' companions and play-mates. We come to recognize ourselves and others in mirrors, to refer to ourselves and to others."[14] Persons are self-conscious and know themselves to be persons among persons. Referring to someone in the "second person" implicitly means that our self-consciousness is connected to addressing that person as "you": "If never addressed, if excluded from the circle of speakers, a child becomes autistic, incapable of using any pronouns or indeed any words at all. The second person, the pronoun of mutual address and recognition, introduces us to the first and third."[15] It's by learning from others that we acquire a sense of our place in *a series of persons*, and that we have special responsibilities to some of them: "We acquire a sense of ourselves as occupying a place in an historical and social order of persons, each of whom has a personal history interwoven with the history of a community."[16]

Baier's approach to personhood is connected with feminist discussions of personhood, mothering, and gender. Her emphasis on interdependence, the embodied nature of human beings, the long dependence of infants on mothers (typically) for their care, and the importance of mutual recognition and responsibility is mirrored in many feminist accounts of the human condition. These differ importantly from the standard Cartesian view of disembodied, rational minds.[17] Central to these feminist approaches is a recognition of the *mutually interdependent* relationship between parent and child, the role of this relationship in making possible a *self*, and the centrality of *caring* to both.

These same themes take center stage in *ST: Nemesis* when Picard is confronted with his younger clone, Shinzon—created by Romulans and raised in the dilithium mines on Remus—and both are confronted with identifying what consitutes humanity.[18] While Shinzon initially suggests he's exactly like Picard, he later remarks that he wants "to know what it means to be human" and recognizes that he's "not quite human." Picard comes to recognize that while the blood pumping in Shinzon's veins may be the same as his own, there's something missing: "Buried deep within you, beneath all the years of pain and anger there is something that has never been nurtured. The potential to make yourself a better man, and that is what it is to be human. To make yourself more than you are."

Picard recognizes a similar quality in Data. As he explains to B-4 after Data's death, Data wasn't human, "but his wonder, his curiosity about every facet of human nature ... allowed all of us to see the best parts of ourselves. He evolved. He embraced change because he always wanted to be better than he was." *Star Trek*'s portrayal of Data, the Doctor, and Seven of Nine recapitulates the process each of us goes through in learning what Baier calls "the arts of personhood." Significantly, *Star Trek* regularly questions and explores these "arts" by showing us different cultures and civilizations, each with different understandings of the arts of personhood. From this perspective, *Star Trek* avoids locating our essence in some fixed, universal nature and suggests a more developmental, dynamic view of our humanity open to ever-shifting, interdependent relationships between nature and culture, human and machine.

## Notes

1. I would like to thank Jason Eberl for his close and careful reading of this chapter and for his seemingly encyclopedic knowledge of all things *Star Trek*.
2. Martha Nussbaum, "Aristotle on Human Nature and the Foundations of Ethics," in *World, Mind and Ethics*, ed. R. Harrison and J. Altham (Cambridge: Cambridge Univeristy Press, 1995), 95.
3. Joel Garreau, *Radical Evolution: The Promise and Peril of Enhancing Our Minds, Our Bodies—and What It Means to Be Human* (New York: Doubleday, 2005), 21.
4. Richard Hanley, *Is Data Human? The Metaphysics of Star Trek* (New York: Basic Books, 1998).
5. Taylor Harrison, ed., *Enterprise Zones: Critical Positions on Star Trek* (Boulder, CO: Westview Press, 1996).
6. For discussion of feminist accounts of human nature, see Alison Jaggar, *Feminist Politics and Human Nature* (Lanham, MD: Rowman and Littlefield, 1988); and Nancy Holmstrom, "Human Nature," in *A Companion to Feminist Philosophy*, ed. Alison Jaggar and Iris Marion Young (Oxford: Blackwell, 1999).
7. Episode references for these relationships include "The Augments" (ENT), "The Schizoid Man" (TNG), "Datalore" (TNG), "Inheritance" (TNG), "Brothers" (TNG), "The Offspring" (TNG), and *ST: Nemesis*.
8. See David Mack, *Star Trek: The Next Generation—Cold Equations: The Persistence of Memory* (New York: Pocket Books, 2012), ch. 9.

9. For further discussion of the importance of *play* in human culture, and not just for children, see Jason T. Eberl's chapter in this volume (Chapter 1).

10. Annette Baier, *Postures of the Mind: Essays on Mind and Morals* (Minneapolis: Univeristy of Minnesotta Press, 1985), 84.

11. Annette Baier, "A Naturalist View of Persons," *Proceedings and Addresses of the American Philosophical Association* 65:3 (1991): 10.

12. Baier, *Postures of the Mind*, 85.

13. For more detail on Q's godlike status (and humanity), see the chapters in the book by Charles Taliaferro and Bailey Wheelock (Chapter 29) and Kyle Alkema and Adam Barkman (Chapter 10).

14. Baier, "A Naturalist View of Persons," 13.

15. Baier, *Postures of the Mind*, 90.

16. Ibid. Another philosopher who's emphasized the need for us to acknowledge our mutual dependency and responsibility for our development as rational and autonomous moral beings—or "independent practical reasoners"—is Alasdair MacIntrye in his *Dependent Rational Animals: Why Human Beings Need the Virtues* (Peru, IL: Open Court, 1999).

17. For additional feminist accounts of personhood, mothering, and gender, see Jane Flax, *Disputed Subjects: Essays on Psychoanalysis, Politics, and Philosophy* (New York: Routledge, 1993); and Nancy Chodorow, *The Reproduction of Mothering* (Berkeley: University of California Press, 1999).

18. For additional discussion of Picard and Shinzon's relationship, as well as ethical issues related to cloning in general, see Jason T. Eberl, "'Killing Your Own Clone Is Still Murder': Genetics, Ethics, and KHAAAAAN!" in *Star Trek and Philosophy*, ed. Jason T. Eberl and Kevin S. Decker (Chicago: Open Court, 2008); and Amy Kind, "Is Ignorance Bliss? *Star Trek: Nemesis*, Cloning, and the Right to an Open Future," in *Bioethics at the Movies*, ed. Sandra Shapshay (Baltimore: Johns Hopkins University Press, 2008).

# 18

# Photons (and Drones) Be Free: Phenomenology and the Life-Worlds of *Voyager*'s Doctor and Seven of Nine

*Nicole R. Pramik*

What's a holographic physician or a recovering Borg drone to do when they've got several years to kill in the Delta Quadrant? A few obvious choices would be exploring alien planets, studying strange space phenomena, and even sampling some of Neelix's cooking. But as interesting as all those trek-related endeavors might be—Neelix's culinary skills notwithstanding—there's yet another journey undertaken by *Voyager*'s not-quite-human crewmembers: the journey into self-awareness. Throughout this trek, Seven of Nine and the Doctor experience various ups and downs as they navigate the deepest reaches of social and emotional interactions. So, as different as they seem at first, the Doctor and Seven of Nine are very much alike as they seek some sort of significance to their "human" experiences or, to get philosophically technical, *phenomena*.

## "Please State the Nature of the Philosophical Emergency"

No, not "phenomena" like wormholes or giant space amoebae capable of devouring whole Starfleet vessels. Instead, as Edmund Husserl (1859–1938) uses the term, *phenomena* are events, from the extraordinary to the everyday, that have some sort of *meaning* to us, even if that meaning isn't immediately obvious.[1] So *phenomenology* studies how we give meaning to the things that happen to us, which is essential to our personalized knowledge of reality.

*The Ultimate Star Trek and Philosophy*, First Edition. Edited by Kevin S. Decker and Jason T. Eberl.
© 2016 John Wiley & Sons, Ltd. Published 2016 by John Wiley & Sons, Ltd.

Typically, when you have ideas and perceptions, you're having *conscious* experiences because you're aware of what you're doing or what's going on around you. These experiences are the "mystery of mysteries" or the "life of consciousness" as your existence consists of subjective, conscious experiences to which you feel compelled to assign some sort of meaning.[2] These experiences, from eating a piece of cheesecake to listening to a piece of music, create what Husserl calls your *life-world*, which comprises the larger context for your sense of identity. Your life-world consists of not just your personal experiences but also how these experiences relate to your placement in the world among other people. Thus, your life-world comprises your unique way of viewing the world and how you interpret and engage the various conscious experiences you have.

Conscious experiences have two basic components: the experience itself and the meaning you derive from it—what it means *to you*. Husserl used two Greek terms, *noesis* and *noema*, to explain these aspects. *Noesis* gives meaning to an experience, as opposed to simply dismissing everyday occurrence as just "things" that happen without any intention or influence. Husserl goes as far as to say that the *noesis* becomes the "real content" of the experience. In contrast, the *noema* is the *actual* meaning of the experience: its point about something, so that the events that happen to us or around us make sense to us in terms of generating personal significance.[3]

Husserl distinguishes between the *content* of an act—what makes an experience meaningful or intentional—from its *object*. In his view, the things that we do, which comprise our experiences, are driven by an *intention* that's separate from the deed itself or any outside object. What we engage is broken down even further into *essences* or *meanings*. Thus, what you understand about an event gives meaning to the event itself and how it relates to you, regardless of whether you're a human, a hologram, or an ex-Borg.[4]

## "The Fun Will Now Commence"

The Doctor and Seven of Nine are always trying to understand the "human" significance of their experiences. While they develop separately as characters, their shared conscious experiences help them formulate a sense of self-awareness en route to becoming unique persons. From the start, both characters were somewhat marginalized: the Doctor was viewed as just a hologram who could initially be turned on and off against his will; and Seven of Nine seen as just a Borg drone detached from the Collective who thus presents a potential threat to the *Voyager* crew. If either of them had been familiar with a certain 20th-century Earth comedian, they might've complained, "I don't get no respect," at least early on.

When the Doctor was initially activated after *Voyager*'s medical staff was killed, he was nothing more than a stoically practical, holographic version of his designer, Dr. Lewis Zimmerman, created to assist in short-term medical emergencies. In time, the Doctor proved that even holograms could be capable of personal change by developing a sense of self-awareness. In his attempts to understand his flesh-and-blood crewmates better, the Doctor sought out new experiences. In doing so, he exercised *noesis*, a purposeful attempt to ascribe meaning to an event, which enabled him to develop a *noema*, an explanation, or ideal meaning, of what happened to him by which he could assign a certain significance to mundane occurrences—or at least as mundane as things can get in the Delta Quadrant. The Doctor further built on these meanings to come to an understanding that possessing them defined him as more of a person rather than just a holographic program. The events of *Voyager*'s seven-year trek through the Delta Quadrant helped create his life-world, which provided the Doctor with knowledge concerning how to further "humanize" his program.

If there's hope for a snarky hologram to develop past his initial limitations, then there had to be some optimism for a former Borg drone with a penchant for metallic bodysuits. Seven of Nine's progress toward self-awareness is akin to the Doctor's journey; so her friendship with him isn't coincidental. Even though Seven is genetically human, her time with the Borg eliminated most of her memories of individual conscious experiences because the Collective dictated what was meaningful for her. When her tie to the Collective was severed, Seven was left to rediscover herself on her own. In a way, Seven possesses what Husserl would label the "transcendental ego," which is developed through personal experiences yet exists solely for its own sake (*"I myself"*).[5] Thus, whenever Seven has encounters with, or flashbacks of her time with, the Collective, her transcendental ego is inhibited because she tries to see her identity as representing a whole, not as a part of herself. But in time, she becomes her own person as well as part of a social group that recognizes her individuality.

While some of Seven's self-discovery is undertaken on her own, it's usually thanks to the Doctor's or Captain Janeway's guidance or prodding. At first, Seven is baffled by the various conscious experiences she faces, seeing them as *noematically* irrelevant. But, over time, she develops *noemata* that allow her to see how her experiences apply to her past, to others, and, more importantly, to her own view of herself. Let's consider a few critical parallels where the Doctor and Seven underwent similar conscious experiences yet carried away completely different *noemata*.

## "Here Begins a New Life"

Seven and the Doctor often use human feelings and sentiments to label their experiences. And this is perhaps never truer than when they're contending with *guilt*. The Doctor comes face to face with guilt in "Latent Image" when he learns to cope with feelings of regret after choosing to save Ensign Kim's life instead of the life of another ensign who had an equal chance of survival. The Doctor doesn't even remember these events at first, so he tries to piece together evidence from his holo-photography collection. This act, in and of itself, can be seen as a sign of a developing self-image as it's undertaken consciously because the Doctor knows something is amiss and wants to uncover what it is.

His attempts to unmask this event's *noesis*, or "real content," possess multiple meanings. First, he assumes aliens are trying to conceal his memories as a form of an attack. Next, he suspects a conspiracy is afoot when his attempt to recover his missing memory files goes cold. Lastly, when the truth is revealed that Janeway purposely deleted his memories to preserve his sanity, the Doctor rightfully expresses anger. He believes his memories are a part of his program and thus his property. So his actual meaning, his *noema*, to the original experience of lost memories pivots on the idea that his personal rights have been violated.

When Seven of Nine comes to his defense, Janeway indifferently compares the Doctor to a replicator, a machine that does only what it's told and nothing more. Seven counters by insisting that she and the Doctor are "not unlike" and claims that if Janeway truly intended for the Doctor's program to evolve, then allowing him to deal with tough choices is a part of that process. Later, Janeway confesses that they did, indeed, give the Doctor a "soul," not just personality subroutines; so she decides it's best for the Doctor to struggle with his emotions.

And struggle he does. The Doctor's conscious experience of dealing with his memories is on "repeat" as he replays and regrets his choices in an emotional-cognitive feedback loop. In the end, he realizes that making hard decisions is a part of his self-awareness, as well as his life-world, and he's not immune to having to live with the consequences of his actions. As the quotation from Dante's *La Vita Nuova* implies, the Doctor's *noema* of the ordeal is that he has a chance to make a fresh start and not allow guilt to guide his feelings from here on out.

## "Now That I Am an Individual, Those Same Voices Frighten Me"

Seven of Nine has a similar conscious experience of guilt in "Infinite Regress," struggling with her past actions as a Borg drone that, like the Doctor's memories, return to haunt her. When an infected Borg vinculum transmits neural patterns of individuals from a variety of species who'd formerly been assimilated, Seven becomes the host body for these congregated voices.

Her experiences with these voices, from a Klingon warrior to a Ferengi wheeler-dealer, become more convoluted when they threaten to destroy her sense of self and, by proxy, her life-world. While Seven isn't consciously aware of what she says and does while under the voices' influence, she's aware when she blacks out and isn't in control of herself; so the *noesis* she attaches to this, the "real content" of the situation, is that something is deeply wrong with her "normal functioning."

When traditional medical assistance fails, Tuvok initiates a mind-meld in an attempt to "isolate her true self and guide it to the surface." Seven's inner self is in disarray as slowly but surely her sense of her individualized self becomes muddled and lost. Yet when the connection to the voices is severed, Seven's personal identity reemerges. After this event, Seven's life-world is fundamentally changed as she understands that a collectivist mindset is no longer the norm. So the *noema* she attaches to these experiences is that her past and her guilt shouldn't control her, but they still remain part of who she is. It's just up to her how much she allows these cognitive and emotional memories to govern her, just as the Doctor's *noema* of his guilt-inducing experience taught him how not to let past choices tint future decisions.

## "I Am One. I Will Adapt"

Seven and the Doctor also contend with forms of social isolation, which develops similar yet different *noemata* for them both. It's no secret that the Doctor and Seven of Nine tend to take social interaction with their crewmates for granted. A case in point is the episode "One" when social chitchat is a little hard to come by as the entire crew, save Seven and the Doctor, is put in stasis while traversing a massive, radioactive nebula. Seven and the Doctor try to adapt to each other's company but begin to grate on each other's nerves. Their individual *noesis* attempts to give meaning to their social isolation while trying to keep *Voyager* operational in the nebula. Yet it's their individual *noemata* that are far more interesting.

The Doctor is further isolated when the nebula causes his program to go haywire, so he's stuck having to ride out the remainder of the trip in sickbay. This forces him to be separated from Seven, which makes running the ship a little harder to coordinate. Thus, his *noema* realizes that his default limitations present not only a potential hazard to the crew but also an inconvenience to Seven as she's now forced to tend to matters alone.

Seven's dealings with her isolation prove far more traumatic but also therapeutic. What she perceives to be the "real content," the *noesis*, of the Doctor assisting her with social interaction exercises is one of disdain; so her *noema* of such activities is that socialization is "ponderous" and serves no purpose. But that changes when her experiences in the nebula cause her to see social interaction as a balm for loneliness. As she endures numerous, and increasingly torturous, hallucinations, she realizes that, while loneliness might be a new and different conscious state of being, it's not a preferred one as it causes her great distress. She tries to let her tingly Borg senses kick in and help her adapt, but they prove no match to her newly formed life-world that now sees loneliness as something to be avoided. In the end, Seven of Nine's *noema* of the event is that social company is far better than isolation.

The Doctor gets to experience loneliness of a different form in "Someone to Watch over Me" when his attempts to get to know Seven better go awry. The Doctor tries to teach Seven the finer points of dating and romance, but the rest of the crew doesn't credit his ability to instruct her: Tom Paris labels his efforts as "the blind leading the blind." The Doctor might not be the ultimate love guru, but he does have ulterior motives for everything he teaches Seven, from singing, to dancing, to how to properly eat a lobster.

Of course, the Doctor's *noesis*, the "real content" of these exercises, is to assist Seven in her social development, but his *noema*, his takeaway meaning, is far different. Rather than keeping his interests detached, the Doctor becomes infatuated with Seven, culminating in his failed attempt to tell her how he truly feels—if only she'd remained in hologram form! Thus, he realizes the *noema* of Seven's lessons—that they're a means to get to know her better as an individual and, perhaps, as a romantic partner.

The Doctor's *noesis* goes through three phases. First, he argues with Paris that there's no difference between "photons and force fields" and "flesh and blood"; so, in his mind, there is no reason why he and Seven couldn't be a couple. Later, the Doctor suspects his growing affections toward Seven are unlikely to lead to a relationship because he assumes she doesn't feel the same about him. Lastly, her rejection provides him with his *noema* of the overall experience: Seven is forever confined to the "Neutral (er, Friend) Zone."

Oddly enough, both the Doctor and Seven interpret this episode's events as failures. Seven believes no suitable mate for her exists onboard—at the moment anyway—so she stops looking; and the Doctor suffers rejection from Seven's lack of romantic feelings toward him. Overall, both of their experiences with various types of isolation generate their respective *noemata* that social interaction is a critical component to one's self-identity, and not everyone with whom they interact will engage them or respond the way they think they should.

## "Until I Spent a Day in Your Skin, I Never Knew What I Was Missing"

The true test of the Doctor's and Seven of Nine's phenomenological development is in "Body and Soul" when the Doctor hides his program inside of Seven to escape detection from hologram-hating aliens. The ensuing experiences allow the Doctor to live vicariously through Seven—much to her dismay—by overindulging in food and drink, and even becoming physically aroused, all of which are aspects of life he can't experience properly. Rather than view eating, drinking, and even flirting as mundane experiences, the Doctor's *noema* is that these are to be enjoyed, not taken for granted. He's seen these events constitute his fellow crewmembers' life-worlds, so he assumes they're normal, even essential, components of his life-world as well.

Through all this, Seven, too, has conscious experiences and they're not exactly positive. She's the one physically suffering from stuffing herself with cheesecake, getting drunk, and enduring sexual arousal despite the fact that, if given the choice, she wouldn't be partaking in any of these activities. Her attempt to gain meaning (*noesis*) is tied up in what the Doctor decides to do through her, though her *noema* is different, especially when she has to suffer the consequences of the Doctor's overindulgences.

This leads to an interesting exchange between the Doctor and Seven as she insists that the Doctor isn't missing out on anything as far as these matters go. But he disagrees. "Indulgences are what make life worth living," he says, insisting it isn't good for her to constantly deny herself new sensations and experiences. "We're quite a pair," he admits. "Me, trapped by the limitations of photons and force fields. You, by a drone's obsession with efficiency. You'd make an excellent hologram." The Doctor's statement is curiously double-sided. On one hand, his *noema* is framed by *envy* towards Seven for her ability to engage in sensations he'd like to experience, yet she willingly chooses not to. At the same time, he recognizes the boundaries of a "normal" hologram that would care more about getting its tasks done and less about enjoying life; and that such a hologram would be more akin to a Borg drone—minus the desire to assimilate others.

In the end, Seven and the Doctor learn from each other and have a communal *noema* of sorts. The Doctor realizes novel experiences through Seven, and his advice encourages her to try new things herself. Seven, on the other hand, comes to define the Doctor's experiences through her as a way to make her more human and to share in some of the pleasures of life that she's denied herself. So both the Doctor and Seven of Nine make amends in terms of "shared experiences" as well as shared *noemata*.

## "To All That Makes Us Unique"

Much like the Doctor's continuous crusade to be recognized as a being with rights, so Seven has struggled to prove herself as more than just a former Borg drone. Their various conscious experiences, undertaken both individually and together, generate meanings that enable them to construct their respective life-worlds.

While the Doctor's voyage to self-awareness is more concerned with how to process social conventions and emotions, Seven's journey is about establishing a sense of personal self-awareness as she'd always had her life-world defined for her by the Borg Collective. Her newly found freedom means she must construct her own life-world by herself. So while the Doctor gives Seven social lessons, Seven, in turn, teaches the Doctor what it means to be an individual who also defines herself or himself by the company she or he keeps.

True to the spirit of *Star Trek*, we see that friendship, loyalty, and other values we take for granted are held up as virtues, not only for the good of others but also for the good of the self.[6] Yet, in light of phenomenology, these events take on a completely different and far more significant meaning in how the Doctor and Seven view themselves as individuals, both separately and as members of a larger social unit that offers a plethora of experiences to embrace, for better or worse. The Doctor and Seven of Nine's shared experiences show that meaning and significance can be found in simple, everyday occurrences, even if you're light years from home.

# Notes

1.  Edmund Husserl, *Logical Investigations* (New York: Routledge, 2001).
2.  Dermot Moran, *Edmund Husserl: Founder of Phenomenology* (Malden, MA: Polity, 2005), 2.
3.  Ronald McIntyre and David Woodruff Smith, "Theory of Intentionality," in *Husserl's Phenomenology*, ed. J.N. Mohanty and William R. McKenna (Lanham, MD: University Press of America, 1989), 147–79.
4.  Husserl spills much ink examining acts of perceiving and conceiving in their noetic and noematic dimensions. In what follows, I'm applying the ideas of *noesis* and *noema* to the human significance of complex social situations in a way Husserl did not. So I have one caveat: Husserl relegates social meaning to the life-world, which for him is the background condition for doing phenomenology. In his book *The Crisis of European Sciences and Transcendental Phenomenology*, trans. David Carr (Evanston: Northwestern University Press, 1970), he suggests that there could be a "science of the life-world," and this chapter should be read as contributing to that idea.
5.  Edmund Husserl, *Ideas* (New York, NY: Routledge, 2012).
6.  For further discussion of the value of various types of friendships, see Jim Okapal's chapter in this volume (Chapter 21).

# 19
# Vision Quest into Indigenous Space

## Walter Robinson

I've always been attracted to books and movies that depict encounters between protagonists and different "others." So it's no surprise that I enjoy *Star Trek*. Indeed, when Gene Roddenberry created *Star Trek*, he referred to it as a "*Wagon Train* to the stars," thus projecting the Western genre into science fiction. An essential motif of the Western is the *frontier* in which people of European descent encounter American Indians as "other." So in *Star Trek* we have "space, the final frontier," where the "other" becomes extraterrestrials.

## "Let's Find out What Life-Forms Are Blessed by This Environment"

When they made first contact with indigenous people, Europeans projected much from Eurocentric imagination onto the "other." Indians were viewed as bloodthirsty savages, despite the fact that Europeans were the primary aggressors. Anglo literature is full of this negative prejudice, which served to justify the cruel and dehumanizing ways in which Indians were treated.

The "bloodthirsty savage" stereotype finds intellectual support in the political philosophy of Thomas Hobbes (1588–1679). According to Hobbes, humanity's "state of nature" is a "war of all against all," such that life is "solitary, poor, nasty, brutish and short."[1] Civil law is a means to get out of a state of nature and escape the conditions of war. American Indians were thought of as being in a pre-civil state

*The Ultimate Star Trek and Philosophy*, First Edition. Edited by Kevin S. Decker and Jason T. Eberl.
© 2016 John Wiley & Sons, Ltd. Published 2016 by John Wiley & Sons, Ltd.

of nature and so living in a state of war. This view is contradicted by Jean-Jacques Rousseau's (1712–1778) theory of the "noble savage," in which he contends that it's *civil society* that's most warlike, and that man in a state of nature is far more at peace.[2] According to Rousseau, humanity was much happier before the advent of civilization; and some within civilization have a romantic longing for that simpler life. This longing is referred to in *Star Trek* as the "Tahiti Syndrome": "a human longing for a peaceful, idyllic natural setting when suffering from the stresses of modern life."[3]

This term *Tahiti Syndrome* is used in the TOS episode "The Paradise Syndrome," which depicts the "noble savage" stereotype of American Indians. Spock identifies the transplanted Indians as a mix of Navajo, Mohegan, and Delaware—"all among the more advanced and peaceful tribes." The village they occupy has what looks to be a large wigwam surrounded by some tepees. Wigwams were commonly used by Indians of the Northeast woodlands, which includes the Mohegan and Delaware. Tepees were used by Indians of the Great Plains, and not by the three tribes that Spock names, so we shouldn't find wigwams and tepees in the same setting. The Navajo traditionally live in wood or clay hogans, which aren't shown. The whole setting is about no real tribe existing in no real place. Appropriate to the fantasy-like nature of the setting, Kirk likens it to mythical utopias like Atlantis and Shangri-La; *utopia* comes from the Greek for "no-place."

Unfortunately, what most Anglo-Americans experience of Indians is through mass media, much of which casts negative stereotypes and causes harm to Indian people and communities.[4] Writing from an indigenous perspective, Sierra Adare reflects on her experience viewing "The Paradise Syndrome" and reports that, despite the superficial depiction of Indians that "reeked of inaccuracy, stupidity, and that generic jumble.... None of that mattered. It was the only time I could remember seeing TV 'Indians' who were not being chased by the cavalry or shot by cowboys and whose intent was not to massacre innocent settlers."[5]

In the eyewitness account of Christopher Columbus's first contact with the Indians noted by Dominican friar Bartolomé de Las Casas (1484–1566), the indigenous people were "by nature the most humble, patient, and peaceable, holding no grudges, free from embroilments, neither excitable nor quarrelsome. These people are the most devoid of rancors, hatreds, or desire for vengeance of any people in the world." As for how the Spaniards behaved toward the Indians, "killing, terrorizing, afflicting, and destroying the native peoples, doing all this with the strangest and most varied new methods of cruelty, never seen or heard of before."[6] The TNG episode "Journey's End" references the Pueblo Revolt of 1680, in which the Spaniards were driven out of modern-day New Mexico after years of tyrannical rule. The Indians' independence was short-lived as the invaders came back in force and retook the Pueblos. We discover that Captain Picard had an ancestor in the Spanish army who, like other mercenaries, was ruthless and brutal.

## "A Very Peaceful, Friendly People, Living on A Primitive Level"

The ethos of the *dominant culture* is symbolically reflected in the relationship Robinson Crusoe has with his Indian companion, whom he names "Friday." Crusoe naming the Indian symbolizes his power over him. When Europeans wanted a justification for slavery, Spanish philosopher Juan Ginés de Sepúlveda (1490–1573) offered one taken from the writings of Aristotle (385–322 BCE). To be human, Aristotle asserts, is to be *rational*, but not all humans are *equally* rational. Men are more rational than women, thus women ought to submit to male domination; and civilized man is more rational than primitives, so primitive people ought to be dominated by the civilized.[7]

Immanuel Kant (1724–1804) adds to this Aristotelian justification for slavery with a *racist* theory of white supremacy, asserting that Europeans are more rational by nature than the other races.[8] Black people are the most inferior, and Indians and "Orientals" are somewhere in between. Georg Wilhelm Friedrich Hegel (1770–1831) expands on Kant by formulating a theory in which cultures develop in stages, European civilization being the supreme accomplishment of cultural progress.[9] American anthropologist Lewis Morgan (1818–1881) had a similar view more suitable for Anglo-cultural imperialism. His taxonomy had three categories of development: savages, barbarians, and civilized. The Anglos have the highest form of civilization, which is offered as a benefit for humanity.[10] This sentiment is expressed by British imperialist Rudyard Kipling (1865–1936), writing that it's the "White Man's Burden" to bring civilization to inferior races and rule over them.[11]

*Star Trek*'s references to social development echo Hegel and Morgan, such as the demarcation of "pre-warp" and "warp-capable" civilizations in many episodes, including "First Contact" (TNG), and the film *ST: First Contact*. This seems like a projection of the distinction between pre-industrial and industrial economies, or the geopolitical dichotomy between "developing" and "developed" countries. But these ethnocentric categories presuppose something like Hegel's view of the historical process as directed toward some predetermined endpoint. The conceit hidden here is that there's some kind of universal principle of evolution dictating that technological development is a natural and inevitable consequence of cultural development. Along these lines, Russian cosmonaut Nikolai Kardashev has proposed a scale for classifying potential advanced civilizations with four levels of development, divided into various types based on use of physical energy and information technology. Type 1 includes terrestrial techno-industrial civilizations, type 2 civilizations have expanded into their respective star systems, and type 3 civilizations have expanded into interstellar space. There are higher types for civilizations that have expanded into galactic and intergalactic space. For example, while the Federation, the Romulan Star Empire, and the Dominion would be categorized at the "galactic" level, the Kelvans of "By Any Other Name" (TOS) would be placed in the higher "intergalactic" category; and the Q would presumably occupy a level all their own.

In the TOS episode "Errand of Mercy," Spock invokes a developmental notion of social evolution in his assessment that the Organians are apparently primitive. They're seen as a nontechnological society somewhat similar in appearance to the Pueblos or a Neolithic community. As it turns out, the Organians are not humanoids at all, but beings of pure, conscious energy. Spock, holding onto his evolutionary paradigm, says of the Organians that they are "as far above us on the evolutionary scale as we are above the amoeba."[12]

Evolution may be an empirical fact (as much as can be reasonably determined by scientific inquiry), but the notion that there's a proper direction to evolution, with "higher" and "lower" forms coexisting, is a metaphysical assumption and not a fact. There's also a significant difference between *biological evolution* and *social development*. Biological evolution explains the adaptation of organisms and communities of organisms to environmental conditions for survival and reproduction. Ecologically, there's no "higher" or "lower," but only differences in form and function that interrelate with system dynamics as a whole. Social development, meanwhile, is a process based on communication between individuals and between communities within a group dynamic. The ways in which societies develop depend on cultural values transmitted in a way that doesn't depend on genetics, and so they aren't limited by biology. There's no predetermined "best way" for a culture to be, and the ranges of possibilities are indeterminate and fluid.

## "And the Children Shall Lead"

*Star Trek* lends itself to a wide range of thought experiments about morality by imagining the possible consequences of adopting different cultural values and priorities. Klingons prioritize war and value warrior discipline; Vulcans prioritize logic and discipline of mind; Betazoids value feelings and empathy. Gene Roddenberry intended various TOS and TNG episodes to be *morality plays*, and the very structure of the *Star Trek* mythos entails a moral philosophy. The Prime Directive is a central ethical precept of Roddenberry's moral vision: it states that one ought not to interfere in the self-chosen values of others, or impose one's own values on others. On this point, there's significant agreement with American Indian values.[13] We can see this in traditional indigenous families, in which children are allowed to grow according to their own innate potentials and capacities without interference from others, but with love and nurturing providing support and safety. There's no interfering with the child's will, although the community's shared values are cultivated in the child's development in terms of interpersonal respect and mutual positive regard.

Western theories of education have historically denied the importance of a child's innate will. John Locke (1632–1704) asserts that a child ought not to have his own will, but must be subdued and improved according to imposed law.[14] Locke echoes a philosophy of education found in Plato, who asserts that a child's will must be subordinated to reason.[15] The Western tradition thus sets up a false dichotomy between reason and will, creating a schizoid condition within the Western psyche. This is the psychological root of the politics of domination in the West.

Furthermore, democracy didn't come across the Atlantic on Europeans boats; it was already here, practiced by many Native American communities. Indigenous government was often based on equal respect for the values and sovereignty of each member of the community. No one has the right to impose their will upon another; rather, one ought to be respectful of others. Governance in most traditional North American Indian communities isn't about ruling *over* subordinates, but about forging *consent* among equals.

Indeed, the oldest continually existing democratic government in today's world is the Haudenosaunee confederation of six Iroquois tribes. Each tribe maintains its own sovereignty based on the self-sovereignty of each member. There's no hierarchical hegemony or dictatorial power. This system of government influenced the founders of both the United States and the United Nations.[16] And, of course, the United Federation of Planets takes its conceptual inspiration from this history. This egalitarian ethos shows up in *Star Trek* in the idea that all intelligent life-forms are afforded equal value, with each person and culture recognized as having the *right of self-determination*.

## "I Knew the Spirits Have Chosen You to Be a Contrary"

The Federation embodies *Star Trek*'s vision of *multicultural liberalism*. Every kind of person finds a place within this vision. In *The Motion Picture*, when the *Enterprise* crew assembles on the rec deck to learn the nature of their mission, we see a wide assortment of species and ethnicities, including American Indians. Commander Chakotay of *Voyager* becomes *Star Trek*'s first major American Indian character. Nevertheless, identifying a character as an Indian inevitably involves *stereotypes*; Chakotay is not only a stereotype, but a generic one at that. He doesn't represent any actually existing tribe. His fictional tribe is called the "Rubber Tree People," who are said to live in the tropical rain forest of Central America. It's suggested that the tribe is Mayan, but the way in which they're depicted has little resemblance to actual Mayans. Rather, it resembles an older culture, perhaps the Olmecs. In any case, they're a fictional people existing only in science fiction.

The VOY episode "Tattoo" offers a profile of Chakotay's family background. We learn that, as a child, Chakotay accompanied his father, Kolopak, on a pilgrimage to learn about their ancestral roots, returning to Earth from their home close to the Cardassian border. It had been revealed in the TNG episode "Journey's End" that some American Indians had chosen to migrate into space in order to preserve their culture from the homogenizing effects of Earth's globalized civilization. It can be psychosocially traumatic, however, for an Indigenous culture to be separated from their ancestral homeland. This is mirrored in the tragedy of the forced removal of Indian people from their homelands by the U.S. government during the 19th century, most visibly in the Cherokee "Trail of Tears" in 1838 and 1839. There are cases, though, in which Indian people have migrated to new lands in order to *preserve* a pattern of culture that's otherwise threatened.[17]

During their pilgrimage, Kolopak and his son have a difference of opinion that creates a rift between them. When they make contact with their jungle-dwelling ancestors, Kolopak embraces them, and as a mark of solidarity, he receives the tribal tattoo. Chakotay, on the other hand, announces to his father that he's made plans to attend Starfleet Academy, exclaiming that "our tribe lives in the past, a past of fantasy and myth." What the young Chakotay didn't understand is that all human beings "live in myth," and even science has its myths. We create stories to tell one another about our relationships to each other and our place in the world. Evidence from cognitive science shows that storytelling is an essential element of our psychological makeup and brain structure.[18] Without myth, we can't function; we become lost. Kolopak tells his son that without the spirits to guide him, he'll be lost, that who he is as a person is connected with his ancestors: "You will never belong to that other life, and if you leave you will never belong to this one. You will be caught between worlds." As learning to live in two worlds has become a necessity for most modern Indians, being caught between worlds has become a problem for them. Chakotay learns the truth of his father's lesson as he matures. While he initially joined Starfleet, his father joined the Maquis and died fighting for his people against the Cardassians ("In the Flesh," VOY). After his father's death, Chakotay embraces his heritage, undertakes a vision quest, and adopts a facial tattoo like his father.

## "You Are a Sacred Person Here, Wesley"

What logic is to Vulcans and empathy is to Betazoids, *vision* is to an Indian. In the VOY episode "The Cloud," Chakotay offers to guide Captain Janeway into a vision so she can acquire a *spirit guide* in the form of a totem animal archetype. To this end he shares with her his *medicine bundle*, which contains the wing of a blackbird; a river stone with the *chamozi*—a healing symbol—carved into it; and a device called an *akoonah* used to facilitate vision. There are a great many ways of undergoing a vision quest according to the diversity of traditions. The most common in North American tribes involves pro-longed solitary fasting and praying in a geographic space sacred to the ancestral spirits. Chakotay uses the *akoonah* instead of psychoactive herbs, another common ingredient of the vision quest. There are a number of psychoactive agents used by Central American Indians. The best known is peyote, which is central to the Huichol Indian culture; another is the psilocybin mushroom used by the Mixtec and Toltec Indians. Probably the most powerful vision-inducing sacrament is the Ayahuasca brew used by Amazonian Indians. The active ingredient in the Ayahuasca brew is dimethyltryptamine, which is also made naturally within the body and interacts with serotonin receptor sites. It's correlated in neurochemistry with *dreaming*—so vision is sometimes called *big dreaming*.

There's more to vision, though, than just an altered state of consciousness. The setting within a culture contextualizes the interactive interpretation, which produces *moral insight*. In "Journey's End," the setting is Dorvan V, the resting place that, for nearly 200 years, its Indian inhabitants searched for. The tribal leader Anthwara states that, upon arriving, they were "welcomed by the mountains, the rivers, the sky.... [This place] holds a deep spiritual significance for us." Into this setting enters Starfleet cadet Wesley Crusher, who's suffering from discontent with his life-path. He's befriended by an Indian named Lakanta, who informs Wesley that he saw him in a vision quest and knew that he would come. Lakanta asks Wesley what he holds as "sacred." Wesley struggles to answer, unclear as to what if anything he holds as sacred. This reflects the moral dilemma of the dominant culture with its priority on materialism and technological conquest. Lakanta tells Wesley that, for an Indian, *everything* is sacred and must be treated with respect, including himself. Wesley realizes that he hasn't treated himself with proper respect. Lakanta then leads him into the holy *habak* chamber to prepare him for his vision quest.

The *habak* is something like the *kivas*, the most sacred ceremonial spaces for Pueblo culture. When Wesley enters, he notices material representations of *mansaros*, which are akin to *Kachinas* or Holy Ones in Pueblo and Navajo cultures. Chakotay, in explaining to Janeway the nature of vision, references psychoanalyst Carl Jung (1875–1961). In Jungian terms, *Kachinas* are culturally specific expressions of archetypal energies of the collective unconscious.[19] Wesley notices that some of the *mansaros* resemble Klingons, Vulcans, and other non-Indian icons. Lakanta responds, "[O]ur culture is rooted in the past, but it is not limited to the past. The spirits of the Klingon, the Vulcan, the Ferengi, come to us just as the bear and coyote, the parrot."

Mythologist Joseph Campbell (1904–1987) draws on Jung in claiming that mythological characters are personifications of energies from the collective unconscious, and that they constitute metaphors for psychospiritual realities.[20] Such energies are alluded to in the Algonquin word *Manitou*, which carries the same meaning as the Lakota word *wakan* or the Polynesian *manna*, referring to mysterious spirit energy. The expression often translated as "Great Spirit" (or "Great Mystery") is *Wakan Tanka*. It's sometimes thought of as equivalent to the idea of *God*, about which Campbell asserts, "God is not a fact but a metaphor."[21] In the context of this chapter, a "fact" indicates something externally observable. The spiritual can't be approached in this way, but must be experienced as inner vision, and so it eludes rational definition. There are realities that can be rationally known and others that can't; the latter constitute the basic features of a spiritual life.

## "If You Have No Spirits to Guide You, I Fear You Will Lose Your Way"

Central to Native American spirituality is the *Medicine Wheel*, utilized in the VOY episode "Cathexis" as "a representation of both the universe inside and outside the mind, and that each is reflection of the other."[22] The Medicine Wheel is a psychospiritual medium through which we may reflect on our life toward the goal of living in harmony and balance.[23] The center of the Wheel forms the axis that connects Mother Earth with Father Sky. Revolving around the axis, the Wheel follows the patterns of time moving through day and night, the seasons, and the life path of people. The four directions of East, South, West, and North symbolize modes of being within patterns of time. The East is associated with the rising sun, the beginning of the day, springtime, and birth. The South is midday, summer, and childhood. The West is sunset, autumn, and coming of age. The North is midnight, winter, and age. Jung's four modes of consciousness—thinking, feeling, sensation, and intuition—can be correlated with the directions of the Medicine Wheel: the North thinking, the South feeling, the East sensation, and the West intuition.[24] The relationship of North and South calls for harmony; and that of East to West calls for balance. The relationship between Mother Earth and Father Sky involves both harmony and balance, which is to say that femininity and masculinity must work together in balance and harmony for the sake of health and goodness.

This framework influences the Indian interpretation of White culture. *Seven Arrows* by Hyemeyohsts Storm has the Cheyenne referring to the White men as "winter-way," suggesting they're cold like a winter wind and lacking the warm feeling of the South. Jung contends that, if your priority is set on thought, then feelings are a lower priority and you may become emotionally underdeveloped. The history of Western philosophy has prioritized reason over, and in opposition to, emotions, and has placed masculinity in dominance and control over femininity. This breeds a culture of violence and disharmony and people in need of healing.[25] People of European descent are infected by this history and in need of the thawing warmth of the South and a vision that harmonizes masculinity with femininity.

*Star Trek* offers motifs of a "hero's journey" in search of self-discovery—a metaphor for the vision quest. Jung's four modes of consciousness play out as different personalities in the drama. In TOS, Kirk is intuition, Spock is thinking, McCoy is feeling, and Scotty is sensation—just consider his love for "green" liquor. The four interact as they adventure away from home. With VOY, the mythological cycle becomes complete with a journey back to Earth. Whereas Kirk had his extraterrestrial first officer with him on his journey away from Earth, Janeway has as her first officer an American Indian on her journey of return. She is a feeling type with Chakotay as the intuition providing vision.

Here, Chakotay as a stereotype becomes an archetype, symbolic of openness to a transpersonal spiritual reality. The same is true of Anthwara and Lakanta in "Journey's End": they are archetypes in the journey of self-discovery and healing. In "Tattoo," Chakotay encounters the "Sky Spirit" people who teach him about his true nature. Wesley likewise discovers his true life-path when Lakanta reveals himself to be the Traveler, an archetype akin to the Sky Spirit. The vision opens up new possibilities that allow both Chakotay and Wesley to overcome the trauma of the past—both involving their paternal relationships—and live in harmony and balance. As a spirit of guidance, the Traveler reveals to Wesley, "You are ready to explore places where thought and energy combine in ways you can't even imagine. And I will be your guide, if you'd like."

## Notes

1. Thomas Hobbes, *Leviathan*, ed. Edwin Curley (Indianapolis, IN: Hackett, 1994), ch. 13.
2. Jean-Jacques Rousseau, *A Discourse on Inequality*, ed. Maurice Cranston (New York: Penguin, 1984).

3. Michael Okuda, Denise Okuda, and Debbie Mirek, *The Star Trek Encyclopedia* (New York: Pocket Books, 1997).
4. Stephanie A. Fryberg, "American Indian Social Representations: Do They Honor or Constrain American Indian Identities?" (2004): http://www.indianmascots.com/education/research/ (accessed June 23, 2015).
5. Sierra S. Adare, *"Indian" Stereotypes in TV Science Fiction: First Nations' Voices Speak Out* (Austin: University Press of Texas, 2005).
6. Bartolomé de Las Casas, *The Devastation of the Indies: A Brief Account,* trans. Herma Briffault (Baltimore: Johns Hopkins University Press, 1974).
7. Lewis Hanke, *Aristotle and the American Indians: A Study in Race Prejudice in the Modern World* (Bloomington: Indiana University Press, 1970).
8. Emmanuel Chukwudi Eze, "The Color of Reason: The Idea of 'Race' in Kant's Anthropology," *Bucknell Review* 38:2 (1995).
9. G.W.F. Hegel, *Lectures on the Philosophy of History*, trans. Ruben Alvarado (Aalten, the Netherlands: WordBridge Publishing, 2011).
10. Lewis Henry Morgan, *Ancient Society* (Tucson: University of Arizona Press, 1985).
11. Rudyard Kipling, "The White Man's Burden," *McClure's Magazine* 12 (February 1899): 290–1.
12. For an analysis of whether Spock's statement is philosophically sound, see Melanie Johnson-Moxley's chapter in this volume (Chapter 20).
13. Viola Cordova, *How It Is* (Tucson: University of Arizona Press, 2007).
14. John Locke, *Two Treatises of Government* (New York: Hafner, 1947), 148; see also Locke, *Some Thoughts Concerning Education*, ed. Ruth W. Grant and Nathan Tarcov (Indianapolis, IN: Hackett, 1996).
15. Plato, *The Laws*, trans. T. Saunders (New York: Penguin, 1970), 85–6.
16. John Mohawk and Oren Lyons, eds., *Exiled in the Land of the Free: Democracy, Indian Nations, and the U.S. Constitution* (Santa Fe, NM: Clear Light, 1992).
17. Beginning in the 18th century, some Cherokee departed from their Appalachian homeland, moving westward to escape from the encroachment of Anglo-Americans. They found a new home in the Ozarks, where for a time it was possible to live the old ways. But the Anglo-American frontier pulled westward, so some of these Ozark Cherokee moved south into Texas, which was then part of Mexico. Then the Anglos in Texas rebelled and separated Texas from Mexico. Some of the Texas Cherokee fled south of the border, and to this day there is a Cherokee community in Mexico.
18. George Lakoff and Mark Johnson, *Philosophy in the Flesh: The Embodied Mind and Its Challenge to Western Thought* (New York: Basic Books, 1999).

19. Vine Deloria, Jr., *C.G. Jung and the Sioux Traditions: Dreams, Visions, Nature and the Primitive* (New Orleans: Spring Journal, 2009).
20. Joseph Campbell, *The Hero with a Thousand Faces* (Princeton, NJ: Princeton University Press, 1972).
21. Joseph Campbell, *Power of Myth* (PBS, 1988).
22. Paul Ruditis, *Star Trek: Voyager Companion* (New York: Pocket Books, 2003).
23. J.T. Garrett and Michael Tlanusta Garrett, *The Cherokee Full Circle: A Practical Guide to Sacred Ceremonies and Traditions* (Rochester, VT: Bear and Company, 2002).
24. Carl Jung, *Psychological Types* (Princeton, NJ: Princeton University Press, 1971).
25. Walter Robinson, *Primal Way and the Pathology of Civilization* (Bloomington, IN: iUniverse, 2012).

# Part IV
# GAMMA QUADRANT: INFINITE DIVERSITY IN INFINITE COMBINATIONS

# 20

# Rethinking the Matter: Organians Are Still Organisms

*Melanie Johnson-Moxley*

Any system of thought based on this earth of ours … is extremely limited in its conceptions…. We know now that our earth is an insignificant planet swinging around a second-rate sun in no very important part of the universe…. I see no reason to suppose that the air about us and the heavenly spaces over us may not be peopled by intelligences, or entities, or forms of life, as unintelligible to us as we are to the insects…. [W]ho knows?—perhaps the nebulae are sentient entities and what we can see of them are their bodies…. My point is, that we are part of an infinite series and since the series *is* infinite, we had better take account of that fact, and admit into our thinking these infinite possibilities.

—Alfred North Whitehead (1861–1947)[1]

The most advanced life-forms in the *Star Trek* universe are portrayed as *incorporeal* beings: creatures who either don't have bodies or at least aren't bound to any physical forms they might assume. This freedom from physical definition seems to be accompanied by distinct advantages in developing intelligence, acquiring information, and achieving interstellar travel and other technological goals. At the end of the TOS episode "Errand of Mercy," in which Kirk and Spock encounter a highly advanced incorporeal species, the first officer observes, "I should say that the Organians are as far above us on the evolutionary scale as we are above the amoeba."

If humanity were to evolve into some staggeringly advanced version of ourselves, into something that would make us the equals of

*The Ultimate Star Trek and Philosophy*, First Edition. Edited by Kevin S. Decker and Jason T. Eberl.
© 2016 John Wiley & Sons, Ltd. Published 2016 by John Wiley & Sons, Ltd.

the Organians, the Bajoran Prophets, or the ubiquitous Q, would independence from our physical bodies be required for this advancement? Does being physical limit our possibilities for developing into better, more powerful beings? Must we shed our bodies if we're to dwell among the stars, not merely as explorers in cleverly designed metal ships, but as superior beings?

## Even Space Clouds Need Food ... and Love

There's no reason to suppose that incorporeality is itself an indication of advanced evolution. The *Enterprise* crews have encountered a number of cloud-beings, electromagnetic field-entities, and other creatures that, while both living and in some sense sentient or intelligent, are sharply limited in other respects.

For example, some of these kinds of creatures do little more than find and consume food, with potentially uncomfortable results for humanoids. Consider the dikironium cloud creature or "vampire cloud" ("Obsession," TOS) that feeds on red blood cells; or the cosmic cloud ("One of Our Planets Is Missing," TAS) capable of converting entire planets into the energy it needs. Spock describes the planet-eating cosmic cloud creature as a kind of intelligent space amoeba, nearly single-minded in its pursuit of nourishment. There are also creatures that feed on emotions they themselves can't generate, such as the Beta XII-A entity ("Day of the Dove," TOS) and the Drella of Alpha Carinae V ("Wolf in the Fold," TOS). There's nothing particularly "godlike" about these creatures; most of them strike us as mindless space monsters, neither malevolent nor benevolent—but simply hungry.[2]

So if not all incorporeal entities are highly evolved, then incorporeality isn't a *sufficient* condition for advanced intelligence and powers. That is, lacking a physical form isn't enough, all by itself, for a species to be judged an advanced life-form. The question remains open whether or not incorporeality is *necessarily* valuable to a species. In fact, there are at least two examples in the *Star Trek* universe in which lack of physical form is a *liability* in some way.

Some species are parasitic or invasive, requiring interaction with— if not complete control of—a physical body in order to function properly. The Zetarians in "The Lights of Zetar" (TOS) were once humanoid; they became incorporeal, not by design or evolution, but through a cataclysmic accident. As energy beings, they retained their memories and desires from their former lives, while acquiring new capacities, such as interstellar travel without need of a vehicle. Rather than finding themselves liberated in these circumstances, the Zetarians sought compatible humanoids whose bodies they could commandeer in order to live out physical lives, resorting to violence in their attempts to achieve this goal.

There's an interesting variation on this with the character Ronin in "Sub Rosa" (TNG), who is an anaphasic life-form that could assume corporeal form by bonding with a host with compatible biochemistry. Though capable of appearing as a male human, he revealed himself as such only to the women with whom he bonded—namely, generations of Dr. Beverly Crusher's family and ultimately, the doctor herself. The bonding wasn't clearly voluntary, which places Ronin in the invasive-parasitic category.

In such cases, the creature's lack of a physical body is detrimental to its capacity for experience, a limitation of function. In other cases, incorporeal beings seem to be somehow dissatisfied with their conventional mode of existence, seeking something more than nourishment or embodiment from physical creatures. Some of the more engaging storylines of this sort are about a highly advanced nonphysical being who encounters and comes to care for an individual or species of humanoids. In some cases, the superior creature, like a god from Hindu mythology, adopts an avatar in order to more fully engage with the other species, giving up some measure of its power in order to do so.

This happens when the Douwd, a possibly omnipotent, millennia-old creature in "The Survivors" (TNG), meets and marries a musician while traveling in the guise of a botany student. He refrains from using his considerable power in order to hide his true nature from her for decades—until tragedy strikes. The sacrifice of power may be permanent, as in the case with the Companion in "Metamorphosis" (TOS), a creature composed of ionized hydrogen and electricity who falls in love with Zefram Cochrane. It ultimately merges with a dying Federation commissioner—after Captain Kirk mercilessly points out the flaw in the cloud–human love connection—in order to experience that relationship as a human being. The sacrifice of power may also result in quite unintended consequences, as when two members of the Q—the parents of Amanda Rogers—adopt human form to live on Earth and are killed by a tornado ("True Q," TNG).[3] In these latter cases, the driving force is a desire for connection or a quality of experience that demonstrates a need for a voluntary recalibration of the entity's interactions with its environment.

## Collapse the Polarity!

All of this can be accounted for by philosophy, because in Alfred North Whitehead's view of the universe, the category of *organism* is broader than we think. His system places amoebas and tribbles, electrons and Klingons, ionized gas particles, and the Q all within this category. According to his system, everything that exists has a *mental* and a *physical* side, and any complex living thing has to have some kind of a body to survive very long. "Body," in this context, doesn't have to be flesh and blood—or silicon and viscous fluid, or whatever—but it'll satisfy the idea of "corporeality" enough to help make the case, not only that advanced life-forms *need* not be purely incorporeal but also that they *could* not be.

In Whitehead's concept of organism, *experience* is ontologically basic and forms the very foundation of reality. The fundamental components of reality are "actual entities." These entities aren't substances or things; they're dynamic "drops of experience," and so are also called "actual occasions," which refers to their happening at some definite time and place. The concept of an actual entity, or occasion, is more fundamental than that of the scientist's atoms, electrons, or quarks (or, for that matter, Quark), since all of these things are *composed of actual entities*.

Whitehead's worldview treats these entities as having a basic kind of decision-making power. This isn't a conscious process like human decision making, but there is a decision made, of a sort, by any actual entity when it realizes one possibility rather than others from a range of real options presented to it. Think of the various possibilities realized in the different parallel universes by Worf in "Parallels" (TNG) or the divergent possibilities that various characters encounter in the universe depicted in "Mirror, Mirror" (TOS) and various mirror universe episodes of DS9. This decision-making power means that every actual entity has a *mental pole*. At the same time, every actual entity is shaped by a multitude of factors. They don't arrive in the universe *ex nihilo* ("out of nothing"). Each is preceded by a history of previous occasions, a series of previous decisions, the influence of factors emphasized or deemphasized, the potentialities and needs of a given environment, and stubborn facts of existence that combine to shape every moment of experience. These constitute an actual entity's *physical pole*.

Every actual entity is *momentary*: as soon as it comes into being, as soon as an occasion arises, it immediately perishes into the past. The moment is gone before it ever really exists—a moment isn't extended in time, and can't be measured—but its influence remains, much like the light from distant stars long since perished as we look upon their traces in the night sky. An act of molecular combination, the path of successive drops of water, the feasting of Cardassian voles all carve the universe into distinct shapes, as it were, but the activities themselves are ephemeral. What persist to various degrees are *facts*: once an occasion has happened, it's forever part of the universe, although the effect of it may fade and become increasingly less important over time. This, again, contributes to the physical pole of future actual occasions.

Any dynamic network of experience is an *organism*. The concept of "organism" applies to more than just biological entities; crystals and planets are also structured societies. The broadest possible background for all activity in the universe is the *extensive continuum*—more expansive even than the Q Continuum. Each identifiable society of occasions also serves as the background for subordinate societies of occasions. So, for example, a living cell is a structured society: it provides the social background for its constituent molecules, which themselves provide the background for constituent electrons, and so forth. On a larger scale, the Milky Way galaxy provides the structured background for both physical societies, such as star systems and the planets they contain, as well as societies such as the United Federation of Planets, the Dominion, and the Romulan Star Empire—each of them in turn providing the macro-level background for their particular civilizations.

The universe thus presents a bewildering complexity of societies that complement and compete with one another. The challenge, Whitehead says, for any society of occasions is to achieve the right proportion of *survival power* and *qualitative intensity*. If a society is underspecialized, it's likely to have survival power, but will lack the intensity needed for the satisfaction of its individual members. On the other hand, if a society is overspecialized, then it may thrive only in a particular and uncommon sort of environment, limiting its long-term survival power. If the underspecialized society is like ontological tofu, unremarkable on its own terms, then the overspecialized society is like the Hajjlaran spice that the *Enterprise* crew encounters in "Oasis"

(ENT)—it's welcome only in precisely the right contexts (and quantity).

This challenge of finding the right mix can be met in a couple of ways. The first way is for a nexus of occasions to minimize unwelcome detail and diversity, overwhelming the collective with uniformity. As a result, changes in the immediate environment are less likely to compromise it. This is what happens with inorganic material bodies such as crystals, rocks, planets, and suns. The second way is for a nexus of occasions to react in novel ways to the immediate environment; this entails creative adaptation and is the primary feature of *living* societies, such as human cells, Tarcanian wildflowers, Loracus devil mites, and Betazoids. In lower organisms, the conceptual initiative is a thoughtless adjustment—a plant bending toward the sun, for example. In more advanced organisms, this initiative "amounts to *thinking* about the diverse experiences."[4]

Whitehead notes that a structured society may have various degrees of life within it, that for some purposes whatever life exists in a society may have only relative importance, and that there's no "absolute gap" between living and nonliving societies—consider the cadmium creatures of Velara III in "Home Soil" (TNG). Furthermore, within a society there will be different strands of occasions that are more or less complex, occupying either a subordinate or a dominant "ruling" position. Just as every actual entity has both mental and physical aspects, every living organism will have both organic and inorganic "nexūs"— organized groups of actual entities. The inorganic nexūs will deal with the challenge of *survival*—in a loose sense, "quantity of existence"— by enforcing uniformity among its actual occasions, so that changes in the immediate environment will not cause it to dissolve. This is similar to how the Borg impose a collective consciousness upon drones in a way that provides a Borg cube with, among other things, the power to resist damage and repair itself. Such enforced uniformity, specifically for the sake of survival, is starkly portrayed in the VOY episodes "Unity" and "Survival Instinct."

The organic nexūs deals with the challenge of *value*—the "quality of existence"—by reacting in novel ways to the environment so that it can achieve different kinds of ends. The Borg also provide a compelling example of the organic nexūs at work, as they have an uncanny ability to analyze and adapt to new situations, much to the *Enterprise* and *Voyager* crews' chagrin. A society is only really living if its organic nexūs are dominant, though a living nexūs requires protection, which the inorganic nexūs provides. In this sense, all forms of life require a kind of material support; a purely mental entity would simply not endure.

An entirely living (but incorporeal) nexus, if unsupported by any inorganic nexūs, would be essentially untethered. Without a complex social environment, it would be deficient both in survival power and its ability to effect change outside of its own immediate activities—akin to a Borg drone like "Hugh" or Seven of Nine when first separated from the Collective ("I, Borg," TNG; and "The Gift," VOY). A living nexus, however, can support a thread of personal order through time, "along some historical route of its members." An enduring entity with such a thread of personal order through time is a *living person*. Along such a historical route, there's a transmission of data from occasion to occasion that gains a depth and robustness (Whitehead calls this "canalization") that ultimately protects the *entire system* of nexūs— the organism as a whole—from destabilization. Without it, "depth of originality would spell disaster for the animal body," Whitehead says. But with it, "personal mentality can be evolved, *so as to combine its individual originality with the safety of the material organism on which it depends.*"[5] In this way, living societies are in fact complex arrangements of the physiological and the psychological.

## The Continuing Voyage

What does it take to reach the level of an Organian, a Prophet, or a Q? Is gaining freedom from physical form a requirement for the highest levels of species advancement? If by "freedom from physical form" we're assuming a *dualism* between mind and matter, and if we suppose that a free entity is a purely mental entity—completely untethered from physical existence—then the answer is "no." In Whitehead's terms, such assumptions would be based on a profound misconception about the nature of reality: nothing is *purely* mental or purely physical, nor could it be. Even if this assertion were modified to fit within the framework of Whitehead's philosophy of organism, such an utterly untethered entity would be an unstable and unsustainable organism. If, however, what we mean is a "freedom from" certain standards of order that might limit the development of life and consciousness, then there may be something to this. In this case, what we really mean by "freedom from physical form" is actually "freedom *of* physical form."

The Q serve as an intriguing case study in this context.[6] In many respects, they seem to be the best candidates for the most evolved life-forms ever to populate the *Star Trek* universe. Q are capable of manipulating matter and energy, and of traveling throughout time and space, without any obvious limits. They exist in their own extradimensional plane of existence, the Q Continuum, without any natural predators or serious adversaries. The Q appear to be omnipotent and immortal, but the fact that they can be killed—at least by each other—compromises this appearance. They also appear to be omniscient, although they can be surprised—at least by certain unpredictable Starfleet officers—and so this idea should be placed in question, too.

While the party line is that the Q have always existed as perfect beings, dissident accounts depict the Q as being originally humanoid, having attained their current state as the result of eons of evolution—a process of development that has long since stalled out, leaving them with a stable but stagnant society. This concern that the species has brought itself to the tipping point of petrification motivates the renegade Quinn to disrupt the order of things by committing suicide in "Death Wish" (VOY), which instigates civil war between the status quo and freedom factions of the Q in "The Q and the Grey" (VOY). The status quo faction is concerned by the influence of human compassion and curiosity on their stable culture; the freedom faction embraces it. In Whitehead's terms, the Q continue to master the balance between survival power and the capacity for creative advance precisely through their engagement in this struggle.[7]

As highly developed as they became, and as well traveled throughout time and space as they were, the Q were somehow *incomplete* precisely because, in a matter of speaking, they were *too* complete. Having seen, done, and said everything there was to say (or so they believed) in their arrested, albeit unfathomably advanced, state of existence, there seemed to be nothing else to do or to become—everyone had even "done the scarecrow." One critical aspect of the solution propagated by the Q's freedom faction was embodied (literally) by Amanda Rogers's parents in their act of voluntary *tethering* to individual physical forms in order to experience the universe differently ("True Q," TNG). The Q's "freedom from" had started to become irrelevant when they ceased exercising their "freedom to" in creative ways; such creativity could be recaptured only by voluntarily assuming corporeality and mortality in order to experience individuality.

The Organians bear some resemblance to the Q. One of their characteristic features is a self-professed aversion to violence and the experience of pain. Like the Q, they structure their society to minimize interaction with—and thus contamination by—the physical and emotional influences of embodied species. But this apparent purity of existence, reinforced by dominant forms of order (tradition), may in fact conceal a certain sterility within the species, as implied by a younger Organian who questions the status quo of his species' approach to observing, but not interacting with, humanoid species ("Observer Effect," ENT). The irony implicit in both Q and Organian attempts to maintain their species' superiority by preventing contamination by inferior species is that they lose the injection of novelty that a society of organisms must have in balanced measure with its canalized forms of order in order to not only endure but also *live*.

Rather than thinking of the necessary characteristics of an advanced life-form in incorporeal terms, we may be better served to think in terms of how effectively such a life-form can engage with its environment to achieve its aims. The temptation to view incorporeal beings as necessarily more advanced may stem from an intuition that freedom and efficiency of thought, "movement," and the exercise of will would all be expanded as the scope of a creature's world horizon is expanded. But we'd be placing emphasis on the wrong thing to insist that being somehow "untethered" is the key component in exercising such power. On the contrary, a more expansive capacity for tethering may be precisely what would enable such power to expand.

## Notes

1. Lucien Price, *Dialogues of Alfred North Whitehead* (Boston: Little, Brown and Company, 1954), 237.
2. Yes, it's certainly possible that a monster may be evolutionarily superior to a human being, but unlikely that a *mindless* monster would be.
3. They were, in fact, the targets of intentional assassination by the Q during events leading toward the Q civil war.
4. Alfred North Whitehead, *Process and Reality*, ed. D.R. Griffin and D.W. Sherburne (New York: The Free Press, 1978), 102.
5. Ibid., 107; emphasis mine.
6. The Q appear in TNG episodes "Encounter at Farpoint," "Hide and Q," Q Who?," "Dèjá Q," "Qpid," "True Q," "Tapestry," and "All Good Things " as well as the DS9 episode "Q-Less" and the VOY episodes "Death Wish," "The Q and the Grey," and "Q2." Pocket Books' *Star Trek* novels featuring Q include *Q-in-Law* (1991), *Q-Squared* (1994), *I, Q* (2000), and *The Q Continuum* trilogy (1998).

7. Examine the chapters in this book by Kyle Alkema and Adam Barkman (Chapter 10) and Charles Taliaferro and Bailey Wheelock (Chapter 29) for more on the philosophy of the Q; as well as Robert Arp's "Mind Your Ps and Qs: Power, Pleasure, and the Q Continuum," in *Star Trek and Philosophy*, ed. Jason T. Eberl and Kevin S. Decker (Chicago: Open Court, 2008).

# "In Search of ... " Friendship: What We Can Learn from Androids and Vulcans

## James M. Okapal

As Spock is dying at the end of *The Wrath of Khan*, he tells Kirk, "I have been, and always will be, your friend." It's an emotionally charged moment. At the funeral, Kirk refers to Spock as his friend and is clearly saddened as his voice breaks. There are many striking similarities here to the end of *ST: Nemesis* when Data dies saving Captain Picard and the *Enterprise*-E. His crewmates are emotionally overcome at the loss, with Counselor Troi breaking into tears as Picard toasts, "To absent friends. To family." What isn't clear, however, is whether Vulcans like Spock, Tuvok, and T'Pol, or androids such as Data, Lal, Lore, and B-4, can form friendships of a deep and moral kind.[1] One obstacle is that each of them has a limited emotional capacity. Another is that each of them tends to reason in a way that focuses narrowly on the consequences of their actions.

### "Never Place Friendship above Profit"

In his *Nicomachean Ethics*, Aristotle (385–322 BCE) distinguishes three types of friendship: for utility, for pleasure, and the genuine friendship shared among the virtuous.[2] Each type of friendship is defined by the value associated with the relationship, based upon the reason that brings the individuals together.[3]

Individuals who share friendships for utility or pleasure, Aristotle says, "do not love each other in themselves, but in so far as some benefit accrues to them from each other. And similarly with those

*The Ultimate Star Trek and Philosophy*, First Edition. Edited by Kevin S. Decker and Jason T. Eberl.
© 2016 John Wiley & Sons, Ltd. Published 2016 by John Wiley & Sons, Ltd.

whose friendship is based in pleasure."[4] These lesser forms of friendship are often referred to together as *instrumental* friendships.[5] In such friendships, the individuals are valuable to each other only as a means to some goal. About friendships for utility's sake, Aristotle says, "Friends of this kind do not indeed request each other's company much, for in some cases they are not even pleasing to each other and therefore have no use for friendly intercourse unless they are mutually profitable."[6] One can't help thinking that Ferengi engage in only these types of friendships. After all, their entire culture is centered on free enterprise, and accumulating more profit is their only goal. Their moral system, enshrined in the "Rules of Acquisition," has many aphorisms that may strike us as morally questionable. We find out in "The Nagus" (DS9) that we should "Never allow family to stand in the way of opportunity"—to the effect that Rom nearly jettisons his brother Quark from an airlock. Ironically, Quark *congratulates* his brother for having "the lobes" to try it. We're told in "Rules of Acquisition" (DS9) that we should "Never place friendship above profit," which is why Quark can't have a relationship with Pel once he learns she's a female and it would cost him dearly to be associated with her. Finally, it's made clear in "Past Tense, Part I" (DS9) that we should "Treat people in your debt like family, exploit them." In such a system, friends and family are merely tools or instruments to be used to gain further profit. At least, this is what the Ferengi system *implies* ought to be the case; in actual practice, Ferengi often violate these rules for the sake of friends and family (even Grand Nagus Zek, after he falls in love with Quark and Rom's mother, Ishka). Perhaps only FCA Liquidator Brunt counts as the model of a truly ruthless Ferengi whose relationships are simply profit motivated.

Friendships for utility aren't limited to business transactions, though. It's possible for Data to form relationships in order to achieve some other goal—namely, to better understand and become more human. Similarly, any treaty between rival governments would be a friendship for peaceful use, such as the creation of the Neutral Zone at the end of the Earth–Romulan war in 2160. Each side manages to avoid further immediate bloodshed, and the Romulans can continue their convoluted plotting against Earth and Vulcan behind closed doors. Later, when the Romulans enter the Dominion War on the side of the Federation, it's only to protect their own interests ("In the Pale Moonlight," DS9). Friendships for utility don't require any emotional overtones since the entire value of the relationship is based on a goal—profit, peace, knowledge, and so on—and none of these require emotional attachments.

Friendships can also be formed for the sake of pleasure and mutual enjoyment during communal activities. Think of how playing the board game Star Trek Catan or going to the San Diego Comic-Con brings people with similar interests together. We see how Julian Bashir and Miles O'Brien, who initially didn't get along well, eventually start spending their free time together playing racquetball and darts, as well as roleplaying in various holosuite programs. Their friendship even develops to the point where O'Brien begrudgingly admits that, while he loves his wife, Keiko, he has more fun with Bashir ("Extreme Measures," DS9).

Can an emotionless individual form friendships for pleasure? It doesn't seem possible. Data isn't able to experience pleasure without his emotion chip. He tells Timothy, the boy he rescued from the *Vico* in "Hero Worship" (TNG), that he can't taste food; he merely analyzes its contents. Once he integrates the emotion chip in *Generations*, though, he's able to taste the "revolting" beverage that Guinan serves him. Without the ability to experience pleasure, any friendship based around shared pleasant experiences would fall short. When Data and Geordi go to the holodeck to solve a Sherlock Holmes mystery in "Elementary, Dear Data" (TNG), Geordi is annoyed that Data knows the Holmes stories so well that he can figure out the mystery with just one clue: "If there's no mystery, there's no game. No game, no fun." The point of the experience for Geordi was to have fun; whereas for Data it was to solve the mystery as a cognitive exercise. Without his emotion chip Data can't have fun, and he can't form friendships of pleasure. With the benefit of his emotion chip in *ST: Insurrection*, however, Data is able to learn how to have fun from Artim on the Bak'u planet.

Virtuous friendships, the finest form of friendship for Aristotle, also require emotions. In these relationships, the bond goes beyond use or pleasure: "one loves the friend for the person she is. ... These include both her character traits ... and her unique perspective on herself and others."[7] Whereas you could exchange the people you interact with in business transactions, make peace accords with, or play darts with, at little or no loss, in a virtuous friendship "the friend cannot be replaced by another, for no other can have her essential features."[8] Such friendships require that the value associated with the friends is *intrinsic* to the relationship, not merely instrumental to other goals, and based in deep emotional states, such as love.

Furthermore, virtuous friendships require emotion to color both sides of the relationship—in particular, *mutual* goodwill: "an active caring and concern for each other's happiness and success."[9] An android without emotions is incapable of caring for another. This is what leads Jenna D'Sora to finally realize that dating Data isn't going to work in "In Theory" (TNG), telling him, "I got out of a relationship with an unemotional man. And I got right back into another one with ... with a man who's ... absolutely incapable of emotion." Data's lack of emotions means that Jenna can't make him happy, while losing her wouldn't make Data sad: "As close as we are, I ... I don't really matter to you. Not really. Nothing I can say or do will ever make you happy or, or sad ... or touch you in any way." After they break up, Data merely deletes the subroutine he devised for their time together.

But suppose all these problems could be overcome. Suppose there was the possibility that Data, before his emotion chip was installed, could form a friendship under some other description. When asked if he has any friends, Data usually mentions Geordi in episodes such as "Data's Day" (TNG) and "Legacy" (TNG). When, in the latter episode, Ishara Yar questions whether Data can have friends given his lack of emotion, he replies, "Even among humans, friends are often more about familiarity." Friendship, for him, is recognizing the absence or presence of someone: "As I experience certain sensory input patterns, my mental pathways become accustomed to them. The input is eventually anticipated and even missed when absent." Even if this allows us to say that Data can form a type of friendship not included by Aristotle's system, we might still think there's something lacking in Data's relationships.

## "Because the Needs of the One Outweigh the Needs of the Many"

Even after Data gets the emotion chip, it might still be difficult for him to form virtuous friendships. Another important requirement of the highest kind of friendship is that the friend must act *out of* friendship, which requires acts to be motivated by the simple fact that someone is one's friend. Motivation to bring about some further end, such as becoming human or having fun, isn't being driven to be a friend in the right way. The problem is that Data, along with the stoic Vulcans and the avaricious Ferengi, seems to act for reasons that make it impossible that he's acting *out of* friendship itself.

When Spock dies in *The Wrath of Khan*, he justifies his sacrifice to Kirk on the following principle: "The needs of the many outweigh the needs of the few ... or the one." Spock is echoing the *consequentialist* idea that an act is right if and only if it produces the greatest good for the greatest number of people.[10] Androids seem committed to a similar way of thinking: in his attempt at forming a relationship with Jenna D'Sora, Data exhibits "the purely instrumental, calculative, unemotional rationality extolled by consequentialism."[11] So what does it mean to act and think in accordance with consequentialism? Why might acting and thinking as if good consequences were the most important thing preclude the possibility of friendship?

Consequentialism is the generalized moral and political theory whose earlier formulations include the utilitarianism of Jeremy Bentham (1748–1832), John Stuart Mill (1806–1873), and Henry Sidgwick (1838–1900).[12] Consequentialism is *teleological* (or goal directed) in its theories of both *right action* and *motivation*. So consequentialists say that whether an action is morally right or not depends upon the value associated with the action's outcome: if the outcome of an action will produce greater value than the outcome of other possible actions, then it's the right action to perform; if the outcome produces less value than other possible actions, then it's the wrong action to perform. We know that, as a cadet, James T. Kirk's solution to the *Kobayashi Maru* simulation was the right consequentialist solution, at least in the timeline in which *The Wrath of Khan* occurs.[13] We might normally think that cheating to make it possible to win a programmed "no-win scenario" is morally unacceptable. Yet Kirk not only wasn't punished but also received "a commendation for original thinking." From a consequentialist perspective, Kirk's cheating was the right action because the outcome's value was positive.

How would thinking like a consequentialist preclude forming virtuous friendships? Consequentialist views about action require that friendships remain merely *instrumentally* valuable:

> [A consequentialist] is forced to justify her personal commitments and concerns, including her friendships, in terms of their ability to maximize the good, and to abandon or compromise them when she cannot so justify them. As a moral agent she must regard her friendships as dependent for their moral worth on the overall good, and thus as sacrificeable to it.[14]

But that isn't how we think of our best friends, who shouldn't be sacrificed for the greater good. This is exactly why Data's actions toward Geordi in "Descent, Part II" (TNG) are particularly horrifying. Lore and Data are carrying out experiments on Geordi to convert biological cerebra into positronic neural nets. If the procedure is successful, the cognitive functions of biological life forms can be improved—an outcome Lore finds valuable on behalf of the Borg. Unfortunately, there's a 60 percent chance that the procedure won't work and Geordi will suffer extensive brain damage. Nevertheless, when challenged by Picard, Data—whose ethical subroutine has been overridden by Lore—responds that "it is for the greater good." Data is willing to sacrifice Geordi, his closest friend, to bring about some collective good; without his ethical subroutine informing his behavior, Data can see Geordi and the rest of humanity only as instrumentally valuable and not as friends.

The *Enterprise* crew in *The Search for Spock*, however, understands how being a friend may require the rejection of consequentialist thinking. After stealing the *Enterprise*, violating the ban on visiting the Genesis planet, destroying the *Enterprise* to defeat the Klingons, and putting their careers in jeopardy, Spock asks Kirk why they would do such things. Kirk's reply could be interpreted as a clear rejection of consequentialist thinking: "Because the needs of the one outweigh the needs of the many." On a nonconsequentialist interpretation, the intrinsic value of a friend will sometimes require that the right action be one that doesn't lead to the greater good and may not even regard consequences at all. If determining the right action doesn't take into account the possible consequences, whether they be good *or* bad, then the action won't be comprehensible from a purely consequentialist perspective. On this interpretation, the actions of Kirk and the others are based on the recognition that "those who have the dispositions of friendship cannot, consistently, be consequentialists, and those who are consequentialists cannot, consistently, be friends."[15] If we accept Aristotle's view of friendship as based on intrinsic value, then consequentialism and friendship are *logically* incompatible. While Spock takes the consequentialist principle as axiomatic, his mother, Amanda, responds, "Then you stand here alive because of a *mistake*, made by your flawed, feeling human friends." Although he may not fully understand or accept Kirk's reasoning, Spock eventually acknowledges his shipmates' sacrifices on his behalf by standing with them in judgment at the end of *The Voyage Home*.

Friendship and consequentialism are also *psychologically* incompatible, for the only states of mind relevant to assessing the value of an act's consequences are states like purposes, goals, and desires.[16] This way of thinking leads to explanations such as "I performed that act for the sake of [insert some purpose, goal, or desire]." When Spock asks Kirk why Kirk saved him at the end of *The Search for Spock*, the explanation could've been "I saved you for the sake of not letting you die a second time" or "for the sake of satisfying my desire to see you again." In neither of these explanations is there any reference to Spock being a friend—they could very well have been said to a red-shirted ensign because they make reference only to either avoiding negative values or achieving positive ones. But by acting *for the sake of* these goals, we ignore that it's possible and worthwhile to act *out of* friendship alone. To act out of friendship is to be motivated to act simply because someone is a friend, regardless of any purpose that might be advanced, goal achieved, or further desire satisfied.

Consider T'Pol's actions in "Twilight" (ENT). Captain Archer, in saving T'Pol, is infected with interspatial parasites that leave him unable to form new memories. This creates an alternative timeline in which Archer is unable to remember that the Xindi have destroyed Earth and spent twelve years hunting down every human they could find. He's also unaware that T'Pol, despite Ambassador Soval's offer to resume her position in the Vulcan High Command, stayed on with the remaining humans on Ceti Alpha V so she could take care of Archer. Why would T'Pol do all this? The answer can only be *out of friendship*. T'Pol's actions aren't for some goal or benefit she might receive from being Archer's caretaker. When they arrive on Ceti Alpha V, he can't be cured; nevertheless, she stays and takes care of him while Dr. Phlox goes back to Denobula to try to find a cure. When Phlox returns years later, he asks why she took care of Archer. She claims it's to repay the debt of saving her life, which would fit a teleological, *for the sake of* explanation. But Phlox knows better: "I can only imagine what it must have been like. Spending all those years in that house. Learning so much about him, yet he remembers nothing about you." T'Pol hasn't been doing this merely *for the sake of* repaying a debt that Archer can't even remember she owes him or strengthening her relationship with him. After all, Archer can't remember any development in their relationship beyond the day he became infected. Doing it for the sake of the relationship would still be a consequentialist reason, but that reason is effectively closed to her. Thus, her only reason for staying, despite her protests, is out of her deep friendship with Archer.

A consequentialist, however, can't admit this is the reason. Instead, a consequentialist would claim it's for the purpose of repaying the life debt or to deepen their relationship. It's clear, however, that these aren't T'Pol's reasons; she's no longer motivated, in this case, by a consequentialist psychology.[17]

## "The Continuing Voyages ... "

What have we learned about friendship from this brief look at the relationships of androids and Vulcans? First, there are multiple forms of friendship, many of which—and the finest of which—require emotion. Second, while some friendships allow us to value our friends *instrumentally*, the finest form of friendship—among the virtuous—requires that we value our friends *intrinsically*. In these virtuous friendships, there's mutual goodwill, acceptance, and a level of caring that's probably hard to achieve very often—hence, Aristotle affirms that we can only have *few* such friendships.[18] Third, there's a difference between acting *out of* friendship and acting *for the sake of* the friendship or some other goal, which suggests that genuine friendships can't be accommodated by consequentialist ways of thinking. But there's so much more we haven't explored in this brief look at friendship.[19] These explorations are part of an "undiscovered country" of possibilities in the continuing voyages of starships, philosophy, and our own lives.[20]

## Notes

1. Dr. Juliana Tainer is an exception. As pointed out in "Inheritance" (TNG), the android version of Juliana Tainer has emotions and the memories of the deceased former wife of Dr. Noonien Soong, and furthermore believes herself to be human.
2. See Aristotle, *The Nicomachean Ethics*, trans. H. Rachham (Cambridge, MA: Harvard University Press, 2003). Books VIII and IX are devoted to the topic of friendship.
3. Many philosophers beyond Aristotle have talked about friendship. See Michael Pakalul, *Other Selves: Philosophers on Friendship* (Indianapolis, IN: Hackett, 1991), for some writings by ancient, medieval, and modern philosophers. For more contemporary views, see Neera Kapur Badhwar, *Friendship: A Philosophical Reader* (Ithaca, NY: Cornell University Press, 1993).
4. Aristotle, *Nicomachean Ethics*, bk. VIII, ch. 3.

5. See Neera Kapur Badhwar, "Why It Is Wrong to Be Always Guided by the Best: Consequentialism and Friendship," *Ethics* 101:3 (1991): 483.

6. Aristotle, *Nicomachean Ethics*, bk. VIII, ch. 3.

7. Badhwar, "Consequentialism and Friendship," 459.

8. Ibid.

9. Neera Kapur Badhwar, "Introduction: The Nature and Significance of Friendship," in *Friendship*, 13.

10. For further discussion of consequentialist moral reasoning in *Star Trek*, see Gregory Littmann's chapter in this volume (Chapter 12).

11. Elizabeth Anderson, *Value in Ethics and Economics* (Cambridge, MA: Harvard University Press, 1993), 40.

12. See Jeremy Bentham, *An Introduction to the Principles of Morals and Legislation,* (Mineola, NY: Dover Publications, 2007); John Stuart Mill, *Utilitarianism*, ed. George Sher (Indianapolis, IN: Hackett, 2001); and Henry Sidgwick, *The Methods of Ethics*, 7th ed. (Indianapolis, IN: Hackett, 1981).

13. In the alternative timeline of Abrams' *Star Trek*, we never find out the official moral judgment of Kirk's solution to the *Kobayashi Maru* as his misconduct hearing is interrupted by Nero's attack on Vulcan.

14. Badhwar, "Consequentialism and Friendship," 492.

15. Ibid., 493.

16. See Michael Stocker, "Values and Purposes: The Limits and Teleology and the Ends of Friendship," in *Friendship*, 245–63; and Michael Stocker, "Moral Schizophrenia of Modern Ethical Theories," *Journal of Philosophy* 73:14 (1976): 453–66.

17. There isn't enough space to adequately go into criticisms of the claims that consequentialism and friendship are either psychologically or logically incompatible. Defenses of their compatibility can be found in Peter Railton, "Alienation, Consequentialism, and the Demands of Morality," *Philosophy & Public Affairs* 13 (1984): 134–71; and Matthew Tedesco, "Indirect Consequentialism, Suboptimality, and Friendship," *Pacific Philosophical Quarterly* 87 (2006): 567–77.

18. See Aristotle, *Nicomachean Ethics*, bk. IX, ch. 10.

19. One topic not explored here is the tension between the values of friendship and equity. For a discussion of this topic, see Judith Barad and Ed Robertson, "Equity and Friendship in *Star Trek*," in *The Ethics of Star Trek* (New York: Harper Collins, 2000), 119–35.

20. I'm grateful to Kevin Decker, Jason Eberl, and William Irwin for the helpful comments and corrections made to this chapter. I would also like to thank my parents, Andy and Mary Okapal, for introducing me to The Original Series and all their encouragement in my endeavors.

# Resistance Is Negligible: In Praise of Cyborgs

## Lisa Cassidy

Resistance is futile.

—The Borg

I would rather be a cyborg than a goddess.

—Donna Haraway

A few years after feminist philosopher Donna Haraway proclaimed she'd rather be a cyborg than a goddess, the Borg marched across television screens in *Star Trek: the Next Generation*. The Borg is an organic–technological hybrid collective that seeks perfection by force-fully incorporating other species into itself. *TV Guide* declared the Borg one of television's all-time scariest villains. But *Star Trek*'s depiction of the Borg as terrifying and atrocious is in sharp contrast to Haraway's sympathy for cyborgs. Haraway declares that being a cyborg is inevitable, yes—but also desirable and liberating. So who's right, *Star Trek* or the philosopher? And what's really so bad about being Borg, anyway? Are there values in being Borg that *Star Trek* is missing?

We first meet the Borg when the mysterious, omnipotent Q deliberately puts the *Enterprise*-D into the Borg's path as a warning to Captain Jean-Luc Picard in "Q Who?" In the confrontation that follows, eighteen crewmembers die, the *Enterprise* is sliced and diced, Picard has to admit his failings to Q, and a new catchphrase— "Resistance is futile"—enters pop culture. In the *Star Trek* universe, no species is so thoroughly terrifying as the Borg. It isn't just the supe-riority of their adaptive weaponry, their mass-produced cube-shaped

*The Ultimate Star Trek and Philosophy*, First Edition. Edited by Kevin S. Decker and Jason T. Eberl.
© 2016 John Wiley & Sons, Ltd. Published 2016 by John Wiley & Sons, Ltd.

ships, or their zombie-like appearance that spooks viewers. It's the idea of actually *being* Borg that's so frightening to us.[1] This is because the Borg don't threaten the Federation with mere death or extinction, but with *assimilation*: "Your biological and technological distinctiveness will be added to our own. Your culture will adapt to service us." Before we decide whether to resist or join them, let's engage with the Borg, maximum warp!

## A Matrix of Three: Locutus

Let us look at three Borg converts who, in their confrontation with Federation values, help us to answer our earlier questions. After the initial confrontation Q orchestrated, TNG features an extremely dramatic encounter with the Borg: Captain Picard himself is kidnapped and transformed into a drone in the "Best of Both Worlds." The former Picard, now sporting Borg prosthetics, implants, and a really tight catsuit, is designated "Locutus"—Latin for "he who speaks." Locutus is fully integrated into the collective Borg consciousness, sharing all of Picard's own knowledge and memories, so that the Borg can more efficiently assimilate humanity.

The Picard/Locutus storyline allows us to explore one of the core values of the Federation: *autonomy*.[2] Confronted with the Borg's plan for cultural assimilation, Picard declares, "My culture is based on freedom and self-determination.... We would rather die" than comply with the Borg. The Borg reply is quite interesting: "Your archaic cultures are authority driven." Despite his protests, Borg nanoprobes are injected and the transformation to Locutus begins. Once Locutus is back onboard the *Enterprise*, he insists to Lieutenant Worf, "Why do you resist us? We only wish to raise quality of life for all species." Worf replies, "I like my species the way it is." In a pivotal scene, Picard and Locutus wrestle each other within one body, a robotic arm and a human one grappling with each other and with Data. The human Picard breaks through as he wills himself to connect with the empathic Counselor Troi.

*Autonomy* is a word from the ancient Greek word *auto*, meaning "self," and *nomos*, meaning "management or rule." Conversely, the antonym of autonomy is rule by others, or *hetero*nomy, although frequently the opposite of autonomy is simply called *slavery*. In Picard's defense of humanity, he seizes on autonomy as the basis of Federation culture. Worf's position is quite similar—by liking Klingons "as they are," he implicitly agrees with Picard that self-rule is essential for a good life. It's only through Picard's personal effort to take command of himself that he metaphorically and literally takes hold of his own body to defeat the Borg.

But what do we make of the Borg's initial reply to Picard that humanity has an archaic culture that's authority driven? This reply can be understood in two different ways: autonomy could mean over-reliance on the authority of the self; it could also mean that the Federation is run by authorities that manipulate us into *believing* we rule our lives, when in reality we don't. Either way, the Borg finds humanity to be less autonomous than Picard, or we, imagine ourselves to be.

## A Matrix of Three: Hugh

A couple years after Picard's experience as Locutus, the *Enterprise-D* crew rescues a Borg drone, the lone survivor of a crash. Dr. Beverly Crusher immediately moves to treat the drone, while the ever-pragmatic Worf argues they should "kill it now." The doctor prevails, the single Borg is returned to function on the *Enterprise*, and Picard dispassionately hatches a plan to use the drone as a walking computer virus to infect the entire Borg Collective.

Hugh's storyline highlights the value of *individuality*. The transformation of an injured Borg *drone*, an "it," that has the Borg *designation* "Three of Five" to a "person," whose *name* is given by Geordi LaForge as "Hugh," is the process of creating an individual. At first, the drone uses only the Borg's collective "we" mode of address. But when the drone discerns the difference between a name and a designation, it asks, "Do I have a name?" This is the first time we've heard an ordinary drone use the first person singular "I," but Hugh soon reverts back to using "we." Frustrated, Geordi explains to Hugh what it's like to be human: "We are all separate individuals. I am Geordi. I choose what I want to do with my life. I make decisions for myself. For people like me, losing that individuality is almost worse than dying." Geordi then tells Hugh that friends ease the loneliness of being an individual. This seems to make an impact on Hugh, who ultimately rejects the Borg assimilation agenda because it would hurt his friend Geordi. Hugh tells the Collective, in the *faux* persona of Locutus, "I will not assist you.... No. I am Hugh." Hugh is eventually returned to the Borg, where his memories of being an individual will be integrated into the Collective. Picard muses, "Every one of the Borg being given the opportunity to experience the feeling of singularity. Perhaps that's the most pernicious program of all. The knowledge of self being spread through the Collective, in that brief moment, might alter them forever."

Being an individual has to do with being a distinct, unique person. The word *individual* is closely connected to *indivisible*—not able to be divided or separated into smaller parts. The Borg Collective, on the other hand, is an integrated collection of smaller parts: drones that aren't valued in themselves, but only for their contribution to the larger whole. Borg drones themselves aren't indivisible, as they're made of swappable spare parts. "The sick and injured are reabsorbed. Others take their place," Hugh explains. Even the memories of a particular Borg drone are divisible in that they can be copied and shared with the hive.

Picard's ultimately correct: the experience of being an individual is "pernicious" to the Borg hive mind. We meet Hugh again in "Descent, Part II." Hugh is with a band of Borg who accidentally assimilated his memories of individuality. These Borg fight for one another and grieve their fallen comrades. Hugh says, "Perhaps in time, we will learn to function as individuals and work together as a group." The *Enterprise* is a model of blending individuality and collectivity, but the fact remains that Hugh—who's experienced the Borg collective, the *Enterprise*, and his own little group—is left speculating if the two values are compatible.

## A Matrix of Three: Seven of Nine

Seven of Nine is the most developed Borg character in the *Star Trek* universe. As the far-flung *Starship Voyager* tries to return to the Alpha Quadrant, Captain Kathryn Janeway finds herself making an alliance with the Borg to defeat a mutual enemy. In the chaos of battle and ensuing victory, *Voyager* is joined by a single drone: Seven of Nine.

Seven experiences autonomy and individuality as challenges, just as Locutus and Hugh do. But we'll focus on how her character demonstrates the value of *authenticity*. "The Gift" shows how a newly liberated Seven struggles to find her authentic self. Seven repeatedly demands that "we" be returned to the Borg collective and her Borg technology restored. "Take me back to my own kind," Seven orders Janeway. "You *are* with your own kind—humans," Janeway responds.

Seven eventually accepts she'll become more human than Borg, now donning small ocular and manual implants, a blond up-do, and an amazingly tight catsuit. She even remembers being a human girl named Annika Hansen—albeit in the third person: "Her favorite color was red," Seven tells Janeway. This memory is poignant because it's true to the girl Seven once was.

*Authentic* is another word we get from ancient Greek and is related to authorship, as in being the true author or original creator of something—think of the Doctor's fight to retain his rights of authentic authorship in "Author, Author" (VOY). Captain Janeway thinks that Seven is authentically human, something the Borg "stole" from her by assimilation. This pits Borg existence as the simulation, the *fake*, against humanity's authenticity. But Seven is, for a long time, ambivalent about which one is her authentic or her simulated self because so much of who she is now really *is* Borg. Her residential quarters, for example, are just a cargo bay retrofitted to *resemble* a Borg ship, complete with regeneration chambers.

The conflict about who Seven authentically is—Borg or human—climaxes in her encounters with the Borg Queen in "Dark Frontier" and "Unimatrix Zero." The Queen was introduced in *First Contact* and is used to great effect as Janeway's foil, the two struggling over where the bona fide Seven belongs. In "Dark Frontier," Seven is tempted to rejoin the Borg Collective or else defend *Voyager* as her personal collective. When Seven voices her objections to the Queen's plan to assimilate humanity, the Queen tells her without any irony, "You're only repeating their words. You sound like a mindless automaton. *Comply*, or we will turn you into a drone." Seven responds, "Proceed, if you wish." The Queen retorts: "You're torn between your desire to be one with us and your loyalty to them.... They were never your Collective." Seven ultimately sides with Janeway, but must use elements of her "true" Borg self to defeat the Queen, wryly noting, "Our thoughts are one," as Seven and Janeway escape the hive.

We've seen that the Borg's terror is that they threaten core values of autonomy, individuality, and authenticity. Without these values, *Star Trek* tells us in many episodes, human life isn't worth living. But is that really true? I will defend a feminist position, inspired by Haraway, that in fact these three values have never really been accessible to all of us insofar as prejudice has barred some people from accessing them. This implies that rival cyborg values—of heteronomy, collectivity, and simulation—might be worth a reboot.

# A Cyborg Manifesto

Perhaps in *Star Trek*'s envisioned future, when injustice and inequality in human society have been eliminated, there'll be little need for feminism. But in our current society, when inequality and injustice are very real, feminism is still very relevant. Feminism is a political and philosophical movement that's broken into historical "waves"— like the transmission of light across light-years. The first wave (Stardate 1860s–1950s)[3] fought for women's suffrage (right to vote) and full citizenship. The second wave (Stardate 1960s–1980s) addressed women's ongoing economic and political inequality. The third wave (Stardate 1980s–present) argues for a more inclusive society by breaking down long-standing cultural barriers to women's freedom based on race, gender, class, and sexuality. In 1985, Donna Haraway published "A Cyborg Manifesto," an essay that came at the forefront of third-wave feminism. After the title, Haraway labels the essay (in all caps), "AN IRONIC DREAM OF A COMMON LANGUAGE FOR WOMEN IN THE INTEGRATED CIRCUIT," which sounds like a Borg command straight from the Queen!

It's impossible to summarize this rich, strange essay without sounding like Data stiffly trying to tell a joke—"I said I kiddillies, diddle I?" Using irony, argument, and deliberately provoked confusion, Haraway gets us to see that the world's categories are more complicated than we've assumed. She wants us to stop dividing the world in terms of simplistic right/wrong oppositional value hierarchies, such as human/animal or human/natural or physical/nonphysical. Things have always been more complex than this—after all, Mr. Spock was *both* Vulcan and human. Today, though, "rearrangements in world-wide social relations tied to science and technology" mean we have an opportunity to reimagine how life itself is organized. Haraway pushes us to embrace "the scary new networks I have called the informatics of domination":

> By the late twentieth century, our time, a mythic time, we are all chimeras, theorized and fabricated hybrids of machine and organism; in short, we are cyborgs. The cyborg is our ontology; it gives us our politics. The cyborg is a condensed image of both imagination and material reality, the two joined centres structuring any possibility of historical transformation. In the traditions of 'Western' science and politics–the tradition of racist, male-dominant capitalism; the tradition of progress; the tradition of the appropriation of nature as resource for the productions of culture; the tradition of reproduction of the self from

the reflections of the other - the relation between organism and machine has been a border war. The stakes in the border war have been the territories of production, reproduction, and imagination. This chapter is an argument for *pleasure* in the confusion of boundaries and for *responsibility* in their construction.[4]

Aside from giving us this iconic image of the cyborg and heralding its new era, Haraway's essay is important because it's pushed feminism in a new direction.

It's intellectually tempting for feminists, seeking to validate women's experiences, to cede the realms of technology, science, and exploration to men, as if those constituted a "boys-only club." Feminists then could claim nature, spirit, and nesting as their own feminine/nurturing turf—think of Deanna Troi's empathic sensibilities or her mother as the galaxy's "Auntie Mame." This strategy of celebrating some mysterious, feminine essence is a major tactical error, however, because it only reinforces the old-fashioned and false idea that human experiences are neatly divided into opposing binaries: man/woman, society/nature, and thought/emotion. For much of the past, women haven't had economic, political, artistic, or scientific power because they were seen as too unruly and untamed to be trusted with the process and products of reasoning.[5]

These divisions, however, as the Borg might say, are now irrelevant. Counselor Troi's model of womanhood—"cosmic cheerleader" outfit included—as a universal ideal is outdated, and it's a mistake for feminists to try cast her or other women as a "goddess of empathy" ("Hollow Pursuits," TNG). Both men and women are already composed of both "natural" and "manmade" materials—your glasses or contact lenses, for example, aren't so different from Geordi's visor.[6] According to Haraway, we shouldn't think of our politics, economics, science, or relationships in terms of dichotomies that need updating so badly.

Haraway contends, "Technology is not neutral. We're inside of what we make, and it's inside of us. We're living in a world of connections—and it matters which ones get made and unmade."[7] In heralding the era of the cyborg, Haraway's essay concludes, "Cyborg imagery can suggest a way out of the maze of dualisms in which we have explained our bodies and our tools to ourselves.... I would rather be a cyborg than a goddess"—whether we're talking about Troi in Barclay's holodeck fantasy or Lieutenant Carolyn Palamas as Apollo's would-be consort in "Who Mourns for Adonais?" (TOS).

## Resistance Was Negligible

If the Borg had a particular existential sense of doubt, it would revolve around their perplexity about why humanity resists assimilation. After all, humanity's biological and technological distinctiveness won't be eradicated, but permanently preserved and encoded into the Borg Collective. Why do you resist us, they ask, when resistance is not only futile but so obviously contrary to humanity's own interests? The battle between the Federation and the Borg isn't really about weapons, technology, and tactics, but *values*. Federation values—autonomy, individuality, authenticity—are challenged by Borg values—heteronomy, collectivity, simulation. It may seem perfectly obvious which values are preferable; but we can nevertheless ask, "What's so bad about being Borg?"

I would say, *nothing much*, once we take seriously Haraway's philosophy. Groups who've endured prejudice—such as women, racial and ethnic minorities, sexual minorities, or disabled people—haven't had ideal experiences of *Star Trek*'s core values. The reason why is that for too long they've existed at the wrong end of the oppositional hierarchies that Haraway identifies—treated as more animal than human, more controlled by body than mind, and so on. For example, women and other minorities haven't had a chance to be *autonomous*, because, for generations, autonomy was denied to them by law insofar as they weren't granted the rights of full citizenship in a putatively democratic society.

While women and minorities today may have the opportunity to be autonomous under the law in most socially developed nations of the world, enduring stereotypes about women and minorities inhibit us from truly being *individuals*. After all, the function of a stereotype is to prevent someone from being understood as the unique individual she is, limiting others' perceptions of her—and possibly her perception of herself—to formulaic and confining parameters. We see negative stereotypes about women even in the *Star Trek* future, when boldly going former Borg drones must still look warp-core hot in their tight catsuits!

*Authenticity* is also complicated in our society, in which some people haven't been really free to rule their own lives and their individuality is threatened by negative stereotypes. How can I be my *true self* when my ability to rule myself and explore my uniqueness is thwarted? Of course, I don't think that living the values of autonomy, individuality, and authenticity is a problem just for women and minorities. These values, appealing as they may be, are still demanding for everyone to live by.[8] Even a cadet fresh from Starfleet Academy, however, knows it's the starship captain who gets to be an autonomous, authentic individual in our cultural script, not the green-skinned damsel in distress. So what's an alien damsel to do?

Borg values pose an alternative. The Borg exist in a *heteronomous* collective, in which the self is governed by others. But these others are inseparable from the individual self, and so there is, in theory, no oppression. Also, the Borg Collective doesn't give a nanoprobe about what's authentic and what's simulated, as long as the hive keeps buzzing along. Every Borg, no matter who they once were, gets to be a *real* Borg and make a contribution to the Collective.

Taken together, these values give us a screenshot of social life that's secure but still dynamic. These values redirect us from the anxious, worried picture of life encoded in *Star Trek*'s values: What should I do? Am I unique enough? Who is the real me? The pressure to constantly choose, create, and maintain oneself as a "me" who's separate from all others disappears. It's replaced by the security of belonging to a network of creatures that are so deeply plugged into me that they are "me-ish." As Commander Chakotay nearly discovers in "Unity" (VOY), being ruled by others isn't a threat to the self if you see that we're all made of other selves. Like Borg drones, we're made of bits and pieces—our biology, technology, family, history, and so on—that've been given to us or that we've scavenged. So when I can play-act a simulated "me," without the fear of being compared against some authentic "me" as a baseline, I am fluid. I am an *explorer*.[9]

To those who object, "But I don't want to be Borg!" there are two sorts of answers. The first, given by the Borg Queen herself in "Dark Frontier," is that when a species is assimilated into the Collective, "They've left behind their trivial, selfish lives and they've been reborn with a greater purpose. We've delivered them from chaos into order." To which Seven sarcastically replies, "Comforting words. Use them next time instead of 'Resistance is futile.' You may elicit a few volunteers." The essential problem with the Borg isn't their values or even assimilation per se, but rather the violent, imperialistic means by which they assimilate. Perhaps the Borg could be brought to reason on these matters.

The second kind of answer to those who don't want to be Borg is that *your objection is irrelevant*, as Haraway pretty much said twenty years ago. Just look at yourself and how you experience values like "individuality." For most of us, modern life is an organic–computer hybrid experience: your downloaded apps, posted status updates, rebuilt knee joint with titanium rods, GPS dropped pins, and naturally and artificially flavored postworkout protein bar— they are all a part of your authentic lifestyle. You can thus ask yourself about the values guiding these experiences: what controls your life—a singular, autonomous self, uncontrolled by outside phenomena, or an evolving, adapting network of interdependent people, ideas, and stuff? Is being an isolated individual really desirable? Wouldn't you prefer to have thousands of "likes" and "friends"? Could you even separate your "authentic" self from your *virtual* one? The answers are obvious, and Borg values are triumphant. You've been assimilated. Resistance was negligible.

# Notes

1. Kevin Decker has written convincingly about how the Borg "freak us out" and are so effective on screen, but curiously were not part of the original *Star Trek* series. The threats technology posed on that show were sort of silly and unconvincing because the technology itself was not integrated into our lives, as it is now. See his "Inhuman Nature, Or What's It Like to Be a Borg?" in *Star Trek and Philosophy: The Wrath of Kant*, ed. Jason T. Eberl and Kevin S. Decker (Chicago: Open Court, 2008).

2. For further discussion of this key concept in light of the Borg, see Barbara Stock's chapter in this volume (Chapter 9).

3. Using the stardate system from *Star Trek* (2009) and *Star Trek: Into Darkness* (2013), of course.

4. Donna Haraway, "A Cyborg Manifesto: Science, Technology, and Socialist-Feminism in the Late Twentieth Century," in *Simians, Cyborgs, and Women: The Reinvention of Nature* (New York: Routledge, 1991), 149–81.

5. See, for example, Genevieve Lloyd's book on how philosophers have aligned men with reasoning and women with unruly, natural passion: *The Man of Reason: 'Male' and 'Female' in Western Philosophy*, 2nd ed. (New York: Routledge, 1993).

6. Further analysis of the natural/technological divide being crossed is provided in Dena Hurst's chapter in this volume (Chapter 25).

7. Hari Kunzru, "You Are Cyborg," *Wired* (1993): http://archive.wired.com/wired/archive/5.02/ffharaway_pr.html (accessed June 24, 2015).

8. Some feminist philosophers, it should be added, have very successfully rethought these *Star Trek* values. See, for example, Diana Tietjens Meyers's work on both autonomy and authenticity in her *Being Yourself:*

*Essays on Identity, Action, and Social Life* (Lanham, MD: Rowman and Littlefield, 2004).

9. Exploring borders, as a metaphor and a way of life, is especially important for third-wave feminists. See Gloria Anzaldua, *Borderlands / La Frontera: The New Mestiza* (San Francisco: Aunt Lute Books, 1987); and Judith Butler, *Gender Trouble: Feminism and the Subversion of Identity* (New York: Routledge, 1989).

# 23

# "Who I Really Am": Odo, Mead, and the Self

## Pamela JG Boyer

Some people find their *self-identity* in their car, house, friends, family, station in life, talents, or job. In DS9's first season, Chief of Security Odo is one who finds his identity in his job, which is a sufficient burden to keep him plenty occupied. *Deep Space Nine*'s security problems stem from being both a port of entry and a military base, leaving Odo in charge of DS9's police as well as its military security—at least when Starfleet security officers such as Lieutenant George Primmin or Lieutenant Commander Michael Eddington don't interfere. Nevertheless, Odo can't find complete self-satisfaction in his identity as DS9's "Constable." As he tells Major Kira in "Emissary," "All my life I've been forced to pass myself off as one of you … always wondering who I really am." For many years, he didn't know if there were any others like him in the galaxy. In a more benign laboratory than what Odo experienced—philosophical instead of exobiological—he presents an ideal case study of George Herbert Mead's (1863–1931) theory of how the *self* is formed and transformed. According to Mead, the formation of the *self* requires social interaction, not isolated growth, in order to develop its identity. Prior to being in a Bajoran lab, Odo's only remembrances are of floating around space as a glob in a small container, all alone. He has no memories of interacting with family members, or what Mead calls *specific others*. Odo's only lab memories are of painful interactions with the Bajoran scientist, Dr. Mora Pol, and later, security-related ones on the station under Cardassian and then Starfleet rule. Odo doesn't remember where he came from or what species he is.

*The Ultimate Star Trek and Philosophy*, First Edition. Edited by Kevin S. Decker and Jason T. Eberl.
© 2016 John Wiley & Sons, Ltd. Published 2016 by John Wiley & Sons, Ltd.

## "It Doesn't Know How ... It's Just a Baby"

Without *language* we'd have no way to articulate, or reason through, interactions with others. According to Mead, language starts with meaningful gestures. When creatures act in coordination through a gesture, signaling that the gesture means the same to them; it becomes language. In "The Begotten," after Odo buys a baby changeling from Quark, Sisko wonders if it's a danger to the station. Odo responds, "When I was first discovered, I didn't know what I was, or have any memory of where I came from. I didn't even know I had the ability to mimic other forms." The Federation wants to study the baby, and Odo is given permission to interact with it. Odo talks to the baby:

> I realize you can't understand a word I'm saying but that doesn't matter. I know you're aware of me. I was once like you. I spent months in a lab being prodded and poked by a scientist who didn't recognize I was a life-form. He thought I was a specimen, a mystery that needed to be unraveled. He never talked to me. I didn't know what I was or what I was supposed to do. I was lost. Alone.

Odo is providing the baby with verbal gestures. It would appear Odo's hopes are to make available the significant symbols, which Mead says are symbols that two creatures agree on having the same meaning. These significant symbols will help the baby gain its *I*. Soon Odo's own teacher, Dr. Mora, arrives to help. Odo, talking to the baby in a soothing tone of voice, insists that Mora can only observe because he doesn't want the baby to go through "Dr. Mora's Chamber of Horrors." Mora calls Odo's soothing talk "incessant chatter," but Mead would say Odo is clearly teaching the baby a language. Later, when Mora and Odo are turning to leave for dinner, the baby comes up out of the dish and forms a face similar to Odo's; when Odo smiles and moves his face side to side, the baby mimics Odo's movement. The baby then reverts back to its liquid form, putting a grin on the faces of Odo and Mora. He compliments Odo on getting the baby to trust him:

MORA: I was wrong. Your approach to communicating with the changeling was sound. Don't you see? It was reaching out to you. It was curious about you. The first time you did anything even close to that was when you formed a tentacle to slap my hand away from the control panel.

ODO:     I remember. I wanted you to stop zapping me.

Odo's gesture was understood by Mora to signal displeasure. In turn, the baby changeling's more positive gesture indicated that Odo's interactions were working. Both gestures were the start of language. Mead calls the first language-users we interact with *specific others*, those closest to us. These specific others teach us our language; and language is the beginning of communications, which is in turn the beginning of social interactions. Both gestures were the start of language, whether between Odo and Mora or Odo and the baby.

Later, Odo and Mora are called to the science lab. It seems the baby had a more serious medical problem than originally thought and it can't be saved. As any parent would, Odo wants to hold the baby before it dies. While he's holding the baby, telling it not to die, the baby integrates itself into Odo. This gives him back his morphing capabilities that had been taken away as punishment by the Founders in "Broken Link." This could also be considered the ultimate way of taking on the attitudes of the other from both the baby's and Odo's point of view.[1]

In "Necessary Evil," we learn more about Odo's past. Not only do we witness the first time Odo met Kira, but also we learn that he left the Bajoran science lab two years prior to living on Terok Nor (the station's Cardassian designation). To solve a murder case assigned to him by Gul Dukat, Odo uses the language he learned in the lab as well as techniques of observation and investigation. However, not all his abilities are learned. During a soliloquy, Odo muses:

> Nobody ever had to teach me the "justice trick." That's something I've always known. A racial memory from my species, I guess. It's really the only clue I have to what kind of people they are.

Mead differentiates between memories and fundamental instincts. We gain memories through experience, but instincts are genetic, like grasping, sucking, and rooting. Although Odo believes his "justice trick" is a "racial memory," Mead would likely say it's an instinct. In "The Search, Part II," Odo finally meets his species—known as "the Founders" of the Gamma Quadrant's interstellar dominion. A female changeling corrects his view on justice, telling him that it's not justice he seeks, but order. The desire for order is fundamentally instinctual, much like his urge to return home was in his genetic makeup.

Memories, on the other hand, are what Odo has from his time in the lab and on the station interacting with the *generalized others*. These are the "organized community or social group the individual"[2] interacts with. Interacting with *generalized others* creates the *me* as an individual objectively distinct from others, and unifies the *self*, understood subjectively. Memory integrates with language acquired in social interaction to give us the ability to expand our array of gestures, vocal or visual, and so we're able to draw on a greater number of gestures to communicate with others. Memory also allows us to remember our past experiences and how we, or others, acted (or reacted) to, a social interaction. Mead contends that the self must comprise the subjective *I* and the objective *me* in order to be whole. If one doesn't have an *I* as well as a *me*, one is only conscious but not *self-conscious*. Consciousness is like awareness. You're aware you're standing on a floor. But being able to reason and articulate who you are in relation to others with whom you interact is self-consciousness. So how does the complex of *I* and *me* make up the emergent *self*?

The *emergence* of one's self integrates language, imagination, and memory of interactions with those around us. For example, Ezri Dax, in "Afterimage," is confused by all the memories she has from the past eight Dax hosts, so much so that we might say she now has nine selves, each with its own *I* and *me*. After all, she didn't train to be a Trill host. She didn't learn how to integrate Dax's past selves into her contemporary identity and thereby separate them from her personal identity as the pre-joined Ezri Tigan. In Quark's bar for the first time, this exchange occurs:

QUARK:  I wondered when you were going to drop by. I can't believe it's really you.

EZRI:   Me neither ... I mean ... of course I can believe I'm really "me" as in Ezri. It's just I haven't gotten used to the idea of "me" as in Dax.

Ezri's problem is that she has too many memories and can't sort them all out, like a child telling one lie to mom, a second to dad, a third to a teacher, a fourth to a sister, a fifth to a brother, a sixth to a friend—soon he doesn't know what he's told to whom. When the *I* just does it, not listening to the *me*, the *self* can get in trouble. Within the *self*, the *I* is the impulsive actor and the *me* is the socially integrated actor. For example, the *I* may want to get drunk while the socialized *me* says no. If the *I* gets drunk and starts a fight, the *I* will throw a punch but the *me* will get knocked out by the return gesture. So, by not listening to the socialized *me* the *I* can cause the *me* of the *self* to wake up hungover and hurt. This dichotomy can be seen explicitly in "Field of Fire" when Ezri uses the Trill "Right of Emergence" to isolate the personas of Dax's previous murderous host, Joran, to help her solve a murder on the station. Joran represents an externally manifested *I* that argues with Ezri's socially integrated *me* as they track the killer.

## Proto-holodeck?

Focused attention is one of the ways we have of influencing the clarity and extent of memories. Think of going to a coffee shop: you take your copy of *The Ultimate Star Trek and Philosophy*, get your coffee, sit down, and focus on your book. You may hear others order coffee, but you focus on the book. Therefore, you have no memory of what others ordered. Mead believes that the imagination serves an important and often overlooked role in creating focus. It's through imagination that we assimilate the attitudes of those around us, be they specific or generalized.

For instance, Nog wants to join Starfleet because he sees in his father a great engineer who can't function in Ferengi society because "A Ferengi without profit is no Ferengi at all" ("Heart of Stone"). Rom can fix anything but never succeeded in business—just sits back and waits for something, either good or unfortunate, to happen to his brother Quark so he can inherit the bar on DS9. But Nog recognizes his father's skills start within his mind, even before picking up a hyperspanner, and he shares his father's attitudes toward fixing things—later reinforced by his apprenticeship under Chief O'Brien, eventually succeeding his mentor as DS9's Chief of Operations when O'Brien leaves to become an instructor at Starfleet Academy.

Watch children at play, and you'll see them assume the attitudes of those they've been watching and from whom they've been learning. Once children learn the language of their parents and siblings, they use their toys to represent their family members' ideas and attitudes. They might take their sick toys to the doctor for a checkup, playing both the parents and the doctor. When playing games with other children, they assume the roles of whatever the game calls for, be it hide-and-seek, mud pies, or commanding a starship.[3] This isn't true only for children: play shows how the imagination helps any of us see into the future in predicting and responding to the attitudes of others.[4] In fact, all of us have learned, and continue to learn, to become what specific and generalized others demonstrate to us. By our use of symbolic gestures and language, our access to memories, and our use of imagination, we learn to become a *self*, just as Odo did. In "The Search, Part II," the female changeling tells Odo, "To become a thing is to know a thing. To assume its form is to begin to understand its existence." Imagination is the same in helping our *self* notice when our *I* and *me* emerge.

## There's No *I* in Team, but There Is in Win

As you've gathered, Mead's use of *I* and *me* differ from our use of them in everyday language. In Mead's sense, the *I* is how we respond to the attitudes of the generalized others; the *me* is the generalized others' attitudes we've internalized:

> The simplest way of handling the problem would be in terms of memory. I talk to myself, and I remember what I said and perhaps the emotional content that went with it. The 'I' of this moment is present in 'me' of the next moment.[5]

In some respect, the *I* exists in the present, while the *me* is the center of my expectations about the future. In the present we're required to respond in certain ways—this is the *me* that's accumulated attitude of others. Yet the part that actually acts is the *I*. In short, the *I* is the *impulsive* part of the self—think again of Joran—that can yet be restrained by all the attitudes the *me*—Dax as an integrated whole—has acquired through interactions with others.

Mead claims we can observe the development of the *self*, gaining its sense of *I* and *me* through playing games. Like Sisko explaining liner time to the Bajoran Prophets, Mead uses playing baseball as an example. In "Take Me out to the Holosuite," when the Niners are first practicing, Ezri and Bashir are in the outfield. Sisko hits the ball. Both call the ball—"*I*'ve got it!"—but neither catches it. They've shown they have an *I*, a distinctive, subjective perspective infused by the desire to catch the ball, but neither took on the attitude of the other, indicating that their sense of *me* as a functional part of the team isn't there quite yet. Sisko shows he has not taken the attitude of the team—a generalized other—when he throws Rom off the team. The rest of the team protests that they'll quit unless Rom is reinstated, showing they've gained the attitude of a team. While there's an individual aspect to baseball—like the *I* of Ezri and her Fancy Dan play, or Nog tagging every Vulcan in their dugout, or hitting the ball like Kira, or bunting like Rom—winning requires the whole team to coordinate their actions as team-orientated *me's*. The Niners were only able to understand and therefore take Sisko's attitude about the upcoming game after Kasidy told them about Captain Solok's constant gloating over a victory won against Sisko while both were at the academy.

Where is Odo in all this? He's the umpire. He has taken on the attitudes of the generalized others he worked with to the point that they're now specific others to him, and he can join in their game. Using his imagination, gained through interactions with them, he accepts Sisko's invitation to be the umpire, a role perfectly suited to an individual who possesses a natural instinct for *justice* that has been sharply honed through his interpersonal interactions. As an umpire, Odo is able to use his *I*, *me*, and integrated *self* that has emerged from his experiences with the station crew. Odo's *I* calls the balls, strikes, safe, or out. However, it's Odo's *me* that feels the poke of both Sisko and Solok. Then it's Odo's *I* that throws Sisko, and subsequently Captain Solok, out of the game. Odo's *self* is fully invested in the baseball game.

DS9's third season sees Odo becoming more multidimensional. At its beginning, Odo finds his people are the Founders in charge of the Dominion. They want him to return, but he doesn't want to be part of their collective—despite his instinctual urge to merge with the "Great Link." In "Heart of Stone," we discover why this is.

Odo and Kira chase a Maquis terrorist to a seismically unstable moon, entering a cave to search for their quarry. Kira's foot gets stuck in a crystalline structure that grows until it's up to her neck and she has problems breathing. To alleviate her fears, Kira wants Odo to talk to her. She says, "Tell me how you got your name." During the occupation of Bajor, the Cardassians insisted that all lab specimens be clearly labeled in Cardassian. He was labeled "unknown sample," translated into Cardassian as *odo'ital*, which literally means "nothing." When they found him to be sentient, the Bajoran scientists still called him Odo Ital, breaking it into a Bajoran name, which was later shortened to Odo.

> But now the thing is, for the longest time whenever anyone would use my name the first thing I would think of was what it meant—"Nothing." What better way to describe me? I had no family, no friends, no place

where I belonged. I thought it was the most appropriate name any one could give me ... and then I met you ... and the others—Sisko, Dax, even Quark. And now ... when I hear one of you call me "Odo" I no longer think of myself as nothing. I think of myself as me.

Through his interactions on the station, Odo comes more fully into his self. When Odo can't find a way to free Kira—really, the Female Changeling in Kira's form—she tells him to leave before the unstable cave collapses. He says he will not, finally confessing his love for her.

## Is All Growing but a Transition?

As Odo's range of interactions with other beings grows, so does his self. In "The Forsaken," he is stuck with Lwaxana Troi in a turbolift, an experience that teaches him the language of trust. In "Necessary Evil," he stands up to Gul Dukat and begins to learn from Kira a language that makes him realize neutrality is truly impossible. In "The Alternate," volcanic gas affects Odo, pushing him to turn his anger language into violence against Dr. Mora. In "Shadowplay," Odo learns the language of concern as he draws close to Rurigan's granddaughter Taya.

Odo's new attitudes, which he learns from his specific and generalized others, mark him as having an ever-evolving *me*. Significant development of Odo's *me* comes from the effects of *conflict*, Mead would say. During times of war a nation, through patriotism, fuses its citizen's self-consciousness together. When a threat to our community of specific and generalized others is apparent, our bond to that community strengthens. In Odo's case, this includes not only Bajor and DS9 but also the whole Alpha Quadrant. The process for him begins with the end of "The Search, Part II," when Odo and Kira find the *Defiant* crew unconscious in a cave on the changeling homeworld:

FEMALE CHANGELING: This will all become clear to you once you've taken your place in the Great Link.

ODO: No. I admit this ... link of yours is appealing but you see, I already have a link ... with these people. Whatever you do to them you are going to have to do to me.

Odo has broken through to what Mead calls an "international" or cosmopolitan *self*. Having been sent by the Founders to seek out and interact with other species, Odo found their attitudes became his attitudes—something his "brother" Laas fails, or is unwilling, to accomplish ("Chimera"). The Founders display their more parochial "national self" by insisting the "solids" are nothing like them; they have to defend themselves by controlling the solids and thus the founding of the Dominion. But later, in "The Die Is Cast," Odo confesses to Garak that he wants to go home to be in the Great Link. Although he tried to deny it, he still wants to be with his people. Garak never divulges this to Enabran Tain, or to Sisko in his after-actions report, because Odo has become one of Garak's "others," with Garak able to understand Odo's perspective and vice versa.

Odo learns the language of attraction and "coupling" when he becomes attracted to Arissa in "A Simple Investigation." This experience makes it possible for him to fully express his love language for Kira in "His Way." Ultimately, though, Odo returns to the Great Link to heal it from a disease inflicted by Section 31. Odo's decision exemplifies Mead's stance on growth: "From the standpoint of the observer the man may be sacrificing himself for others; from his own he is realizing the meaning of his identity with his whole group." [6] This all comes into question in "Behind the Lines" and "Favor the Bold," when the Dominion takes over the station and Female Changeling pays Odo a visit. The two fully link, and Odo acquires a different *self*—that of the Link. He learns the Link's attitude of being "One. And many. It depends on how you look at it." Yet, when the station's resistance cell is in trouble in "Sacrifice of Angels," Odo once again takes on his "station" *self*, telling Kira, "The Link was *paradise*. But it appears I'm not ready for paradise." But in "What You Leave Behind," Odo ultimately chooses to heal the Great Link and help his people learn attitudes of the solids from whom he's learned.

## Only Change Doesn't Change

Over the arc of *Deep Space Nine*'s tales, all the characters change. But Odo goes from being a one-dimensional to a multidimensional character by learning languages—in the broadest sense of the word—from those who start out as generalized others, but become specific others as time goes on. After leaving Dr. Mora's lab, Odo experiences social interactions with Kira and others who treat him, not as a specimen, but as an individual with a *self* composed of an *I* and a *me*—although the Cardassians with whom he initially interacts are more interested in his "neck trick." Odo's station-mates use his name, and he begins taking on their attitudes. Kira's attitude becomes one of friendship that grows into one of love. Quark's attitude is one of suspicion, treating Odo as the zealous enforcer of justice that he is; Odo responds with his own suspicion of Quark's underhanded dealings. But, in a way, Quark becomes Odo's most intimate confidant, as evidenced in episodes such as "Crossfire" and "The Ascent." We see Odo act upon new languages, memories, and imagination by gaining attitudes from those around him. Assimilating these attitudes changes him over time, while his interactions with others change those with whom he interacts—particularly Dr. Mora, whose attitude about Odo evolves from seeing him as a curious "unknown sample" to his ersatz "child." And so it is with us.

## Notes

1. George H. Mead, *Mind, Self, and Society: From the Standpoint of a Social Behaviorist*, ed. Charles W. Morris, (Chicago: University of Chicago Press, 1934), 139 footnote.
2. Ibid., 154.
3. In the *Star Trek: The Next Generation* novel *Cold Equations: Silent Weapons* (New York: Pocket Books, 2012), 34–5, Dr. Beverly Crusher observes that her and Captain Jean-Luc Picard's preschool son, René, acts as a natural leader and is treated deferentially by other children by virtue of his being "the captain's son." She worries that this could lead René to develop unhealthy attitudes if he's socialized to function in that role with its attendant pressures.
4. For further discussion of the essential value of play—or, more generally, *leisure*—in the cultivation of not only self but also *cultural* identity, see Jason Eberl's chapter in this volume (Chapter 1).
5. Mead, *Mind, Self, and Society*, 174.
6. Mead, "The Psychological Basis of Internationalism," in *G. H. Mead: A Reader*, ed. Filipe Carreira Da Silva (New York: Routledge, 2011), 283.

# 24

# Is Liberation Ever a Bad Thing? *Enterprise's* "Cogenitor" and Moral Relativism

## William A. Lindenmuth

*Star Trek* is fundamentally about the triumph of the human spirit. It represents a utopian destiny, a realization of Carl Sagan's remark, "The sky calls to us. If we do not destroy ourselves, we will one day venture to the stars."[1] *Star Trek* envisions a future in which humans have put away their petty differences to explore the cosmos, supported by an egalitarian society founded on the dignity of individuals and the loftiness of the human spirit, all the while boldly moralizing through progressive ideas. While there will always be controversy concerning moral disagreements between cultures, it isn't difficult to see in our own history an emerging pattern of greater respect for the rights and dignity of human individuals and freedom from irrational prejudice. That said, another aspect of progress is the notion that no single group can decide what's absolutely best for everyone else. In the *Star Trek* universe, this is reflected through a general discouragement of lecturing other cultures on what their values and laws should be. As a result, Starfleet came up with a foundational principle: the Prime Directive— also known as General Order One—which says that Starfleet personnel, regardless of their positive intentions, must refrain from interfering with the natural development of societies.[2]

This directive wasn't yet in place for Captain Jonathan Archer and his crew, piloting the *Enterprise* NX-01 in Earth's first long-range exploration of the galaxy. This *Enterprise's* mission is primarily "first contact"—the initial encounter between new life forms. It's not an easy mission, as the crew often meets species that are quite different than us. One such species is trisexed, and the dominant males and females

*The Ultimate Star Trek and Philosophy*, First Edition. Edited by Kevin S. Decker and Jason T. Eberl.
© 2016 John Wiley & Sons, Ltd. Published 2016 by John Wiley & Sons, Ltd.

treat the third sex like a thing to be used: more or less as a reproductive slave. How could an advanced race do this? It seems uncontroversial to add slavery to our list of things that are clearly immoral. Isn't it, then, our moral duty to fight such bondage and affirm the dignity of every sentient being? The ENT episode "Cogenitor" raises these questions in a challenging way.

## "So Much for the Little Training Cruise"

While exploring a hypergiant star, the *Enterprise* encounters the ship of an unknown species: the Vissians. We quickly learn that their species has a third gender, called a *cogenitor*. Making up about 3 percent of their population, the cogenitors apparently secrete an enzyme that makes reproduction possible between the males and females. The Vissian ship's chief engineer and his wife are attempting to have a child, and so have a cogenitor assigned to them who is being used to help them procreate—and that's all. The cogenitor doesn't have an identity or receive an education. When Commander Charles "Trip" Tucker III tries to introduce himself to the cogenitor, he's told that it doesn't have a name. So begins Trip's obsession with this new being.

Trip decides to investigate this third reproductive member, inquiring insistently about it to the Vissian engineer. He's clearly uncomfortable with even the concept of a third gender—Dr. Phlox tries to describe the mating process, but the squeamish Trip doesn't want to hear it. Trip insists to anyone who'll listen that his real problem is that the cogenitor is treated "like a pet." When T'Pol reminds him that they aren't here to judge the customs of other cultures, Trip claims that this isn't a simple issue like "taking off your shoes when you enter someone's house," but a "question of human rights." "They are not human," T'Pol responds.

## "Keep an Open Mind, Commander"

Philosophers such as Immanuel Kant (1724–1804) and Plato (c. 428–348) imagine morality as timeless and changeless, something that any rational being can understand. David Hume (1722–1776), though, argues that "reason is, and ought only to be the slave of the passions, and can never pretend to any other office than to serve and obey them."[3] People feel a moral intuition *first*, and reason about it *second*, according to Hume. We see someone help an elderly person, and we think, "That's nice! It's good they're doing that." Likewise, when we see someone littering, we think, "That's terrible! They shouldn't do that."

Hume famously distinguishes "is" statements from "ought" statements: "Vice and virtue may be compared to sounds, colors, heat and cold, which, according to modern philosophy, are not qualities in objects, but perceptions in the mind."[4] Hume believes that "facts" and "values" are always separate things. This means that nothing *is* ethically right; it just *feels* right. Reason arrives later to validate our feelings and ensure we have all the proper facts to inform them. The role of reason is simply to help us reach our goals. Reason can't tell us what to want or how to want it, but merely how to get it. After all, Hume claims, values lie "in yourself, not in the object."[5] Value is not *in* the world; it's simply *applied* to the world. Our passions and desires determine our goals, and reason helps us achieve those goals. Unlike many other philosophers, Hume is less interested in *prescribing* morality to us than *describing* it.

On Hume's view, Trip feels a negative intuition about the cogenitor's situation, and then seeks a reason to confirm his discomfort. Dr. Phlox and T'Pol both make this case. From another perspective, bioethicist Leon Kass argues that there's "wisdom in repugnance," that a strong negative intuition is an indication of something amiss.[6] Trip's reason—so he thinks—is that he objects to the treatment of the cogenitor, not to its mere existence. Yet this isn't what his actions reflect.

## "Insufficient Facts Always Invites Danger"

Trip dines with the Vissian couple, not to learn about them or exchange ideas—and he can't hide his distaste for their food—but to covertly take a brain scan of the cogenitor to confirm it's as mentally capable as the male and female Vissians. Secretly meeting with the cogenitor, who's initially resistant, Trip insists, "You're as capable as they are, as smart as they are.... You have the same rights to learn, to choose how you're gonna live. To *have a name*." It is, in fact, impressive how quickly the cogenitor learns in just a few hours. We see a consciousness emerging, reflected through expressions and open body language that indicate wants, interests, and desires replacing the doubts and fears of this previously nameless being. The cogenitor takes Trip's name "Charles." as its own. Instead of seeing the dangers apparent from this rapid imprinting—as Data does in "Hero

Worship" (TNG)—Trip is simply flattered. He doesn't tell Charles how names are chosen or how important they are, or that maybe he isn't the right person to model an identity upon. He sneaks the cogenitor aboard the *Enterprise*, giving it a tour and losing at a board game. Trip's response to his primary intuition could be seen as positive, as he's trying to help the cogenitor. However, his actions become more and more suspect when we see that his way of helping is to make the cogenitor more like *himself*. Trip is oblivious to the fact that he's in over his head. Humanity has a long history of cultures "helping" other cultures by telling them who the right gods were, how to dress, how to speak, what to eat, and where to work.

Perhaps we could defend Trip's actions by noting that the Vissians might suffer from a massive moral blind spot in not recognizing cogenitors as worthy of self-determination and respect. He obviously felt that he had to research the cogenitor's intellectual abilities in secret, because their culture seems dismissive about any such inquiries. It certainly seems that they fail in an absolute moral sense in this fashion if we follow Kant's "categorical imperative" that persons, as rational and autonomous beings, cannot be used merely as a means toward some other end—as the Vissians use "Charles" and other cogenitors merely as a means toward reproduction.[7] But is that the same thing as *proving* them wrong? Trip never tries to find out. We never see him poring over Vissian historical data—which they would've freely shared; or speaking to other Vissians about their customs; or at least waiting for Captain Archer to return from exploring the hypergiant with the Vissian captain. Then Trip could've informed Archer about what he had found out, and discussed how to proceed. This kind of caution seems warranted because the facts of their biology compel the Vissians to make choices that we and other bigendered species haven't had to make.

## "We're Out Here to Meet New Species, Not Tell Them What to Do!"

Archer returns and T'Pol informs him there's been an incident. Considering the productive and pleasant time he had with the Vissian captain, he's livid about what's transpired in his absence. Trip tells Archer, "I did exactly what you'd do, Captain! It's not like I had much choice." Archer takes great issue with this, as he should: situations such as these aren't at all clearly decided by moral absolutes. But we've never seen Archer this outraged before … why? Consider this: in the earlier episode "Fortunate Son" (ENT), Archer says "Human beings have a code of behavior.… Just because someone isn't born on Earth doesn't make him any less human." Maybe one of the reasons why Archer is so angry is that he *might* have done a similar thing, or at least felt the way Trip does. On this occasion, though, he's been able to get some distance and perspective. It's precisely dilemmas like these that make positions asserting the universal nature of certain moral values so difficult to maintain. Trip, for some reason, can't see this. He equates his own teaching the cogenitor to read to Archer sharing the ship's books and movies with the Vissians. "Giving them books is *a lot different* than suggesting they defy their culture!" Archer replies. Trip admits that the cogenitor didn't ask for any of the things he provided. Archer asks, "Sneaking into her quarters, bringing her on *Enterprise*, lying about where you were going, *why?*"

Trip says nothing, but we can speak for him. It's reasonable to think he believed the cogenitor was a neglected rational being who was systematically oppressed, mistreated, and denied self-determination by their culture through indoctrination. He saw someone in need of liberation, a suffering individual whose autonomy and rights were not being recognized. After all, if something is simply *customary*, that doesn't make it right, does it? For Trip, sometimes it does. In a lighthearted exchange early in the episode, Trip eats ice cream sundaes with two Vissian officers. Before they begin, Trip counsels: "You gotta eat the cherry first." When asked why, he responds, "You just do." In a conversation with Dr. Phlox, Trip says, "I'm not interested in discussing their habits. I'm concerned with the way they treat this cogenitor." Phlox responds, "They're mostly one and the same." Trip retorts, "Yeah, well, that doesn't make it right."

Here we have a classic case that might make us wonder whether or not morality *is* relative in some way: whether culture, circumstance, perspective, or a number of other factors can alter standards of right and wrong. Trip evinces moral absolutism—that is, the view that such factors may change, but right and wrong hold fast. Trip sees the cogenitor as being treated unfairly, and acts accordingly to change it. Dr. Phlox evinces a moral relativist attitude, echoing the famous anthropologist Ruth Benedict (1887–1948): "Mankind has always preferred to say, 'It is morally good,' rather than 'it is habitual' … [but] the two phrases are synonymous."[8]

Trip, as he sees it, is doing his moral duty. He's showing compassion to someone who needs it. He's nurturing class consciousness and emancipating someone who has no voice. The utilitarian philosopher John Stuart Mill (1806–1873) observes, "Bad men need nothing more to compass their ends, than that good men should look on and do nothing."[9] How could Tucker's attempts at liberation be a bad thing?

The cogenitor Charles asks Archer for asylum, and he replies, "It's not our place to tell you what rights you have." Archer purports to speak for his own culture. Yet from our own human philosophical tradition, we have brilliant philosophers like Kant who would say, "You're right! *Reason* tells us what rights we *all* have! A cogenitor can clearly reason, and therefore can autonomously guide their actions by what they believe they have the best reasons for doing, and should therefore be treated with respect." A religious intellectual like St. Thomas Aquinas (c. 1225–1274) would argue that God determines the rights we have, and that the human laws we make must square up with the objective principles of *natural law*, accessible through the Holy Spirit, scripture, and reason.[10] Both of these systems of belief hold that morality is clear-cut and easily accessible to every rational being. Of course, not everyone agrees with this. Thus problems abound when conflicting cultures think that their way of doing things is the only right way, and that everyone must conform. Is there any way to figure out who is right?

## Trying out One's New Phaser

Philosopher Mary Midgley thinks that we *can* make judgments about other cultures, and do so fairly. She rejects what she calls *moral isolationism*, the idea that we cannot and should not criticize cultures outside our own since we can't understand them. Midgley contends that this is mistaken: while a moral isolationist seeks to respect other cultures, she also overlooks the fact that you must understand something in order to respect it. Respect comes *from* judging, not the other way around; once you understand a culture, you're able to praise or decry aspects of it. Beings outside our culture can criticize us, the way that Vulcans, Klingons, and Ferengi do. And we can do the same to them. Consider Quark's speech to Sisko in "The Jem'Hadar" (DS9) about his apparently negative attitude toward Ferengi culture:

I think I figured out why humans don't like Ferengi.... The way I see it, humans used to be a lot like Ferengi: greedy, acquisitive, interested only in profit. We're a constant reminder of a part of your past you'd like to forget.... You're overlooking something. Humans used to be a lot worse than the Ferengi: slavery, concentration camps, interstellar wars. We have nothing in our past that approaches that kind of barbarism. You see? We're nothing like you, we're *better*.

Sometimes, it takes an outsider to help you see something you've been missing about yourself—this is one of the most important messages of *Star Trek*.

Midgley offers the example of the concept of *tsujigiri* in feudal Japan, which means "trying out one's new sword on a chance wayfarer."[11] It was common practice among the Samurai to cut through a random lower-class person in one slice to ensure one's blade was battle-ready. Some will say we can't judge that practice because we don't comprehend Samurai culture, and that if we only understood discipline, devotion, and the caste system of the Japanese Sengoku period, we'd also appreciate their moral attitude. Midgley points out that this is doing exactly what some are telling us we can't do: comprehend a foreign custom sufficiently to judge it. She stresses that "we ought to avoid forming—and expressing—*crude* opinions, like that of a simple-minded missionary, who might dismiss the whole Samurai culture as entirely bad, because non-Christian."[12] But this doesn't prevent us from making assessments about each other and the things that we do. The Japanese themselves eventually came to see the practice as wrong and outlawed it.

Perhaps this is the problem we have in "Cogenitor." Trip thinks that even if he doesn't understand Vissian culture, he still has a clear grasp of right and wrong. Trip is essentially saying, "There is no possible morally acceptable account of the way this cogenitor is being treated." It might very well turn out that the Earth, its allies, and the Vissians won't be able to get along because of the moral turpitude of their treatment of the cogenitors. It may be that this otherwise friendly and advanced race has somehow gotten to the stars while still harboring a repugnant attitude toward members of their own species. But should we make that judgment on *the very first day we meet them*, as Trip does, and immediately begin covertly undermining their belief structure?

Archer sits down with the Vissian captain and couple to discuss the asylum request, which Archer says he must take seriously. The

Vissian engineer (and potential father) objects to their even having this discussion, and demands the cogenitor's immediate restitution:

ENGINEER: You have no right to judge us. You know nothing about our culture. What if one of your stewards, the men who are forced to serve you food, what if they should ask us for asylum?
ARCHER: They're not forced to do anything.
ENGINEER: I apologize. But it's easy to misunderstand someone when you know nothing of their culture.

Archer regretfully returns the cogenitor to the Vissian ship. They later learn that the cogenitor has committed suicide. Trip takes responsibility, and Archer agrees: "You knew you had no business interfering with those people. You thought you were doing the right thing. I might agree if this was Florida, or Singapore, but it's not, is it? We're in deep space, and a person is dead. A person who'd still be alive if we hadn't made first contact." We can condemn certain things in the familiar places that Archer mentions because we understand enough about their cultures. We can look back on the history of racism in the United States and condemn it and legislation supporting it as a poor representation of the type of people we aspire to be. We can also see how long it's taken to begin to lift ourselves out of the racist mindset and acknowledge that we're still working on it.

## "Is Your Entire Species So Ill Mannered?" — "Nope ... Just Me"

Trip shows Charles the film *The Day the Earth Stood Still*, a 1951 sci-fi story in which aliens arrive on Earth with a warning against spreading violence to the stars. Charles asks why there was so much fear toward the aliens in the film. Trip explains, "Well, before we made first contact with the Vulcans, the people of Earth were pretty violent. They had a hard time trusting things they didn't understand. The characters in the film knew nothing about Klaatu—who he was, where he came from—so, they tried to kill him."

Trip routinely has a hard time trusting things he doesn't understand. He knows nothing about the cogenitor—what it is, where it came from—and tries to "save" it. Interestingly, perhaps tellingly, he never once inquires about the potential child. As I've suggested, his actions could've come from an after-the-fact rationalization of his discomfort, from misguided self-interest, a genuine sense of compassion, or a sanctimonious belief that he knows a culturally independent set of standards of right and wrong of which the Vissians are ignorant. Compare this to the hasty conclusion he makes about the mother weaning her son in "Broken Bow" (ENT). T'Pol warns him, "Humans can't refrain from drawing conclusions. You should learn to objectify other cultures, so you know when to interfere and when not to."

By no means are the Vissians free from our condemnation if in fact they're unjustly treating an intelligent and autonomous member of their own species like a thing. It appears that *this* couple treats *this* cogenitor immorally, which might be indicative of a greater cultural attitude that eventually won't allow us to ally ourselves with the Vissians. It's unclear at present what the wider consequences of Trip's actions will be down the line, but it's unlikely that the suicide will have any positive effect on the Vissian culture; more likely, it will be detrimental to future contact with humans or perhaps other species as well—unless it's just swept under the rug. Conversely, consider what might've happened if the cogenitor *hadn't* committed suicide. Charles could conceivably have become the Vissian version of Gandhi or Martin Luther King, Jr., leading a cultural revolution that would've secured rights for all cogenitors such that they can become educated, choose whether and with whom they wish to procreate, and play an active role in raising the children they help produce. Given that the cogenitors make up a small fraction of the Vissian population, the natural balance would likely be disrupted, and reproductive levels might fall drastically—and so the outcome of Trip's well-intentioned, but not well thought-out, intervention may very well have been the eventual extinction of the Vissians!

Apart from these utilitarian concerns, the Vissians are an advanced race and deserve the benefit of the doubt before others make crude judgments and act as Trip does. Cultures aren't free from criticism and judgment, and beliefs, as dear as they may be, are not unassailable. But we also need the ability to explain disagreements and remain open to the possibility that we are mistaken.

## "You Had No Business Interfering with Those People"

Someday my people are going to come up with some sort of a doctrine: something that tells us what we can and can't do out here—should and shouldn't do. But until somebody tells me that they've drafted that directive, I'm going to have to remind myself every day that we didn't come out here to play God.

So says Captain Archer in "Dear Doctor" (ENT) when the *Enterprise* visits a planet with two species, one far technologically superior to the other but ravaged by a disease, while the supposedly inferior race is immune. It turns out that the former species is at a sort of evolutionary dead-end, whereas the latter species stand poised to surpass the former. Dr. Phlox can cure the disease, but believes it's unethical and obtrusive to do so. Archer feels compelled to give them the cure, but after considering Phlox's objections, decides against it, giving them only something to help ease the symptoms instead.

Between *Enterprise* and TOS, Starfleet devises a doctrine that states a principle of noninterference with cultures, especially ones with a pre–warp drive level of technology. The Prime Directive serves to protect cultures from the fallacy of good intentions, from do-gooders making things worse on a planet they were ostensibly trying to help by introducing technology or pharmaceuticals, inspiring a religion, or siding with a faction in a war. As Captain Picard explains in "Pen Pals" (TNG), "The Prime Directive has many different functions, not the least of which is to protect *us*. To prevent us from allowing our emotions to overwhelm our judgment." But, in that episode, they treat a plea for help as something that should override the directive; in the cogenitor's case, the appeal is rejected. Most of *Star Trek* is an allegory for what we struggle with on Earth today. This very minute, there are cultures that don't treat everyone with respect and appreciation. Should we make a list of them and go there, guns drawn if necessary, and "fix" them? We've tried that many times before and for many different reasons, with varying amounts of "success"—and how do we define *that*?

In "Symbiosis" (TNG), Picard explains, "The Prime Directive is not just a set of rules. It is a philosophy, and a very correct one. History has proven again and again that whenever mankind interferes with a less developed civilization, no matter how well intentioned that interference may be, the results are invariably disastrous." Of course, the Vissians are not "less developed"—unless, according to Trip, we're speaking morally.

If we act as if the only choices open to us are either moral relativism or absolutism, we ignore the possibility that morality and its truths can be *reasonable*. Evidence can be given to show something to be good or bad regardless of someone's feelings about it. When we deliberate between moral judgments, we should be considering relevant information, weighing that evidence, and making the most reasonable choice possible. It should take more than a day before we condemn an entire culture—a benefit that we have because we don't need to wrap up our ethical dilemmas at the end of a forty-two-minute television broadcast. Of course, in this episode it's *not* resolved. Rather, it ends with Archer indignant, Trip aghast, and the audience—us—haunted.

# Notes

1. Carl Sagan, *Cosmos* (1980), ep. 7.
2. For another perspective on the Prime Directive, see the chapter in this volume by David Kyle Johnson (Chapter 5).
3. David Hume, *A Treatise of Human Nature* (London: Penguin, 1969), 462.
4. Ibid., 469.
5. Ibid., 468.
6. Leon Kass, "The Wisdom of Repugnance," *The New Republic* 216 (1997): 17–26.
7. For a detailed description of Kant's moral rule, the "categorical imperative," see the chapter in this volume by Alejandro Barcenas and Steve Bein (Chapter 10).
8. Ruth Benedict, "Anthropology and the Abnormal," *Journal of General Psychology* 10 (1934): 59–82.
9. John Stuart Mill, "1867 Inaugural Address at the University of St. Andrews," in *Littell's Living Age*, ed. E. Littell, 4th series, vol. IV (Boston: Littell and Gay, 1867), 664. Also available at http://www.scribd.com/doc/55699265/John-Stuart-Mill-Inaugural-Address-at-St-Andrews (accessed June 1, 2015).
10. See Thomas Aquinas, *Treatise on Law*, trans. R.J. Henle (Notre Dame, IN: University of Notre Dame Press, 1993).
11. Mary Midgley, "Trying out One's New Sword," in *Heart and Mind: The Varieties of Moral Experience* (Brighton: Harvester Press, 1981).
12. Ibid.

# 25

# Resistance Really Is Futile: On Being Assimilated by Our Own Technology

## Dena Hurst

In "The Best of Both Worlds, Part I" (TNG), Captain Jean-Luc Picard is captured by the Borg and is told in no uncertain terms:

> Strength is irrelevant. Resistance is futile. We wish to improve ourselves. We will add your biological and technological distinctiveness to our own. Your culture will adapt to service ours.... Freedom is irrelevant. Self-determination is irrelevant. You must comply.... Death is irrelevant.

The Borg look toward a bleak, *transhumanist* future where humans and machines become one. The fear the Borg represent is that the integration of humans and machines will yield a creature more machine than human: emotionless, calculating, task-driven, craving the efficiency of the Collective more than the freedom of the individual. The Borg, however, are much more than elements of a dystopian vision of our future. They're the embodiment of the concept of *technology* put forth by philosopher Martin Heidegger (1889–1976), and, as such, they signify our likely end.

The Borg are precisely what Heidegger warns us about: technology that has the purpose of preserving and propagating itself at any cost. Heidegger argues that technology isn't *neutral*, to be used for good or evil, depending on the intent of the user: "Everywhere we remain unfree and chained to technology.... But we are delivered over to it in the worst possible way when we regard it as something neutral."[1] When we fall into this way of thinking, we make the

*The Ultimate Star Trek and Philosophy*, First Edition. Edited by Kevin S. Decker and Jason T. Eberl.
© 2016 John Wiley & Sons, Ltd. Published 2016 by John Wiley & Sons, Ltd.

horrendous mistake of thinking we're in control of technology. We become blind to the *essence* of technology, and therein lies the problem.

## "I Am the Beginning. The End. The One Who Is Many. I Am the Borg."

By "technology," Heidegger is referring to modern *industrial* technology, as opposed to "older handicraft technology," or craft.[2] More significantly, Heidegger doesn't see technology merely in terms of machines and mechanical processes. Even though he focuses on the machine technology of his time, he acknowledges that modern machines are more complex variations of the simple machines of earlier times. So his definition of technology can't be linked solely to particular machines. Rather, technology is composed not just of machines and processes, but also the *use* of machines and processes, and the *needs* and *ends* serviced by the machines and processes.[3]

The Borg fit this definition: they're an amalgamation of the technology of all of the species they've assimilated over the thousands of years they've existed, and many of these societies were more advanced than civilizations of Earth. They are constantly in motion, driven to acquire more technology. As Q tells Picard in "Q Who?" (TNG), "You can't outrun them. You can't destroy them. If you damage them, the essence of what they are remains. They regenerate and keep coming. Eventually you would weaken. Your reserves will be gone. They are *relentless*." The Borg are technology acting upon technology, both the means and end of applied scientific knowledge.

This, though, isn't the limit of Heidegger's definition of technology. This view of technology offers only a look at what we might term *technological fetishism*, the worshipping of technology for its own sake, or when cultures bestow upon it power simply because it's seen as indispensable. Seeing technology as a *means* driven by needs and ends is accurate, Heidegger claims. But limiting ourselves to this view means that we overlook the relationship between all the things that technology has done for us and the ways in which technology—as a mindset—*governs* how we view everything. This includes things we may consider nontechnological, such as religion, history, or nature. The real nature—the essence—of technology extends beyond its uses.

The essence of technology is a way of revealing things, "a challenging ... which puts to nature the unreasonable demand that it supply energy that can be extracted and stored as such."[4] What does this mean? Heidegger offers some examples: "Agriculture is now the mechanized food industry. Air is set upon to yield nitrogen, the earth to yield ore, the ore to yield uranium."[5] Technology gives us a way of viewing the world and everything in it as *resources*, the purpose of which is to serve further applications of technology.

This is how the Borg view the universe, as raw material (Heidegger calls it "standing reserve") that they can assimilate into the Collective to feed their quest to continually assimilate more. Q is again instructive here: "The Borg is the ultimate *user*.... They're not interested in political conquest, wealth, or power as you know it. They're simply interested in your ship, its technology. They've identified it as something they can *consume*." Heidegger would say the Borg are the "challenging," the "setting upon," the way of revealing the world solely through technology.

> Such challenging happens in that energy concealed in nature is unlocked, what is unlocked is transformed, what is transformed is stored up, what is stored up is in turn distributed, and what is distributed is switched about ever anew ... the revealing never simply comes to an end.[6]

This passage from Heidegger neatly describes the endless process of Borg assimilation. The instruments and bodies of countless civilizations are taken over and added to the Collective, a process that transforms the Borg into something better. The Borg seek *perfection*, and their process of achieving perfection requires taking in the best of every civilization they encounter. As Locutus queries Worf in "The Best of Both Worlds, Part II" (TNG), "Why do you resist? We only wish to raise quality of life."

## "Toward a State of Perfection"

The Borg also view the assimilation of species as an improvement, not only of the Collective, but also of the species being assimilated. We learn from "Hugh" (or Third of Five), in "I, Borg" (TNG), that the Borg view the assimilation of other species as a way of gaining more knowledge; thus, any species assimilated gains the knowledge of the Collective—while, of course, losing their identity as that former species. In addition, the shared consciousness creates a deep sense of being connected to others, a feeling that's comforting, based on Hugh's initial loneliness at being separated from the Collective. We see this, too, in Seven of Nine's transformation from Borg to a more human state in "The Gift" (VOY). Seven is initially angry at losing her connection to the Collective, having been assimilated as a child and raised by the Borg.[7]

In this revealing action of technology—providing a view of the world in which we see nature and people merely as raw materials for technology—everything loses its unique form and independence. Individuals assimilated by the Borg lose all sense of identity. Their physical appearance changes: implants are added to the body and brain, and physical indications of gender are removed. The collective voices of all Borg, as we learn in "Dark Frontier" (VOY), overwhelm any thoughts an individual may initially have other than those of the Collective.

Removing individuality allows for greater interchangeability. In "Q Who?" (TNG), a Borg drone boards the *Enterprise* and begins scanning its systems. When killed by Worf, another drone immediately beams aboard and picks up the task. When a Borg drone is injured beyond repair or killed, the Collective repurposes its parts. Heidegger claims that this *interchangeability* is a symptom of technology. When nature and people are seen as resources to be used by technology, individuality counts for much less than *function*. Individuality leads to irreplaceability, and a resource that's irreplaceable is of limited usefulness; use it once and there's no more. Thus, *similarity* and *conformity* are of greater value to technology. When one tract of land is used up, another can be provided. This same idea is embodied in the design of Borg ships, which don't have central locations, such as a bridge or engineering section, with the result that a Borg cube, as Commander Shelby says, "could continue to function effectively even if 78 percent of it was inoperable." Heidegger claims that by treating nature as a reserve of resources, technology creates a world of things with merely *instrumental value* based on their usefulness. If something serves no purpose, then it has no value and is of no concern. For instance, the Borg ignore intruders on their ship and remain focused on their tasks unless the intruders begin interfering.

The Borg also show us that humans aren't exempt from becoming resources for technology. Heidegger claims this happens to a lesser extent among humans because we drive the development and use of technology. We're both the means through which technology is used, and we define the ends for which it's used. The Borg represent a further evolution, where technology itself becomes its own driving force.

While species are assimilated into the Collective, the Collective itself becomes greater than the sum of the individual drones. Together the Borg, through their collective consciousness, can accomplish what a group of individual drones could not—witness the struggles of the individual drones separated from the Collective in "Survival Instinct" (VOY). They're separate parts of one body, led by one mind, rather than individual bodies under a central control; when Data asks the Borg Queen in *First Contact*, "Do you control the Collective?" she responds, "You imply disparity where none exists. I *am* the Collective." Technology, in Heidegger's view, acts in a manner similar to that of the Borg collective consciousness. Technology orders human beings to challenge nature and secure resources to serve technology,[8] just as the Borg Collective orders each drone to challenge nature, to assimilate resources to serve the Collective.

The Borg bring us face-to-face with the reality that we're not in control of technology; it controls us. We're under the illusion that we control technology; but in reality any attempt to control technology is regulated by our relationship *to* technology. We're attempting to control technology within the confines *of* technology. This is shown in the repeated attempts at engaging the Borg in battle. The Borg are capable of adapting to any new technology that they encounter. Modulating phaser frequencies and evasive maneuvers to escape the Borg's tractor beam, even on a random rotation, work only temporarily.

The Borg can't be conquered using Federation technology because the Borg have the advantage of the knowledge and technology of all of the species they've ever conquered. The *Enterprise* doesn't fight the Borg per se, but rather all of the species the Borg has assimilated. Battling the Borg within normal protocols proves ineffective because the *Enterprise* crew can only see this confrontation as if the Borg were any other enemy. The crew's limited perspective is the whole reason why Q propels them to the Delta Quadrant for their first encounter with the Borg. It's an attempt to shift Picard's perspective on what the desire to encounter new species may lead to—to provide, as Picard puts it, a "kick in our complacency."

Similarly, in Heidegger's view, we must understand our human relationship to the essence of technology, not just the machines and processes, but also the connections it creates between the parts and the whole, the uses it assigns to resources, and the ordering of human beings to gather those resources for the benefit of technology. If we fail to understand our relationship to the essence of technology, we face grave consequences. We'll continue down the path of becoming *standing reserve* like any other resource while at the same time believing we have greater control over other resources, meaning the natural world. We'll see ourselves as master over all, with a world we've created in our image, and be unable to see the world as it really is.

## Just Ask Guinan

Heidegger's solution to the problem at hand is quite simple. We can't change the essence of technology, but once we become aware of our relationship to it, we can change the way we think and talk about technology. In other words, to escape the hold of technology, we have to make ourselves aware of the danger. Since technology can't be mastered, we must learn to see technology differently, within its own limits but not confined to those limits.

The Borg's assimilation of Picard shows how a shift in our perspective can help us change our relationship to technology, and might offer some hope that technology may not be able to sustain the challenging of all of nature. Picard, as "Locutus of Borg," is appointed spokesperson for the Borg in their attempt to conquer humanity. The Borg reason that humans are an "authority-driven" culture and Picard represents the ideal of authority by virtue of leading "the strongest ship in the Federation fleet"—they rate Picard's value by reference to the technology he commands. He thus should be able to convince humans to be assimilated peacefully. Picard also provides a tactical advantage; by assimilating him, the Borg gain knowledge of human nature, Starfleet tactics and protocols, and specific information about the *Enterprise* crew's plans to attack the Borg.

Using Picard's knowledge, the Borg are able to avoid the *Enterprise*'s newly designed weapon and head toward Earth, defeating a contingent of Starfleet and Klingon ships in the Battle of Wolf 359 on the way. Left on their own to stop the Borg, Riker—the field-promoted captain of the *Enterprise*—and the rest of the crew try to plan as best they can, knowing that the Borg have all of Picard's knowledge. While Picard himself is irreplaceable, drone-like conformity to his way of commanding the *Enterprise* won't win the day. Riker must assert his own individuality as captain, as he learns from Guinan:

GUINAN: There can only be *one* Captain.
RIKER: It's not that simple. This was his crew. He wrote the book on this ship.

GUINAN: If the Borg know everything he knows, it's time to throw that book away. You *must* let him go, Riker. It's the only way to beat him. The only way to save him.

With this shift in perspective, Riker devises a plan that takes advantage of Picard's knowledge, effectively using it against the Borg. Picard is thereby rescued and the tables are turned. The crew is able to attain knowledge of the Borg through Picard's continued connection to the Collective and the Borg's weakness is revealed: their *interdependence*.

This change in perspective, beginning with Riker, allows for a change in the way the crew views the relationship between the Borg Collective and its drones, and their own relationship with the Borg. While the Borg's nature doesn't change, the new perspective allows for the *Enterprise* crew to avoid the danger the Borg pose. Likewise, Heidegger asserts that mere awareness of our relationship to the essence of technology—to the relationships it cultivates and the way it focuses our view of all things in the world—is enough for us to avoid the dangers technology poses.

## "Resistance Is Futile"

We could ask whether this change in perspective suffices for us to change our relationship with technology. I suggest we skip that question, though, because it's too late to ask it—like Kirk admonishing Scotty in *The Search for Spock* for fully automating the *Enterprise*'s systems a mere 2.1 hours before arriving at Earth, "You've fixed the barn door after the horse has come home." To support this claim, we have only to look at recent technological advancements. We have the technology to clone mammals, to generate self-perpetuating stem cell lines from which we may soon be able to grow functioning human organs, and to 3D print tissue and bone. We implant chips in brains to control seizures and restore movement. And we've created *synthetic life*.[9] In other words, we're "boldly going where no one has gone before" without even leaving the planet!

Contemporary philosopher Slavoj Žižek has addressed the dangers of technology, supporting and extending Heidegger's concerns.[10] Žižek warns about the creation of new life, contending that we're entering a "new terrain of unknowns."[11] We create a new life form, but we have no idea how it will act. Further, such biogenic research takes place in the "absence of any public control."[12] With different countries pursuing different research agendas, what's outlawed in one country may be permissible, even encouraged, in another: "in such a global situation legal prohibitions are becoming meaningless."[13]

We could argue that technology, as defined by Heidegger, has caught us within its domain, making it impossible to for us to shift our perspective. Society is being ordered on a global level so as to enable faster technological developments. Heidegger and Žižek's concern is that this slippery slope will sever our human connections and prevent us from relating to the world as it really is: "relations between computers and things are replacing relations between persons."[14] In addition, Žižek cautions about a more pragmatic danger, the perpetuation of *class division*: "there is a social demand for the creation of a new servant sub-class" using the technology that has created synthetic life.[15]

Contemporary philosophers Andy Clark and David Chalmers claim that our consciousness is being extended by our reliance on "smart" devices.[16] They've become our *memory*, remembering for us where we are to go, with whom we are to associate, what we are to do, and so on. They're even, to an extent, our *identities*. Our photos, stories, activities, family and friends, financial information, interests, and more are kept on our devices. Today, most of us carry our devices; very soon, more of us will wear them. It isn't far-fetched to imagine that one day these devices will be implanted and become *part* of us.

The Borg prompt us to wonder how this will be done and to what purpose. *Are we being gradually assimilated by our own technological creations?* More than a commentary on transhumanism, the Borg show us what could happen if we don't recognize the essence of technology—the relationships it creates among us, one to another, and between us and the world we inhabit, and the ways in which technology orders our thinking so that we view everything through its lens. Current technological developments indicate that we are, for the moment at least, unwilling to heed Heidegger's warning.

## Notes

1. Martin Heidegger, "The Question Concerning Technology," in *Martin Heidegger: Basic Writings*, ed. David Farrell Krell (San Francisco: Harper, 1993), 311.
2. Ibid., 312.

3. Ibid.
4. Ibid., 320.
5. Ibid.
6. Ibid., 322.
7. For further discussion of how Seven's childhood assimilation affects her self-development once separated from the collective, see Dennis Weiss's chapter in this volume (Chapter 17).
8. Heidegger, "The Question Concerning Technology," 323.
9. See the work of Craig Venter. For example, http://www.ted.com/talks/craig_venter_unveils_synthetic_life?language=en (accessed May 31, 2015).
10. Slavoj Žižek, *Living in the End Times* (Brooklyn, NY: Verso Books, 2010).
11. Slavoj Žižek, "Apocalyptic Times," Clore Theatre Lecture, November 24, 2009: http://backdoorbroadcasting.net/2009/11/slavoj-zizek-apocalyptic-times/ (accessed May 31, 2015).
12. Ibid.
13. Ibid.
14. Ibid.
15. Ibid.
16. See Andy Clark and David Chalmers, "The Extended Mind" *Analysis* 58 (1998): 10–23, available at http://consc.net/papers/extended.html; and David Chalmers, "Is Your Phone Part of Your Mind?" https://www.youtube.com/watch?v=ksasPjrYFTg (both accessed May 31, 2015).

# Part V

# BEYOND THE GALACTIC BARRIER: THE FUTURE AS THE FINAL FRONTIER

# Life on a Holodeck: What *Star Trek* Can Teach Us about the True Nature of Reality

## *Dara Fogel*

Philosophers and other thinkers have pondered tough questions about the nature of reality for thousands of years. Many of them have shared the view that our daily life is actually some sort of appearance or simulation, a dramatic presentation within which we interact and exist, but that isn't itself fundamental reality. Now, science seems to be discovering increasing support for this ancient concept, and *Star Trek*'s holodeck technology offers us great insights into understanding both old and new theories about what's *real*.

Every historical period has its own version of the idea that reality isn't what it seems to be; and the level of available technology influences the form the idea takes. In Plato's (428–348 BCE) "cave allegory," shadows cast upon a wall create an ever-changing drama enacted for chained prisoners, who mistake the shadows for reality since they're all the prisoners have ever perceived. Plato believed there existed both the realm of illusions inside the cave—analogous to the world we perceive with our senses—and the true reality outside of the cave—analogous to what we can understand with our intellect.[1] Hinduism[2] and Buddhism[3] both rely on the idea of *maya*—the illusory appearance of the world that contrasts with the indestructibility of consciousness. The Judeo-Christian Bible speaks of a perfect, ever-present, eternal, but invisible realm beyond the physical world. René Descartes (1596–1650)[4] and Immanuel Kant (1724–1804)[5] claimed that this nonmaterial realm is somehow the ultimate cause of the effects we experience and observe, regardless of physical appearances.

*The Ultimate Star Trek and Philosophy*, First Edition. Edited by Kevin S. Decker and Jason T. Eberl.
© 2016 John Wiley & Sons, Ltd. Published 2016 by John Wiley & Sons, Ltd.

Often, this other realm is couched in religious terms, but recent scientific discoveries and TNG's Lieutenant Commander Data can help us discover a material, secular perspective on this age-old notion.

## Of Humans and Holograms

*Quantum physics* lends compelling new support for the ancient dualistic view that there's both a physical realm we can perceive with our senses, as well as a level of reality we can't directly perceive. The accumulation of data over the last twenty-five years from a variety of scientific fields reveals that our reality seems to be *holographic* in nature— that is, the "reality" in which we live, move, and have our being may actually be a three-dimensional projection of a two-dimensional surface, such as a piece of holographic film that originates in another, higher dimension.[6] Scientific study seems to confirm what much earlier philosophers and religious figures intuited, with far-reaching, mind-boggling implications that challenge our ordinary ways of thinking about reality and free will.

The animated *Star Trek* series introduced the holodeck as a total immersion, three-dimensional entertainment technology that provides computer-generated environments, characters, and dramatic contexts. "The Practical Joker" (TAS) pioneered the idea of an interactive, virtual reality technology designed for exercise, entertainment, and educational or problem-solving purposes. The holodeck in TAS began as a recreation center for the crew to reconnect to simulated natural landscapes while on long missions. Using photonic energy, combined with both transporter and replicator technologies to project a three-dimensional interactive environment, holodecks could be programmed to re-create a wide variety of settings for the crew to enjoy.[7]

By the inception of TNG, holodeck technology had evolved, offering programs as simple as a backdrop of a scenic location, or as complex as a narrative that unfolds as crewmembers enact roles in a story, as when Data and Geordi LaForge pretend to be Holmes and Watson in "Elementary, Dear Data" and "Ship in a Bottle." In DS9, Dr. Julian Bashir plays a James Bond–like 1960s-era spy in "Our Man Bashir," and also fights in various famous historical scenes with Chief Miles O'Brien. Finally, in VOY, Lieutenant Tom Paris and Ensign Harry Kim play in the Buck Rogers–inspired "Captain Proton" serial holo-program, complete with ray guns and rockets, as they battle the evil

Chaotica ("Bride of Chaotica"). *Voyager*'s whole crew even gets into the act when Paris creates a charming Victorian-era Irish village ("Fair Haven" and "Spirit Folk"). In pursuit of their own interests, Captain Kathryn Janeway apprentices herself to the quintessential Renaissance man, Leonardo da Vinci, in "Scorpion, Part I" and "Concerning Flight"; and Kim battles Beowulf in "Heroes and Demons."

## The Holographic Hypothesis

Philosopher Nick Bostrom has hypothesized that we could be part of an elaborate computer simulation being run by intelligent creatures, perhaps the descendants of the creatures we, as inhabitants of the simulation, are modeled upon.[8] Just as Data's Holmes and Bashir's spy holoprograms are re-creations of past eras, so might our "reality" be a historical holonovel being run by unimaginably advanced people. Bostrom calls these "ancestor" simulations, further positing that there could likely be many more simulations of history than "real" lived histories. As with the several different Holmes-type stories Data and Geordi run, serial holoprograms illustrate how each "player" can have multiple permutations, with changing stories, themes, settings, and featured characters in their sagas.

Bostrom observes that there are basically only three possible responses to the question of whether we live in a computer simulation or not. One of these *must* be true: (1) it's impossible; (2) if it's not impossible, then it's unlikely; and (3) if it's not unlikely, then it's almost certain. Bostrom claims that we lack the evidence to fully accept the first option, so we can't rule out the possibility that we live in some kind of computer-generated world. In fact, if simulated worlds are possible for advanced civilizations and such civilizations are inclined to run them, then there would be many simulated worlds and only one real world. The odds would thus be that any being is much more likely to be in a simulated world than in the real world. Although Bostrom offers no empirical data to support his ideas, his conclusions result from valid arguments, meaning that we must at least allow for the *possibility* that our reality is a computer simulation.

Recent research in quantum physics converges with Bostrom's hypothesis in reporting that "behind" physical reality lies an energetic field that could be compared to a holodeck matrix grid with the capacity to transform into the myriad forms of physical reality. This subatomic field is sometimes called "the Zero Point Field" or simply "the Field."[9] The Field contains limitless power potential and can collapse into all the discrete physical units we call *matter*, but it's not composed of matter itself. The famous "Double Slit" experiment illustrates how particles can either manifest as waves of energy (the Field) or coalesce into concrete points of matter that make up our physical world.[10] It isn't a far stretch to think of the Field as the holo-matrix through which some cosmic holodeck generates the scenarios and characters that constitute our reality.

Of course, holodecks manipulate optics and matter, generating vir-tual space on demand that far exceeds the room's apparent dimen-sions. The same could be true with our own scientific discoveries—the more we look into the physical nature of "reality," the more "empirical evidence" is generated by the holodeck at both the quan-tum and physical scales. But all of these "discoveries" would still only be computer-generated probabilities inside the holomatrix. This could actually explain many of the paradoxes of quantum physics. Perhaps so-called *limit conditions* in nature, such as the speed of light or the Planck length, are telltale signs of our holodeck's processing boundaries.[11] Maybe these universal standards aren't truly "univer-sal" outside the simulation. They could be merely dictated by our real-ity's particular holomatrix, and so they're true only within this current holoprogram.

Increasing evidence indicates that our universe is *digital* in nature. Theoretical physicist S. James Gates recently found computer code in the mathematics used to describe string theory in quantum physics. Specifically, he found "Block Linear Self Dual Error Correcting Code" embedded *inside* his string theory equations. This wasn't just a set of similar numbers, but the *actual* code! This is the very same algorithm used by the Google search engine to monitor and correct received digi-tal information.[12] This embedded code serves as more evidence under-writing the possibility of holodeck informational processing constitut-ing our world.

Neuroscientist Karl Pribram (1919–2015) has discovered that brains behave like holograms. For instance, *memory* is infused throughout the whole brain and not in discrete locations, allowing those with damaged or even mostly missing brains to still have recall. Pribram and other researchers suggest that the brain itself may be part of a hologram-decoding system. Our brains act as filters on the millions of sensory inputs each of us experience all the time, allow-ing us to recognize, understand, and interact with the continuous patterns within the holoprogram—akin to how Geordi's brain filters the "visual frenzy" presented to him through his VISOR ("Heart of Glory," TNG). The human brain's structure is consistent with the design specifications necessary to exist and function within a holographic universe. The brain functions by looking for and identifying discernible regularities in our environment. This allows us to recognize and engage with the universe's many recurring patterns, such as the widespread occurrence of *pi* and the "golden ratio" in nature, ranging from the orbits of subatomic particles to the spiraling arms of galaxies. This is sort of like how Data keeps encountering odd occurrences of the number "3" when he receives a subconscious signal from his past self in "Cause and Effect" (TNG); his positronic brain is hardwired to pick up and interpret the signal. This is a new, scientific understanding akin to the ancient Hindu belief that humanity is the microcosm to the creator's macrocosm. Perhaps that was also a low-tech expression by the ancients to describe the recurring algorithms used to create our holoprogram and our participation within it.

If this "holodeck hypothesis" is an accurate model of our own existence, then *Star Trek* can help us to understand both our metaphysical predicament and how this impacts our moral obligations to each other and to ourselves. Issues like holo-addiction, which challenge Reginald Barclay, Tom Paris, and Geordi La Forge in different ways, may give us insight into our own psychological addictions to drama. The creative aspect of holoprograms, such as "Captain Proton," Bashir's spy adventures, or *Voyager*'s Emergency Medical Hologram, raises serious questions about our own reality and offers a fresh perspective on many ancient beliefs and traditions.

## Is Reality an App?

If our reality is a holographic projection, then who or what programmed it? Holoprograms and holonovels require an author/ programmer of some kind, while the "player" interacts with the program through their own physical presence. Virtual reality, of course, requires that programming and processing take place outside of the reality generated. The technology that creates manifest images on the holodeck must exist separately from the projected holomatrix, as must the programmer/operator of that technology—unless *self-awareness* occurs *within* the program, as occurs when Dr. Moriarty becomes self-aware within Data's Sherlock Holmes program and is able to seize control of both his holo-environment and the *Enterprise*.

While traditional religions offer a deity to fulfill the function of holoprogrammer, *Star Trek* points us toward a creator-artist, who designs holoprograms and novels for enjoyment, self-expression, and learning. Barclay, LaForge, and Paris all dabble with creating their own holoprograms; and Bashir procures his customized holoprograms from his off-screen friend, Felix, whose name comes from the Latin word for "happiness."[13] Even *Voyager*'s EMH creates his own ideal holofamily in "Real Life" and later pens a controversial holonovel in "Author, Author" about his experiences as a sentient holoprogram entitled "Photons Be Free."[14]

In each of these cases, someone who's not part of the holomatrix originated the program, except in the few cases where the holodeck was used as a problem-solving tool, recursively manipulating images and brainstorming from inside the holodeck. A good example of this is "A Matter of Perspective" (TNG) in which the holodeck is used to re-create a crime scene from the points of view of several witnesses. Another example of holoprogramming on the fly occurs in "Booby Trap" (TNG) when Geordi uses the holodeck to re-create the Utopia Planitia shipyard drafting room where the *Enterprise* was designed. Geordi ends up with more holoprogram than intended, when the computer includes a simulacrum of the *Enterprise*'s engine designer, Dr. Leah Brahms. But these in situ programming sessions are the exception, not the general rule of how the holodeck is utilized. Holoprograms are thus similar to apps for our smartphones or tablets: all apps must have programmers and users, as well as an operating system on which the app runs. These conditions are separate from the "matrix" of the app itself.

Some physicists, like Niels Bohr (1885–1962) and Richard Conn Henry, have claimed that the universe is basically *mental* in nature.[15] If so, then the structure of our brains as "holographic decoders" is our prime interface with the world and indicates a direction for future research. Others liken our universe to a multiplayer computer game.[16] Likewise, *Star Trek*'s holodeck is primarily for recreation and entertainment. The parallel implies that there may be an inherent purpose to human life, but not one that's been popular with philosophers and theologians in the past. Instead, we're here to *play the game*—just as Q tests the *Enterprise* crew through "a deadly game" he constructs in "Hide and Q" (TNG). Hinduism claims this is the underlying reason for the creation of *maya*, or illusion, and calls this "playing at life" *lila.* What if our own reality is more like a video game or an app than the random happenstance of matter in motion described by scientific materialism? The implications are paradigm shattering.

First, it would mean that we don't live in a universe without *reason.* The cycles and patterns of nature are evidence of recurring templates and algorithms. Thus, everything we experience—physical bodies, the natural world, the complexities of cultures, governments and societies, and even our own personal relationships—must have been previously coded by this unknown creator-artist of our own holographic novel. Mystic traditions of the past have appeal in no small part due to their explanatory power for the *purpose* of existence. Science has been notably silent when it comes to ascribing purpose or meaning to the universe, due to lack of any unbiased, physical evidence sufficient to meet the scientific method's burden of proof. But quantum physics is beginning to make incursions into territory once firmly held by religion, offering new science-based interpretations of ancient teachings.

If the holographic hypothesis is borne out, it may provide a scientific framework for understanding what might be ancient empirical discoveries buried under eons of religious tradition and superstitious misunderstanding. The holographic hypothesis can expand our comprehension of human potential and limitations, once we understand our status as characters in the larger ongoing story of the holoprogram—perhaps William Shakespeare, as Q notes to Picard in "Hide and Q," was pronouncing a literal truth when he wrote, "All the world's a stage." This interpretation has profound implications for who we think we are and for our capacities to control or change our lives and our world.

## Can't Tell a Soul without a Program

Another implication of living in a cosmic video game is that our "free will" is merely apparent, as characters in a computer game or holonovel can do nothing that's not already coded into their program. While playing Sherlock Holmes, Data must limit himself to only what the fictional Victorian-era sleuth is capable of doing and knowing, or else the illusion is destroyed and the game is over. In fact, this is what gets him and Geordi into trouble in "Elementary, Dear Data" when the latter, frustrated that Data has memorized all the extant Holmes stories, instructs the computer to program Holmes's nemesis, Professor Moriarty, to be a match for *Data*, not Holmes.

Playing the game is possible only by continuing some pretense of the artificial limitations of our circumstances. This would explain why, if our world is a simulation, you can't fly without technological help, nor magically manifest a million dollars in your checking account by just wishing. It also explains the failure of many personal development techniques, such as the "Law of Attraction" originating in early 20th-century "New Thought" or personal affirmations. Unless possibilities are coded into the program, no special techniques within the program can "make it so."

Sometimes, however, games have secret shortcuts and "easter eggs." Pre-programmed surprises can be bad as well as good—like the "jack-in-the-box" feature in Bashir's casino program featuring holo–lounge lizard, Vic Fontaine. When holoprogrammer Felix decides to shake things up, the mob takes over Vic's casino ("Badda-Bing Badda-Bang," DS9), and the crew has to outsmart the program to restore their favorite holo-hangout.

Perhaps there are features of our reality that serve like shortcuts, "easter eggs," or "jacks-in-the-box." The social and psychological fabric of our lives contains common elements of mythic structure, drama, and storytelling that we seem compelled to enact. Most of us have seen the "fingerprints of the editor" in our lives—those reoccurring archetypal themes, last-minute saves, beatings of impossible odds, and unlikely miracles that make up some of the content of our daily lives— the same stuff as myths are made of.[17] So, while it would seem that we don't normally get to determine the plot from inside our holoprogram, there does appear to be some kind of cyclic and mythic shaping to the story we experience.

In this way, ancient traditions propose that we can gain some degree of freedom, if we're willing to devote sufficient time and attention to self-development. Many, such as Buddhism and Hinduism, offer rigorous training systems claiming to accomplish such self-realization. The holographic hypothesis gives us a means for evaluating the accuracy and effectiveness of these traditional training programs. Perhaps we, like the DS9 crew, can find shortcuts to outsmart our own holoprograms.

But we must also be willing to face the possibility that the idea of transcending one's programming is but another layer of programming in the holonovel, and in reality, there's no independent consciousness. It may be that there's no way for creatures like us ever to escape the confines of the holodeck. Perhaps the cycles and predictability of nature were programmed by yet another program, without the intervention of what we'd consider an *ultimate intelligence*. This line of reasoning only defers answering the question of who programmed the holodeck, and doesn't resolve any questions about the origin or purpose of the simulation.

On this view, we're as firmly fixed within our own storyline as any *Star Trek* character is enmeshed in the plots they inhabit. As authoritative and intelligent as Picard may be, he doesn't exist apart from the *Star Trek* universe. It matters not at all how capable or determined he might imagine himself to be; he can't transcend the script. Indeed, such an intention on his part could only exist within the context of a *Star Trek* script or novel, and is constrained by his very own manifestation as a character within the ongoing *Star Trek* saga. Stepping down from the meta-level, Vic Fontaine is a self-aware hologram, which gives him a certain degree of freedom within the holoprogram he inhabits—he can end his own program, create new characters within the program, and even move himself into other concurrently running programs—yet he's also aware of his built-in limitations as a holographic representation of a 1960s-era lounge singer ("His Way" and "It's Only a Paper Moon," DS9).

Talmudic tradition within Judaism holds that we have no choice *but* to believe in our own free will. Perhaps this is correct, and free will is just another feature of the pre-programmed human holographic characters. Some may find the idea that they have absolutely no control over their lives comforting, and there are whole belief systems and religions dedicated to precisely this view, but others find it obnoxious. For them, the idea that the universe is like an interactive computer game is immensely more attractive.

## Who's Playing What?

On the holodeck, there are two types of people: "players"—like Data pretending to be Henry V or Sherlock Holmes—and "non-player characters" (NPCs)—holographic people created to interact with the players. Does this imply some of the people we interact with on a daily basis might not be real? Your coworkers who you never see outside of work might just be NPCs. What about those neighbors whose name you don't know, but wave to occasionally when you both happen to be outside at the same time? Or maybe even those kooky family members you only see at Christmas? They might be NPCs making recurring cameo appearances, like Janeway's Leonardo da Vinci or Riker's Minuet ("11001001" and "Future Imperfect," TNG).

How do we know if the person we're dealing with is "real" like us, or an NPC created to fill out the details of our story, making it seem more plausible? It would seem that we can't. In "Ship in a Bottle" (TNG), Data realizes they're in Moriarty's holographic version of the *Enterprise* only when subtle computer glitches tip him off. Before then, Picard believes he's actually communicating with crewmembers on the bridge, not suspecting them to be holodeck facsimiles of the crew. In "Homeward" (TNG), Worf's brother Nikolai Rozhenko fools the pre-industrial tribal Boraalans as he and Worf lead them on a fictitious exodus through the holodeck, while the *Enterprise* races to find them a new planet to replace their ravaged world. Even Captain Janeway falls for a computer-generated hunk on the holodeck, fully knowing he's an NPC, in "Fair Haven," as does Geordi with the holographic Leah Brahms—leading to a rude awakening for him when me meets the *real* Leah Brahms in "Galaxy's Child" (TNG).

It's notable that most NPC holocharacters at first fail to realize that they're not real. Picard explains this peculiar metaphysical fact to NPC mobster Cyrus Redblock, breaking briefly out of character as 1940s-era private-eye Dixon Hill in "The Big Goodbye" (TNG). And he confronts Moriarty with the same facts when the enhanced holovillian expresses the desire to leave the holodeck. Inside the holodeck, what appears to be real is what passes for reality.

How do you know that *you're* "real," by these standards? We currently have no way to determine this, as our science is likely to be keyed to physical laws of the holodeck program and not representative of physics outside of the holomatrix. Ancient traditions tell us that the persona we experience ourselves to be is just another part of the illusion—that we're actually immaterial consciousness beyond any physical manifestations. Perhaps what's been traditionally called the *soul* or *consciousness* is analogous to operating in a fully immersive role-playing computer game. Could it be that we've become so caught up in the fun and drama of the world as "holonovel," we've forgotten our true identity as individuals whose lives are rooted outside of the holodeck?

But in the end, we can't even know if this is the truth or not. Our whole existence might be nothing more than energy pulses, our self-awareness (or lack of it) just an expression of a random algorithm. At the conclusion of "Ship in a Bottle" (TNG), having outwitted Moriarty into thinking that he and his beloved Countess have left both the holodeck and the *Enterprise* in a shuttlecraft, Picard raises a nagging epistemic question:

PICARD: In fact, the program is continuing even now inside that cube.
CRUSHER: A miniature holodeck?
DATA: In a way, Doctor. However, there is no physicality. The program is continuous but only within the computer's circuitry.
BARCLAY: As far as Moriarty and the Countess know, they're half way to Meles II by now. This enhancement module contains enough active memory to provide them experiences for a lifetime.
PICARD: They will live their lives and never know any difference.
TROI: In a sense, you did give Moriarty what he wanted.
PICARD: In a sense. But who knows? Our reality may be very much like theirs. All this might be just an elaborate simulation running inside a little device sitting on someone's table.

Or perhaps—as Sisko and the rest of the DS9 crew may very well be—we might just be characters in a story being written by an author like Benny Russell ("Far Beyond the Stars" and "Shadows and Symbols," DS9).

## Cogito Ergo Sum?

Finally, we might ask about the metaphysical and ethical status of self-aware holograms, such as Moriarty, VOY's EMH, and DS9's Vic Fontaine. Do they count as "real" people? Or are they merely computer-generated NPCs? And if they are just virtual people, does their self-awareness grant them some special status or wisdom? Does their added self-consciousness make them worthy of *rights*? More than once, *Star Trek* has sought to address the metaphysical question of personhood for holographic sentients. These holocharacters are aware that they're photonic projections, their parameters designed by someone else. Yet they're able to transcend their original programming, to learn and even change the holomatrix determining their own character and story.

Could these sentient holocharacters be analogies of human capacity? Traditional mystical approaches offer us the examples of prophets, saints, and saviors as similar to these holocharacters; with some traditions even providing teachings and techniques for individuals who seek to overcome their own "holoprogramming." Perhaps these "real" prophets and sages somehow managed to achieve this goal, surpassing their programming and emerging into a new level of being. Such a conclusion would be consistent with ancient mystical traditions—such as Buddhism, Kabbalah, and Hinduism—according to which this potential for realization resides within each of us. But again, this so-called "transcendence" could just be a new screen or level of play in the ongoing game.

*Star Trek* provides an instructive allegory for understanding both ancient and current, cutting-edge concepts of reality. The holodeck hypothesis suggests that perhaps taking hold of our destiny depends upon the realization that we're fictional characters playing a role in an ongoing narrative in a cosmic "holodeck." As players, we can't exceed the parameters of the original design—unless we, like Moriarty, the EMH, or Vic Fontaine, can figure out how to transcend our own programming. But whether we can escape the holomatrix altogether is the topic of an entirely different sci-fi franchise ... [18]

# Notes

1. Plato, *Republic*, trans. Harold Bloom (New York: Basic Books, 1991).
2. *The Bhavagad Gita*, trans. Juan Mascaro (New York: Penguin Books, 1962).
3. *The Dhammapada*, trans. Juan Mascaro (New York: Penguin Books. 1973).
4. René Descartes, *Meditations on First Philosophy*, 3rd ed., trans. Donald A. Tress (Indianapolis, IN: Hackett, 1993).
5. Immanuel Kant, *Groundwork of the Metaphysics of Morals*, trans. H.J. Paton (New York: Harper & Row, 1964).
6. Bob Yirka, "New Work Gives Credence to Theory of Universe as a Hologram": http://phys.org/news/2013-12-credence-theory-universe-hologram.html; Michael Talbot, *The Holographic Universe* (New York: HarperCollins, 1991); and Brian Whitworth, "Quantum Realism": www.brianwhitworth.com/bw-vrt.1.pdf (both websites accessed June 19, 2015).
7. "Holodeck," *Memory Alpha*, http://en.memory-alpha.org/wiki/holodeck (accessed June 19, 2015).
8. Nick Bostrom, "Are You Living in a Computer Simulation?" *Philosophical Quarterly* 53 (2003): 243-55; http://www.simulation-argument.com (accessed June 19, 2015).
9. Lynn McTaggart, *The Field: The Quest for the Secret Force of the Universe* (New York: HarperCollins, 2001).

10. Mike May, "The Reality of Watching," *American Scientist* (July-August, 1998): https://www.americanscientist.org/issues/pub/the-reality-of-watching (accessed June 19, 2015).

11. Whitworth, "Quantum Realism."

12. S. James Gates, "Symbols of Power," *Physics World* 23:6 (2000): 34-9.

13. For an analysis of whether holodecks could actually make one "happy," see Philip Tallon and Jerry L. Walls in "Why Not Live in the Holodeck?" in *Star Trek and Philosophy: The Wrath of Kant*, ed. Jason T. Eberl and Kevin S. Decker (Chicago: Open Court, 2008).

14. A different take on the opportunities for self-realization that the Doctor's efforts offer can be found in Nicole Pramik's chapter in this book (Chapter 18).

15. Richard Conn Henry, "The Mental Universe," *Nature* 436 (July 7, 2005): www.henry.pha.jhu.edu/The.mental.Universe.pdf (accessed June 19, 2015).

16. Silas R. Beane, Zohreh Davoudi, and Martin Savage, "Constraints on the Universe as a Numerical Simulation": http://arxiv.org/pdf/1210.1847.pdf (accessed June 19, 2015).

17. This thesis lends credence to Joseph Campbell's theory of the "monomyth" that's played out in various mythological dramas throughout various times and cultures. See his *The Hero with a Thousand Faces*, 3rd ed. (Novato, CA: New World Library, 2008). John Thompson critically engages *Star Wars* creator George Lucas's reliance on Campbell's "monomyth" in his "'In That Time...' in a Galaxy Far, Far Away: Epic Myth-Understandings and Myth-Appropriation in *Star Wars*," in *The Ultimate Star Wars and Philosophy*, ed. Jason T. Eberl and Kevin S. Decker (Malden, MA: Wiley, 2016).

18. See William Irwin, ed., *The Matrix and Philosophy* (Chicago: Open Court, 2002); and William Irwin, ed., *More Matrix and Philosophy* (Chicago: Open Court, 2005).

# 27

# Which Spock Is the Real One? Alternate Universes and Identity

*Andrew Zimmerman Jones*

Of all the crew to serve on a starship *Enterprise*, none has had such a convoluted line of existence as the venerable Mr. Spock. He was born, died, and resurrected, and he is the only member of his universe to survive into the timeline altered by Nero in *Star Trek* (2009). Indeed, the threads of his existence are so tangled that one could reasonably ask whether Spock is really still Spock when all is said and done. Is the Spock represented by Leonard Nimoy in the 1966 *Star Trek* pilot the same person portrayed by Zachary Quinto in 2013's *Star Trek Into Darkness*? If they're not the same person, then in what ways are they similar? If they are the same, then what features are constant? In this chapter, we'll explore what the various incarnations of Mr. Spock can tell us about the nature of reality, existence, and personal identity.

## The Search for Which Spock?

It's always useful to begin with clear definitions of the objects under discussion. This is even more important and logical when the objects you're discussing are all named "Spock." Let's call the character in the TOS pilot "The Cage" portrayed by Leonard Nimoy "Spock-Prime." And let's call the character portrayed by Zachary Quinto in the J.J. Abrams films "Spock-2."

These aren't the only versions of Spock to consider, however. In the classic episode "Mirror, Mirror" (TOS), Kirk ends up in an alternate universe where the Federation is replaced by a barbaric empire. There

*The Ultimate Star Trek and Philosophy*, First Edition. Edited by Kevin S. Decker and Jason T. Eberl.
© 2016 John Wiley & Sons, Ltd. Published 2016 by John Wiley & Sons, Ltd.

he encounters another version of Mr. Spock, sporting a stylish yet sinister beard. Let's call this incarnation of Spock, logically, "Mirror-Spock." In the expanded universe of *Star Trek* comic books set within the timeline established in *Star Trek* (2009), many original storylines are once again encountered. This includes the original "Mirror, Mirror" storyline, in which the comic introduces us to an alternate reality version of the sinister, bearded Mr. Spock. We'll reference this Spock as "Mirror-Spock-2." That seems to be all of the Spocks we need to worry about for the moment—unless we consider the *infinite* number of Spocks contained within these four, as we'll discuss later in this chapter.

Spock-Prime refers to all incarnations of the character as portrayed by Leonard Nimoy (except for Mirror-Spock), so it refers to the Vulcan who was appointed science officer on the *Enterprise*, the Vulcan who was present when tribbles overran the *Enterprise*, the Vulcan who saved the whales, the Vulcan who negotiated peace with the Klingons, the Vulcan who served as a secret ambassador to the Romulans, and the Vulcan who was pulled through time just after Romulus's destruction. The implicit assumption at work here is that all of these Vulcans are the *same person*. I'm taking it for granted that it makes sense to refer to them all with the single name "Spock-Prime." But since we're questioning the nature of identity, perhaps it's worth taking a moment to consider this assumption, logical though it may seem.

What exactly does it mean to say that two people at different points in time are the same? For most of us, this is a relatively unambiguous question, because we live in terms of a clear path through space and time. One moment of our existence is connected to another moment in a way that seems clear and unbroken. Even when we don't have conscious awareness of that stream of existence, like during sleep, we see other people sleeping and yet continuing to exist, so we typically don't question whether we cease to exist during this time.

But this assumption of *physical consistency* through time is largely an illusion. Our cells die and are lost on a regular basis. After about fifteen years, a completely different set of cells composes one's body. So all of Spock-Prime's cells at age thirty were different than the ones that belonged to his newborn self. Pointing at thirty-year-old and newborn Spock-Prime at two different points in time and saying they're the same person is an identity claim that seems to make sense, but is difficult to explain. For example, we can't rely on the fact that both Spock-Primes have the same *genetic information* because of counterexamples like cases of twins, clones, or transporter malfunctions, all of which produce two individuals who have identical genetic information but are clearly not the same person.[1] The fundamental "Spockness" (or "Spock-Primeness") that connects newborn Spock-Prime to thirty-year-old Spock-Prime isn't based strictly on genetic properties, nor can it be based on the physical and mental characteristics that we identify as Spock-Prime's.

Philosopher David Lewis (1941–2001) addresses this metaphysical conundrum by arguing that existence—and thus identity—is a result of "Humean supervenience."[2] Lewis points to the Enlightenment thinker David Hume (1711–1776), who makes the point that what we directly perceive about the world is the correlation between *natural properties*—sights, sounds and other appearances—rather than directly perceiving the causes connecting those properties.[3] Lewis thinks identity works in much the same way. We don't directly perceive that a thing remains the same; instead, we compare two adjacent instances of the thing in space and time. If the objects contained within those adjacent moments contain basically the same natural properties, then it's appropriate to say they're identical to each other.

Consider three versions of the starship *Enterprise*: the original Constitution-class vessel commanded by Captains Pike and Kirk in TOS; the refitted *Enterprise* that Kirk usurps from Captain Will Decker in *The Motion Picture*; and the *Enterprise-A* given to Kirk and company at the end of *The Voyage Home*. While the *Enterprise* Kirk commandeers in *TMP* differs greatly from the TOS version, Scotty and the spacedock crew had spent eighteen months "redesigning and refitting" what Scotty treats as the *same* vessel. Each part of the TOS *Enterprise* had been swapped out for an upgraded replacement part, so through this process the ship would've been composed of an ever-shifting set of both old and new parts. By contrast, once the refit *Enterprise* is destroyed over the Genesis planet in *The Search for Spock*, there are no old parts remaining that can be used to construct the *Enterprise-A*: the two are *wholly different* ships. Analogous to the TOS *Enterprise* and its refitted version, personal identity can be retained despite the loss of old cells and the creation of new ones, because at any given point the moment-by-moment, cause-and-effect transformation is slow enough—with one's body comprising both old and new cells at any given moment—to retain the sense of identity.

Lewis's resolution, though likely good enough in most cases, is still problematic in the Spock-Prime case. At about age fifty-five, Spock-Prime implanted his *katra* (Vulcan soul) into Dr. Leonard McCoy via a mind-meld, died, and was seemingly resurrected with a new, completely rejuvenated body on the Genesis planet. While most people replace their bodies at a rate of a few years, Spock did it here at the rate of a few days! And, for a period of time, there was a younger Spock running around Genesis without his soul. If we take into account the relationships in space and time of the various elements of Spock-Prime's identity during this time—particularly the separation of his body and *katra*—it's hard to believe he retains his identity, but it's easier to treat this like the case of the *Enterprise* and the *Enterprise*-A, where the two similar things are the same in name only.

But consider another analogy. What if, before destroying the *Enterprise* over Genesis, Scotty had downloaded all of its main computer's software—including both operational programs and the ship's logs— onto an external drive? He later loads the software package into the *Enterprise*-A's main computer—maybe that's why it's functioning so badly in *The Final Frontier*! Yet we might be inclined to claim that the *Enterprise*-A's computer still isn't the same computer as the destroyed *Enterprise*'s, despite having identical programming. Similarly, it's hard to see how the Spock-Prime who dies at the end of *The Wrath of Khan* is the same person who's recovering on Vulcan at the beginning of *The Voyage Home*, though moving forward I will make precisely this claim. For our purposes, the label of "Spock-Prime" can be applied meaningfully to these different manifestations. It seems illogical to do anything else.

## Kiri-kin-tha's First Law of Metaphysics

At the beginning of *A Voyage Home*, Spock undergoes a memory test following his resurrection. Among the computer's quick series of questions is "What was Kiri-kin-tha's first law of metaphysics?" Spock answers, "Nothing unreal exists." But what does it mean to say that something *exists*?

Lewis argues for the metaphysical theory of *modal realism*: all "possible worlds" are as real as the "actual world."[4] In science fiction parlance, this philosophical concept of "world" is more often called a *universe*. Thus, Earth and Vulcan are both part of the same "world" depicted in *Star Trek*. The central question Lewis addresses is whether our world is the only real world, or whether other possible worlds could also be considered real.

So what is this "actual world" in Lewis's theory? Our world is clearly distinct from worlds that are *not part of our world*, whether or not these other worlds are ultimately considered "real worlds." This label used for this distinction is that our world is the actual world, and any world that is not part of our world is not the actual world. To say that a world is not part of our world is the same thing as to say that each world has its own internal coherence and consistent history of ordered, actualized possibilities, but that these are different for both. This allows us to draw a distinction between our world and other possible worlds, but to do so without making a premature judgment on whether those other worlds are "real" or "exist." The view of modal realism is that these possible worlds are real worlds, but they're not *actualized*. Only our world is actual *for us*, and the world of *Star Trek* is actual for Spock-Prime, because that's the possible world in which he exists. This assumes, of course, that the *Star Trek* world falls within the set of all possible worlds—but, after passing into Abrams's hands, that status is less clear.

Lewis is not saying that the world of *Star Trek* is an actual world from *our* perspective. From our perspective, the only world that's actualized is our world—in which Spock-Prime doesn't exist, but an actor named Leonard Nimoy did, until recently, exist. Any other possible world that isn't part of our world isn't actualized as far as we're concerned: "This makes actuality a relative matter: every world is *actual at* itself, and thereby all worlds are on par. This is not to say that all worlds are actual—there's no world at which that is true, any more than there's ever a time when all times are present."[5]

Think of Lieutenant Worf's experience in "Parallels" (TNG). He finds himself slipping into different worlds in which different possibilities have been actualized: in some he's married to Counselor Troi, in some Geordi is dead, and in some Captain Picard remained assimilated by the Borg and Riker commands the *Enterprise*. Each of these worlds is "real" in that they have their own internal coherence and consistent history of ordered actualized possibilities: because Picard isn't rescued from the Borg in one world, Riker's field promotion to Captain in "The Best of Both Worlds, Part II" becomes permanent, and Worf is subsequently promoted to be Riker's First Officer. None of these worlds, however, are actualized *for Worf* until his transition to that world is effected by an inadvertent signal from Geordi's VISOR.

Consider instead what it would mean if our world were somehow *absolutely* actualized, in a way that other possible worlds aren't actualized. Lewis argues that this would be incredibly fortunate for us, as we would exist in the only possible world that's actualized, and everyone except us exists in possible worlds that aren't actualized. There's a sense in which the *Copernican principle*—the idea that we don't have an inherently privileged position within the universe—forces Lewis to concede the status of being "actual" onto these other possible worlds, so that he can allow himself to claim that status for our own world.

Lewis extends this same reasoning to the idea of "existence," because if a world is "actual," that suggests *it must exist*. And if something exists within your world, then that means it's actual. Using this approach, we get to the idea that a thing exists if it's part of your world, if it's actualized. Thus, by defining Kiri-kin-tha's first law of metaphysics in terms of Lewis's modal realism, we get a good starting point to figuring out which Spock is the real one: *nothing unreal (in your world) is part of your world.*

## "I Liked Him with the Beard Better"

When Kirk and his landing party undergo a transporter malfunction to find themselves in an alternate reality in "Mirror, Mirror," they're faced with a bearded Spock. This Mirror-Spock is among the most humane denizens of a barbaric alternate reality, where the Federation is replaced by a brutal empire; but even he punishes Mr. Kyle with an "agonizer" for a simple transporter error. Is this *really* Spock? Or is the real Spock the one back on the Federation's *Enterprise*, dealing with the evil Kirk and his associates? Are they *both* real? Are they both *actualized*?

If these universes had remained isolated from each other, neither could've been considered actualized by inhabitants of the other. In this case, Spock-Prime and Mirror-Spock would be "counterparts" of each other: beings that exist in different possible worlds but that contain some sort of *inherent property* that makes them similar to each other. But exactly what this property is can be a bit hard to pin down. David Kaplan coined the term *Haecceitism* (from the Latin *haec*, or "this") to describe the idea "that a common 'thisness' may underlie extreme dissimilarity or distinct thisness may underlie great resemblance."[6] There's much dispute over what the "thisness" may consist of, a dispute summed up in the problem of *transworld identity*. This problem manifests as the question: in what sense, if any, are Spock-Prime and Mirror-Spock *identical* to each other? What's the fundamental "Spockness" that underlies the two beings?

The most obvious commonality is that the two men look like each other, but there are many ways they could look alike without being identical—Commander Riker and Lieutenant Riker look alike when the latter is discovered in "Second Chances" (TNG), but they're certainly two *different* men by this point. Spock-Prime and Mirror-Spock presumably were both born in the year 2230 on the planet Vulcan, to Vulcan father Sarek and human mother Amanda Grayson. But how many details about them would need to differ? For example, if Amanda Grayson went into labor prematurely in the Mirror universe and Mirror-Spock was born in 2229 while visiting Earth, they'd still be counterparts. These incidental facts about their existence can't be the thing that makes them alike; there must be something more fundamental.

Perhaps the issue is that Spock-Prime and Mirror-Spock don't have transworld identity, because they're just *too different*; but they might be identical if the worlds were basically identical to each other. If this were the case, though, it's possible to consider a pair of other possible worlds that are essentially identical to the Prime and Mirror worlds, except that the Spock-Prime and Mirror-Spock counterparts are just a tiny bit more like each other—say, Mirror-Spock lacks a goatee. It's then possible to imagine another possible world where they are, again, a little bit more like each other—say, Spock-Prime's logical nature is more similar to Mirror-Spock's cold ruthlessness. And so on, through more possible worlds, until you arrive at a possible world where they've switched places. There's a possible world in which all the properties of Spock-Prime are held by a being that has the identity of Mirror-Spock, and a possible world where all the properties of Mirror-Spock are held by a being with the identity of Spock-Prime. In all particulars, it would seem that these worlds are identical to the original Prime and Mirror universes, except that the identities of the Spocks have somehow reversed.

This problem of transworld identity, also known as *Chisholm's paradox*, was developed by metaphysician Roderick Chisholm (1916–1999) the same year that "Mirror, Mirror" aired on television. Chisholm argues that we should be strongly skeptical about any sense of transworld identity and Haeccetism. But if Mirror-Spock and Spock-Prime aren't related to each other by identity, they're certainly related to each other by some sort of strong *similarity* relationship. They are, after all, *counterparts* to each other. Or are they?

The term *counterparts*, in this context, refers to two entities that are part of different possible worlds. It's important to think carefully about how we're distinguishing between "possible worlds." "Mirror, Mirror" depicts two possible timelines that are clearly different but not entirely isolated from each other. Kirk, Bones, Scotty, and Uhura travel between the worlds, which means that Kirk—more specifically, Kirk-Prime—is a possible individual within the Mirror universe. For however brief a time, Kirk-Prime coexists in a clear spatiotemporal relationship with Mirror-Spock. In Lewis's terms, this makes the two of them *worldmates*. Spock-Prime and Mirror-Kirk are also worldmates. This worldmate status contains a *transitive* property that allows it to extend to all members of the two worlds—including beings who actually cross over from one universe to the other, like *Deep Space Nine*'s Major Kira Nerys and Dr. Julian Bashir, but even beings like *Voyager*'s Commander Chakotay who never actually exist within the Mirror universe.[7]

Therefore, when talking about the possible worlds in this context, we aren't talking about two different possible worlds, but about one single possible world that contains both the original *Star Trek* timeline and the Mirror universe timeline. Though Spock-Prime and Mirror-Spock don't ever directly meet each other, they're worldmates to each other: in this enlarged sense of "world," Mirror-Spock is a part of Spock-Prime's world and vice versa. So the two versions of Spock are both actualized to each other, though neither is actualized in relation to our world (it's just a TV show, after all!).[8]

In this way, the problem of discovering transworld identities ceases to be a problem, if it ever really was one. Spock-Prime and Mirror-Spock aren't identical to each other, because they're different beings within the same world. At no point are they ever the same by being identical to each other. The same can't be said, however, for the relationship between Spock-Prime and Spock-2.

## "I Have Been and Always Shall Be … "

In the year 2230, on the planet Vulcan, a child was born to the Vulcan, Sarek, and his human wife, Amanda Grayson. He grew up, initially, with an older Vulcan half-brother, Sybok. These details are relevant, because they would've been true for both Spock-Prime and Spock-2. After all, the Romulan ship *Narada* didn't arrive from the late 24th century until the year 2233, when James T. Kirk was born. So for at least the first three years of life, Spock-Prime and Spock-2 would seem to be identical to each other. They shared a spatiotemporal existence, with everything about their world and their experiences absolutely in accord with each other. The newborn Spock-Prime was identical to the newborn Spock-2. In other words, the newborn Spock grows up to become *both* Spock-Prime and Spock-2.

Logically, though, this creates a problem, which gets to the idea of why these questions have such philosophical importance. Earlier, I made clear an assumption: that I was using the term *Spock-Prime* to refer to both newborn Spock-Prime and the elderly Spock-Prime as identical beings across time. But if the same newborn shares an identity through time with *two different people*—elderly Spock-Prime and Spock-2—doesn't that mean that those two different people are, in fact, identical?

Lewis argues that this isn't the case. In fact, newborn Spock-Prime and newborn Spock-2 aren't actually identical to each other, though they're "excellent counterparts" to each other. Indeed, they are exact *duplicates*, and even share completely the spatiotemporal relationship within duplicates of the same physical universe. Lewis illustrates this bizarrely counterintuitive claim with the analogy of a highway. Two highways—say, U.S. Interstate 70 West and Interstate 65 South— may overlap for a period, using the same physical road surface for both—as they wind through the city of Indianapolis, Indiana—but this doesn't mean the two highways are identical. They're different highways that are superimposed upon each other. When the overlapping stretch of highway ends, they break apart into different road surfaces—one heading due west and the other due south—their distinct identities becoming apparent. The highways would only be identical if they comprised the whole length of the same road surface. Overlapping road surfaces for a limited stretch doesn't make the highways identical.

The same is true for the two Spocks. Spock-Prime and Spock-2 shared a spatiotemporal existence up until the time when Nero's arrival in 2230 caused changes in their experience. At this point, like the highways, their paths through space and time began to diverge from each other, and their experiences becoming more and more distinct, the similarities in their traits diminishing with greater distance.

One curious question regards precisely *when* the split between Spock-Prime and Spock-2 would've occurred. The original timeline began to diverge immediately upon the *Narada*'s arrival, but does that mean Spock began diverging at the moment? Or did he only diverge later, when the consequences of those events changed things for him locally? I know of no good philosophical answer to this question.

Regardless, it's clear that Spock-Prime and Spock-2 continued to have many points of commonality—both teased by other Vulcan boys for their human provenance, both choosing a career in Starfleet instead of the Vulcan Science Academy to their father's chagrin, and both eventually serving alongside Captain Kirk on the Starship *Enterprise*—like a highway that branches off into two roads that travel near each other, through a common countryside. The same could be said for Mirror-Spock and Mirror-Spock-2.

With this reasoning, the answer we arrive at is one in which logic matches common sense and intuition, which is always a good outcome in philosophy, and all too rare when considering questions of transworld identity. When Spock-2 and Spock-Prime converse, they're not two identical beings speaking to each other, but two similar beings that have shared common experiences. Rather than being abstract counterparts, they're instead *individuals*, each formed out of their own successes and failures, rivalries and friendships, passion and pain.

## Notes

1. For further discussion of how malfunctioning transporters—and even perfectly functioning ones—raise puzzles of personal identity, see William Jaworski's chapter in this volume (Chapter 14).
2. David K. Lewis, *On the Plurality of Worlds* (Oxford: Blackwell, 1986).
3. David Hume, *Enquiries Concerning Human Understanding and Concerning the Principles of Morals*, ed. L.A. Selby-Bigge, 3rd ed. (Oxford: Clarendon Press, 1975).
4. Lewis, *On the Plurality of Worlds*.
5. Ibid., 93.
6. David Kaplan, "How to Russell a Frege-Church," *The Journal of Philosophy* 72:19 (1975): 716.
7. Later *Star Trek* episode stories that concern the Mirror universe—sometimes, but not always, involving crossovers with the Prime universe—include the DS9 episodes "Crossover," "Through the Looking Glass," "Shattered Mirror," "Resurrection," and "The Emperor's New Cloak"; the ENT two-part episode "In a Mirror Darkly"; and various comics, games, and novels—such as the TNG novel *Dark Mirror* by Diane Duane (New York: Pocket Books, 1993). VOY doesn't include any episodes concerning the Mirror universe.
8. Two early *ST* publications are of note here. In the first *ST* fanzine *Spockanalia*, Ruth Berman offered us "Visit to a Weird Planet," in which Kirk, Spock, and McCoy beamed from an *Enterprise* transporter room onto the

Desilu studio set of *Star Trek*. Its sequel, published in one of the earliest official publications of original *ST* fiction, *Star Trek: The New Voyages*, is "Visit to a Strange Planet Revisited," by Ruth Berman, in which William Shatner, Leonard Nimoy, DeForest Kelley, and James Doohan step onto a transporter room set and emerge on the actual *Enterprise*; *Star Trek: The New Voyages*, ed. Sondra Marshak and Myrna Culbreath (New York: Bantam, 1976).

# 28

# "Strangely Compelling": Romanticism in "The City on the Edge of Forever"

## Sarah O'Hare

During suppers with my parents as a child, I often traveled into the future and deep into space with my Starfleet friends toward *our* next adventure. *Star Trek* is a successful popular cultural endeavor because it allows for exactly this kind of imaginative escapism—the possibility of joining in on an alternative narrative. In "The City on the Edge of Forever" (TOS), the *Enterprise* orbits a mysterious planet, where on its surface someone or something is causing temporal and spatial displacement. The central crisis revolves around Dr. McCoy's accidental cordrazine[1] overdose while tending to Mr. Sulu on the *Enterprise* bridge. Now in a hyperparanoid state, the doctor flees the ship and beams down. McCoy jumps through the Guardian of Forever in an effort to escape, ultimately changing the course of "Old Earth's" history—a momentous change that leaves Captain Kirk, Mr. Spock, and the other landing party members stuck without a past and without a future. Without any historical points of reference, Kirk and Spock have "no alternative" but to journey through the Guardian in order to restore history and rescue McCoy.

This chapter uses Romanticism as a philosophical gateway to the sublime experience that is the Guardian of Forever. *Romanticism* names an intellectual, literary, and artistic movement in Europe from 1770 to 1850, which was born out of reaction to the Industrial Revolution and the Enlightenment's overreliance on reason and rationalization of nature. Standing upon a historical precipice between a shared crisis and the possibility of a resolution, Romantic thinkers treated the imagination as a worthy source of critical authority, and in so

*The Ultimate Star Trek and Philosophy*, First Edition. Edited by Kevin S. Decker and Jason T. Eberl.
© 2016 John Wiley & Sons, Ltd. Published 2016 by John Wiley & Sons, Ltd.

doing were able to break away from the traditional forms of classical realism and representation in literature and art. Romantic thinkers shared a secular reverence for the beauty of the natural landscape, and latched on to the aesthetic and moral implications of concepts like memory and oblivion, darkness and light, death and love, horror and beauty, and nature and industry. Of course, many of these themes also find expression in episodes of *Star Trek*. Examining how these contrary concepts illuminate each other fascinates Trekkers and Romantics alike because, as the Romantics first discovered, a concept can't be thought of without its opposite: they're thus inseparable, while their fundamental opposition is irresolvable. This seems like a paradox, but for the Romantics, its truth points to a thread of irrationality that exists in all nature.

## "The Source of All the Time Disturbance"

The idea of time travel is itself a Romantic notion (in the late 19th century, H.G. Wells's *The Time Machine* and other early works of sci-fi "scientific romances" emerged); however, Romantic thinkers didn't think about time in the logical or mathematical ways that many philosophers had before. Their philosophy of time was concerned with how we *narrate history* in time. From this perspective, the idea of traveling through time provides the possibility of making change through human action in something that already seems fixed and finished, just as Dr. McCoy disrupted the course of history and caused a dramatic change in a fixed time. This occurrence is mirrored in the real experience of the Romantic reaction against the Enlightenment, a movement that the Romantics saw as stifling the possibilities for change.

One study of the genre of time travel fiction calls it a "fundamental condition of storytelling itself, even its very essence."[2] The structures of fiction that alter our perception of the passage of time—pauses at the end of chapters, parallel action, and flashbacks—allow readers or viewers to travel through the narrative with the characters without living it out in real time. In the 21st Street Mission, Spock explains, "There could be some logic to the belief that time is fluid, like a river, with currents, eddies, backwash." So has McCoy created an eddy? Well, the *very act of going back in time* should make some kind of alteration to the timeline. The traveler arriving in the past wasn't there before, and so their presence should impact history.[3] We're often told in time travel stories that small changes don't make a difference, but from a "god's-eye perspective" encompassing all events past, present, and future, no action is more or less relevant to the shaping of history. Luckily for us, our desire for escapism isn't constrained by the laws of physics, and so "The City on the Edge of Forever" takes place at a "focal point" in history, an idea that really has no scientific sense when we talk about the space–time manifold, but means everything to the Romantics, as we'll see.

The Guardian of Forever—"a gateway to your own past if you wish"—is the cause of the spatial displacement and ripples in time that shake the *Enterprise* at the episode's beginning. In Harlan Ellison's original teleplay draft, the Guardians of Forever referred to several giant, ancient, cloaked beings that stood guard in front of the pillars that held "forever." In the final aired version, however, these cloaked beings are replaced by the stone arch ruin of the Guardian, which speaks for itself.[4] The Guardian returns in "Yesteryear" (TAS), in which Kirk and Spock conduct time travel research with Starfleet historians. Alarmingly, when they return through the Guardian, no one but Kirk recognizes Spock. In this episode, Spock's seven-year-old self is the focal point in history. When "our" Spock goes back in time to Vulcan in 2237, he disguises himself as a distant cousin "Selek," whom he later remembers saved his young life from a ferocious *le-matya* during his *kahs-wan* ritual.[5] The young Spock is saved, and his pet *sehlat* dies. Most importantly, a turning point in Spock's personal history is preserved: his success in completing the ritual forestalled the disappointment his father Sarek had in his half-human son—having commented immediately upon his birth, "So human" (*ST V*). This is also the moment when Spock chooses his philosophy of life. He could've chosen the human traditions of his mother Amanda, but instead, by "logically" letting his mortally wounded pet I-Chaya die peacefully, Spock chooses a Vulcan way of life. Spock's experience fits the Romantic philosophy according to which no story we tell about ourselves is merely a record of events. Rather, narratives are constructed to convey the *meaning* we look for—and often find—in our developing identity.

When asked if it is a being or machine, the Guardian replies, "I am both and neither. I am my own beginning, my own ending." The Guardian further explains that it can present time only in a moving, chronological manner. Kirk finds this opportunity "strangely compelling," to "lose oneself in another world." In fact, this is exactly what McCoy does. As a result, the Guardian explains, "Your vessel, your beginning. All that you knew is gone." Realizing that his ship, Starfleet, and the Earth he once knew have all disappeared, Kirk is alarmed.

"We're totally alone," he says with a suggestion of existential horror in being unmoored from history. This is the ultimate *nihilist* moment: to experience forever without reference points. *Nihilism* means many things, but here it suggests this ultimate sense of *meaninglessness*. If we try and imagine our position within an eternal span of time, without the traditional signposts of birth, education, maturity, and even death, we can feel the creep of nihilism. With no pressing limit to our measure of life, we wouldn't be compelled to pass it on in the form of a record or memorial. And we certainly wouldn't have cause to reexamine our lives and the choices we've made.[6]

Romanticism urges us to see that as the times and culture change, inevitably taking points of reference away from our life story, the only response is to find new meaning by creating new reference points. Of course, Kirk can't live with being erased from history—he's a Romantic! The trip he and Spock take into the Guardian is human action expressing itself by reconstructing a narrative of the past. It's in this sense that Romanticism is filled with meaning, reacting against the void of nihilism. In the face of crisis, Romantics acknowledge the pieces of culture they're losing, while also finding a way to move forward without these familiar, iconic concepts. Moving forward toward an opportunity while simultaneously acknowledging what you stand to lose is exactly what Kirk does in losing Edith Keeler and what Spock does in "Yesteryear."[7]

## "Modern Museum Perfection"

According to Georg W.F. Hegel's (1770–1831) philosophy of history, cultures attempt to "hold their own time in thought," capturing the essence of their times through art, history, and philosophy. But we don't always realize that we're doing this, either as representatives of our culture or as individuals. Hegel suggests that individuals feel *compelled* to make and read history because we have a sense of our own mortality and live with an implicit fear of death. When we die, we'll be gone from this time, our consciousness gone from this place. We must ask ourselves, then, for what do we want to be remembered? These concerns compel us to move forward and record our path as we go along. For if there's no record to remember us by, it would seem our lives have little meaning.[8]

In this perspective, we can consider what Edith Keeler will be remembered for. Kirk prevents McCoy from saving Edith from being hit by a truck. Thus, Kirk serves as a *medium* of the movement of history because, with Spock's help, he foresaw the dire consequences of Edith's survival. From Hegel's perspective, everyone has a role to play in history—but your role may not be the role you would have wanted to play.[9] Edith believes her role is to be a visionary leader for world peace. Ironically, her conscious efforts, in the wider landscape of history, would do more harm than good as Spock and Kirk see the result of Nazi world domination on their "future-viewing video device."[10] As strange as it seems, and though she's unaware of it, Edith's actual role in history is to die young in a traffic accident. This is both tragic and ironic. Though Hegel didn't see any aesthetic appeal in irony—calling it a form of evil[11]—irony is an important Romantic notion. Yet seeing irony makes it more difficult to try to "Romanticize" the world—that is, to act with the knowledge "that humans can *participate* in the dynamic power of nature, through invention, creativity, imagination, [or] art," because moments like Edith's death and Kirk's subsequent heartbreak seem unfair on a cosmic level.[12]

"Romanticizing" the world extends to the ways in which we make, record, and interpret history. For Hegel, history's meaning is twofold. It includes events that happened as we experienced them *and* the human-made narrative record: "Change is historical when those involved in it understand it as fitting into a narrative scheme of things, when they are conscious of its having historical significance."[13] But being conscious of our own history is a responsibility that is today more honored in its breach than its observance, and we can only hope this will be different in the 23rd century. The responsibility implies we must have an *awareness* of what's considered historically significant and what isn't. The Romantics, of course, had a keen awareness of this. When the Guardian begins to show images of "Old Earth's" history, the landing party is captivated. However, they're shown only brief clips from human history that audience members are likely to identify as pivotal moments. But why shouldn't the Guardian show everyday images? Why not show an Inca family tying knots in a calendar, an aristocrat enjoying teatime in St. Petersburg, or a fisherman out on his sea? Popular opinion might have it that, while these moments may have seemed important in the short run, their impact wasn't significant enough to be understood as a "focal point" in history. This clarifies a distinction many of us recognize: some moments or people are common and unimpressive, and others are revolutionary or "world-historical," as Hegel would've named them.[14]

Spock displays his Romantic awareness when suddenly he realizes he's failed at his responsibility to record the history the Guardian shows: "I am a fool! My tricorder is capable of recording even at this speed. I've missed taping centuries of living history." Spock's quick thinking leads to his efforts to Romanticize his world: he shows an *awareness* of history by recognizing the images in the Guardian as having value, and so he begins to record the history. The moment those images were perceived to be valuable, they immediately were *made to be* Romantic. The famous scenes of history are seen to be valuable because we recognize them, as does Spock, as being *connected* to wider narratives of history. The ability to travel into a valued moment in recorded history is a familiar wish "to step through there and lose oneself in another world"—this is the escapism of the imagination at work. Standing before the Guardian of Forever and imagining the possibilities would, as Kirk said, be "strangely compelling." Indeed, the Romantic Novalis (1772–1801) contends that all the world *should* be made to be Romantic: "the world must be made Romantic. In that way one can find the original meaning again. To make Romantic is nothing but a qualitative raising to a higher power." We can make the world more Romantic by seeing a higher value in even the most mundane moments in life and history, by treating "the ordinary with a mysterious respect."[15] When we do this with history, we're highlighting the human element in the narrative record as well as forming a *relationship* to history and thereby cultivating a better self. Spock quite literally does this by bettering himself in "Yesteryear" when he offers his pet *sehlat* I-Chaya a path of diminished pain and offers his younger self valuable advice. Indeed, if we don't choose to make the world Romantic, we're more likely to fall victim to the meaninglessness of nihilism that awaits us in the shadows.

## "Stone Knives and Bearskins"

We can indeed Romanticize *Star Trek*. After all, Kirk, Spock, and McCoy are *Star Trek*'s Romantic trio, and not in the sense of a bromance! We can see each of them as representing particular archetypes from Friedrich Nietzsche (1844–1900) who, while not a Romantic, co-opted the Romantic use of short aphorisms, irony, and the suspicion of certain forms of reason in his own philosophy. Nietzsche, in his writings on Greek history, also adopted the Romantic attitude toward the past by suggesting there are certain meaningful archetypes in the Greek past: in the context of "City on the Edge," Kirk represents the "Tragic Hero," Spock the "Apollonian" figure, and McCoy the "Dionysian" figure.[16] Nietzsche defines a Tragic Hero as the one who takes the suffering of the world onto their shoulders for the benefit of everyone else. Kirk bears the burden of letting the woman he loves die in front of him, entailing immense personal suffering to ensure that the millions more who would've died under Nazi world domination would be saved.

Nietzsche describes the Apollonian character in terms of logic and symmetry, peace and beauty, and the Dionysian character as chaotic, emotional, and impulsive. Kirk is often caught between the Apollonian and the Dionysian extremes of Spock and McCoy, respectively.[17] Logical and calm, Spock is the prime example of an Apollonian temperament, whereas McCoy is more emotionally driven and compassionate, which is what led him to save Edith Keeler in the first place and thereby unwittingly change all of history for the worse.

The moment Edith is killed, the extremes of these Greek characteristics come out in our three protagonists. McCoy, driven by temper and profession to care for the well-being of others, darts into the street to save her life. Spock waits, watches, and hopes for the logical good to come about, for history to be made rational again. And Kirk is stuck in the middle. As he's in love with Edith, he wants more than anything in the world to be able to keep her alive, but he also knows the consequences of her well-meaning pacifism. The dramatic climax proves to be a (re)turning point for all of history with Edith Keeler as the focal point, and Kirk must make the painful but life-affirming decision to grab McCoy and hold him back from saving her. In the restoration of history to its original trajectory, there's *beauty* in her death. This idea, as strange as it may seem, isn't a contradiction, since, for Romantics, there can't be beauty without death; this is a point about the impermanence of beautiful things and how the recognition of that makes us melancholy. In this way, the focal point in history around which the future of humanity revolves, Edith's brief life and death (at the historical "edge of forever") also serve as a Romantic focal point in history. The choice of life or death puts Kirk into a position to create a meaningful narrative despite tragedy. Regardless of the outcome, the decision will have a lasting effect *forever*. At this decisive moment, Kirk emerges from the center of the struggle between the Apollonian and the Dionysian as the Tragic Hero. This pattern of ethical struggle is found over and over again during the course of these three men's mission through space. And their shared experiences have bonding effects, just as the early Romantic thinkers bonded together in facing crises through Romantic action.[18]

## "I Am ... My Own Ending"

As a child, *Star Trek* taught me a valuable lesson: difficult decisions must be made, even if we humans are underqualified to do so. Sometimes those decisions are ethically challenging or painful, sometimes life-changing, and to *choose* not to make a decision is still very much a decision. Turning points in history lead one way or another because choices and actions and times change accordingly; people make history as much as history makes them. By boldly going toward where no one has gone before, the *U.S.S. Enterprise*—like the Romantics[19]— goes "out there, thataway" to create new points of cultural reference after the old points have fallen away.[20] The lesson for us is that as we advance toward the *Star Trek* era, we must be mindful of the importance of our understanding and interpretation of historical narratives so that we too can create points of cultural reference and meaning in our lives.

## Notes

1. As defined in *The Star Trek Encyclopedia*, ed. Michael Okuda, Denise Okuda, and Debbie Mirek (New York: Pocket Books, 1994), 58: "cordrazine. Extremely powerful pharmaceutical stimulant used by Federation medical personnel." Dr. McCoy prescribed 2 ml of cordrazine to Lieutenant Sulu, who suffered serious electrical burns when the ship was investigating time-distortion waves in 2267 near the Guardian of Forever. Another time wave caused McCoy to receive an accidental overdose of cordrazine, whereupon he experienced extreme paranoid delusions and fled to the planet's surface ("The City on the Edge of Forever" [TOS]). McCoy also used cordrazine to revive Ensign Rizzo when he was attacked by the dikironium cloud creature ("Obsession" [TOS]). Dr. Beverly Crusher used 25 ml of cordrazine in a last-ditch effort to save Worf's life when his body rejected genetronic replication therapy in 2368 ("Ethics" [TNG]).
2. David Wittenberg, *Time Travel: The Popular Philosophy of Narrative* (New York: Fordham University Press, 2013), 1.
3. This is exemplified to the greatest extent in *Star Trek* (2009).
4. For more information on the controversial "Cordwaine Bird" rewrites, see Harlan Ellison, *The City on the Edge of Forever: The Original Teleplay That Became the Classic Star Trek Episode* (Stone Mountain, GA: White Wolf Publishing, 1996); and Herbert F. Solow and Robert

H. Justman, *Inside Star Trek: The Real Story* (New York: Pocket Books, 1997). And for the record, the original draft from Ellison wasn't rewritten because Scotty was dealing drugs—a misconception I had long held, but have now rectified!

5. The *kahs-wan* is the ritual Vulcan maturity examination for all children.

6. Such existential meaninglessness seems to plague the eternal Q—or at least one of them who subsequently desires to be made mortal so he can commit suicide in "Death Wish" (VOY).

7. The Guardian also plays a central role in A.C. Crispin's Pocket Books *Star Trek* novels "Yesterday's Son" (1983) and "Time for Yesterday" (1990).

8. Such concern fuels Dr. Beverly Crusher's angst as she perceives all of her shipmates to tragically disappear with no one having any memory of them in "Remember Me" (TNG), as well as the perpetual recollection implanted in the minds of passersby of the atrocity that occurred on Tarakis in "Memorial" (VGR).

9. G.W.F. Hegel, *The Hegel Reader*, ed. Stephen Houlgate (Malden, MA: Blackwell, 1998), 45–124.

10. Wittenberg, *Time Travel*, 163.

11. G.W.F. Hegel, *The Hegel Reader*, 353.

12. Curtis Stone, *The Science Delusion* (Brooklyn: Melville House, 2013), 85.

13. Stephen Houlgate, *An Introduction to Hegel: Freedom, Truth, and History*, 2nd ed. (Malden, MA: Blackwell, 2005), 19. Of course, sometimes the "made" historical narrative doesn't correspond to what's actually experienced, as seen in "Living Witness" (VOY).

14. G.W.F. Hegel, *The Hegel Reader*, 285.

15. Novalis, *Novalis: Philosophical Writings*, trans. and ed. Margaret Mahony Stoljar (Albany: State University of New York Press, 1997), 60.

16. The Tragic Hero, the Apollonian, and the Dionysian characters are described in Friedrich Nietzsche, *The Birth of Tragedy: Out of the Spirit of Music*, trans. Shaun Whiteside, ed. Michael Tanner (London: Penguin, 1993).

17. The discussion held in Kirk's cabin about the development and use of the Genesis device in *ST II: The Wrath of Khan* is particularly good at pointing this out, and the film again presents Kirk as a Tragic Hero.

18. The after-effects of this tragic decision, as well as what happened to McCoy in the altered history he inadvertently created, are explored in the "Crucible" series of Pocket Books *Star Trek* novels by David R. George III: *Provenance and Shadows* (2006), *The Fire and the Rose* (2006), and *The Star to Every Wandering* (2007).

19. #RomanticsLLAP.

20. This chapter is for Leonard Nimoy, 1931–2015. You lived long and you prospered, sir.

# 29

# It Is a Q of Life: Q as a Nietzschean Figure

*Charles Taliaferro and Bailey Wheelock*

> One must still have chaos in oneself to be
> able to give birth to a dancing star.
>
> —Friedrich Nietzsche[1]

> To learn about you is, frankly, provocative.
> But you're next of kin to chaos.
>
> —"Q Who?" (TNG)

The self-proclaimed omnipotent rapscallion Q embodies some of the values celebrated by the great German philosopher Friedrich Wilhelm Nietzsche (1844–1900). At the forefront of their shared values is the importance of seeking to enhance life at a level of intensity and quality that transcends ordinary morality. Along these lines, Q pushes the crew of the *Enterprise*-D, and Captain Jean-Luc Picard in particular, toward personal greatness and higher knowledge. Although Q makes other appearances in the *Star Trek* universe, we'll focus on TNG, as these are the best set of episodes for looking at Q through the lens of Nietzsche's revaluation of conventional values, reflecting Q's own stance on questions of moral conduct.

## To Cultivate One's Individuality

Nietzsche is sometimes interpreted as someone who rejects all morals and values, a mistaken impression amplified by the title of one of his more famous books, *Beyond Good and Evil*. But Nietzsche was

*The Ultimate Star Trek and Philosophy*, First Edition. Edited by Kevin S. Decker and Jason T. Eberl.
© 2016 John Wiley & Sons, Ltd. Published 2016 by John Wiley & Sons, Ltd.

neither a *nihilist* nor someone who thought there was no such thing as good or evil. Nietzsche only challenges *conventional morality* as codified and practiced in particular systems of *Christian ethics* and *utilitarianism*.[2] These challenges emerge from the fact that Nietzsche, like Q, deplores systems of ethics that weaken us by promoting pity— such as Christianity's compassion for others—or by seeking egalitarian happiness—such as utilitarianism's principle of promoting the greatest happiness for the greatest number. Instead, Nietzsche affirms the values of *life-enhancing strength*. Human excellence should be sought through the pursuit of powerful vitality by the strongest among us. Nietzsche thus challenges us to ask whether our ideas of good and evil are "a sign of the distress, poverty and degeneration of life? Or, on the contrary, do they reveal the fullness, strength and will to life."[3] Nietzsche calls us to transcend, move beyond, and even reverse the kind of ethical thinking that focuses on caring for the weak, and implores us to not hold back the strong in their pursuit of a higher order of life—as exemplified by beings such as Q. The pursuit of such vitality isn't safe: those who pursue individual greatness must be willing to take profound risks and endure the suffering that most people go to lengths to evade. Nietzsche observes, "The discipline of suffering, of great suffering—do you not know that only this discipline has created all enhancements of man so far?"[4]

Nietzsche teaches that we must accept the past suffering that's gone into making us who we are. We shouldn't live life with regret; rather, we should learn to "love our fate" (*amor fati*).[5] To develop, refine, and temper one's identity require one to engage with chaos and uncertainty, for it's only through trials that one may flourish or "give birth to a dancing star."[6] Sometimes, it's easier to see what Nietzsche stands for by comparing it to what he rejects, and one of Nietzsche's great drives is his opposition to mindless *collectivism*, in which individuals are absorbed into a system and robbed of the passion that the strong rely upon to individuate themselves. As he says, "It belongs to the conception of 'greatness' to be noble, to wish to be apart, to be capable of being different, to stand alone, to have to live by personal initiative."[7]

Key to this new perspective on values is Nietzsche's idea of the "superman" or *Übermensch*—sometimes pictured as an isolated man on top of a rugged alpine peak, a powerful solitary figure looking out upon the world below. But Nietzsche's ideal spiritual aristocrat wouldn't necessarily be isolated and alone. Nietzsche, in fact, wrote movingly of friendship and marriage, and even thought that the best marriage relied on friendship. So if we compare Q to Nietzsche's super-man, we needn't think Q embodies the secluded, life-enhanced power of an *isolato* to the exclusion of others who share the need for, and love of, the companionship that can exist between friends—or between fathers and sons once Q has a son ("Q2," VOY).

The trials through which Q puts Picard and his crew suggest a Niet-zschean philosophy of values. Q shares some of Nietzsche's outlook insofar as he, too, looks beyond social prescriptions about safety and timidity that prevent us from developing the higher skills and pow-ers through which we individuate ourselves. In "Q Who?" Q places the *Enterprise* crew into a life-threatening struggle that they barely escape, and eighteen crewmembers die as a result. When confronted by Picard's indignant objection to his apparent ruthlessness, Q replies: "If you can't take a little bloody nose, maybe you ought to go back home and crawl under your bed. It's not safe out here." Q seems to share Nietzsche's opposition to herd-like, mindless living. Indeed, he appears prepared to go to great lengths to train individuals and enhance their strengths. Beyond this, Q seeks out friendships (often prickly ones) with individuals who, like Picard, have developed these strengths. Indeed, Q prizes the highly refined companionship that would exist among Nietzsche's rigorously self-mastered "supermen."

The *Enterprise* crew initially meets Q in TNG's first episode, "Encounter at Farpoint," in which Q comes across as a completely self-fixated creature, who would presumably have *no* interest in any-one or anything outside himself. Remarkably, though, Q is interested in the crew of the *Enterprise* and especially Picard. Contemptuous about what he and others in the Continuum regard as humanity's bar-baric, childish ways, Q contends that the human race is so dangerous that it ought to be destroyed. Nonetheless, he's willing to give human-ity a chance to prove otherwise. Q thus presents Picard and his crew with trials at which they may succeed—which includes successfully learning the lessons these trials are designed to teach—or fail. The enduring and important role of these trials is made explicit in the last episode of TNG, "All Good Things … ," when Q remarks to Picard, "The trial never ends."

## Existential Trials

Though Q might think of himself as omniscient, he clearly doesn't know all details of the future, particularly the free actions that will be taken by Picard and others. Were he omniscient, he wouldn't need to put people through trials to discover what his subjects are like. In "Encounter at Farpoint," the *Enterprise* crew is deemed at least temporarily worthy of being saved from destruction because they've saved an alien "star-jelly" that had been kidnapped. In "Hide and Q," Riker is further tested by Q to see if he might be able to evolve beyond humanity.

In "Q Who?", perhaps in an effort to measure the extent to which he and Picard might form a bond between supermen, Q announces he's willing to give up his powers in order to act as a cosmic guide, assisting humans in meeting future challenges. Picard responds with a firm— and, it turns out, overconfident—refusal of Q's offer, saying that he and his crew have no need of assistance as they face the unknown, and that Q's presence is neither desired nor required. Q responds by transporting the Enterprise 7000 light-years into uncharted space, where they first encounter the Borg.

Despite their power, the Borg represents the quintessence of everything Nietzsche despises. We gradually learn that individual, cybernetic Borg drones don't have independent minds; instead, they're controlled by the Borg Collective—a kind of hive mind.[8] It turns out that the Borg can assimilate other organisms into this ghastly cyborg system by injecting living creatures with nanoprobes. Without individual voices of their own, they're employed by the Collective to deliver such cheerful messages as "Resistance is futile."

Picard learns the lesson that there are many circumstances in which he might indeed need Q to save him and his crew. This may seem to put Picard in a peculiarly non-Nietzschean position. In this situation he isn't the rugged, self-sufficient *Übermensch* who towers over his inferiors; but since Nietzsche's superman welcomes love and friendship, as well as rugged self-sufficiency, the model fits. In fact, in *Thus Spoke Zarathustra*, where Nietzsche articulates his vision of the superman in most detail, he centers on what he *loves* about this individual. It'd be odd to aspire to love the superman if it were impossible or unlikely for this superperson to love you back.

Q's concern for individuals is especially keen in "Hide and Q," in which Q gives Commander Riker Q-like powers. Riker finds himself in a position, engineered by Q, in which he must use his new powers to save his fellow crewmembers. Although he promises his crewmates that the power won't corrupt or change him, his actions prove otherwise as he tries to win the support of the others by granting them "wishes." While Picard is upset about all this, Q believes that, having converted Riker to his side, he's won. Q tries to convince Riker not only to use but also to *enjoy* his new powers, but he's disappointed when Riker realizes he must abandon Q's power and remain human, limited and weak. Q is disappointed in Riker for being unable to transcend his "merely human" capacities, and for his failure to transform Riker, Q is banished back to the Continuum, never to interfere with the *Enterprise* again. Consigned to a fate that seems to realize one of his worst fears, Q desperately pleads for a second chance.Promoting the Nietzschean "love of fate," Q instructs Picard in "Tapestry" on the significance of reflecting on how his identity is shaped by his past and accepting that legacy. Given the opportunity to change some key events from his youth, Picard is disappointed in the man he turns out to be as a result. Q provides this perspective:

> The Jean-Luc Picard you wanted to be, the one who did NOT fight the Nausicaan, had quite a different career from the one you remember. That Picard never had a brush with death, never came face to face with his own mortality, never realized how fragile life is, or how important each moment must be. So his life never came into focus. He drifted through much of his career with no plan or agenda, going from one assignment to the next, never seizing the opportunities that presented themselves.... And no one ever offered him a command. He learned to play it safe and he never, ever got noticed by anyone.

Q tells Picard to embrace his past—even events that Picard looks upon as mistakes—as essential to making him the person he is today. Without his brash actions as a hot-headed ensign, he'd never have become the Captain Jean-Luc Picard capable of facing up to, and eventually befriending, Q and of proving the worth of humanity when put on trial.

## The Necessity of Q

Should we approve of Q's methods or, by extension, of Nietzsche's theory of values? There are at least two ways to think about it. In the context of Q's role in the fictional world of *Star Trek*, the fusion of the entertaining trials he forces Starfleet crews to endure and his exemplification of Nietzschean philosophical ideas is brilliant. Dramatically, a character like Q may be essential to upsetting our expectations about what's ordinary and normal, stretching our imaginations through wild thought experiments on the nature and limits of what it is to be human—particularly when Q himself is made human in "Déjà Q." In both fiction and the real world, there exist all sorts of life-denying, collective entities that can rob us of our individuality like the Borg; both Q and Nietzsche take exception to these. There's genuine wisdom in how Nietzsche and Q get us to think about how suffering and hardships in life are crucibles indispensable to the making of who we are, philosophical reflections that can help reconcile us to past harms rather than live in resentment of them.

But in the real world, ordinary morality shouldn't be set aside for the sake of an aristocratic pursuit of excellence that countenances coldness and cruelty. Q's putting the *Enterprise* in danger, leading to the death of innocent persons, wasn't worth the price of Picard's education. Imagine if we cut through Q's bombastic claim from "Q Who?" to reveal what's really going on: "If you can't take the bloody death of eighteen crewmembers in the course of my teaching Picard to be humble, then you ought to go back home and crawl under your bed." To that we should reply: according to the moral intuitions many of us share, the death of eighteen innocent persons isn't equivalent to getting a "bloody nose" in the course of teaching someone humility. Given such a choice, we'd be well advised to take Q's advice and go home to enjoy John de Lancie playing the *character* Q in a fictional series we love. We can't bring ourselves to agree with Nietzsche's dictum: "The weak and ill-constituted shall perish ... and one should help them to do so."[9] Instead of crawling under the bed or following Nietzsche, we prefer a dictum such as: When you encounter the weak and ill-constituted and you can help them find health and healing, do so. But, notwithstanding our qualms about Nietzsche's advice on how to address those of us who are weak and ill-constituted, we can certainly learn from Q, even if we can't boldly go where he is on the scale of cosmic values.[10]

# Notes

1. Friedrich Nietzsche, *Thus Spoke Zarathustra*, trans. Walter Kaufmann (New York: The Viking Press, 1954), 129.
2. For a discussion of *utilitarianism*, see Greg Littmann's chapter in this volume (Chapter 12).
3. Friedrich Nietzsche, *On the Genealogy of Morals*, trans. Walter Kaufmann and R.J. Hollingdale (New York: Vintage, 1967), 3.

4.   Friedrich Nietzsche, *Beyond Good and Evil*, trans. Walter Kaufmann (New York: Vintage, 1989), 225.
5.   Friedrich Nietzsche, *The Gay Science*, trans. Josefine Nauckhoff (Cambridge: Cambridge University Press, 2001), 276.
6.   Friedrich Nietzsche, *Thus Spoke Zarathustra*, trans. Walter Kaufmann (New York: The Viking Press, 1954), 129.
7.   Friedrich Nietzsche, *Beyond Good and Evil*, in *The Complete Works of Friedrich Nietzsche*, trans. Helen Zimmern (1909–1913), 212.
8.   For an analysis of the value of *autonomy* in the face of Borg assimilation, see Barbara Stock's chapter in this volume (Chapter 9).
9.   Friedrich Nietzsche, *The Antichrist*, trans. H.L. Mencken (New York: Alfred A. Knopf, 1918), 43.
10.  We are grateful to Meredith Varie for comments on an earlier version of this chapter.

# A God Needs Compassion, but Not a Starship: *Star Trek*'s Humanist Theology

## *James F. McGrath*

*Star Trek* creator Gene Roddenberry's *humanism* is well known.[1] It's expressed in many ways, including his decision that the *Enterprise* didn't need a chaplain—although it has a nonsectarian chapel suitable for ceremonies like weddings ("Balance of Terror," TOS). And yet, for a show depicting a secular future, there is still a *lot* of talk about God and gods. Why should this be, and what does it tell us about the vision of the universe *Star Trek* offers?

It's been suggested that attention to religious themes constitutes mere pandering to the audience:

> Roddenberry's well-documented views on religion played a major role in the representation of religion in the Original Series, *Next Generation*, and the early films. Yet he was keenly sensitive to the religious proclivities of the American audience, and he was not above pandering so as not to offend viewers, sponsors, and the network. The Original Series and *Next Generation* reflect not only the views of Roddenberry and his many writers but also the complex and changing role of religion in American life.[2]

Yet Roddenberry took a firm stance on a number of matters about which he felt strongly. And so, while it may be that the *inclusion* of talk about gods reflected the interest in religion in his own time, the *way* that the show talked about gods reflects a "humanist theology" that's at least compatible with, and perhaps an expression of, Roddenberry's own vision.

*The Ultimate Star Trek and Philosophy*, First Edition. Edited by Kevin S. Decker and Jason T. Eberl.

Humanism is often viewed as a synonym for *atheism*. But no matter how much overlap there may be between the two worldviews, they're distinct. Humanism means placing the focus on human values and on the value of humans, and there's a long history of religious humanism. Not even all *secular* humanists are atheists, since personal religion or spirituality is compatible with a secular vision for society.[3] So was Gene Roddenberry an atheist as well? According to biographer Joe Engel, the answer is yes:

> Not all humanists are necessarily devout atheists. But Rodenberry certainly was, and in his atheism he exhibited the same certainty that religious fundamentalists do. By definition, such absolute certainty precludes the ability to examine or accept the validity of opposing viewpoints. Thus, pure reason and pure faith are mirror images. If, to evangelicals, he was an unrepentant sinner, then to him they were foolish and superstitious. Neither position leaves any room for accommodation.[4]

Whether this depiction fits the evidence depends on a number of things, such as what's meant by the word *god*, and whether atheism need entail the rejection of any and all gods. Must an atheist reject the possibility that powerful beings like Q could exist in real life? Or is it enough to refuse to call such beings "gods" or deny them worship?[5]

Fortunately, we needn't speculate, since we have Roddenberry's own words: "I believe I am God; certainly you are, I think we intelligent beings on this planet are all a piece of God, are becoming God. In some sort of cyclical non-time thing we have to become God, so that we can end up creating ourselves, so that we can be in the first place."[6] This represents an intriguing science-fictional theology, relying on the possibility of time travel or temporal loops for human beings to, as Roddenberry says, "become God" and create ourselves. But it also raises questions, such as whether the God we become then disappears after this act of creation—as Deistic believers in a nonintervening God insist—or whether God, as future human possibility, loops around and becomes present and active in guiding the development of "God-to-be."

## "Do You Have Any Gods, Captain?"

So what does *Star Trek* demonstrate through its exploration of divinity as the potential for humanity's future? The first mention of a god occurs in the second TOS pilot, "Where No Man Has Gone Before."

As a result of crossing the galactic barrier, Lieutenant Commander Gary Mitchell and Dr. Elizabeth Dehner begin transforming into more powerful beings, who soon come to look upon human existence with disdain and describe what they're becoming as "gods." The episode "Charlie X" also features a person with powers beyond what ordinary humans have. And a similar entity named Trelane is central to "The Squire of Gothos." In each of these stories, beings who are essentially *children* within the context of their own civilization use their godlike powers to act on their whims, including playing with humans as toys for their entertainment. Such beings continued to be a feature of *Star Trek*, most famously with Q in TNG.[7] Indeed, the *Star Trek* universe appears to be teeming with various godlike life-forms, at least from our perspective: the Metrons, the Excalbians, the Organians, and the Traveler, to name just a few.

But if the godlike beings inhabiting the heavens bring *Star Trek* close to the historic domain of religion, Roddenberry also took steps to demote them. In "Who Mourns for Adonais?" the *Enterprise* finds itself literally in the grip of the ancient Greek god, Apollo. Kirk says unequivocally, "Apollo's no god," adding, "But he may have been mistaken for one, once." Kirk offers an explanation in the vein of the "ancient aliens" theory in which Apollo and others of his species visited Earth some 5000 years earlier, forming the basis of Greek mythology. Kirk comments that most mythology has some basis in fact.

Adopting this approach to all of Earth's religions renders them true, at least on one level. Whereas skeptical scholars might treat the stories of ancient gods as merely folktales with no basis in fact, Kirk isn't a skeptic about the *reality* of the beings like Apollo. The ancient Greek stories might be factual accounts of actual events and encounters with powerful entities. What Kirk denies is the *divinity* of those beings, which raises a question about Kirk's definition of *divinity*. He might be presuming that any being that's part of the natural, physical world doesn't deserve to be called a god, and so has no right to demand worship. Indeed, it's the demand for worship that's the crux of the matter for Kirk, rather than the nature of the entity he encounters on Pollux IV. Asserting unjustified authority over humans or demanding veneration is what Kirk regards as inappropriate, no matter how powerful the being in question may be. Yet, after destroying Apollo, Kirk laments that humanity might've owed Apollo and his kind a debt of gratitude: "They gave us so much. The Greek civilization, much of our culture and philosophy came from a worship of those beings. In a way, they began the Golden Age. Would it have hurt us, I wonder, just to have gathered a few laurel leaves?"

It's here that we begin to see *Star Trek*'s humanist theology becoming clear. Beings that demand worship, that treat humans as insignificant playthings, have no legitimate claim to the designation *god*. But what about a being who's full of *compassion*, as Kirk challenges Mitchell? Is the very possibility of divine beings excluded altogether, regardless of their motivation? Or is divinity, as Roddenberry suggests, a potential that humanity has and can strive to fulfill? Does Kirk's defeat of humanity's erstwhile "god" Apollo show that, by the 23rd century, we're well on our way? Or would a wiser and more compassionate—and thus arguably more divine—humanity "have gathered a few laurel leaves"? Is Kirk's regret over destroying one of Earth's ancient gods simply an indication that, even in that future era, humanity still has more growing up to do? Perhaps it's simply the feeling of genuine loss at the innocence of the childhood one has to leave behind in order to mature.

Robert Asa, commenting on Apollo as a tragic figure in the episode, writes, "Only at the end does he realize that threats of violence are ineffective against those who wield god-like powers themselves. Instead of creating worshipers he creates enemies."[8] Asa explores the streams of theology in the late 1960s of TOS, which also saw the "death of God" movement, the development of secular wings within Christianity and Judaism, as well as the increasing popularity of secular humanism. It isn't only Apollo that humanity is depicted as having outgrown:

> [T]he traditional idea of God found in Western religion suffers a significant pummeling in Classic *Star Trek*. Even if the existence of God is not categorically denied in a literal way, God is still denied symbolically and pragmatically. Symbolically, god-figures are consistently disappointing, decadent, and/or dangerous. Pragmatically, God does not function in any clear or meaningful way in the *Star Trek* universe or in the lives of Federation members. Despite Kirk's brief comment to Apollo that "we find the one [God] quite adequate," in the twenty-third century the God of traditional theism is dead. There is no transcendent, personal Deity who exists independently of humanity.[9]

Interestingly, Spock is the one who defeats Apollo, using the *Enterprise*'s phasers. As a Vulcan, he's not susceptible to the emotional reactions Apollo evokes among humans. And Vulcans are usually depicted as practitioners of a philosophical spirituality seemingly modeled on

Buddhism in that their beliefs don't revolve around a personal god.[10] It may be that humanity, too, is en route toward a future of logic and reason; nevertheless, *Star Trek*'s humanistic vision doesn't demand the rejection of spirituality any more than it requires rejection of the literal existence of Apollo. Powerful beings can exist, and so can spirituality. But human beings who've matured sufficiently will refuse to prostrate themselves before such power, because they understand that humans are powerful, and becoming more so. Mere power doesn't make a being worthy of worship, and *Star Trek* considers it possible that godlike power might one day become an aspect of the lives of human beings—or our distant descendants.[11]

## "Well, Don't Just Stand There. God's a Busy Man!"

On the other hand, the plot of *ST V: The Final Frontier* bears an uneasy relationship to Roddenberry's convictions. The original screenplay was drafted by William Shatner, and Roddenberry expressed his reservations. In a letter to Shatner, Roddenberry wrote of his deep disappointment: "I simply cannot support a story which has our intelligent and insightful crew mesmerized by a 23rd Century religious charlatan. I had thought from our discussion that you were going to reconsider using religion and God as a subject matter, particularly with what has been happening to public attitudes in that area."[12] In a letter to the head of Paramount Pictures, Roddenberry described himself as "the Paramount-proclaimed 'conscience of Star Trek'" and declared that, as such, "I must disassociate myself from this story."[13] Roddenberry was reacting to a story that differed in important ways from the film that was eventually released—for example, in the first draft, it's revealed that Spock had formerly been a seminary student![14] By the time the script had undergone serious revisions, many of Roddenberry's initial concerns had been addressed. But he still felt that the religious focus was inherently problematic for *Star Trek*. In a memo to executive producer Harve Bennett, Roddenberry wrote,

> We long ago got rid of the idea of our dealing with anything suggesting the traditional Judeo-Christian God. It is vital to *Star Trek* that we deal properly with the attitudes of our crew regarding this question.... It seems to me the only possible answer to this is throughout the script to stay a mile away from revealing or even hinting at what our people believe about God. I was generally successful in doing this in the original *Star Trek* series. A few things did slip by, but not many, at least not many

serious variations of my policy to keep *Star Trek* free of serious religious themes.[15]

Yet we've also seen that, despite his qualms and reservations, Roddenberry's own convictions about God do come through in the series. His idea of godhood as a possibility for humanity's future meshes well with the theological dialogue on the show we've surveyed so far.

This message of theological humanism, of course, is that humanity can become God in the future. But to do so, we need to cultivate compassion. Raw power isn't enough. The potential unlocked in Gary Mitchell, void of compassion, was turning him into something other than divine; and the immature Charlie Evans used his telekinetic powers only to serve his petulant, selfish desires. Humanity becoming God is depicted as a mere *possibility*; it isn't inevitable. Roddenberry's suggestion that humanity is "an infant God, an infant race" allowed him to see even some of humanity's worst atrocities as part of a process of growing up.[16] It also allows us to see stories like "The Squire of Gothos" in a different light. For all his childish play with the *Enterprise* crew, Trelane's actions are more mature, less malevolent, and less deadly than many of humanity's own works. If the *Enterprise* encounters godlike beings who lack maturity and compassion, we're forced to look at our own selves, and consider how much further we have to go toward relative perfection. On the other hand, at least by the 24th century, Captain Picard sees compassion as one of humanity's central features. When Q, with newly restored powers after having suffered a period of penance as "a normal, imperfect, lumpen human being," saves the people of Bre'el IV from a falling moon, Picard muses, "Perhaps there's a residue of humanity in Q after all"—although Q is quick to retort, "Don't bet on it" ("Déjà Q," TNG).

If the relationship of *Star Trek* to humanism has been unambiguous, its relationship to, and view of, "posthumanism" is less clear. *Posthumanism* usually refers to the expectation that the future of humanity or its descendants will be something other than "human," whether due to the changes biological evolution brings or because humanity transitions from a flesh-based to a silicon-based existence. However, posthumanism can also refer to the notion that an all-embracing ethos of the kind offered by "humanism" ought to be reconfigured to incorporate other beings besides terrestrial ones. Diana Relke has described "*Star Trek*'s unique way of dealing with the posthuman" as "expanding the definition of human so that the posthuman can be embraced within it."[17]

There are hints of this expanding definition in *Star Trek*, but they're somewhat minimal and piecemeal. The crew of the *Enterprise* in TOS was cutting edge in its inclusion of many races and nationalities of humans. But it was scarcely plausible as representative of the United Federation of Planets. There was a token half-Vulcan on board, but throughout the *Star Trek* franchise there's rarely been more than one representative of a nonhuman species as a central member of the crew.

When it comes to the other, more widespread definition of posthumanism, *Star Trek*'s stance has been even less open. Transcending fleshly existence by moving in the direction of becoming cyborgs, eventually transferring entirely to a mechanical and computerized existence, is viewed in an entirely negative manner. This move represents, not the next step in humanity's future, but a threat to that future. We see this in "What Are Little Girls Made Of?" when Kirk makes the judgment regarding the android version of Dr. Roger Korby that "Dr. Korby was never here." And we see it in the depictions of the Borg as representing a form of existence that integrates biology with technology, as well as collectivizes, but, as a result, obliterates individual distinctiveness and thus is to be rejected.[18] *Star Trek*'s ethos is encapsulated by the Vulcan dictum, "Infinite Diversity in Infinite Combinations"; but there's one type of entity that has no place in this vision: a creature that's unwaveringly committed to the obliteration of diversity.

This negative attitude toward human–machine union isn't consistently articulated, however. *ST: The Motion Picture* ends with Will Decker becoming one with V'Ger, a human technological creation that had achieved sentience and transcended its original nature—another example of Roddenberry's theme of human self-transcendence toward divinity. Perhaps it's the uniqueness of this union, and that it's formed by mutual consent, which allows it to escape *Star Trek*'s normal antiposthuman bias. Be that as it may, it's noteworthy that this unique human–machine unification—viewed as "possibly a next step in our evolution"— is never revisited.

## "For All Our Knowledge, All Our Advances, We're Just as Mortal as You Are"

This brings us back to the depiction of humanity's godlike potential. Whether we're considering Gary Mitchell and Elizabeth Dehner, or Apollo and Q, the divine future of humanity and other species that get there before us never involves so complete a departure from physical and social modes of human existence—as we're familiar with them—that all semblance of recognizable humanity is lost.[19] And advanced capacities to heal oneself and others, to manipulate matter and energy, to move unhindered through space and time, seem most "godlike" when envisaged as products of biological evolution rather than technological support.

But these hopes seem to be based in a romantic view of evolution that's not supported by science, as well as in the idea that the paranormal is genuinely capable of scientific explanation. Such views, although they remain popular and widespread, are viewed by the scientific community as implausible and unfounded. And even if we might be capable of manipulating our genes to endow us with such abilities, doing so could prove to be to our own detriment.[20] Whatever means might or might not lead to future godlike powers for human beings, the difference between humans and those who already have such powers is always one of *degree* and not of *kind* in the *Star Trek* universe. While sometimes viewed as "hard science fiction" that seeks to be scientifically realistic, *Star Trek* regularly imagines technological and biological situations unsupported by what science currently considers realistic—whether it be the transporter, faster-than-light travel, or the possibility of interbreeding between humans and beings from other worlds.[21] This isn't a final judgment, however, since the short recorded history of humanity has regularly witnessed the supposedly impossible becoming possible—science *fiction* may yet become science *fact*.

Even if it is unrealistic and unscientific at times, *Star Trek*'s vision of humanity's future doesn't for that reason lose its value. *Star Trek* depicts a universe populated by not just beings with human-like capacities and powers but also beings who can be *mistaken* for gods, even if that label is withheld from them and its appropriateness questioned. In depicting these pseudo-gods as really existing, *Star Trek* gives expression to the conviction that such beings are possible, and that humanity has reason to hope for a future characterized by transcendence of one sort of another, even if it's through means other than those of traditional human religions.

*Star Trek* offers a humanist theology of the divine potential of humanity as a possibility that may or may not be actualized, rather than giving a definitive answer. It's unclear whether technological enhancements, biological interventions, natural processes, or some combination of these can bring us closer to the divinity toward which many of us aspire. But even if technology can't deliver on the optimistic promises that *Star Trek* has often made, the show offers a challenge that retains its value. We can't know for certain what our near and distant future holds for us as a species, and whether this includes warp-capable starships, or might even eventually render starships superfluous as we become able to travel in a flash like Q or transdimensional Travelers like Wesley Crusher do. While starships may be part of our human future, a god ought not to need a starship, as Kirk points out toward the end of *The Final Frontier*. It's not only Kirk, and through him Roddenberry, but also many theological systems that would assert, "Above all else, a god needs compassion!" And if compassion is the defining attribute of a god, then *Star Trek's* humanist theology encourages us not only to believe that divinity is a real possibility for humanity in the future, but also to recognize it as a possibility already open to us in the present.

# Notes

1. See James F. McGrath, "Explicit and Implicit Religion in *Doctor Who* and *Star Trek*," forthcoming in *Implicit Religion*. See also Michael A. Burstein, "We Find the One Quite Adequate: Religious Attitudes *in Star Trek*," in *Boarding the Enterprise*, ed. David Gerrold and Robert J. Sawyer (Dallas: BenBella, 2006), 87–99.
2. Ross Kraemer, William Cassidy, and Susan L. Schwartz, *Religions of Star Trek* (New York: Basic Books, 2009), 5–6.
3. For further details on social secularization, see Kevin Decker's chapter in this volume (Chapter 31).
4. Joel Engel, *Gene Roddenberry: The Myth and the Man behind Star Trek* (New York: Hyperion, 1994), 156.
5. Kraemer et al., *Religions of Star Trek*, 56.
6. David Alexander, *Star Trek Creator: The Authorized Biography of Gene Roddenberry* (New York: ROC/Penguin, 1994), 568; from an interview originally published in Terrence A. Sweeney's *God* (Minneapolis: Winston, 1985). See also Roddenberry's description of his aim to be able to talk about controversial subjects like this on *Star Trek* by setting them among aliens on distant worlds (Alexander, *Star Trek Creator*, 570).
7. Trelane is revealed to be, in fact, a member of the Q Continuum in Peter David's novel *Q-Squared* (New York: Pocket Books, 1995).
8. Robert Asa, "Classic *Star Trek* and the Death of God: A Case Study of 'Who Mourns for Adonais?'" in *Star Trek and Sacred Ground*, ed. Jennifer E. Porter and Darcee L. McLaren (Albany: SUNY Press, 1999), 38.

9.  Ibid., 45.

10. For an in-depth exploration of Vulcan philosophy and spirituality, and its links to non-Western views, see Walter [Ritoku] Robinson's chapter, "Death and Rebirth of a Vulcan Mind," in *Star Trek and Philosophy*, ed. Jason T. Eberl and Kevin S. Decker (Chicago: Open Court, 2008).

11. The episode "Hide and Q" (TNG), in which Riker is given godlike powers by Q, is also relevant here. Q says that the human "compulsion" to grow and learn sets them on a course to become like the Q in the future, and perhaps even surpass them. There's also Wesley Crusher's personal evolution from being an annoying teenager who saves the *Enterprise*-D on a weekly basis to becoming a "Traveler" able to manipulate space and time by mere thought ("Where No One Has Gone Before," "Remember Me," and "Journey's End," TNG). On the question of power and its relationship to worthiness to be worshiped in another science fiction franchise, see Aaron Smuts, "'The Little People': Power and the Worshipable," in *Philosophy in The Twilight Zone*, ed. Noël Carroll and Lester H. Hunt (Malden, MA: Wiley-Blackwell, 2009), 155–70.

12. Memo sent June 3, 1987, quoted in Alexander, *Star Trek Creator*, 520. It's interesting to compare the concepts in *Star Trek V* to elements in the screenplay "The God Thing," which Roddenberry wrote and which influenced *The Motion Picture*. See further http://www.well.com/~sjroby/godthing.html (accessed June 19, 2015).

13. Alexander, *Star Trek Creator*, 523.

14. Although a *Vulcan* "seminary" could still be in line with Roddenberry's vision—perhaps this was referring to Spock's having been an adept of the Kolinahr in *The Motion Picture* (in which Roddenberry was heavily involved).

15. Ibid., 531.

16. Ibid., 572.

17. Diana M.A. Relke, *Drones, Clones, and Alpha Babes: Retrofitting Star Trek's Humanism, Post-9/11* (Calgary: University of Calgary Press, 2006), 89. Posthumanism—aka *transhumanism*—is also discussed in this volume by Dan Dinello (Chapter 8), Dena Hurst (Chapter 25), and Dennis Weiss (Chapter 17).

18. For more on the Borg as a post/transhumanist threat, see Dinello's and Hurst's chapters (Chapters 8 and 25, respectively), as well as Lisa Cassidy's (Chapter 22), in this volume. See also Kevin S. Decker, "Inhuman Nature, or What's It Like to Be a Borg" in *Star Trek and Philosophy* (2008).

19. Melanie Johnson-Moxley discusses the value of corporeal and socially integrated existence in her chapter in this volume (Chapter 20). The closest thing to beings that have moved so far in the direction of "divinity" that they can't understand human existence—at least without baseball

metaphors—are the incorporeal and atemporal wormhole aliens known as "the Prophets" in DS9.

20. See, for instance, the TNG episode "Unnatural Selection," in which the immune systems of genetically enhanced human children attack unenhanced humans.

21. Although it's revealed in Diane Duane's *Spock's World* (New York: Pocket Books, 1988)—and discussed in *The Big Bang Theory* (https://www.youtube.com/watch?v=KW2nJBj3TTI)—that Spock's parents required genetic engineering assistance in order to conceive him; and Bashir has to provide assistance in order for Worf and Jadzia to potentially conceive in "Tears of the Prophets" (DS9).

# 31

# "The Human Adventure Is Just Beginning": *Star Trek*'s Secular Society

*Kevin S. Decker*

> When in doubt, Gene [Roddenberry] always had Kirk get into a fight with God.
>
> —David Gerrold[1]

American life in the late 1960s wasn't short on spirituality, with flower power, instant karma, even an entire "Summer of Love." Yet there were also powerful signals in the culture that its millennia-old love affair with religion was cooling off. The public's commitment to treating justice and good government as based wholly on divine order was challenged by seismic changes in the nature of religion itself. These included increasing religious diversity in the United States, an emerging "religion" of international interdependency that was an outgrowth of the dread of global nuclear holocaust, growing ecumenical cooperation between religious traditions, and the acknowledgment by the Catholic Church of a plurality of Christian faiths in Vatican II. Against the background of the civil rights movement and the Vietnam conflict, "theology became primarily an ecumenical matter of social activism and involvement and theological thinking became largely a reflection on social change.... God became the instrument for social change, a further symptom of an emerging secularism in religion."[2]

As the creator of *Star Trek*'s ethos, Gene Roddenberry riffed on the Enlightenment—with its emphasis on reason, progress, and individual self-determination—as much as the new spiritualistic and religiously liberal upheavals just mentioned. Roddenberry's vision of the future rejected the monstrous moral implications of a creation myth in which

*The Ultimate Star Trek and Philosophy*, First Edition. Edited by Kevin S. Decker and Jason T. Eberl. © 2016 John Wiley & Sons, Ltd. Published 2016 by John Wiley & Sons, Ltd.

"an all-knowing all-powerful God ... creates faulty Humans, and then blames them for his own mistakes."[3] *Star Trek*'s central character, Captain James T. Kirk, was created to be a paradigm of the anti-authoritarian, individualistic, skeptical, and libertarian mindset that defined *secular humanism* in the late 1960s and early 1970s. This mindset, in turn, was a product of the "disenchantment" of the world perceived to come along with the rise of industry, technology, war, and atrocities like the Holocaust.[4] Secularists like Roddenberry and his sci-fi creation embraced an idea of political power as used for the common good—including the securing of important freedoms—but also as needing no transcendent higher law or power to guarantee its legitimacy.[5] This is the philosophical dimension of secularism that permeates *Star Trek*.

In their short runs, both the original and animated *Star Trek* series boast no fewer than *fifteen* encounters with would-be gods—aliens with god-like powers—interested in subjugating the *Enterprise* crew.[6] Themes of religious belief, freedom, and authority run through *Star Trek: The Motion Picture* and *Star Trek V: The Final Frontier*, and countless TNG, DS9, VOY, and ENT storylines, each of which adds a layer of complexity to our answer to the question: what is the relationship between faith and secularism in the future society *Star Trek* depicts? In this chapter, I'll chart *Star Trek*'s course in wrestling with issues of political and social *secularization*.[7] Any debate about secularization is a set of arguments about the best relationship between religious beliefs and institutions on the one hand, and political, social, and economic structures on the other. So I'll provide several moral arguments as to why liberal democracies like the United States should pursue greater secularism in the future.

## "I Never Met a God Before" — "And You Haven't Yet"

What exactly *is* a religion? Robert Audi's work on religion in the public sphere isolates nine distinctive features:

1   Belief in one or more supernatural beings
2   A distinction between sacred and profane objects
3   Ritual acts focused on those objects
4   A moral code believed to be sanctioned by the god(s)
5   Religious feelings (awe, mystery, etc.) that tend to be aroused by the sacred objects and during rituals

6  Prayer and other communicative forms of conduct concerning the god(s)
7  A world view according [to] adherents a significant place in the universe
8  A more or less comprehensive organization of one's life based on the worldview
9  A social organization bound together by (1) through (8).[8]

Notice that those in favor of a secular society could *agree* on (1) through (8) with believers who favor an active role in the public sphere for religious beliefs and attitudes; they differ about (9). The real friction over the place of religion in the public sphere, though, has to do with conflicts between *political democracy*—"government of, by and for the people under republican or parliamentary institutions"—and *civil liberties*—"under which all individuals and groups have the right to free speech, due process of law, and equality before the law."[9] Freedom of (and *from*) religion is an important civil liberty; yet, as we'll see, some uses of that freedom can endanger political democracy in turn.

A popular but particularly unhelpful way of framing this debate is in terms of "religion *versus* reason." Everyone—even the most evangelical of religious fundamentalists—sees their strongly held beliefs as *rational*. Instead, political debates about secularization, like all political exchanges, should be seen as attempts to define what Benedict Anderson called an "imagined community." An *imagined community* is a cultural framework that has authority because it provides a taken-for-granted system of reference against which politically "rational" claims are judged; its shape is negotiated by voices both inside and outside the community.[10] In *Star Trek*, Starfleet personnel often find themselves as outsiders in imagined communities, and they may find it difficult to sort out the line between religion and politics. "The Omega Glory" (TOS) is merely one example of this, in which Cloud William, leader of the tribe of "Yangs," treats an ancient U.S. flag as sacred and excoriates Kirk, "Freedom? That is a worship word. Yang worship. You will not speak it." The politics of the Yangs and their enemy, the Kohms, is a thinly veiled, stagnated version of the Cold War; but as the lifeblood of a more vigorous imagined community, political life represents what Paul Kahn defines as "a structure of the imagination that makes sense of experience by embedding it in narratives."[11] There are many such narratives in any nation that don't all cohere with each other. In "The Omega Glory," Kirk points out that the principles of freedom and equality the Yangs worship are spelled out in the U.S. Constitution as applying to *everyone*—and so diagnoses an incoherency in the Yangs' imagined community that makes possible peace with the Kohms. Similarly, unless we're willing to countenance complete political *relativism*, we should treat politics philosophically by looking for fatal incoherencies in political narratives premised upon religion or any other systematic worldview.

In TOS, Roddenberry's secular voice is often heard speaking through Captain Kirk, who emphasizes the core value of *free striving* animating the Federation's imagined community when confronting patronizing, god-like beings such as Apollo ("Who Mourns for Adonais?"), Trelane ("The Squire of Gothos"), and Landru ("Return of the Archons"). Despite his affinity for humankind, the Megan Lucien, in "The Magicks of Megas-Tu" (TAS), assumes this mantle when he condescends to greet the *Enterprise* crew: "Ah, humans. Lovely, primitive humans. Can't you do anything right?" Kirk's famous line from *ST V: The Final Frontier*, "What does God need with a starship?" is a classic opening line of criticism focusing on the apparent incompatibility between "divine" power and the neediness or immaturity of the god-like creatures confronting him.[12] In this same regard, Captain Jean-Luc Picard and the *Enterprise*-D crew can't make much sense of celestial beings they encounter in TNG, from the "Justice" of the Edo god to Q's efforts to put humanity on trial ("Encounter at Farpoint" and "All Good Things … ") to Nagilum's casual disregard for human lives ("Where Silence Has Lease"). These antagonistic encounters encapsulate what we might call the distinctively "Roddenberry attitude" about the need for secularization: despite any charms it might have, religious authority is inevitably *tyrannical*, and Federation citizens like the notably nonreligious Kirk and Picard shouldn't turn their back on the progress that's been made up to their time.[13]

## "You Don't Understand Something So You Become Fearful"

The militant "Roddenberry attitude" toward religion began to be complicated as his influence on TNG was tempered over time by producers like Jeri Taylor and Ronald D. Moore.[14] In this slow change, "Who Watches the Watchers" is a particularly important episode that turns the dynamic of "Roddenberry attitude" stories on its head by placing Picard in the role of ersatz deity to the proto-Vulcan

Mintakans. Scrambling to undo the cultural damage wrought by the exposure of a Federation "duck blind" cultural observatory, the *Enterprise* crew returns one of the injured natives, Liko, to the surface after a failed memory wipe. Liko believes he's been to the Mintakan equivalent of heaven, which is governed by "the Picard" who also gave him back his life. After Liko tells his story, both enthusiasm and skepticism about the return of the gods is raised in his primitive but secular community. When Counselor Troi, posing as a Mintakan native, is seized, Picard must decide, with the aid of anthropologist Dr. Barron, whether to risk further cultural contamination by beaming down to rescue her:

PICARD: Doctor, do you believe the Mintakans are capable of harming Counselor Troi?

BARRON: They are not normally a violent people but these are extraordinary circumstances. They're trying to comprehend what they believe to be a god.

PICARD: Recommendations?

BARRON: The Mintakans wish to please the Overseer, but they can only guess what he wants. They need a sign.

PICARD: Are you suggesting …

BARRON: You must go down to Mintaka Three.

RIKER: Masquerading as a god?

PICARD: Absolutely out of the question. The Prime Directive …

BARRON: Has already been violated. The damage is done. All we can do now is minimize it.

PICARD: By sanctioning their false beliefs?

BARRON: By giving them guidelines. Letting them know what the Overseer expects of them.

PICARD: Doctor Barron, I cannot, I will not, impose a set of commandments on these people. To do so violates the very essence of the Prime Directive.

BARRON: Like it or not, we have rekindled the Mintakans' belief in the Overseer.

RIKER: And are you saying that this belief will eventually become a religion?

BARRON: It's inevitable. And without guidance, that religion could degenerate into inquisitions, holy wars, chaos.

PICARD: (*quietly*) Horrifying. Doctor Barron, your report describes how rational these people are. Millennia ago, they abandoned their belief in the supernatural. Now you are asking me to sabotage that achievement, to send them back into the Dark Ages of superstition and ignorance and fear? No! We will find some way to undo the damage we've caused.[15]

When confronted by public policy fueled by religious beliefs and attitudes in a liberal democracy, those in favor of further secularization may not jump to the drastic conclusions that Barron does, but they likely share Picard's concern. To take two contemporary examples: the multiple Christian doctrines lumped under the name of *creationism* are considered by many to be a faithful account of the origin of the universe, yet empirically supported cosmology and the science of evolution place substantial obstacles in the way of rational belief in these accounts.[16] By using political levers to introduce creationism as an alternative to empirical science in both traditional public and charter schools, creationists are diluting students' understanding of the significance of the scientific method in favor of a view that leads to epistemic relativism about human origins.[17] If the biblical account of creation is suitable for instruction as "science," then should schools avoid arbitrariness by teaching every creation story in science classrooms—such as the Greek mythology that *Trek* speculates may have been inspired by powerful extraterrestrials visiting Earth millennia ago ("Who Mourns for Adonais?")? That would, of course, leave little time for actual science.

The secular–religious divide in public policy is even less visible in the case of abstinence-based sex education. Since 1996, most American tax revenue set aside for sex education has been spent on exclusively abstinence-*only* approaches—as contrasted with "comprehensive" approaches. A meticulous recent correlation of the type of sex education in the United States with teen pregnancy rates is telling:

> After accounting for other factors, the national data show that the incidence of teenage pregnancies and births remain positively correlated with the degree of abstinence education across states: The more strongly abstinence is emphasized in state laws and policies, the higher the average teenage pregnancy and birth rate. States that taught comprehensive sex and/or HIV education and covered abstinence along with contraception and condom use ... also referred to as "abstinence-plus," tended to have the lowest teen pregnancy rates, while states with abstinence-only sex education laws that stress abstinence until marriage ... were significantly less successful in preventing teen pregnancies.[18]

This study shows that, overall, the pregnancy rate in the years 2002–2005 per 1000 teenage girls in the United States was 72.2; by comparison, the figure for our neighbor to the north (birthplace of William Shatner and Jimmy Doohan) was 29.2 per 1000 teens. The sexually more liberal Netherlands? 11.8 per 1000. Even before we consider the human cost of abstinence-only education, we have to at least admit that, as public policy, it fails at its appointed goals.

Or at least a purely cost–benefit approach would draw this conclusion. An ethical approach would likely consider the consequences for the health, education, and welfare of teens and others affected by higher pregnancy and abortion rates (including the unborn children aborted) resulting from a lack of comprehensive sex education. The fact that abstinence-only sex education is the *only* option in half of U.S. states seems to indicate, though, that for many religious legislators, parents, and interest groups, the restriction to abstinence-only serves a *moral* purpose, regardless of what social harms it might bring along. This kind of reasoning is characteristic of creationists as well; but it's reasoning that secularists reject, and we'll see why next.

## "We Can All Be Counted upon to Live Down to Our Lowest Impulses"

*Deep Space Nine* is the *Trek* series in which one society's religious interests and the Federation's secular commitments create the most friction. In the premiere episode, Commander Benjamin Sisko assumes command of a former Cardassian space station orbiting—for the moment—the recently liberated planet Bajor. Almost immediately, he's told by the Bajoran Kai—akin to the Roman Catholic Pope or the Dalai Lama of Tibetan Buddhism—that he's the "Emissary of the Prophets" foretold in Bajoran scripture. Sisko reluctantly tolerates this exalted status, hoping that doing so will help further Bajor's admittance to the Federation. DS9's first season ends with a version of the creationist controversy when the power-hungry Vedek Winn and other Bajorans boycott Keiko O'Brien's physics-based teaching about the "wormhole aliens"—whom the Bajorans worship as "Prophets" residing in a "Celestial Temple"—in the station's school.

Sisko, who respects Bajoran faith, responds to his son Jake's aspersions that belief in the Prophets is "stupid" by saying, "You've got to realize something, Jake. For over fifty years, the one thing that allowed the Bajorans to survive the Cardassian occupation was their faith. The Prophets were their only source of hope and courage" ("In the Hands of the Prophets").

The Prophets exist in a *timeless* state in the wormhole, allowing Sisko to make a compelling argument in favor of Winn's religious interpretation:

JAKE:    But there were no Prophets. They were just some aliens that you found in the wormhole.

SISKO:    To those aliens, the future is no more difficult to see than the past. Why shouldn't they be considered Prophets?

JAKE:    Are you serious?

SISKO:    My point is, it's a matter of interpretation.

Further confirming their unique status according to Sisko, the Prophets are able to communicate accurate future knowledge to the Bajorans through their hourglass-shaped "orbs" that had been sent to Bajor over the course of millennia.

These orb revelations are important, because they provide one answer to what Michael Martin questions concerning the justification of actions, including public policies, according to the authority of *divine commands*. Martin writes that this sort of justification

> supposes that morality is based on God's commands, [but] the question arises of how one knows what God's commands are. There are three issues to consider here. First of all, there are several apparent conflicting religious sources of God's commands—the Bible, the Koran, the Book of Mormon. How does one choose the correct source? Second, even within the same source, e.g., the Bible, there seem to be conflicting moral commands. Third, there are different interpretations of the same command, e.g., thou shall not kill.[19]

Even if we were sure that our religious leaders were in contact with divinities that knew facts about our future, there would still be a question about the human interpretation of these facts. Thus, any citizen could still challenge these interpretations. If there were no other evidence confirming a particular interpretation of an alleged divine revelation, purported knowledge about the future would have no more political legitimacy than other empirically supported claims.

This fact doesn't provide a *moral* argument, though, that political and social decisions should be made on a secular basis. For this, we need to look to a later DS9 episode, "Accession." One of Bajor's greatest poets, Akorem Laan, emerges from the wormhole in a lightship; he's been gone for only a few days in his own subjective time, but has missed more than 200 years of Bajoran history. He's missed the Cardassian occupation and the Bajoran resistance movement, as well as Bajor's initial steps toward membership in the Federation. Akorem soon claims the title of "Emissary," as he seems to fit a certain interpretation of Bajoran prophecy better than Sisko does—and Sisko is happy to relinquish the title. In his first major public speech, however, Akorem proclaims:

> Ever since the Prophets returned me to my people, I've asked myself the same questions over and over again. Why did they keep me with them for so long? Why did they return me to my people now? I now know the answers. Bajor suffered a great wound while I was with the Prophets. The Cardassian occupation. The Bajor I have returned to has lost its way. People no longer follow the path the Prophets have laid out for them. They no longer follow their D'jarras.

Adherence to a *caste* system like the D'jarras—abandoned by Bajor since the occupation—isn't a strictly religious idea: Plato suggested it in his *Republic*, and pre-Christian civilizations from the Roman Empire to the Chinese dynasties flourished under it. For Plato, a person's place in society was supposed to be dictated by the composition of their soul, which also indicated what work they would be best at—whether, in the broadest categories, a craftsperson, a warrior, or a political leader. But for Akorem, in his appeal to Bajoran tradition, castes are segregated by both division of labor *and* family tradition:

> Artists have become soldiers. Priests have become merchants. Farmers have become politicians. We must heal the wounds of the occupation. We must return to our D'jarras. We must reclaim what we were and follow the path the Prophets have laid out for us. It is their will that the farmers return to their land, painters to their canvasses, priests to their temples.

"Accession" isn't merely about the evil of castes—members of unclean castes may be killed for disobedience, and even the Prophets call the D'jarras "of the past"—but also an allegory about how narrow religious education and practice can debilitate civil society. In concentrating solely on sacred texts and religious ceremonies as their main source of information and culture, future citizens are robbed of the cultural resources that make civil society a better place in which to live and work. The contrast, in the minds of fundamentalists, between the inerrancy of the Bible or Koran versus the falsehoods and distractions of secular culture is held to be a basic, value-laden distinction between sacred and profane culture.[20] The humanist Corliss Lamont believes, however, that the right of access to, and appreciation of, a wide variety of cultural resources—music, films, and public events—is implied by the First Amendment to the U.S. Constitution:

In my judgment civil libertarians have stressed too much the undoubted fact that freedom of expression is the best way for men to arrive at the truth. The justification for free speech goes deeper than that. For the realm of significant meaning and cultural creativity is far wider than the realm of truth. Novels, poetry, and art do not need to be true in a factual or scientific sense; the human imagination cannot permit itself to be fettered by fact.[21]

Nor, we can add, should human imagination permit itself to be fettered by the narrow limits of a particular religious perspective taken as *fundamentally true* without regard for alternative worldviews. Criticism of fundamentalists who disdain Lamont's right of access to their own culture isn't the only moral argument in favor of a secular society.[22] Robert Audi summarizes a number of other characteristics of religious thought that often have polarizing effects on civil society, including the dangers of the believers' inflated sense of self-importance according to doctrine and organized religion's "passionate concern with outsiders"—that is, evangelical or exclusionary behavior toward "those who don't believe like us."[23]

Some characteristics of religious thinking are quite antagonistic to political principles of a liberal democracy. Belief in the guidance of an infallible supreme authority, along with condemnations of those who hold contrary beliefs, works against the "leveling" effect of democracy on popular opinion and political action, expressed succinctly in the idea of "one person, one vote." Can citizens of a democracy, for example, be said to be truly equal when some of them are assured that God backs their arguments, while opponents are quite literally demonized?

Earlier, I mentioned the difference between *political democracy* and *civil liberties*. These forms of democratic life are *interdependent*: institutions by which people are self-governing are strong to the point that opportunities for free speech, association, and worship are protected, but there are many uses of this freedom that undermine political democracy. Aside from the use of religious reasoning in cases where more broadly ethical or scientific thinking is called for—like sex education and the teaching of creationism in schools—the hierarchical and sacred power embraced by religious attitudes and behavior erodes a genuine sense of *equality* between people, that important "regard for whatever is distinctive and unique in each, irrespective of physical and psychological inequalities."[24] Of course, there are many religious believers who are exceptions, and organized religions aren't the only impediments to democratic equality; but certain characteristics of the religious—especially fundamentalist—mindset that Audi identifies have been, and continue to be, corrosive to secular democracy, as Sisko found out in the worst possible way in "Accession."

## "This Would Be the Second Time Lucifer Was Cast Out"

At the end of "Accession," Akorem and Sisko confront the Prophets together, and "the Sisko" is named by them as the true Emissary. Akorem is sent back to his own time, his memory of the future erased. What best qualifies Sisko for the role, at least from the perspective of his friends, is his ability to synthesize his personal respect for faith traditions with his own record of secular decision making and policy creation, in an effort to actualize their shared goal: Federation membership for Bajor. Sisko's experience, in turn, is based in the Federation's tradition of secular democracy. This tradition urges every one of us to examine religious faith in our society in the light of one undeniable fact about all civilizations, as true today as it will be in the 24th century:

> [W]e are … faced with the quite elementary and yet quite staggering anthropological fact that there are thousands of religions with conflicting revelations, most of them claiming ultimate truth in matters of religion. Which one are we to choose? Why should we think, as finite men, historically and ethnically bound, that our religion and our tribe alone should have the one true revelation? We are members of one historically bound culture on a minor planet in an unbelievably vast universe. Why should it be that in these matters we have a unique hold on the truth? To think that we do is to have a fantastically unrealistic picture of the world.[25]

One of the challenges—and charms—of *Star Trek* is its provocation to recognize that as we take our place in the universe, the number of our discoveries of conflicting revelations of ultimate truth is likely to grow with every new species, every new culture with which we might interact.[26] Long since grown out of the antagonistic "Roddenberry attitude" toward religion in the public sphere, secularism in the later *Star Trek* series reminds us "the human adventure is just beginning."

# Notes

1. "Interview with David Gerrold": http://www.startrekanimated.com/
   tas_david_gerrold.html (accessed April 21, 2015).
2. Dean William Ferne, *Contemporary American Theologies: A Critical
   Survey* (New York: Seabury Press, 1981), 27–8.
3. Roddenberry, quoted in *Free Inquiry* (Autumn 1992). For more details
   on Roddenberry's humanism, see James McGrath's chapter in this book
   (Chapter 30).
4. The use of the word *disenchantment* to describe modern, bureaucratic,
   secularized Western societies, as opposed to the "enchanted" mysticism
   of traditional societies, was coined by Max Weber in *The Sociology of
   Religion* (Boston: Beacon Press, 1993). In *A Secular Age,* Charles Taylor argues that modern societies transform religion rather than abolish-
   ing it, so this might be called "re-enchantment"; Taylor, *A Secular Age*
   (Cambridge, MA: Harvard University Press, 2007).
5. Charles Taylor, *Modern Social Imaginaries* (Durham, NC: Duke Uni-
   versity Press, 2004), 96.
6. I include in this group "The Cage," "Where No Man Has Gone Before,"
   "The Corbomite Maneuver," "The Menagerie," "The Squire of Gothos,"
   "Arena," "The Return of the Archons," "Errand of Mercy," "Who
   Mourns for Adonais?" "The Apple," "The Gamesters of Triskelion,"
   "Spectre of the Gun," "Plato's Stepchildren," "The Savage Curtain,"
   "The Magicks of Megas-Tu," and "How Sharper Than a Serpent's
   Tooth," meaning that sixteen out of the 101 episodes featuring the orig-
   inal crew (15%) turn on this single plot theme!
7. One phenomenon I won't have time to explore is America's so-called
   civil religion, a set of common religious metaphors "expressed in a set of
   beliefs, symbols and rituals" that, while "sharing much in common with
   Christianity, was neither sectarian nor in any specific sense Christian";
   Robert N. Bellah, "Civil Religion in America," *Daedalus* 96:1 (1967): 4,
   8. See also Richard A. Couto and Eric Thomas Weber, "Civil Religion,"
   in *Political and Civic Leadership: A Reference Handbook* (Washington,
   DC: Sage, 2010), 505–12.
8. Robert Audi, *Religious Commitment and Secular Reason* (New York:
   Cambridge University Press, 2000), 35.
9. Corliss Lamont, *The Philosophy of Humanism* (New York: Continuum,
   1990), 264.
10. Benedict Anderson, *Imagined Communities*, rev. ed. (New York: Verso,
    2006).
11. Paul Kahn, "Philosophy and the Politics of Unreason," Yale Law
    School Faculty Scholarship Series, http://digitalcommons.law.yale.edu/
    fss_papers/317, 396.

12. Intriguingly—and that word isn't used much in discussing *Star Trek V*— director William Shatner talks at length about how his original idea for the film was itself "secularized" in the process of story development. "Basically, with Harve [Bennett, executive producer] and the studio suits both worrying that my story, featuring appearances by both God and Satan, would more than likely offend a lot of moviegoers, Harve came up with the idea that perhaps we should alter the story and turn God and Satan into an evil alien pretending to be God for his own gain. This was a HUGE change, lightening the script considerably, and as I look at it now I can clearly see my acceptance of this most basic revision as my first mistake"; William Shatner with Chris Kreski, *Star Trek Movie Memories* (New York: HarperCollins, 1994), 227.

13. Q, for example, appears to legitimate his tyrannical authority to judge humanity's alleged "savagery" based on his own *power*, as opposed to any evident "superior morality" to which his conscience is bound; see Kyle Alkema and Adam Barkman's chapter in this volume (Chapter 10).

14. After working on both TNG and DS9, Moore would go on to create the reimagined *Battlestar Galactica* series, which would further adopt a complex, but thoroughly un-Roddenberry-*esque*, attitude toward religion. For discussion of religious and philosophical themes in Moore's BSG, see Jason T. Eberl, ed., *Battlestar Galactica and Philosophy: Knowledge Here Begins Out There* (Malden, MA: Wiley, 2008).

15. Compare Picard's serious, thoughtful reaction to this situation to the way in which the sight of the *Enterprise* by the Nibiru in the teaser for *Star Trek Into Darkness* is played for laughs. This comparison makes sense of James Hunt's critical comment, "For its hardcore fans, *Star Trek* doesn't have to be about a specific crew, or certain aliens, or a particular starship. At its core, it has to be about how the application of reason, knowledge and understanding in the face of the unknown can make the universe a better place. Whatever you think of Abrams' movies, they weren't about that. If longtime fans don't like the current incarnation of *Star Trek*, it's because the current incarnation doesn't resemble *Star Trek*"; James Hunt, "Does *Star Trek* Need Its Old Fans?" *Den of Geek*: http://www.denofgeek.us/movies/star-trek/242126/does-star-trek-need-its-old-fans (accessed May 20, 2015).

16. If you'd like to delve into these debates yourself, a couple of good starting points that offer multiple perspectives are William A. Dembski and Michael Ruse, eds., *Debating Design: From Darwin to DNA* (New York: Cambridge University Press, 2004); and William Lane Craig and Quentin Smith, *Theism, Atheism, and Big Bang Cosmology* (New York: Oxford University Press, 1993).

17. See http://thehumanist.com/magazine/may-june-2014/church-state/a-charter-for-controversy. You might rewatch "The Chase" (TNG) and "The Paradise Syndrome" (TOS) for their comparisons of religious and

scientific creation stories for humanoid races in the Alpha and Beta quadrants.

18. Kathrin F. Stanger-Hall and David Hall, "Abstinence-Only Education and Teen Pregnancy Rates: Why We Need Comprehensive Sex Education in the U.S.," *PLoS One* 6:10 (2011): http://www.ncbi.nlm.nih.gov/pmc/articles/PMC3194801/ (accessed May 21, 2015).

19. Michael Martin, *Atheism, Morality and Meaning* (Amherst, NY: Prometheus Books, 2002), 128

20. This isn't universally true of all believers; harmony between religious and secular culture has been sought and achieved in many different ways, from the Christian humanism of Desiderius Erasmus (1469–1536), to the Jesuits, to the "classical education" homeschooling movement.

21. Lamont, *Philosophy of Humanism*, 264. Lamont's idea coheres with religious philosopher Josef Pieper's exhortation on the essential importance of *leisure* as a basis for human culture. For elucidation of Pieper's thesis, see Jason Eberl's chapter in this volume (Chapter 1).

22. The classical statement of the moral importance of robust access to "cultural capital" is in John Stuart Mill, *On Liberty* (New York: Penguin, 2007); see also Bryan S. Turner, "Outline of a General Theory of Cultural Citizenship," in *Culture and Citizenship*, ed. Nick Stevenson (Thousand Oaks, CA: Sage, 2001), 11–32.

23. Audi, *Religious Commitment and Secular Reason*, 100–5.

24. John Dewey, "Search for the Great Community," in *The Essential Dewey*, vol. 1, ed. Larry A. Hickman and Thomas M. Alexander (Bloomington: Indiana University Press, 1998), 296.

25. Kai Nielsen, *Ethics without God* (New York: Prometheus Books, 1999), 99.

26. Such interaction will raise challenges concerning not only purported religious truths but accepted scientific and moral truths as well. William Lindenmuth addresses the challenge of moral *relativism* in his chapter in this volume.

# Contributors
## Federation Ambassadors to Babel

**Jerold J. ("J. J.") Abrams** is Associate Professor of Philosophy at Creighton University in Omaha, Nebraska. Abrams is the editor of *The Philosophy of Stanley Kubrick* (University Press of Kentucky, 2007), and the author of many articles on philosophy of film. Abrams also shares his name with the famous director of *Star Trek* and *Star Trek Into Darkness*. Early in their respective careers, the college professor was often asked whether he was, in fact, the yet-to-be-famous director. Over the years, his response has always been, "No. He's the cool one. I'm the other one." But no one really asks him that anymore.

Before his adventures in philosophy—which has resulted in a number of chapters in popular culture and philosophy volumes, such as *The Ultimate Star Wars and Philosophy* (Wiley-Blackwell, 2015), *Batman vs. Superman and Philosophy* (Open Court, forthcoming), and *It's Always Sunny and Philosophy* (Open Court, 2015)—**Kyle Alkema** studied biochemistry hoping to invent a food replicator, a hope that was eventually dashed in nearly the same manner as Captain Kirk's head by the boulder thrown by the Gorn.

**Alejandro Bárcenas** teaches history of philosophy at Texas State University. He's the author of *Machiavelli's Art of Politics* (Brill, 2015) and a contributor to *The Daily Show and Philosophy* (Wiley-Blackwell, 2007). His research focuses on political theory and classical Chinese philosophy. Nowadays, he spends most of his time writing philosophy subroutines for Data and The Doctor.

*The Ultimate Star Trek and Philosophy*, First Edition. Edited by Kevin S. Decker and Jason T. Eberl. © 2016 John Wiley & Sons, Ltd. Published 2016 by John Wiley & Sons, Ltd.

**Adam Barkman** is Associate Professor and Chair of the Philosophy Department at Redeemer University College in Canada. He's the coeditor of four books on popular culture and philosophy, including *Manga and Philosophy* (Open Court, 2010) and *Downton Abbey and Philosophy* (Open Court, 2015), and the author of five books, most recently *Making Sense of Islamic Art & Architecture* (Thames & Hudson, 2015). For Barkman, the motto "To boldly go where no man has gone before" is very near the thrust of all philosophy.

**Steve Bein** is Assistant Professor of Philosophy at the University of Dayton, where he's a specialist in Asian thought. He's also a novelist, and his science fiction short stories have been used in philosophy and science fiction courses nationwide. His books include *Compassion and Moral Guidance* (University of Hawaii Press, 2012), *Purifying Zen: Watsuji Tetsurō's Shamon Dōgen* (University of Hawaii Press, 2011), and the *Fated Blades* novels from Penguin Roc. He's perpetually mystified when *Star Trek* fans get angry whenever he tells them, "May the Force be with you."

**David Boersema** is Professor of Philosophy at Pacific University. He teaches in the Philosophy Department and the Peace and Social Justice Program. He's former Executive Director of the Concerned Philosophers for Peace. He's published in the areas of pragmatism, philosophy of science, philosophy of art, philosophy of language, and philosophy of human rights, and he is the general editor of the journal *Essays in Philosophy*. To the dismay of all those around him, he frequently bursts into song whenever he plays his homemade CD of "Lt. Kevin Riley's Greatest Hits."

**Pamela JG Boyer** did her master's work in American Studies at Montana State University. She is a twenty-two-year Navy retiree. She also believes that, as it's been established in *Star Trek VI: The Undiscovered Country*, Shakespeare was Klingon, and Søren Kierkegaard must have been a Bajoran due to his work in existentialism—because only Bajorans can understand his work.

**Lisa Cassidy** is Associate Professor of Philosophy at Ramapo College of New Jersey. Her research focuses primarily on responsibility and the family, and she also writes about teaching philosophy. She's published articles on who should have children, to whom we should donate our organs, and how being a lousy knitter has made her a better philosophy teacher. Lisa's only remaining concern about the upcoming Borg assimilation of Earth is how she'll squeeze into the regulation Borg catsuit.

**Tim Challans** received his bachelor's degree from West Point and his master's and doctorate in philosophy from Johns Hopkins University. He's taught at West Point, the Army Command and General Staff College (CGSC), the School of Advanced Military Studies (SAMS), and the National Defense University (NDU). His publications include a previous contribution to *Star Trek and Philosophy* (Open Court, 2008) and the award-winning book, *Awakening Warrior: Revolution in the Ethics of Warfare* (SUNY Press, 2007). He's currently working behind the scenes to help set the conditions for the implementation of the Prime Directive here on Earth.

**Kevin S. Decker** teaches philosophy at Eastern Washington University, where he often lectures about the phenomenology of peaches and the rights of vampire citizens. He's the editor or coeditor of several anthologies of philosophy and popular culture, including the original *Star Trek and Philosophy* (Open Court, 2008) and *Star Wars and Philosophy* (Open Court, 2005), as well as *The Ultimate Star Wars and Philosophy* (Wiley-Blackwell, 2015)—all with Jason T. Eberl. He's also the author of *Who Is Who? The Philosophy of Doctor Who* (I.B. Tauris, 2013). He's proficient with both the lirpa and the ahnwoon, and doesn't need any tri-ox compound to fight with them either. As if!

**Dan Dinello** is Professor Emeritus at Columbia College Chicago. The author of *Technophobia: Science Fiction Visions of Posthuman Technology* (University of Texas Press, 2006) and *Finding Fela: My Strange Journey to Meet the Afro-Beat King* (Shockproductions, 2011), he's also written chapters for *Avatar and Philosophy* (Wiley-Blackwell, 2014) and books about *Battlestar Galactica*, Ridley Scott, Philip K. Dick, the Rolling Stones, and the Who, among others. An award-winning filmmaker, Dan directed several episodes of the Comedy Central TV series *Strangers with Candy*. He runs the website Shockproductions.com while awaiting neural implant surgery that will transform him into the first Borg with a sense of humor.

**Jason T. Eberl** is the Semler Endowed Chair for Medical Ethics and Professor of Philosophy at Marian University in Indianapolis. He teaches and publishes on bioethics, medieval philosophy, and metaphysics. He's the editor of *Battlestar Galactica and Philosophy* (Wiley-Blackwell, 2008); coeditor (with Kevin S. Decker) of *The Ultimate Star Wars and Philosophy* (Wiley-Blackwell, 2015), as well as the original *Star Trek and Philosophy* (Open Court, 2008) and *Star Wars and Philosophy* (Open Court, 2005); and coeditor (with George A. Dunn) of *Sons of Anarchy and Philosophy* (Wiley-Blackwell, 2013) and *The Philosophy of Christopher Nolan* (Lexington, forthcoming). He's also contributed to similar books on Stanley Kubrick, J.J. Abrams, *Harry Potter*, Metallica, *Terminator*, *The Hunger Games*, *The Big Lebowski*, and *Avatar*. Ever the pluralist, he finds no inconsistency in Gandalf having trained Harry Potter to become a Jedi so that he might one day rise to captain a Federation starship and save the natives of Pandora from the crushing tyranny of the Capital with its army of T-1000s.

**Jeff Ewing** is a doctoral candidate in Sociology at the University of Oregon. Recently, he's written chapters on the concept of Hell (Palgrave Macmillan, 2015), demonology (forthcoming), the Devil (Open Court, 2014), *Jurassic Park* (Open Court, 2014), and *Frankenstein* (Open Court, 2013). He spends most of his spare time trying to figure out a way to set phasers to "classless society." So far little luck, but he did "accidentally" get a replicator permanently stuck on making infinite copies of the *Communist Manifesto*.

**Dara Fogel** teaches philosophy at the University of Central Oklahoma and has designed several courses on *Star Trek* themes. She's also the author of four books exploring philosophy and fiction. As a kid, she watched the original *Star Trek* on her dad's knee, later going on to win multiple fan convention costume contests with her Orion Slave Girl cosplay (complete with Klingon handlers). Although she no longer paints herself green, she still attends conventions and is a popular panelist on all things *Trek* and *Doctor Who*.

**Victor Grech** is Associate Professor of Paediatrics in Malta and is an interdisciplinarian. His first PhD thesis was entitled *Congenital Heart Disease in Malta*. His second PhD was in the humanities, with the thesis entitled *Infertility in Science Fiction*. He's currently completing his third PhD thesis, *A Review of Global Secular Trends and Latitude Gradients in Sex Ratios at Birth over the Past 50 Years*. He's also just boldly gone into his 50s, as will *Star Trek* in 2016. When painting, a pastime that creates impressionist/expressionist scenes (including starships from *Star Trek*), he wonders how long it'll be before the men in white (or, more hopefully, in black) will come to take him and his friend Benny Russell away.

**Dena Hurst** completed her doctorate in philosophy at Florida State University, where she currently works as a researcher and special projects manager. She recently contributed a chapter to Wiley-Blackwell's *Supernatural and Philosophy*. She's a certified fellow of the American Philosophical Practitioners Association. Her philosophical interests include social and political philosophy and philosophy of technology. After being kidnapped by Ferengi and abandoned on Earth, Dena awaits the day she's able to return to her home planet of Vulcan to complete the *kolinahr* and live a life of pure logic.

**William Jaworski** was Associate Professor of Philosophy at Fordham University until 2009, when he accidentally stepped into a transporter thinking it was a restroom. His replica succeeded him and is the author of *Philosophy of Mind: A Comprehensive Introduction* (Wiley-Blackwell, 2011) and *Structure and the Metaphysics of Mind: How Hylomorphism Solves the Mind-Body Problem* (Oxford University Press, forthcoming). He lives in New Jersey with Jaworski's family, who say, "It could've been worse."

**David Kyle Johnson** is Associate Professor of philosophy at King's College in Wilkes-Barre, Pennsylvania. He's written on many pop culture topics, including *The Daily Show*, *The Colbert Report*, *Doctor Who*, *South Park*, and Quentin Tarantino. He publishes regularly in journals on philosophy of religion and all his articles are available, for free, on academia.edu. He also edited *Inception and Philosophy* (Wiley-Blackwell, 2011), produced two courses (*Exploring Metaphysics* and *The Big Questions of Philosophy*) for *The Great Courses*, and authored *The Myths That Stole Christmas*. He largely credits Spock and Data for his love of logic, mostly blames Jeri Ryan for his desire to join the Borg Collective, and is still waiting for the episode that explains how Captain Janeway ended up in a 21st-century prison with a Russian accent.

**Melanie Johnson-Moxley** teaches philosophy at Columbia College and the University of Missouri. Her philosophical interests include A.N. Whitehead's process philosophy, field–being studies, and women in the history of philosophy. As a child, she cherished her Engineer Scotty action figure and whispered encouragingly to it to "beam her up" out of awkward social situations.

**Andrew Zimmerman Jones** never attended Starfleet Academy, but he studied physics at Wabash College and minored in mathematics and philosophy, then went on to earn a master's from Purdue University in Mathematics Education. He's coauthor of *String Theory for Dummies* (Wiley, 2010) and Physics Expert at About.com, as well as a full-time freelance writer in the areas of science communication and educational publishing. His work on science, philosophy, and popular culture has appeared on the "PBS *Nova*: The Nature of Reality" blog, *Black Gate* fantasy magazine, and several anthologies of philosophy and popular culture, including *The Avengers and Philosophy* (Wiley-Blackwell, 2012) and *Ender's Game and Philosophy* (Wiley-Blackwell, 2013). In high school, he received the award "Most Likely to Have Been an Alien in *Star Trek* in a Former Life" during his senior year at the Indiana Academy for Science, Mathematics, and Humanities.

**Courtland Lewis** teaches at Owensboro Community and Technical College. He's contributed chapters and edited several books on popular culture and philosophy, including *Doctor Who*, *Futurama*, *Divergent*, and *Red Rising*. He regularly speaks at conventions in order to spread philosophy's love of wisdom. Spock inspired him to study logic, and when he isn't practicing the Klingon martial art of *mok'bara*, he enjoys drinking prune juice and reciting android poetry.

**William A. Lindenmuth** is Associate Professor of Philosophy at Shoreline College. He received his MA in philosophy in New York City from the New School for Social Research, and his BA in English from Saint Mary's College in California. He's had success in getting students to ask questions like "What does God need with a starship?" in New York, Las Vegas, Seattle, and Rome, Italy. He specializes in normative ethics and moral psychology, particularly through the mediums of literature and film, arguing that our stories show us both who we are and who we'd like to be. He's contributed to the forthcoming *The Philosophy of Christopher Nolan* (Lexington), *Jane Austen and Philosophy* (Rowan and Littlefield), and *The Ultimate Star Wars and Philosophy* (Wiley-Blackwell, 2015). You can find him online in the MOOC "Philosophy and Film" at Canvas.net.

Spock raised an eyebrow and said, "Fascinating, captain. I've never seen readings like this before. **Greg Littmann** is Associate Professor of Philosophy at Southern Illinois University Edwardsville, an M-class university with a breathable atmosphere. He has published on

metaphysics, the philosophy of professional philosophy, and ... "
Spock's eyebrow rose higher. "The philosophy of logic. He has also
contributed numerous chapters to books relating philosophy to
popular culture, including volumes on *Doctor Who, Dune, Ender's
Game, Game of Thrones*, and *Star Wars.*" Kirk readied his phaser.
"Is it dangerous, Spock? I thought philosophers were a species with
fangs!" "Once, captain," Spock replied. "The species lost its fangs
through evolution. This specimen is quite harmless."

**Trip McCrossin** teaches in the Philosophy Department at Rutgers
University, where he works on, among other things, the nature, history, and legacy of the Enlightenment. The present essay is part of
a broader effort to view the debate regarding the nature of personhood in the 18th century and beginning again in the second half of the
20th, through the lens of literature and other forms of popular culture
since the beginning of the 19th. He sometimes wonders if perhaps, as
Kirk was touched that Spock gave him as a birthday gift a copy of
*A Tale of Two Cities,* he wouldn't have been equally touched, though
in a different way, to receive on an earlier occasion a copy of *Bleak
House.*

**James F. McGrath** is the Clarence L. Goodwin Chair in New Testament Language and Literature at Butler University in Indianapolis.
He's the editor of *Religion and Science Fiction* (Wipf & Stock, 2011)
and coeditor (with Andrew Crome) of *Time and Relative Dimensions
in Faith: Religion and Doctor Who* (Darton, Longman & Todd,
2013). He blogs about religion and science fiction, as well as his
other research interests in the New Testament, at "Exploring Our
Matrix" (http://www.patheos.com/blogs/exploringourmatrix/). It was
his interest in solving the "Synoptic Problem" that led him to turn his
attention from the Christian Gospels to *Star Trek* in his search for the
elusive Q.

**Sarah O'Hare** is studying Critical Theory and Creative Research at
Pacific Northwest College of Art. She completed her undergraduate
studies in philosophy and art at Eastern Washington University, where
she studied the sublime landscape of foggy pine trees and wrote aphorisms among the roses that grow beneath the cypresses. This is her
first publication, and in celebration she continues to engage her flip
phone as a communicator device and proudly sports the ultimate pair
of "Starfleet-approved" boots.

**James M. Okapal** is Associate Professor of Philosophy, Chair of the Philosophy and Religion Department, and Chair of the History and Geography Department at Missouri Western State University. He is also the Area Chair for Philosophy and Popular Culture at the National Pop Culture Association/American Culture Association Conference. He's interested in the intersections of ethics and pop culture, especially in science fiction and fantasy. He's published articles on ethical issues in *Harry Potter* and in *The Ultimate Star Wars and Philosophy*, and presented papers on the works of Philip K. Dick, Orson Scott Card, and Roger Zelazny. He's never entirely forgiven his parents for not naming him James Tiberius, but is nevertheless proud of being named after the alternate universe version of his mother where she was the eldest son of Bob and Beck (Materni) Weber.

**Nicole R. Pramik** is a published novelist and poet as well as a former Humanities and English Instructor. She's served as a contributor for *SpongeBob SquarePants and Philosophy*, *The Devil and Philosophy*, and *Dracula and Philosophy*. In her spare time, she shares intel about Earth with the Obsidian Order in exchange for crates of yamok sauce.

**Walter Robinson** (Cherokee) is on the faculty of the Department of Philosophy, as well the Native American and Indigenous Studies Program, at Indiana University-Purdue University Indianapolis. He earned his PhD in Philosophy and Religion from the California Institute of Integral Studies. His specialty is non-Western (East Asian and Native American) religious philosophy. He's an ordained Zen Buddhist priest in the Soto lineage. Much of his psychospiritual existence is dedicated to indwelling in Vision, in which he interplays with multidimensional life forms such as "The Traveler" and "wormhole entities," among others.

**Nina Rosenstand** is Professor of Philosophy at San Diego Mesa College, teaching courses in ethics and social philosophy, philosophy of human nature, philosophy in literature, and philosophy of women. She was born in Copenhagen, Denmark, Planet Earth (Stardate: classified), and is a naturalized U.S. citizen, but she's had her eyes on the stars since she was Wesley Crusher's age, resulting in her appreciation for the capacity of science fiction to explore the ethics of possible and alternate futures. Her dissertation focused on the philosophy of Henri Bergson; in addition, she's written *The Concept of Myth* [*Mytebegrebet*] (Gad, 1981), as well as a number of articles and blog posts on ethics, human nature, and philosophy of film and literature. She's also the author of two textbooks in philosophy: *The Moral of the Story*, 7th ed. (McGraw-Hill, 2012), and *The Human Condition* (McGraw-Hill, 2001). She's happy to converse at length about whether Data is a moral agent, and in what sense he's "human."

**Barbara Stock** is Associate Professor of Philosophy at Gallaudet University, having completed her graduate work at Syracuse University. She team-teaches one of her favorite courses with a physics professor: philosophy and physics through science fiction. Other teaching and research interests include ethics, early modern philosophy, and disability studies. Although not born in time to watch the first run of *Star Trek* TOS, she was exposed prenatally via her Trekkie mom. Upon arriving at Gallaudet, where the language of instruction is American Sign Language, she tried unsuccessfully to have the Vulcan salute become her name-sign.

**Charles Taliaferro** is Professor and Chair of Philosophy at St. Olaf College. He's the author or editor of over twenty books, including (with Chad Meister) the forthcoming six-volume work, *The History of Evil*. He's contributed to philosophy and popular culture volumes on *Star Wars*, *Harry Potter*, the Olympics, the Rolling Stones, and other topics. When in trouble, he often yells to the heavens, "Beam me up, Scotty!"

**Dennis M. Weiss** is Professor of Philosophy at York College of Pennsylvania, where he regularly teaches courses on human nature, technology, film, and popular culture. He's the editor of *Interpreting Man* (Davies Group, 2003) and coeditor of *Design, Mediation, and the Posthuman* (Lexington, 2014). His work explores the impact of technology on the human condition, and in this vein he's authored articles on Philip K. Dick, *The Twilight Zone*, William Gibson, and *Star Trek*. He's pretty sure he's not posthuman, though his students have often observed (or complained about) more than a passing resemblance to an overly logical and utterly unemotional human–Vulcan half-breed.

**Bailey Wheelock** studied philosophy and neuroscience at St. Olaf College. She's an EMT in the Twin Cities and has interests in bioethics and science fiction. She hopes to someday follow in the footsteps of Leonard "Bones" McCoy and become a doctor aboard the *U.S.S. Enterprise*, but will settle for an Earth hospital.

# Index

*The Ultimate Star Trek and Philosophy*, First Edition. Edited by Kevin S. Decker and Jason T. Eberl.
© 2016 John Wiley & Sons, Ltd. Published 2016 by John Wiley & Sons, Ltd.